*Practical Risk Analysis*

# *Practical Risk Analysis*

## *An Approach Through Case Histories*

**David Hertz**
*Formerly a Director and Partner of McKinsey & Co*
*Now Counsel Leva, Hawes, Symington, Martin and Oppenheimer and Professor, University of Miami, Coral Gables*

and

**Howard Thomas**
*University of Illinois at Urbana-Champaign*



JOHN WILEY & SONS

Chichester · New York · Brisbane · Toronto · Singapore

***Library of Congress Cataloging in Publication Data:***

Hertz, David Bendel, 1919–
Practical risk analysis.

Companion volume to: Risk analysis and its applications/ David Hertz and Howard Thomas.
Bibliography: p.
Includes index.
1. Risk—Case studies. 2. Risk management—Case studies. 3. Decision-making—Case studies. 4. Capital investments—Case studies. I. Thomas, H. (Howard) II. Title. III. Title: Risk analysis.

HD61.H418 658 81-16056

ISBN 0 471 10144 3 AACR2

***British Library Cataloguing in Publication Data:***

Hertz, David B.
Practical risk analysis.
1. Risk management 2. Risk
I. Title II. Thomas, Howard
658.4′03 HD61

ISBN 0 471 10144 3

Typeset by Activity Limited, Salisbury, Wilts.
Printed by the Pitman Press, Bath, Avon.

# *Contents*

# *Preface*

This volume is intended to be a companion volume and course material complement to *Risk Analysis and its Applications*. During the textual monograph we presented a number of cases involving risk analysis in order to examine the nature of the approach more fully.

We believe, however, that there is a considerable demand from practitioners, college professors, students and managers alike for a series of practical applications to be presented in a rigorous and wide-ranging format. Whilst we have drawn primarily from our own experience in building up this collection of case studies, we have taken the opportunity of drawing upon other published sources to expand the collection in useful ways. However, every application has been written up in case history form in order that both the formulation and implementation problems involved in real applications are fully presented. Thus, in case history form many of the necessary analytical calculations have been carried out and presented for the reader. Although we regard an ability to perform the analytical aspects of risk analysis as essential, we firmly believe that equal emphasis must be given to the nature and character of the entire risk analysis process. For example, information of a probabilistic type may be difficult to derive and sensible organizational procedures for obtaining such measurements may need to be developed. Further, the 'people' problems of implementation of risk analysis in organizational contexts are by no means easily soluble and we strongly believe that the literature should direct more attention towards feasible approaches for handling implementation issues.

In addition, we have developed a series of notes which can be used for generating additional case discussion. These teaching notes seek to demonstrate how we believe these case histories should be used in developing a thorough understanding of the issues, problems and drawbacks in carrying out practical risk analyses.

In any endeavor of this type we would wish to express our appreciation to fellow practitioners and colleagues who have worked with us over the years. We have acknowledged, where appropriate, individual contributions during the course of this case volume. Needless to say, any errors or omissions that may remain are our responsibility. We would, however, welcome correspondence and comments from interested readers.

*July 1983*
*New York* D. B. Hertz
*Champaign, Illinois* H. Thomas

# *Acknowledgements*

We would formally like to thank those individuals who have provided us with help, encouragement, suggestions and contributions to improve the quality of this volume. We have acknowledged the sources and original authorship of each of the cases in the footnotes to each chapter. We are especially grateful to those contributors who have permitted us to use and adapt material for this volume.

We would also like to recognize the important contributions and intellectual debt we owe to students, scholars and consultants with whom we have been associated over the years. Notably, Professor Peter Moore of London Business School, Professor Gordon Kaufman of MIT, Professor Larry Phillips of Brunel University and the London School of Economics, Professor Howard Raiffa of Harvard Business School, Professor Robert Winkler of Indiana University, Dr. Rex Brown of Decision Science Consortium, Dr. Michael Menke formerly of SRI and Dr. Ralph Keeney of Woodward-Clyde. Members and associates of the Decision Analysis Group at the London Business School in the 1970s, namely Richard Bell, Derek Bunn, Peter Burville, Geoffrey Easton, Juliet Hampton, John Hull, Andrew Lock and Paul Morris also deserve particular mention. In addition, colleagues at the Australian Graduate School of Management such as Ray Ball, Philip Brown, Jeremy Davis, Jean-Roch Dubourdieu, George Foster, Paul Greenwood and Danny Samson also provided valuable assistance and encouragement.

*Chapter 1*

# *Introduction – The Book, Issues, Definitions and Scope*

## 1.1 WHAT WE UNDERSTAND BY THE TERM 'RISK ANALYSIS'

The companion text to this volume, *Risk Analysis and its Applications*, contains a discussion about the role for risk analysis in the context of organizational decision-making. However, while not wishing to duplicate material already presented, we believe that some repetition of that discussion may be valuable.

### Decision and Risk Analysis as Strategic Thinking Frameworks

Decision and risk analysis (Hertz and Thomas 1983; Moore and Thomas, 1976; Thomas, 1972; Raiffa, 1968) can be viewed as having two major roles. Firstly, it offers a broad perspective for structuring the process of decision-making, and secondly, it provides a set of techniques for evaluating the worth of alternative decision options. Both analytic approaches involve the stages of *decomposing and structuring the problem*, assessing the *uncertainties and values* of the possible outcomes, and the *determination of the preferred strategy* in terms of some specified choice criteria.

We believe that within the organizational context there is a close connection between decision and risk analysis, and policy and strategy formulation. Further, we believe that risk analysis adds a valuable contribution by providing strategic thinking input for the process of policy dialogue about the decision situation. Such input should encourage entrepreneural activity through a better awareness of risk while at the same time providing flexible and adaptive 'thinking structures' for policy/strategy problems. It is further contended that there is no meaningful distinction between analytic approaches such as risk analysis – which develops an awareness of the impacts of risk and uncertainty on decision problems – and processes of policy/strategy formulation concerned with the resolution of these problems. They should both be seen as valuable parts of *policy dialogue* prior to final decisions being taken. Chapter 2 illustrates the role of risk analysis in strategy dialogue through an examination of a recent new product diversification problem.

**Risk analysis defined**

The term 'risk analysis' is used here to denote methods which aim to develop a comprehensive understanding and awareness of the risk associated with a particular variable of interest (be it a payoff measure, a cash flow profile, or a macroeconomic forecast). In other words, a forecast is obtained for a variable of interest in the form of a probability distribution. Two solution techniques are most commonly used to generate the required forecast probability profile. An analytical approach might be adopted. Using this technique, individual forecasts are combined (according to a specified structural model) using statistical distribution theory (often in relation to such standard distributions as the normal distribution) to calculate the mean, variance and possibly skewness parameters of the probability distribution of the final criterion variable (usually a payoff measure). The other technique most frequently used is to adopt a Monte-Carlo-type simulation approach using the structural model. This model specifies the set of equations required to combine the input probabilistic variables into the distribution of final payoff measure.

Typically, not all of the inputs need to be specified as probabilistic variables because a preliminary *sensitivity analysis* is often used to screen and identify those input variables which need to be specified in probabilistic form.

Risk analysis has, perhaps, found the greatest immediate acceptance in the area of investment project appraisal. The reason for this may be that it is in such areas that managers frequently have to confront the possibility of making the wrong decision and experiencing 'negative' outcomes such as financial loss. Although risk analysis is useful in this area, it is possible that many of the readers of the original *Harvard Business Review* article by David Hertz (1979) wrongly interpreted risk analysis as an argument in methodology about investment decision-making. Unfortunately, by concentrating on this aspect, some people may have missed the broader perspective of risk analysis: that is as a vehicle for examining the data surrounding a decision problem (which might very often be an investment proposal) given the pervasive uncertainties in both business and other environments. In other words, we see a broad role for risk analysis in terms of strategic thinking about decision problems. Risk analysis is as important a vehicle in planning, forecasting, understanding and handling uncertainty as it may seem to be in the area of financial decision-making.

Risk analysis has a valuable role to play in the management of the strategic process through its input into such areas as: *forecasting and planning*, *risk positioning* for the firm, *scanning* of the uncertain business environment, *scenario development* in relation to potential social, political, economic and technological futures, and the *handling of risk and uncertainty*, which are increasingly stressed in modern strategic management paradigms, e.g. Hofer and Schendel (1978).

It should be noted that the risk analysis method emphasizes the value of managerial judgment in both input estimation and decision. Our experience suggests that the variety of information available from a risk analysis is useful in two main areas. Firstly, it is a valuable aid in clarifying managerial assumptions about the nature of the decision problem and consequent implications, and secondly, it is an invaluable tool for improving communication, debate and dialogue about the problem (i.e. its assumptions, structure, etc.) amongst the managerial team, and also between managers and analysts. We believe this improved communication to be one of the major benefits to be gained as a result of using risk analysis.

However, we are not suggesting that risk analysis should ever be considered as a meaningful substitute for managerial judgment. The contribution which risk analysis can make is to help managers' thinking processes, and this is done in the first instance by forcing them to confront the structure of the decision problem in a relatively unemotional manner. After the problem has been defined, a 'first-pass' risk analysis can facilitate various activities: it can successively assess the range of uncertain variables deemed important, gather any information required which bears on the resolution of the problem, exhaustively evaluate the cross-impacts amongst the uncertain variables, and combine key uncertain variables to identify viable decision paths and options for the organization in terms of specified preference and choice criteria. Ultimately, it enables the decision-maker – business executive, government administrator, scientist, legislator – to examine, discuss, and eventually understand why one course of action might be more desirable than another.

## 1.2 SOME DEFINITIONS

### Risk and Uncertainty

As used in this book, *risk* means both uncertainty, and the results of uncertainty. That is, risk refers to a lack of predictability about problem structure, outcomes or consequences in a decision or planning situation. Risk is therefore related to concepts of chance such as the probability of loss or the probability of ruin. However, the definition of risk here is broadened to include both the lack of predictability about outcomes and also *all* of the elements of problem structure. This includes such factors as the relevance of assumptions, the generation of strategic alternatives, the level of organizational information about the problem, the importance of consequences and the ability to attain various organizational goals.

## 1.3 THE NATURE OF A CASE HISTORY

Throughout the companion text volume we stressed the value of working through applications of the risk analysis approach. The book included a number of examples, and four case histories were presented in Chapter 6.

This text contains a further series of case histories. Over the years many practitioners have indicated how useful they have found this approach, and have frequently asked for additional examples. We believe that the desire for further case histories stems mainly from the view that managers can become better able to solve problems through reading or experiencing successful applications. Thus, a manager can become more aware of problems and problem types to which risk analysis has been applied and learn vicariously through such experiences. This 'external learning' is made much more useful if the problems are presented in 'case history' form, cataloguing the problems involved in applications. That is, they can throw light upon the issues of problem identification, as well as indicate the measurement and assessment problems associated with risk analysis. A further feature of case histories is that they often present the results of a 'first-pass' analysis in order that readers can question the role of analysis in the process of policy dialogue.

Such 'external learning', however, has limitations. It must be reinforced by 'internal learning', which managers and analysts can only obtain in actual organizational decision-making contexts. In this way, they can further appreciate the problems of implementation and the potential influence of, for example, organizational structures on strategy formulation and the strategic thinking process.

Case histories can, therefore, alert managers only to applications performed in other organizations and by consultants. However, since applications have increased in scope through time, managers can now read of an increasing number of applications to ill-structured, complex and strategic types of problems.

### The use of case histories in training

Basically, case studies and case histories can provide a series of different problems or problem-types, e.g. new product, manufacturing, etc., which the manager can review early in the problem formulation stage. Thus, he can attempt to 'match the problem to problem-type' and go through a form of pre-diagnosis of the problem. In this 'matching of problems', the manager relies on recognizing familiar problem patterns and in this sense, practise with case studies might help him more with the diagnosis of well-structured, programmed problems than with ill-structured problems.

However, as more case studies of ill-structured problems are developed, the manager can learn more about the crucial role of problem formulation and also the role of 'first-pass' analysis in the development and implementation of a successful risk analysis application.

We recommend that 'trainers' – be they designers of executive programs or MBA/BBA business school instructors – should use these case histories in the following manner:

(i) to alert students to a range of real-life programmed and unprogrammed management applications;
(ii) to illustrate implementation issues from problem identification to dialogue about the choice of preferred alternative options;
(iii) to assign students one of a number of possible roles:

  (a) replication and subsequent criticism of the analytic approach suggested in most instances;
  (b) discussion of the range of questions suggested at the end of the case history.

Trainers should therefore realize that in most situations some part or parts of the structuring and analysis have been carried out in order to focus upon the issues involved in implementation of risk analysis. However, sufficient information about problem formulation and input data has been presented for students to be able to attempt the technical features of the analyses.

A case manual has been produced and is available for trainers who adopt the text and case book. The manual gives detailed teaching notes for each case, and also suggests directions for the design of courses in this area. To that end, a number of course outlines are provided.

## 1.4 SCOPE OF THE BOOK

### Aim of the book

The book attempts to demonstrate the ever-widening application of risk analysis to business and public sector decision problems. We believe that managers and students can learn about the risk analysis process by confronting the issues of problem identification, measurement and implementation raised in virtually every case history and case study. Such 'learning by doing' can only improve the experience base of the manager and potential analyst.

Our selection of case histories reflects our concern to report as wide a range of applications as possible. In this manner, we believe that the book provides a comprehensive review of risk analysis applications and demonstrates the power of the approach in strategic thinking.

### Relationship to *Risk Analysis and its Applications*

The companion text volume presents a comprehensive treatment of the theoretical and measurement foundations of the risk analysis approach, illustrated with a range of case examples. The purpose of this volume is to provide an extensive set of case examples, which not only throw light upon the issues raised in the text, but in addition provide the opportunity for managers to gain practical experience of a series of real applications. Thus, they can attempt to reproduce analytical results presented and also discuss the value of the approach and the issues raised in each case history.

**Case histories included: brief 'thumbnail' sketches**

*Strategic Risk Analysis and Policy Dialogue*

This chapter illustrates the role of risk analysis in policy dialogue about a new product diversification situation.

*A Strategic Reorganization Problem*

This case describes an extensive reorganization of some subsidiaries of a British industrial holding company, Ferguson Industrial Holdings. The case outlines every phase of risk analysis from problem formulation to choice. It also gives some indication of the manner in which the dialogue and discussion about policy developed.

*A Diversification Problem at Egg n' Foam*

The case outlines a diversification situation for Egg n' Foam, the company described previously in Chapter 6 of *Risk Analysis and its Applications*. It examines the role of risk analysis in acquisition strategy and compares the approach with a number of alternative approaches for appraising the acquisition opportunity.

*Strategic Sensitivity Analysis: An Electricity Generation Project*

The case examines the role of sensitivity analysis in highlighting the key features of, and uncertain variables associated with, a major plant investment decision in a publicly-owned Australian electricity utility. It is argued that the tabular output of the sensitivity analysis phase is a valuable prelude to the formulation of a concise, well-specified risk-analytic approach to the problem. This 'first-pass' sensitivity analysis also suggests some strategy options available to the electric utility.

*XYZ: A Risk Management Scenario*

XYZ Ltd. is a major Australian trading bank. Its concern is to identify, analyze and measure areas of corporate risk, e.g. risk of loss of cash, risk of physical damage, etc. The aim is to manage risk better and adopt sensible strategies to mitigate the effects of risk.

*Fincomsoc: Computer Security Assessment*

The Fincomsoc case treats the problem of the risk of computer fraud potentially confronting a financial services company. The case invites the reader to question how assessments concerning the occurrence of such potentially rare events as computer malpractice can be made. Further, it examines the issue of developing sound risk-management principles.

*Globair: Insurance Premium Setting*

Globair is a large Australian airline which is assessing the accident/crash risk from the viewpoint of its liability as an employer. Certain scenarios leading to a crash/injury/fatality situation are assessed, and judgments made about the appropriate premiums which should be paid for insurance purposes.

*Austrans: Determination of Risk-management Policies*

Austrans is a large fleet haulage company which is reviewing the risk inherent in its operations in order to judge the effectiveness of its risk-management policies. These relate not only to insurance covers against accidents, but also actions designed to anticipate the effects of labor disputes upon its operations.

*Smith, Tyne and Georges: Simulating Alternative Premium Structures*

Examines the role of a consultant in assessing the risks of crashes/accidents which would affect the operations of a large Australian airline. The consultant is asked to examine the current hull insurance cover held by the airline with an insurance company. A simulation approach for comparing premium covers is suggested as a basis for the reappraisal of the existing arrangements.

*Cassida: New Product Marketing*

This involves a new product situation in a multinational food and detergent company. It is presented primarily as an example of decision-structuring. The problem's structure can quickly become complex, and the reader is encouraged to address the trade-off between having a manageable structure and including sufficient realism about the set of underlying assumptions and key problem features.

*J. Sainsbury: Bidding*

This case illustrates an unique, real-life competitive bidding situation in a major British food-retailing chain. A solution is presented, but the reader is encouraged to question every facet of the problem. In particular, it might be useful to assess whether the problem's solution may have been confounded by the analyst's desire to produce an elegant analytical solution, and whether simulation should be considered a realistic alternative.

*Quantock Plastics: Facilities Investment*

This situation involves a facilities planning problem in relation to plant investment in the plastics industry. A structured decision-analytic approach forms the basis of the case history. However, questions can be raised both about the problem's structure and assumptions and about the value and wisdom of the solution approach presented.

*Risk Analysis of Chemical Plants: Investment Decision-making*

A risk analysis approach for investment in a new chemical plant and facility is presented. The case includes a comprehensive analysis of the problem structure and formulation and gives a step-by-step development of the entire analytic process.

*The Hewitt Ingot Problem: An Operations Management Problem*

The case describes a difficult problem encountered in the operations management of a metal ingot production process. The case history discusses a manager's wish to examine the effectiveness of inventory policies for analyzed residues known as 'recovered melts.'

*Industrial and Chemical Processes Ltd.: A Diversification Decision*

This case history involves a diversification decision by the company into the area of automated car crushing and scrap metal equipment.

*The Rheumatogen Situation: Pharmaceutical R & D*

The case examines the question of appraising research and development opportunities in the context of a pharmaceutical company. It should be interesting for the reader to compare this R & D environment with the more turbulent environment of technological obsolescence examined in the Aztech case, where the electronics industry is discussed (see the companion text: *Risk Analysis and its Applications*).

*Risk Analysis in Mining Ventures: Mine Evaluation*

The case examines the potential purchase of a copper/nickel mine. A risk analysis approach is used to evaluate the potential of the mining operation.

*Sand/Gravel: Exploration Investments Involving Uncertainty*

The case examines the judgment by a mining company of the worth of two potential exploration projects. The two projects, Penrose and Tremoe, are compared during the course of the case.

*The Sandy Creek Problem: A Coal-mining Case Study*

Examines the profitability on a twenty-year basis of a major coal seam in N. Queensland, Australia. The appraisal is a prelude to a potential investment/joint venture decision by a multinational company.

*National Feeds: A Bargaining Decision*

This case examines an animal feeds company which has made a major facilities planning decision and then has to implement the decision with the labour unions. The case attempts to model the bargaining negotiations for the company and anticipate the future actions of the unions.

*Simulating the Civil Litigation Process*

This case illustrates the structure of a model developed to improve the flow of the civil litigation process in the courts. It uses simulation to indicate the critical system variables.

*Investment in Indonesia: An International Business Problem*

This case examines the options open to a multinational company in formulating its policy with regard to manufacture in Indonesia (not the country in the real situation, and merely selected as a disguise). The company had no manufacturing operation in Indonesia and was exporting to that country.

## 1.5 CHAPTER ORGANIZATION

Each chapter contains a case history of a risk analysis application. Each case history is introduced and explained in outline, and occasional references are also given to other sources in order to provide the widest possible perspective for examination of the case history.

After each case history has been described, a series of questions and issues for discussion are posed for the reader. These should raise some of the main issues, however they do not by any means exhaust the range of critical comments which might be made. Readers are encouraged to examine and criticize the assumptions and nature of each and every application.

Our main hope is that these case histories will provide readers with considerable insight into areas of application and thereby enable them to examine and understand the rationale of the risk analysis approach.

Finally, we would be grateful to receive not only comments, but also cases and areas which readers feel ought to be included in any subsequent revision.

## REFERENCES


Hertz, D. B. *Risk Analysis in Capital Investment*. Harvard Business Review Classic, Volume 57, September/October 1979, pp. 169–181 (reprinted in its entirety from *Harvard Business Review*, 1964).

Hertz, D. B. and H. Thomas (1983). *Risk Analysis and its Applications*. Chichester: John Wiley and Sons Ltd.

Hofer, C. W. and D. E. Schendel (1978). *Strategy Formulation: Analytical Concepts*. St. Paul, Minnesota: West Publishing Company.

Moore, P. G. and H. Thomas (1976). *Anatomy of Decisions*. London: Penguin.

Raiffa, H. (1968). *Decision Analysis*. Reading, Mass.: Addison-Wesley.

Thomas, H. (1972). *Decision Theory and the Manager*. London: Pitman Publishing.

*Chapter 2*

# *Strategic Risk Analysis and Policy Dialogue: New Product Diversification**

## SUMMARY

This chapter aims to illustrate the role of strategic risk analysis in the process of policy dialogue. An example of a new product diversification demonstrates the role of risk analysis in clarifying problem assumptions and in understanding the impact of uncertainty on decision-making. Risk analysis is seen as an adjunct to problem formulation and resolution and not an end in itself.

## 2.1 STRATEGIC RISK ANALYSIS AND POLICY DIALOGUE

The role of strategic risk analysis in policy formulation and choice should be to force hard thinking about the problem under consideration. That is, it should highlight what alternatives should be considered, should examine changing secondary effects and anticipate the nature and extent of the impact of uncertainty for contingency planning. Thus it is recognized that an initial risk analysis is no more than a first attempt at problem understanding. It should encourage controversy and allow members of the decision-making group to find out where basic differences exist about problem assumptions, values and uncertainties. This controversy should enable critical comment and review to be obtained, and through policy dialogue force the re-analysis, re-examination and sensitivity testing of the problem solution. Thus, after considerable dialogue, the quality and level of debate about the problem should be improved. This should facilitate compromise and consensus around a reasonable problem solution.

An example of the use of strategic risk and decision analysis follows, and insights gained summarized in the conclusions section.

*This chapter, and the associated case study, were developed jointly by David Hertz and Howard Thomas.

## 2.2 NEW PROJECT DIVERSIFICATION EXAMPLE

This case considers the decision problem faced by a US chemical company about whether to invest in a newly developed synthetic product. (*Note*: the example and company are real although some of the chronological and assessment features of the problem have been disguised). Management was faced with a seemingly attractive product, but was unsure about the longer-term competitive viability of the product. In particular, given the high capital investment requirements, there was concern about the decreasing prices of competitive products and the increasing possibilities of additional entries into the market.

It was decided that a risk analysis evaluation of the new product opportunity should be undertaken. The key assumptions of the model are outlined in Figure 2.1 and the flow chart for the risk analysis model is shown in Figure 2.2. An important point to note is that management decided that they

KEY ASSUMPTIONS

Ten-year projections for profit and loss statement and balance sheet

Fifteen-year calculations for discounted cash flow (DCF)

Straight-line depreciation
- −15 years for equipment
- −40 years for buildings

R & D prior to 1966 not included in DCF

Investments to be made in 1967

Product introduction in 1968

Figure 2.1 Key Model Assumptions

wanted the new product opportunity evaluated in terms of a series of indicator variables or criteria, rather than in terms of a single rate of return, performance measure such as internal rate of return or net present value. In fact, six performance measures were suggested and each was calculated over its entire range of probable values. The following measures were calculated for the indicated periods:

- — Total dollar sales (1968–1977)
- — Cash flow (1966–1977)
- — Gross profit as a percentage of sales (1968–1977)
- — Net profit after taxes (1968–1977)
- — Net profit as a return on investment (1968–1977)
- — Discounted return on investment (1966–1981).

The probability profiles of some of these performance measures are presented in Figures 2.4 to 2.7.

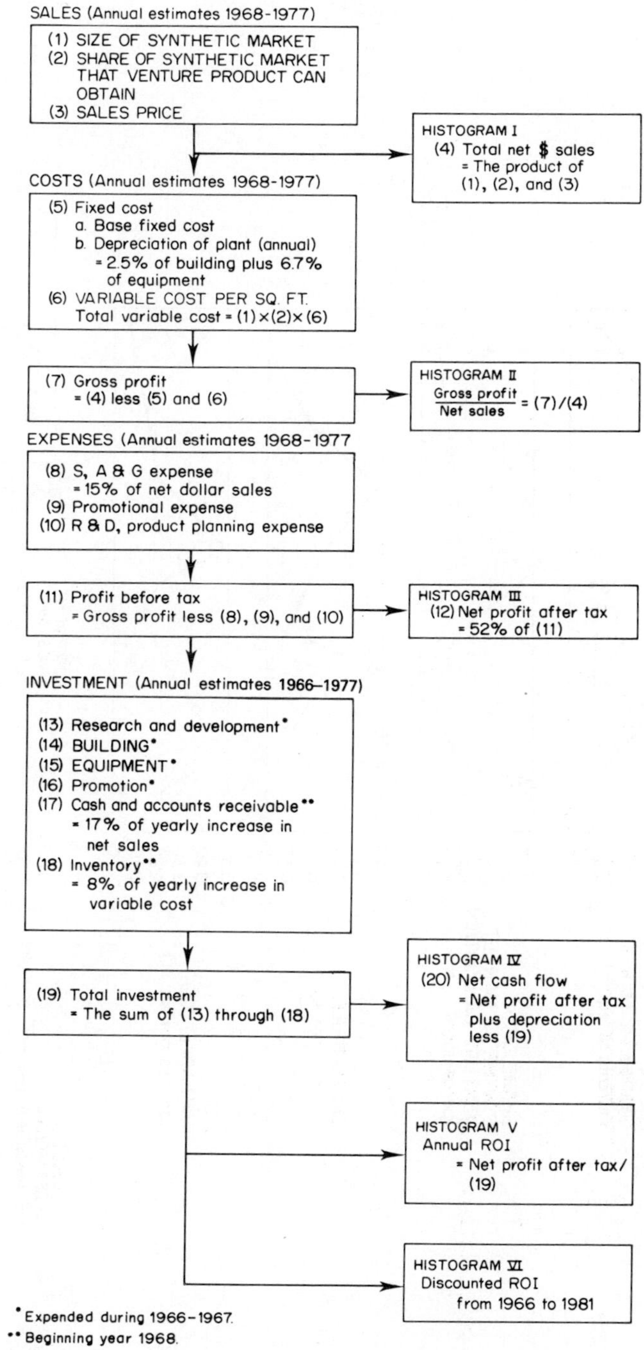


Figure 2.2 Flow Chart of the Risk Analysis Process

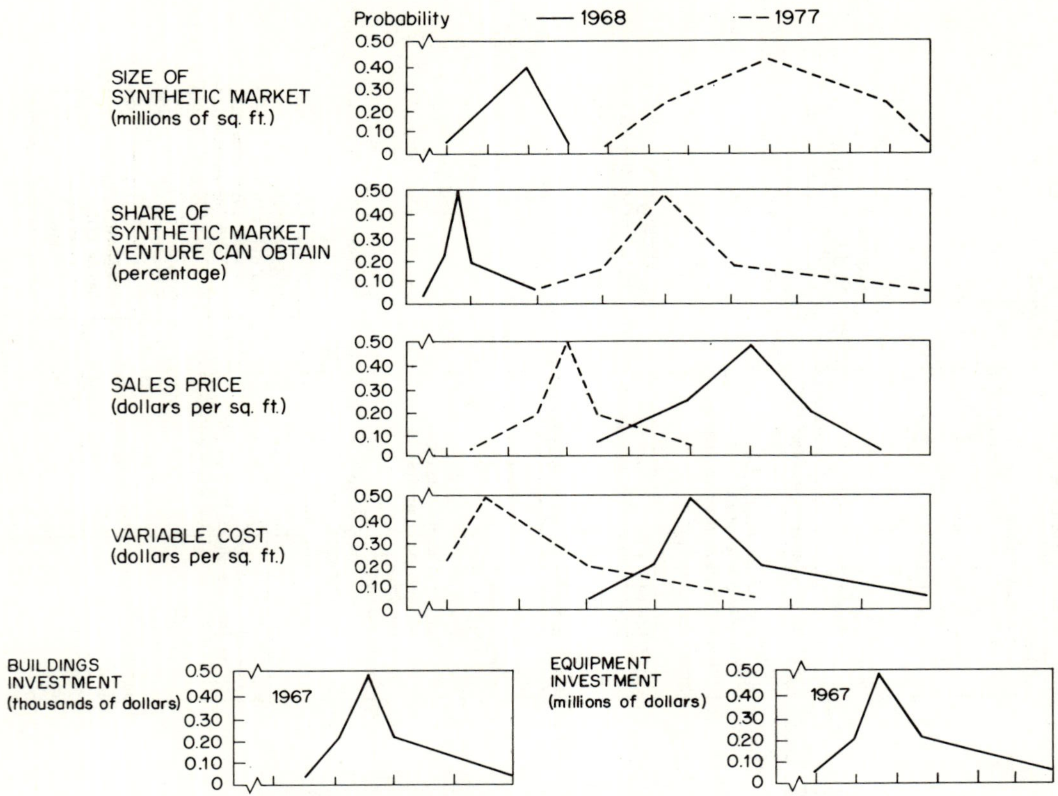


Figure 2.3(a) Probability Assessments for Uncertain Variables

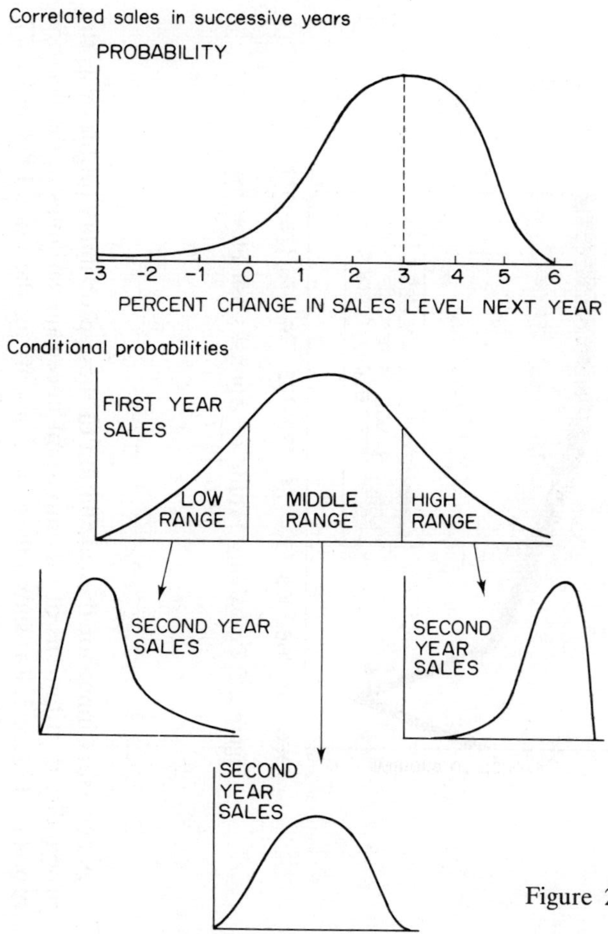


Figure 2.3(b) Handling Correlation Effects in the Risk Analysis Process

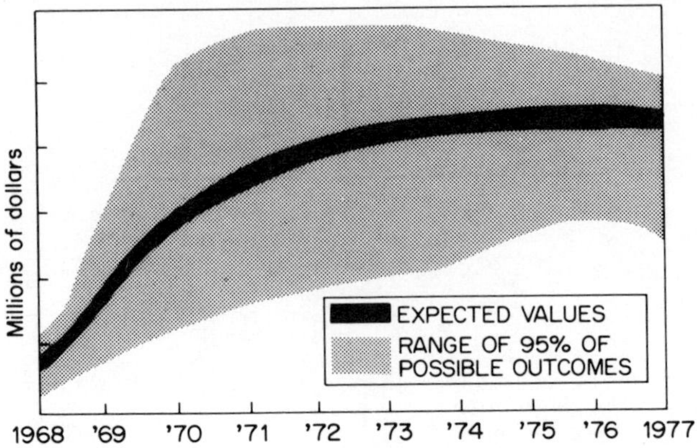


Figure 2.4 Probability Profile of Sales Per Year 1968–1977

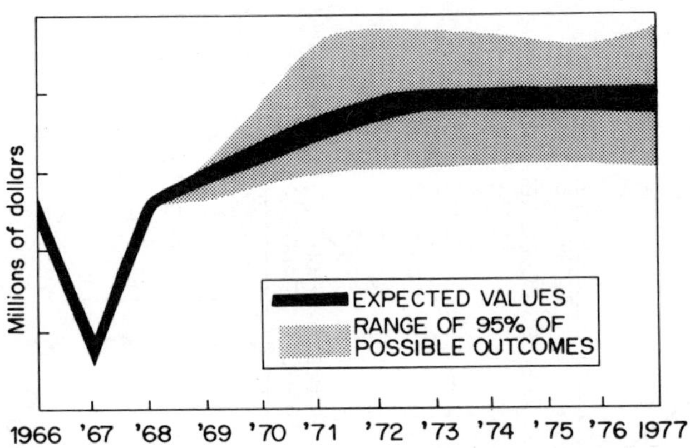


Figure 2.5 Probability Profile of Annual Cash Flow for 1966–1977

A necessary input for the calculation of these probability profiles was the probability distributions of the important uncertain variables in the decision problem. Figure 2.3(a) shows these assessments for the years 1968 and 1977. It is interesting that the distributions for 1977 are much more diffuse or 'spread out,' confirming the proposition that the management team were uncertain about the future and had difficulty in confronting and assessing these future events. Figure 2.3(b) shows how this risk analysis model handled correlation effects. The figure shows how the procedure works in relation to correlated sales in successive years of the product's life. If first-year sales are sampled

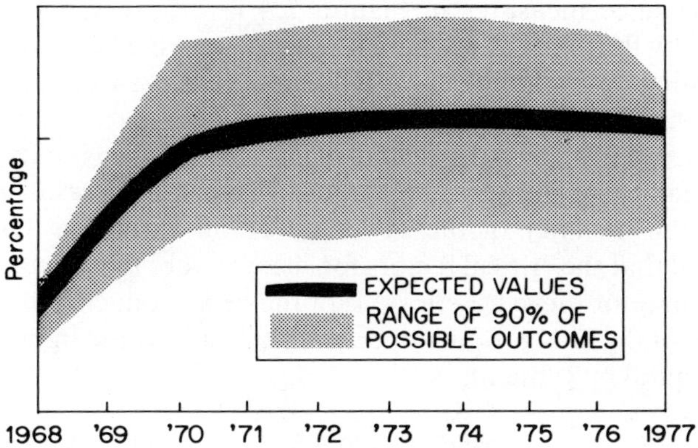


Figure 2.6 Probability Profile of Net Profit as ROI, 1968–1977

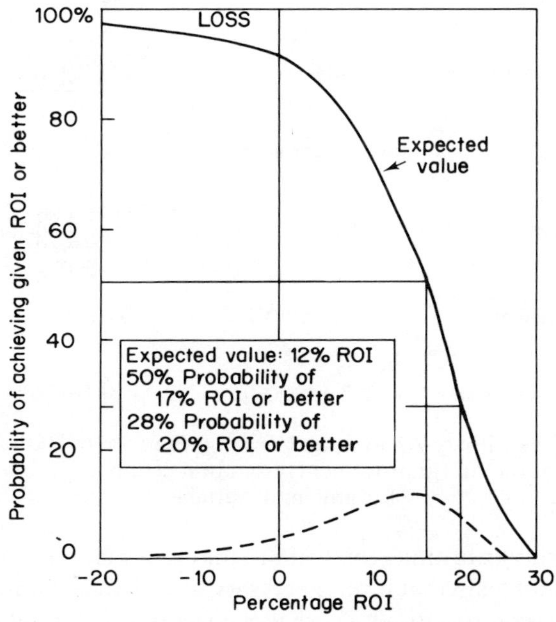


Figure 2.7 Probability Profile of Overall Discounted ROI, 1968–1981 (Note: Heavy line denotes cumulative density function and broken line denotes probability density function)

from the low range of the distribution, then the model samples a value for second-year sales from the second year sales distribution assessed conditional on low sales in the first year. Similarly, if first-year sales are in the middle or high range, then the second-year sales value is obtained by sampling the appropriate conditional distribution as shown by the arrows in the figure.

The performance measures in Figures 2.4 to 2.7 were eagerly examined and discussed by the management team. The team wished to undertake further sensitivity testing, even though it was felt that the cash generation potential and the DCF return of the project were adequate.

Figures 2.8 and 2.9 show the results of one form of sensitivity testing, that is the examination of the effects on rate of return as a result of percentile changes in each member of the set of uncertain variables. This sensitivity testing showed that the critical factors for success were the size of the synthetic market, the share of the synthetic market the new product is likely to obtain, the sales price of the final product, the variable costs and the financial resources involved in capital investment.

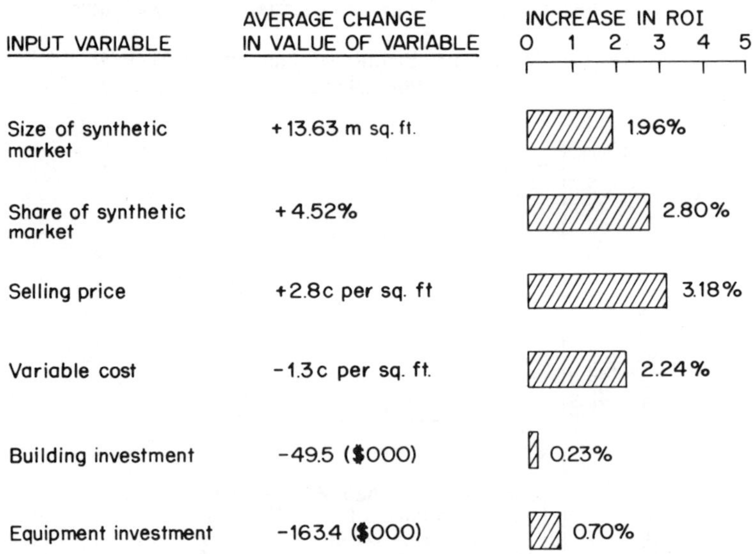


Figure 2.8 Sensitivity Analysis and Testing: Increase in ROI as a result of a 25% deviation (improvement) from best estimate (50th percentile) for any input variable

What this sensitivity testing achieved was the confirmation to many members of the management team that it was necessary to look even more closely at this new product decision situation. There was concern both about the realism of the problem assumptions and the influence of contingencies on policy diversifications into synthetic product areas.

It was decided that attention should be focused very firmly on the objectives underlying diversification moves as well as the portfolio effects on the organization. Further re-analysis was considered necessary to aid formulation and it was felt that, in the meantime, the critical factors should be monitored and re-assessed. Such factors included the size of the synthetic market and environmental influences on the generation of competing products. It was decided, therefore, to postpone an irrevocable policy decision for several

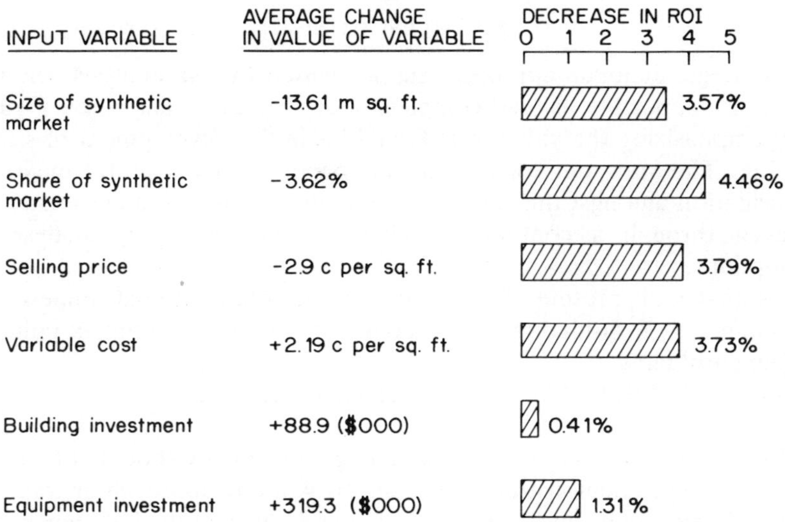


Figure 2.9 Sensitivity Analysis and Testing: Decrease in ROI caused by a 25% deviation (decline) from best estimate (50th percentile) for any input variable

months, particularly given the high potential exit costs associated with failure of such a diversification move.

In some ways, the greatest benefit of the analysis seemed to come from its contribution to organizational processes in terms of the reduction of controversy and the improvement of communication.

## 2.3 THE NATURE OF THE STRATEGIC DIALOGUE

There should be recognition of the role of strategic risk analysis in the policy dialogue process. First, it was clear that the value of the iterative, cyclic process of dialogue was that it forced a more *focused* questioning of assumptions, scenarios and product/market concepts. It was decided, for example, that some extreme 'what-if' scenarios related to the growth of the synthetic market should be included in order that the team could examine and challenge project assumptions. Second, the value of sensitivity analysis (Rappaport, 1967) lies in relation to its simplicity and the speed and economy with which it is undertaken. It can quickly highlight crucial uncertain areas and focus attention on contingency planning. It is thus a complement and a necessary adjunct to the application of risk analysis. Therefore, the dialogue process about six performance measures does no more than recognize that there is no single 'best' criterion, or set of criteria, by which strategic management of the firm's strategic diversification should be handled. Rather it encourages all members of the management team to understand more fully policy alternatives before a choice decision had to be made.

## 2.4 CONCLUSION

This strategic dialogue approach, supplemented by risk analysis, should be viewed as supportive of, and complementary to, an earlier paper (Wagner, 1980) emphasizing the value of risk analysis in the development of strategic thinking. The view put forward in this paper is that a useful measure of reconciliation amongst the various viewpoints in a management team can be achieved through a continuous policy dialogue involving analyses and assumptions.

Risk analysis is presented, therefore, as a useful additional framework for understanding, formulating and resolving ill-structured, complex policy and planning problems.

Mason and Mitroff (1981; p. 302) put it another way:

> 'In our view the risk of policy, planning and strategy should not consist of attempting to demonstrate the superiority of one approach or framework for all situations but rather of showing their mutual dependency ... Whatever methods are used they should always aid in challenging strategic planning assumptions.'

## REFERENCES

Mason, R. O. and I. I. Mitroff (1981). *Challenging Strategic Planning Assumptions*, John Wiley and Sons: New York.

Rappoport, A. (1967;). 'Sensitivity analysis for decision-making', *Accounting Review*, July, pp. 441–456.

Wagner, G. R. (1980). 'Strategic thinking supported by risk analysis', *Long Range Planning,* **13** (June), pp. 61–68.

## QUESTIONS FOR DISCUSSION

1. Examine and critique the role of analytic modelling approaches in the policy debate and dialogue process.
2. How can consensus in relation to policy choice be achieved in managerial debate about competing strategic alternatives?

*Chapter 3*

# *A Strategic Reorganization Problem**


## SUMMARY

The role of decision and risk analysis in the context of business policy is explored with the aid of a case study of a reorganization situation involving subsidiaries of a British company, Ferguson Industrial Holdings Ltd. The case study provides insights about the implementation of analytic models in the policy field. It also indicates guidelines for managers to follow in discussing the implications of the analytic results for the resolution of the reorganization problem.

A unique feature of this case study is the presentation of the entire set of data and assumptions upon which the analyses were carried out. In addition, an appendix gives the logic and details of the decision analytic calculations.


## 3.1 INTRODUCTION

After looking at the problems facing the three Ferguson subsidiaries in Hull, it was felt that decision and risk analysis techniques could usefully be applied. This would involve:

(1) Looking at the feasible alternatives.
(2) Deciding what were the key areas of uncertainty.
(3) Structuring the problem in a decision tree framework.
(4) Assessing subjective probabilities for the key areas of uncertainty.
(5) Estimating future costs and revenues.
(6) Evaluating the strategies by the analytic process of 'averaging out and folding back' the tree.

This project was worked on from February to May 1973 and involved about eight days in Hull for information collecting, at various times throughout the period.


*This contribution was originally developed by Richard Bell and Howard Thomas whilst at the London Business School. Thanks are also due to Dennis Vernon of Ferguson Industrial Holdings. It was written around the 1972/73 time horizon.

On 12th April 1973, one of the subsidiaries, Henry Smiths, had a serious fire which destroyed about half their warehouse space and stock. An appendix to this project shows what implications this fire has to the overall conclusions. Unfortunately the fire came after the bulk of the analysis had been completed. It is fortunate that the implications of the fire support rather than contradict the main conclusions.

## 3.2 THE EXISTING SITUATION

Ferguson Industrial Holdings are a firm of builders' merchants in the North of England. The company has four principal trading divisions (Table 3.1).

Table 3.1

| | | Turnover % | Profits before interest and tax % |
|---|---|---|---|
| 1. | Builders' and plumbers' merchants | 79 | 63 |
| 2. | Architectural and marine ironmongery | 9 | 10 |
| 3. | Industrial heating equipment | 7 | 17 |
| 4. | Engineering supplies | 5 | 10 |

The company has a turnover of about £10m and pre-tax profits of over £460,000. In Hull, the company has three subsidiaries:

James Darby Ltd. (Darbys)
Henry Smith (Merchants) Ltd. (Smiths)
King and Company Ltd. (Kings) – the latter only recently taken over in January 1972 and has a separate division in Darlington.

### (1) James Darby

James Darby are glass merchants. They occupy an old two-storey building in the north of Hull (see map p. 90) which is rented from the Borough Council at a nominal rent. The glass is delivered to Darbys by Pilkingtons; Darbys cut the glass to size and deliver it to customers.

*(a) Sales*

(i) 92 per cent is trade sales.
(ii) More than 90 percent is delivered.
(iii) 60 percent of sales are for new housing work.
(iv) 10 percent of sales are double glazing.

(v) There are contracts with Edenlight and Crittal-Hope to supply greenhouse glass for domestic greenhouses in the Humberside area. This amounts to about 10 percent of sales.

(vi) Many of the customers are the same as Henry Smith's customers. It is a peculiarity of the Hull area that plumbers also do glazing work.

*(b) Buildings*

James Darby's warehouse is not suitable for a glass merchant because the access height is not sufficient. They cannot accept the larger sizes of float glass from Pilkingtons. Also they have not the space to install overhead lifting gear, so that loading and unloading lorries becomes very time-consuming. Although no penalties have been incurred as yet for the delay caused to delivery lorries, these may well occur in the future.

Darby's offices are attached to the warehouse. In the entrance there is a small display of double glazing, though the site and the surroundings are not likely to attract much retail trade.

*(c) Staff*

(i) office staff (2 part-time; the accounts are done centrally at Kings);
(ii) 3 drivers;
(iii) 4 cutters;
(iv) 1 warehouseman.

*(d) Transport*

(i) 2 5-ton } box vans
(ii) 1 1¾-ton }

**(2) Henry Smith (Merchants) Ltd.**

Smiths are plumbing and heating merchants. They supply domestic boilers, standard sanitary fittings (not luxury models), gutters, downpipes, etc., iron and copper tubes and fittings, brassware and water tanks. They are situated on the east side of the River Hull, about a mile from the centre of Hull.

*(a) Sales*

(i) Sales are mainly to firms of plumbers – both one-man and larger firms – though 20 percent are to local councils. About 7 percent of sales are direct (i.e. straight from factory to customer).

(ii) Traditionally Henry Smiths have been very strong in Lincolnshire, going as far south as Spalding. They also deliver as far north as Thirsk and Whitby. They are comparatively weak in Hull.

(iii) They have no showroom facilities and retail trade amounts to only 5 percent.
(iv) Similarly over 90 percent of sales are delivered, but they have an active trade counter and many sales made at the trade counter are subsequently delivered.

*(b) Building*

Henry Smith's buildings, which are freehold, are old and cramped. They have an amazingly high stock turnover and it is felt that sales cannot be increased much, due to congestion, except through direct sales. At present they have 10,300 sq. ft. of space. They could do with nearly double this in the longer term.

*(c) Staff*

Henry Smith's staff amount to 40:
(i) 3 representatives (who also represent Darbys);
(ii) 5 drivers;
(iii) 10 warehousemen;
(iv) 9 sales office;
(v) 13 secretaries/typists.

*(d) Transport*

(i) 2 7-ton lorries;
(ii) 1 6-ton lorry;
(iii) 1 5-ton lorry.

Smiths run regular deliveries, with some of the Lincolnshire trips lasting 2 days.

**(3) King and Company**

King and Company are situated in the old business center of Hull. Their sales are organized into a number of divisions

(i) *Architectural Brassware*. This is high-grade ironmongery. About one-third of the sales are contract sales to architects. There has been considerable rationalization of stock since the takeover, in 1972. It is the largest division, accounting for 40 percent of the net operating profit.
(ii) *Heating*. This division supplies industrial (schools, offices, etc.) heating equipment and also designs and fits the systems. This latter service is unique to the Ferguson Group.
(iii) *Tools*. 90 percent of sales are of small hand tools, 10 percent are of power tools with stands.

(iv) *Catering*. Originally this division supplied industrial catering equipment though the trend is now toward domestic sales.

(v) *Sanitary Ware*. Since the takeover Kings have concentrated on selling at the luxury end of the market, leaving Smiths to supply standard products. This division has a large first-floor showroom nearing completion.

There is also a ground-floor retail shop which is shared by all divisions.

*(a) Sales*

Historically Kings had an excellent reputation in Hull for service and being able to supply virtually anything from stock. However, mismanagement and neglect have eroded their goodwill over the last 12 years, although they are now beginning to regain profitability.

About 7 percent of King's sales are retail and as many as 30 percent are collected rather than delivered. Their customers cover all Yorkshire, particularly in the Hull region. They are not so strong in Lincolnshire.

*(b) Buildings*

Kings occupy a 1¼-acre site in the 'old town' of Hull. It is a rambling building on many levels and is not suitable for its present use. It is situated in a block, part of which is a scheduled historic building (school) and part a telephone exchange owned by the council. Access to the site is very difficult for large vehicles since:

(i) there is no access on South Churchside;
(ii) Vicar Lane and Fish Street are very narrow;
(iii) the Mytongate access will be closed as it is the line for the new South Orbital road (see map pp.90, 91).

*(c) Staff*

King's staff has been very much reduced since the takeover, from 100 down to about 75. This figure of 75 includes 18 heating fitters and 5 drivers.

*(d) Transport*

(i) 1 5-ton lorry;
(ii) 4 1½-ton vans.

The vans undertake regular deliveries around Hull. The lorry has 3 loads a week and one to Darlington, the location of the other King's division.

Table 3.2 Summarized Financial Statement of the Hull Subsidiaries, 1972/73

| | King and Co. (*Hull*) | Henry Smith (£'000) | James Darby |
|---|---|---|---|
| Sales[a] | 554 | 635 | 157 |
| Gross profit[a] | 134 | 115 | 62 |
| less: Total expenditure[a] | 110 | 70 | 30 |
| Net operating profit[a] | 24 | 45 | 32 |
| less: Interest[a] | 2 | 1 | 0 |
| Profit before tax[a] | 22 | 44 | 32 |
| Fixed assets | 119 | 26 | 1 |
| Debtors | 108 | 118 | 32 |
| Stocks | 115 | 65 | 16 |
| Creditors | 72 | 81 | 23 |
| Average net assets | 270 | 146 | 27 |
| Return on net assets (net operating profit/net assets) | 8.9% | 33.6% | 126% |
| Stock turnover[a] | 4.8 | 10.0 | 10.0 |
| Debtor turnover (months) | 2.4 | 2.2 | 2.4 |
| Salaries (as % of sales) | 12.4% | 6.4% | 11.7% |
| Gross margin | 24% | 18% | 40% |

[a]11 months data grossed to 12.

## 3.3 THE FUTURE

All three companies need new premises. Darbys could possibly rebuild on their existing site – but it has no great geographical advantage. Smiths and Kings could rebuild but it would cause a huge amount of disruption to their trading. Kings are also likely to have difficulty in obtaining planning permission for a suitable warehouse at South Churchside. Another possibility would be to amalgamate Smiths and Kings on one site, and possibly Darbys as well, though Darby's business is very different and amalgamation would not be such an obvious move.

**Advantages of Rebuilding** (K = Kings, D = Darbys, S = Smiths)

(1) Less maintenance (K, S, D).
(2) Better stock control, stock handling, etc. (K, S, D).
(3) Can cope with increased demand (K, S, D).
(4) Access height advantages (D).
(5) Easier access to building (K, S).

**Disadvantages**

(1) Higher rent (D and K, S if not on own land).
(2) Loss of some retail and collect trade (if on new site).

**Advantages of amalgamation**

(1) Slight saving in transport costs – combined deliveries, etc.
(2) Saving in warehousemen/office staff through common stocks, stock control, accounting, etc.
(3) Reduction in stocks that were held in common.
(4) Improved management – one manager to coordinate all Ferguson's subsidiaries in Hull. This is perhaps the major advantage of amalgamation.

**Disadvantages**

(1) Loss of corporate identity, effect on morale, etc.

**Likely changes in the market**

The Building and Civil Engineering EDC (part of NEDO) recently published the result of a pilot study entitled 'Regional forecasting for construction in Yorkshire and Humberside'. This study predicted an above average growth rate in construction of 4.5 percent per annum in real terms. This is well above the average predicted for the whole country. Factors which influence this are:

(i) Humberside's designation as an intermediate development area.
(ii) The Humber Bridge (starting 1973, due to finish 1976).
(iii) The M62 and other trunk roads, which will link Hull directly with Liverpool and Manchester and also to the M1 and A1 (see Appendix III p. 92).
(iv) The growth of container/freight traffic to the EEC.

This growth on Humberside is, however, likely to attract other builders' merchants to the area. UBM already have a glass merchant, Baxendale Kyall (which is changing its name to Rycroft's). Thomas Tilling are rumored to be thinking of moving into the area.

**Likely changes in Hull**

The map in Appendix III shows the new roads planned in Hull. At present the South Orbital road is the only one being built. The others should be completed in the next ten years.

The South Orbital road goes very close to Kings. In fact the area of the town where Kings is situated is likely to become more of a shopping and commercial centre over the next decade.

(i) The old market place has been cleared and plans have been passed for a supermarket, multistorey car park and Holiday Inn Hotel to be built on the site.
(ii) Whitefriargate, a street just north of Holy Trinity Church, has been made a pedestrian precinct and is beginning to regain its place as one of the major shopping areas of Hull.
(iii) The council have compulsorily purchased a number of buildings near Kings with an obvious eye to redevelopment.

It seems then that Kings could be a very valuable site for development as offices and shops, but not as a builders' merchants. It is possible though that this value could not be realized until the redevelopment of the area becomes more apparent. The fact that:

(i) part of the block is a scheduled historic building, and
(ii) the building faces Holy Trinity church,

might mean that the redevelopment value is limited. Also at present part of the block is occupied by the telephone exchange.

Henry Smith's building is likely to have only *site* value, rather than any intrinsic worth. This is obviously going to increase, but the site does not have the same potential as Kings.

James Darby's building is only rented from the Council, and that at a very nominal rent.

## 3.4 DECIDING ON THE TREE STRUCTURE

Obviously all possible permutations of:

(i) rebuilding site;
(ii) which companies amalgamate;
(iii) when they rebuild;

would lead to thousands of different possibilities. By discussion with people directly concerned, it was possible to narrow down the alternatives to a group of feasible strategies that could be analyzed in a decision tree framework.

(1) *The site*?
It was decided that any rebuilding should be on a *new site* outside the centre of Hull. A site to the *west of Hull*, near the approach roads to the Humber Bridge, would give the highest sales but an alternative site of Sutton Fields, an industrial estate *north of Hull*, was also suitable and was considerably cheaper in terms of land rent.

(2) *When*?
An immediate decision would still involve about 6 months of planning and then about a further 12 months building. The earliest a new building could be opened would be January 1975. As a latest date, it could be argued that a decision should be postponed until the bridge was opened, and the full effect of the improved communications on Humberside properly assessed. This would mean a decision in mid-1976 and moving in, say, January 1978. As a compromise a decision could be delayed until late 1974 and the move would then take place in July 1976, just about to coincide with the bridge opening.

(3) *Which Companies*?
Kings and Smiths are in many ways similar and could amalgamate apart from Darbys. However, if an immediate decision was taken it would seem sensible to amalgamate all three onto one site, so that building costs would be minimized. Darbys felt they had much to gain from rebuilding and have gone ahead with their own plans to rebuild. If it is then decided to wait as far as Kings and Smiths are concerned, Darbys could be built on a new site and the extra land acquired in preparation for a later move by Smiths and Kings.

This leaves seven strategies:

(1) Status quo.
(2) Darbys build, moving late 1974.
(3) Smiths, Kings and Darbys build, moving January 1975.
(4) Smiths, Kings and Darbys build, moving July 1976.
(5) Smiths, Kings and Darbys build, moving January 1978.
(6) Darbys build, moving late 1974. Kings and Smiths build, moving July 1976.

(7) Darbys build, moving late 1974. Kings and Smiths build, moving January 1978.

For the last five there is also the decision whether to move to North or West Hull.

Set out as a decision tree, this looks like Figure 3.1.

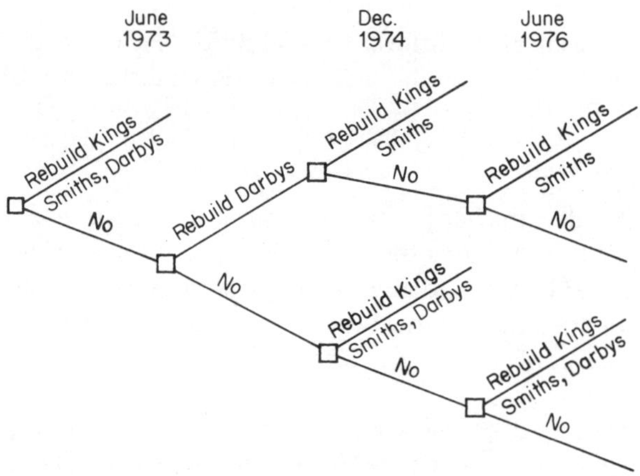


Figure 3.1 Decision tree

## Uncertainties

Within the decision period there are a number of uncertain events which might occur. The outcome of these events could very well change the decision that will be taken. These uncertainties include:

(1) Growth in overall market for building materials on Humberside.
(2) Growth of competition.
(3) How the value of King's site will change.
(4) How the value of Smith's site will change.
(5) How quickly the bridge and road building program will progress.
(6) How the gross profit margin is likely to change.

It was felt after considerable discussion with managerial staff in Hull that the three key uncertainties were:

(1) Overall growth of market.
(2) Growth in competition.
(3) Change in value of King's site.

The first two variables were combined to give a single market growth variable. The margins were somewhat uncertain but it was felt that the historical trend could be extrapolated with reasonable confidence. One caveat that should be noted is that a drop in sales would increase costs as a percentage of sales, since fixed costs would not be reduced in the short run. However, it can be seen later that even under pessimistic assumptions sales are predicted to increase, so this was not considered.

Subjective probability estimates were then obtained from the managers in Hull. These were the managers of each of the three subsidiaries and, in addition, Stephen Martin, a non-executive director of Ferguson Industrial Holdings, who lived in Hull and had close knowledge of King and Company. The method used is described later. What was required was growth in *profits* but since these were found difficult to predict, it was decided to get estimates of sales growth and then, using separate profit margin estimates, to translate this into profit figures.

A seven-year horizon was chosen as this encompasses all decision periods and allows an extra two years for transitional effects to iron themselves out.

In summary, therefore, assessments for growth in sales and the change in Kings value were obtained on the following basis:

(1) Growth in sales of
- (i) Kings;
- (ii) Smiths;
- (iii) Darbys (old site);
- (iv) Darbys (new site);
- (v) Kings and Smiths together.

It was felt that Darby's sales growth depended only on whether they rebuilt or not, *not* on amalgamation.

(2) Change in value of King's building
- (i) January 1975
- (ii) July 1976
- (iii) January 1978

This then leaves a decision tree looking like Figure 3.2.

## 3.5 PROBABILITY ASSESSMENT

As was discussed in the previous section on the decision tree structure, the two key uncertainties are the rate of market growth and the value of Kings, probably as a site for potential shop/office development.

Subjective probability assessments for these two key factors were determined directly to give the CDF.* The method used was to present the assessors with two fictitious bets and to alter the bets to obtain indifference between the two. An example is given below:

*Analyst*

Imagine there is an opaque jar containing 50 red and 50 black balls. You are to choose one ball, without looking in the jar. If you choose a black ball then you win £20, a red ball will win you nothing. Let's call this 'bet number 1'.

*Cumulative probability Distribution Function.

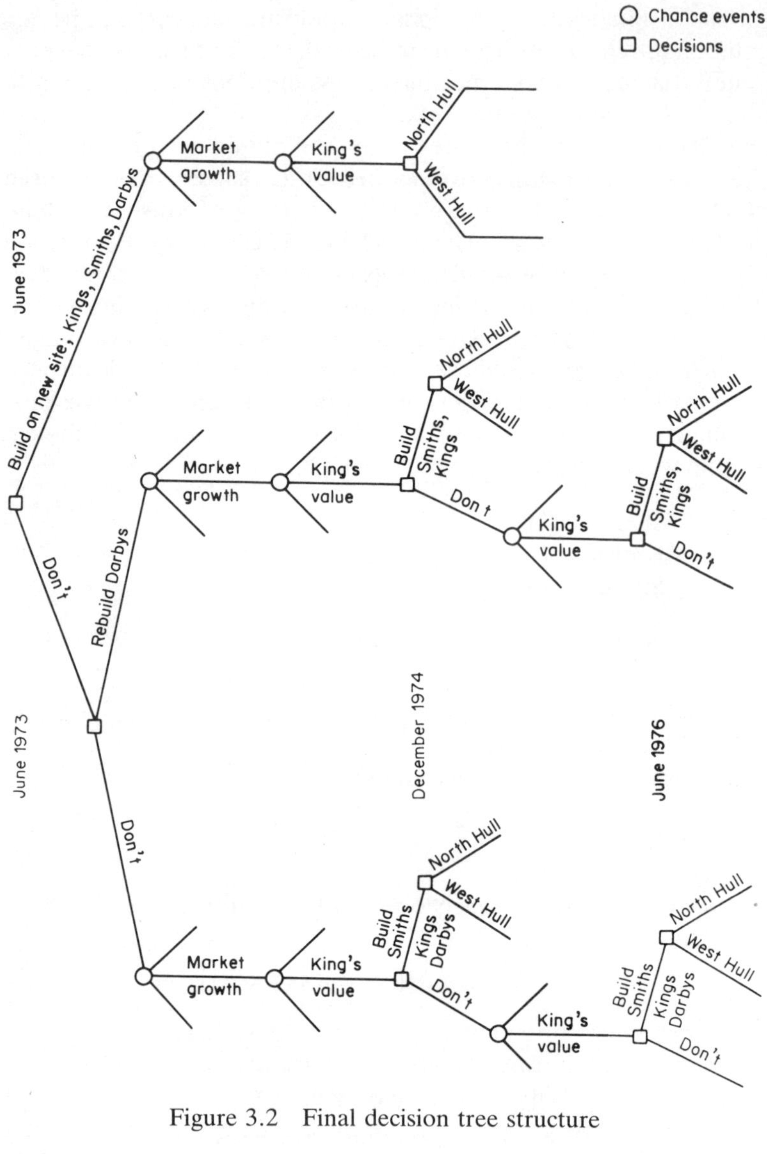


Figure 3.2 Final decision tree structure

Now there's another bet in which you must consider the annual growth rate of *X*'s sales over the next seven years assuming they carry on trading in the same line of business and from the same premises. In considering the growth of sales you must consider the possible effects of inflation. This may mean that just to stay still, sales will have to show an apparent growth equal to the rate of inflation. There is also the fact that the NEDO regional construction forecast predicted a higher than average rate of growth for the Humberside construction industry. You should also consider the possible effects of competition. For example it is rumored that Thomas Tilling are planning to come to Humberside.

This second bet is as follows: if *X*'s sales growth exceeds 11 percent per annum, you win £20, if not, you win nothing. These two bets can be illustrated thus:

| | Bet 1 | Bet 2 |
|---|---|---|
| 50 black<br>50 red | £20<br>win, black<br><br>lose, red<br>£0 | £20<br>win, sales growth *more* than 11% p.a.<br><br>lose, less<br>£0 |

Which bet do you prefer?
*Assessor*: I think I'd go for bet 1, 11 percent seems a bit steep.
*Analyst*: Imagine then a new choice.

| | Bet 1 | Bet 2 |
|---|---|---|
| 30 black<br>70 red | £20<br>win, black<br><br>lose, red<br>£0 | £20<br>win, sales growth *more* than 11% p.a.<br><br>lose, less<br>£0 |

*Assessor*: Well, this time bet 2 seems a better choice.

Eventually, by altering either the number of red and black balls, or the percentage growth rate, a point can be achieved where the assessor is 'indifferent' between the two bets – he cannot choose between them.

| | | | |
|---|---|---|---|
| For if, | £20<br>*x* black<br><br>(100 − *x*) red<br>£0 | ~ is indifferent to | £20<br>sales growth more than θ%<br><br>less<br>£0 |

then Prob. {growth > θ%} = $\left[\dfrac{x}{100}\right]$, where θ% represents target sales growth

In this way a cumulative distribution function can be obtained since by by altering $x$ in the range, say, 5 → 95 a complete distribution could be obtained.

**Problems encountered in practice**

*(a) Untrained Assessors*

Although this method tries to minimize the difficulty of putting across probabilistic ideas to someone who is unaccustomed to them, even so some distributions were rather peculiar. For example, Don Smith was surely not quite as certain of the future of Henry Smith as his CDF made out.

This problem could have been solved partially by presenting the assessors with a graph of the CDF (or preferably the probability *density* function) and letting them adjust their original estimates if necessary. The analyst could help the assessor by offering him further bets (based on his CDF) as a consistency check. (See Hertz and Thomas ((1983), p. 160) for further details)

In practice certain of the distributions were altered slightly where it was felt that major errors were likely.

*(b) Second Opinions*

For two of the distributions, that involving the sales trend for Kings, and for Kings and Smiths combined, both Stephen Martin and Brian Spencer assessed CDFs independently. In each case, but especially in the combined case, these were somewhat different. Each time Stephen Martin was less certain (i.e. there was a wider spread) and more optimistic. One way to resolve this would have been to have a discussion involving both of them and for them to come to some agreement. However, this would bring in interpersonal factors so that a better solution would not necessarily be achieved. A possible approach to arrive at a consensus based on the 'Delphi' method was considered but rejected because of time pressures as it involved repeated adjustments.

In practice it was decided that some weighting of the two CDFs would be used. It was felt that Stephen Martin's assessment of the degree of uncertainty involved was more realistic and his CDF was weighted more heavily.

*(c) Conditional Assessments*

In assessing King's value, it was assumed that a valuation of Kings would be undertaken at three points in time, January 1975, July 1976 and January 1978. The CDF of each of these valuations was required. However, there was a further assessment problem since if, say, a high valuation resulted in 1975 a high valuation was *more* likely in 1976. In practice, managers found it very difficult to think about conditional probabilities, and only a small allowance was made for them as they did not appear to change the overall analysis significantly. This issue is discussed on page 44. However, in the analysis only the centre branch of the tree is used and there the probabilities do not deviate by more than 10 percent from the norm of 0.25 – High, 0.5 – Medium, 0.25 – Low.

*(d) Growth Rates*

What was required was an assessment of the average annual growth rate over the next seven years. In practice a number of assessors found it difficult to think in terms of percentage growth *rates* so tables were prepared which translated growth rates into sales on an annual basis. The assessor was then asked to consider the £-sales amount in five years' time. The CDF was then prepared as before and the *x*-axis was converted, again using the tables, to percentage rates of growth.

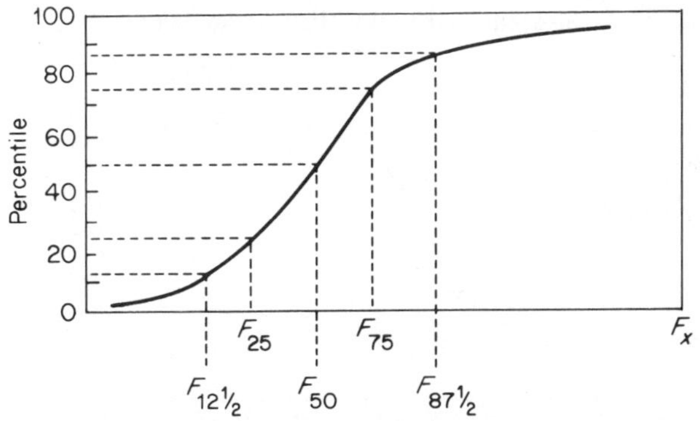


Figure 3.3 Obtaining the high-medium-low (¼, ½, ¼) Estimates from the Cumulative Distribution Function

A subjective distribution function was obtained, as has been described previously. It was then required to split up this continuous distribution into three discrete probabilities, so that it could be fitted into a decision tree framework. Since in some cases several rates of growth are combined (e.g. Kings, Smiths and Darbys),* the set of three probabilities had to be the same for each case. The probabilities of 0.25, 0.5 and 0.25 were chosen. The point estimate for the medium value of the distribution was chosen as $F_{50}$ for obvious reasons (the real value is equally likely to be above or below this figure). Since a probability of 0.5 was being assigned to this value, the range $F_{25}$ to $F_{75}$ was chosen as being the appropriate range. An 'average' of $F_{12\frac{1}{2}}$ was chosen as being the point estimate for the low values (below $F_{25}$) and similarly a value of $F_{87\frac{1}{2}}$ was given to the high values (see Figure 3.3).

**Results of Probability Assessments**

Table 3.3 Growth Rates of Sales, %(p.a. over next 7 years)

| | | *Probabilities* | |
|---|---|---|---|
| | 0.25<br>High<br>% | 0.5<br>Medium<br>% | 0.25<br>Low<br>% |
| Kings (on existing site) | 16 | 12 | 7 |
| Smiths (on existing site) | 11 | 9 | 7 |
| Darbys (on existing site) | 14 | 10 | 6½ |
| Darbys (on new site) | 20 | 16 | 12½ |
| Kings and Smiths (on new site) | 18 | 13½ | 9 |
| *King's value* | | | |
| January 1975 | £150,000 | £110,000 | £90,000 |
| July 1976 | £180,000 | £140,000 | £100,000 |
| January 1978 | £220,000 | £160,000 | £120,000 |

*It was assumed that these growth rates were dependent, i.e. if Smiths and Kings had low sales growth, so did Darbys.

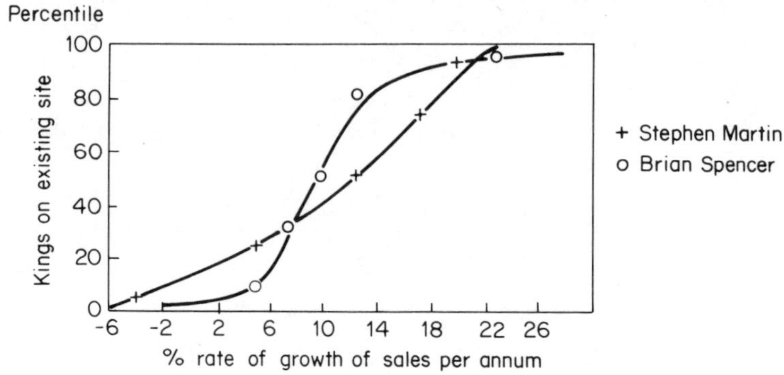


Figure 3.4 Cumulative Distribution Functions for Sales Growth for Kings on existing site

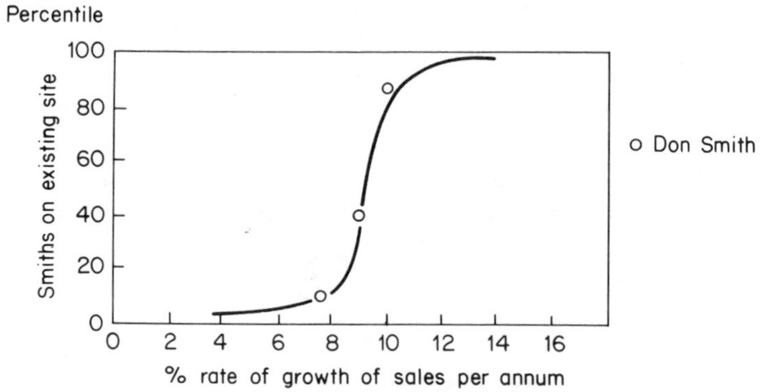


Figure 3.5 Cumulative Distribution Function for Sales Growth for Smiths on existing site

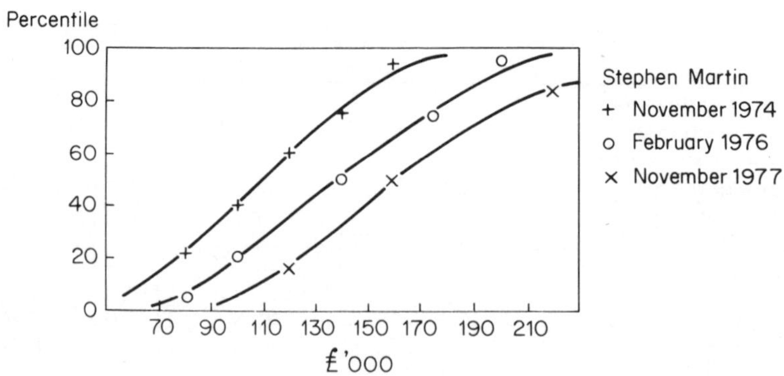


Figure 3.6 Cumulative Distribution Functions for Kings value

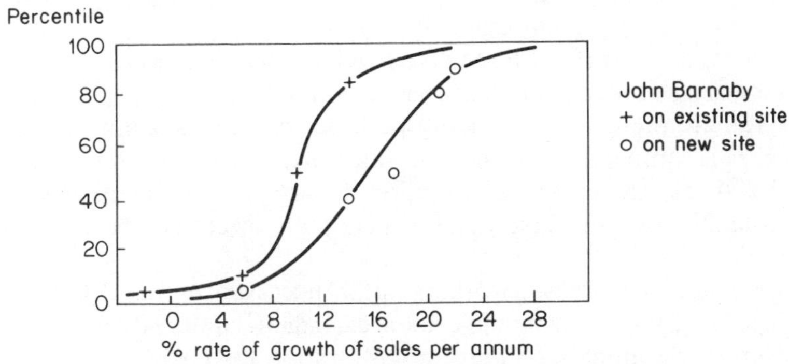


Figure 3.7 Cumulative Distribution Functions for Sales Growth for Darbys

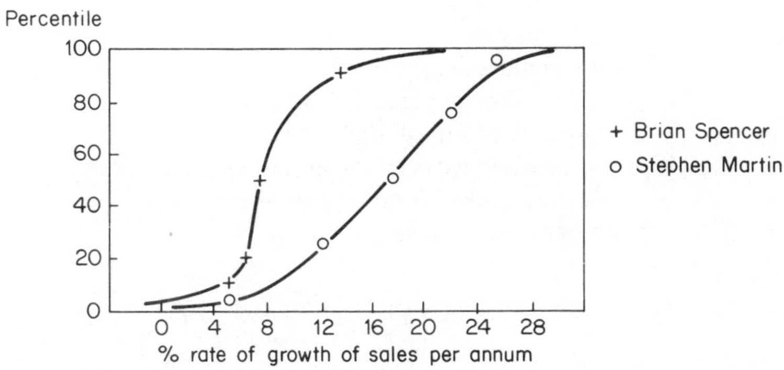


Figure 3.8 Cumulative Distribution Functions for Sales Growth for Kings and Smiths new site (W)

## 3.6 COST ESTIMATION

As was explained in the introduction, the form of the analysis involves finding expected costs and revenues for each different strategy. It was decided that the most reliable way to do this was as follows:

(a) Take the sales estimates for that year, or if a move is involved in that year, for the parts of the year before and after the move.
(b) Deduct a fraction (1½ percent was used), if the original sales figure assumed a site in West Hull, in order to obtain likely sales in North Hull.
(c) Deduct a figure to represent collect-sales lost during the first two years of operation on a new site. This was taken as half the collect sales in year one and a quarter in year two, based on estimated fraction of collect sales in 1972/73.
(d) Estimate the: (1) gross margin;
(2) cost of selling;
using an amalgamation of:
(i) historic trends (Hull and Tyne Tunnel);

(ii) management estimates;
(iii) NFBPM data (trade association data).

(e) Hence obtain the profit before interest and tax.
(f) Estimate the depreciation allowable for tax. (This is not very great as there is comparatively little investment in plant and machinery and since the firms are in the distribution industry, regional grants are not available despite Humberside being an intermediate development area.)
(g) Estimate the increased working capital necessary to support the increase in sales (again by using the evidence available under (d) above).
(h) Hence, assuming a 50 percent corporation tax (Advance Corporation Tax and Mainstream Tax) payable on average a year in arrears, the annual cash flow from operations was obtained if:

$r$ = discount rate;
$S_t$ = sales in year $t$;
$\alpha_t$ = gross margin in year $t$;
$c_t$ = selling cost in year $t$ (assumed slightly dependent on sales growth);
$\Delta WC_t$ = increase in working capital in year $t$;
$D_t$ = depreciation for tax purposes in year $t$.

Cash flow from operations in year $t$ is

$$X_t = [S_t(\alpha_t - c_t) - D_t]\left[1 - \frac{0.5}{(1 + r)}\right] + D_t - \Delta WC_t$$

Cash flow from capital transactions (buying and selling land and buildings etc.) is $Y_t$ in year $t$.

Terminal value of fixed assets = $F_T$;

Initial value of working capital = $WC_0$;

Final value of working capital = $WC_0 + \sum_{t=1}^{T} \Delta WC_t$

Hence, discounting at $r$ percent,

$$\text{NPV} = \sum_{t=1}^{T} \frac{(X_t + Y_t)}{(1 + r)^t} + \left[\frac{F_T + WC_0 + \sum_{t=1}^{T} \Delta WC_t}{(1 + r)^T}\right]$$

NOTES

(1) King's value has been treated separately.
(2) Smith's building is assumed to have a value of:
£35,000 in January 1975;
£40,000 in July 1976;
£46,000 in January 1978;
£60,000 in December 1979.

(3) Working capital is valued at balance sheet prices. It has been found that at the Tyne Tunnel operation, working capital has increased as 16 percent of sales. This figure was used in the analysis.

(4) Depreciation was taken as a percent on sales (though of course in the short run it would be fixed).
Depreciation = 0.4% of sales at Darbys;
0.75% of sales at Kings;
0.3% of sales at Smiths;
0.4% of sales at the new site.
(This last figure is obviously higher in the first year after the move since 100 percent write-off is allowed on certain items.)

(5) Graphs (Figures 3.9 and 3.10) showing the expected costs and margins are shown on pages 39 and 40. Table 3.4 shows relevant historic data for these costs.
Tables of cost data are also shown in Appendix II.

It is felt that, as in the past, the trend will be towards lower gross margins, but Ferguson Industrial Holdings' increasing size will give it the buying power to help counteract this trend.

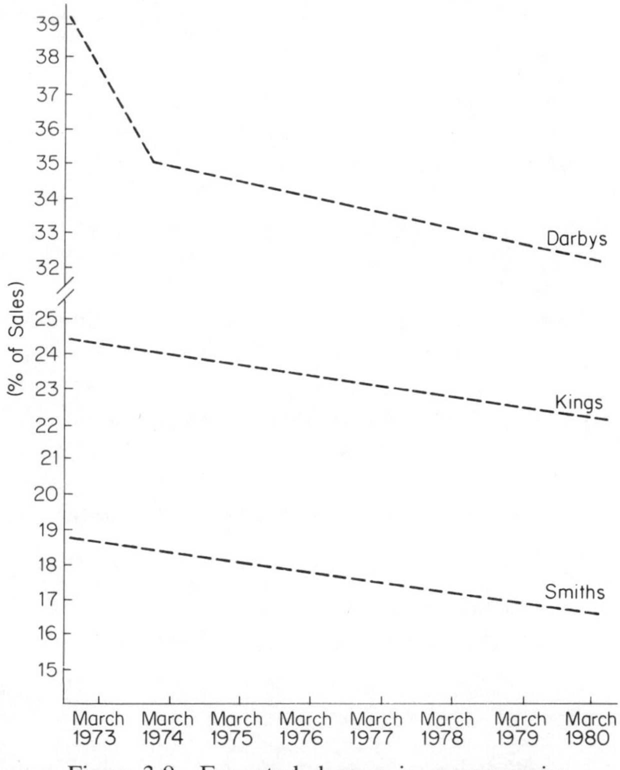


Figure 3.9 Expected changes in gross margins
It is assumed that the business cycle does not have a significant effect.

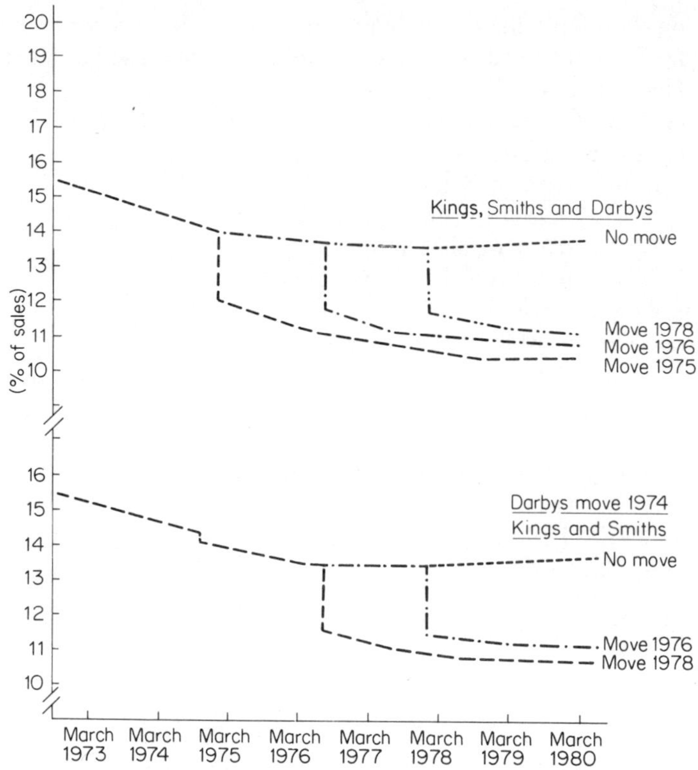


Figure 3.10 Expected costs as percentage of sales

There will be an initial gradual improvement in selling costs irrespective of any move, but in the absence of a move it is felt costs will rise again in the late 1970s due to wage inflation.

At the time of the move a sharp drop in costs should occur as the economies of a combined operation under one roof, which were mentioned previously, are achieved. It is hoped that the experience of the move at Tyne Tunnel could prove instructive and keep the costs of moving to a minimum. The temporary loss of part of the collect trade is, however, virtually inevitable.

(6) The value of the business at the end of the seven-year period analyzed is taken to be merely the building value plus working capital.

(7) *New building*

(i) Costs increase at 6 percent p.a.

(ii) Present cost of single frame, specially built warehouse is £4.25 per sq. ft.

Required for Kings and Smiths.

(a) Kings at present have 75,000 sq. ft., but in a *suitable building* could need only about 35,000 sq. ft.

Table 3.4 Profit margins

| | | 1972/3 | | 1968/9 | 1969/70 | 1970/71 | 1971/2 | 1972/3 |
|---|---|---|---|---|---|---|---|---|
| | Kings | Smiths | Darbys | Ferguson-Foster at Tyne Tunnel | | | | |
| Sales (actual) £'000 | 553 | 633 | 157 | 974 | 1127 | 1429 | 1457 | 2099 |
| Sales (on a percentage base) | 100 | 100 | 100 | 100 | 100 | 100 | 100 | 100 |
| Gross profit (on a percentage base) | 24.4 | 18.3 | 39.4[a] | 15.4 | 15.9 | 14.8 | 16.8 | 16.9 |
| Costs (on a percentage base) | 20.0 | 11.1 | 18.9 | 13.7 | 15.2 | 11.9 | 12.2 | 10.3 |
| Net profit (on a percentage base) | 4.4 | 7.2 | 20.5 | 1.7 | 0.7 | 2.9 | 4.6 | 6.6 |

[a]The gross margin of Darbys in 1972/73 was abnormally high due to a price rise affecting existing stocks.

(b) Henry Smiths have 10,300 sq. ft. but could use more at present and should thus allow for 20,000 sq. ft. in a new building.

This implies a new building of say 60,000 sq. ft. including office accommodation.

With Darbys an extra 10,000 sq. ft. may be needed, including an entrance height sufficient for the large sizes of float glass.

Obviously it would be more expensive to build a separate building for James Darby unless the height differential proved difficult to overcome.

The land cost varies considerably between North Hull (e.g. Sutton Fields) and West Hull (British Rail land). Annual rent (reviewable every 5 years):

(i) North Hull £1,500 per acre;
(ii) West Hull £2,500 per acre.

About 4 acres would be required. It may be possible to obtain a 999-year lease.

*New building costs*

(1) Smiths and Kings and Darbys:
70,000 sq. ft. at £4¼ £298,000
(2) Smiths and Kings, Darbys separate would cost an additional £10,000. (Rate higher than £4¼ for small building.)
(3) Land – North Hull £6,000 p.a.
West Hull £10,000 p.a.
(assume rising to £10,000 North / £14,000 West after 5 years)
(4) Fixtures and fittings £30,000

## 3.7 RESULTS AND RECOMMENDATIONS

The completed decision tree, analysis based upon the structure of Table 3.4 is shown in Appendix I. This shows three trees in which the NPVs of the various strategies have been calculated using alternative discount rates of 11%, 13%, 15%.

It is thought that Ferguson's cost of capital after tax is in the region of 13 percent in view of the high growth rate expected and the high coupon rate on the debt. The other two rates show the sensitivity of the result to changes in discount rate.

It can be seen that the net present values are all positive, and lie within a fairly tight range. At 13 percent the range is from £736,000 to £501,000.

However, it is more valid to compare these NPVs with the value of the three subsidiaries at present, not with zero. The book value of the three subsidiaries is about £450,000 at the moment.

**Choices**

Basically the choices open to Fergusons at the moment are:

(1) To rebuild Smiths, Kings and Darbys on a new site.
(2) To rebuild Darbys on a new site, and wait as regards Smiths and Kings.
(3) To wait for all three (see Table 3.5).

Table 3.5

| | NPV at | | |
|---|---|---|---|
| (£'000) | 11% | 13% | 15% |
| Rebuild in North Hull[a] | 716 | 636 | 566 |
| Rebuild in West Hull | 706 | 627 | 557 |
| Darbys rebuild | 692 | 620 | 556 |
| Wait | 693 | 623 | 562 |
| Present book value | *c.* 450 | *c.*450 | *c.* 450 |

[a]Optimal decision.

An alternative way to look at these figures is as a kind of opportunity cost. That is to say how much would one lose by not taking the optimal decision.

| £'000 | 11% | 13% | 15% |
|---|---|---|---|
| Rebuild in North Hull | 0 | 0 | 0 |
| Rebuild in West Hull | 10 | 9 | 9 |
| Darbys rebuild | 24 | 16 | 10 |
| Wait | 23 | 13 | 4 |

On an expected present value criterion the best choice is to decide to rebuild on a site in North Hull immediately, leading to a move in, say, January 1975. This seems relatively insensitive to changes in discount rate.

However, the expected differences between the various strategies are *not* great – only a few thousand pounds. One reason why the real difference may well be *greater* than this, is as follows.

The 'wait' decision assumes that Fergusons can benefit through waiting because they can see what the trend in market growth is likely to be, and hence alter their decision accordingly. On the other hand the 'market growth factor' depends on both internal and external forces. Moving early will both expand the market and deter competition, thus enlarging the difference in present value.

Rather than use an expected present value criterion, Fergusons might feel they are risk-averse and want to minimize the worst outcome. At 13 percent discount rate, *low* market growth and *low* King's value would give a present value of £553,000 if a rebuilding decision were adopted now. On the other hand, rebuilding just Darbys and waiting as far as Smiths and Kings are concerned, would give a minimum present value of £560,000.

But: (1) because of the 'self-fulfilling' nature of the effect of King's and Smith's move on sales growth,

(2) because the Hull subsidiaries are only *part* of the Ferguson group, it is felt that this risk-averse criterion is NOT appropriate.

**Effect of changes in the uncertainties**

At present the 'market growth' chance fork is:

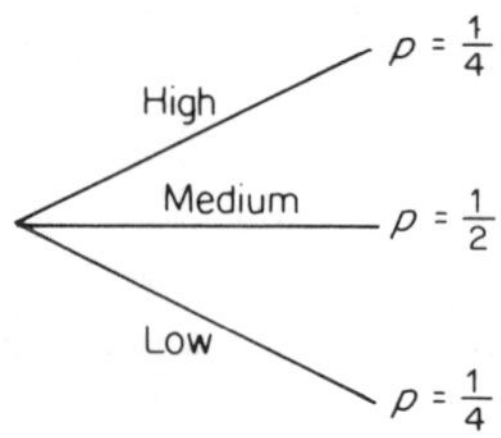


If this changes to:

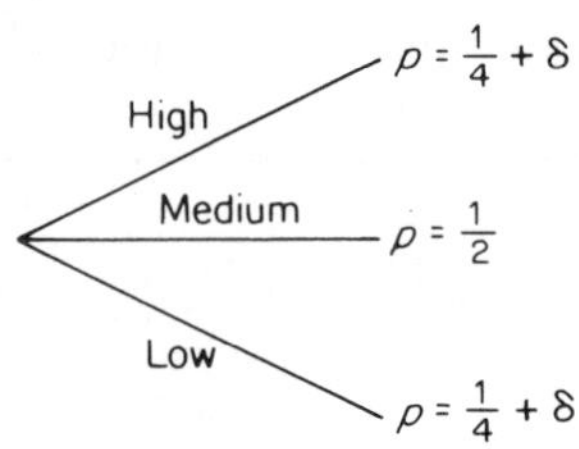


The important issue is how large can δ be before a change in optimal strategy would occur?

It is found that even were δ to be as much as ¼ or as little as −¼, the optimum decision would not change.* So this optimum strategy is relatively independent of changes in *market growth*.

## 3.8 DISCUSSION OF IMPLICATIONS

**(1) Sutton Fields**

Sutton Fields is an industrial estate to the north of Hull (see map, Appendix III). It has good road communications with the North and West and is generally very suited to Ferguson's needs. There is, however, one drawback. Hull Corporation have insisted up to now that no retailing be carried out from the estate. If this clause were to be rigidly enforced the whole range of possible retailing activity, from a retail counter, to showroom, through to cash-and-carry, might be endangered. It is worth considering the implications of this, not so much for the immediate future, but for the longer term when cash-and-carry may be the norm. So far the figures produced by other publicly quoted builders' merchants have been inconclusive, so that at present it is not possible to tell exactly what benefits cash-and-carry entail.

Other sites that are currently available are shown on the map in Appendix III. Apart from Sutton Fields, 'I', 'C', and 'J' seem most suitable, being between the Hessle Road and the Humber. However, until the South Docks Road is completed by the late 1970s (with luck!) the benefits in communication will not occur. The analysis shows that the additional cost of these sites (50 per cent or so) is not justified by the estimated 1.5 percent increase in sales. An increase of 3.5 percent would be needed to make the decision swing the other way.

### (2) Retailing

When Fergusons moved out of the centre of Newcastle to their new premises on the Tyne Tunnel trading estate they kept a showroom in the centre of Newcastle to display fires, boilers, kitchen and bathroom units. In view of the previous comments about Sutton Fields, it is worth considering:

If Kings were developed for shops and offices, it might be worth keeping a lease on a ground-floor area for a similar showroom and possibly a retail shop as well. Alternatively another central site could be chosen.

(a) Kings already have more people coming into their shop/showroom in a day than the Newcastle showroom has in a week – the Newcastle showroom is very much in a backwater.

(b) With the surrounding development, Kings is likely to become a central shopping and commercial part of Hull.

(c) Keeping a store at Kings would alleviate the problem of lost collect-sales over the move.

### (3) Heavy-side

Fergusons do not provide a full buidlers' and plumbers' merchants service in

---

*Proof:

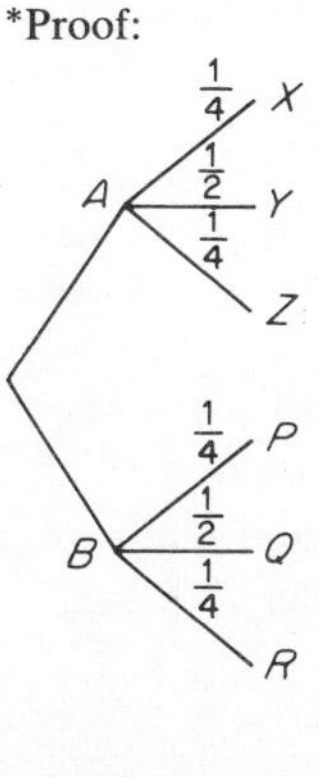


$X.\tfrac{1}{4} + Y.\tfrac{1}{2} + Z.\tfrac{1}{4} = P.\tfrac{1}{4} + Q.\tfrac{1}{2} + R.\tfrac{1}{4} + (A-B)$

At change-over, $X.(\tfrac{1}{4} + \delta) + Y.\tfrac{1}{2} + Z.(\tfrac{1}{4} - \delta) = P.(\tfrac{1}{4} + \delta) + Q.\tfrac{1}{2} + R.(\tfrac{1}{4} - \delta)$

Therefore, $X.\delta - Z.\delta = P.\delta - R.\delta + (B - A)$

or $\delta = \dfrac{B - A}{(P + Z - R - X)}$; for $r = 13\%$, $\delta = 13/24$ which is $> \tfrac{1}{4}$.

Hull. The heavy-side (bricks, sand, cement) and timber is not catered for. Recently Fergusons were looking at Douglas Williams with a view to possible acquisition so that they would then have a complete range of services in Hull.

If Fergusons move to a new site, the addition of the heavy-side (and possibly timber as well) would be a natural progression. This, however, could be developed from existing skills, not necessarily by acquisition.

### (4) Kings

It may be felt that an immediate move would be unwise because being seen to have to sell Kings might mean having to sell it at a reduced price. If this price were below book value, repercussions might occur when the annual accounts are published. However, Fergusons do not necessarily have to sell Kings immediately they move out. It may be profitable to leave it empty for a year or two to achieve a higher offer.

### (5) Heating

The heating design and installation side at Kings seems to be rather an anomaly in the Ferguson group. It does not contribute much to King's profits and it should be examined closely to see if divestment is a worthwhile option.

### (6) The amalgamation process

Even if a decision were made immediately to go ahead and rebuild, a move could not occur before December 1974 or January 1975. During this time it would seem sensible gradually to change the image of the firms to that of a single company. A progression could be:

(i) Emphasize on invoices and stationery that the individual companies are part of the Ferguson Group, e.g. put 'A member of Ferguson Industrial Holdings'.
(ii) Register 'Ferguson Humberside' or some other name for the new company.
(iii) Bring the companies' lettering and colours into line with Fergusons.
(iv) Introduce 'Ferguson Humberside' into the invoices and stationery and let the original names become divisions of the overall company.
(v) Drop the original names altogether at the time of the move.

### (7) Management

A general manager to supervise all three companies in Hull should be appointed without delay. He should not concern himself too much with the day-to-day running of the companies but should organize and plan the move and become managing director of Ferguson Humberside when it is formed.

# Appendix 1: Decision Trees:

### Summary

Three figures, namely 3A.1, 3A.9 and 3A.17, summmarize the 'foldback' analysis of the strategy options for discount rates of 11%, 13% and 15% respectively. These results are reproduced in Table 3.5 earlier in this chapter.

The remaining figures present the details underlying the entire set of calculations. Thus, Figures 3A.2 to 3A.8 analyse branches A through G when the assumed discount rate is 11%. Similarly, Figures 3A.10 to 3A.16 and 3A.18 to 3A.24 analyse branches A through G for assumed discount rates of 13% and 15% respectively.

### Glossary of Symbols Used in Figures 3A.1 to 3A.24

| | |
|---|---|
| ○ | Chance fork |
| □ | Decision fork |
| $(\frac{1}{3})$ | Probability assignment |
| 432 (boxed) | Expected NPV at that stage in the tree, in £'000 |
| —//— | A branch from a decision fork that is not taken; i.e. it is dominated by another branch |
| ——D | Indicates the decision tree is continued on branch D |

Note: the numbering 1 through 200 is a means of identifying end-points on the decision trees in Figures 3A.1 to 3A.24. It was used by the authors as a procedure for checking the accuracy of the calculations.

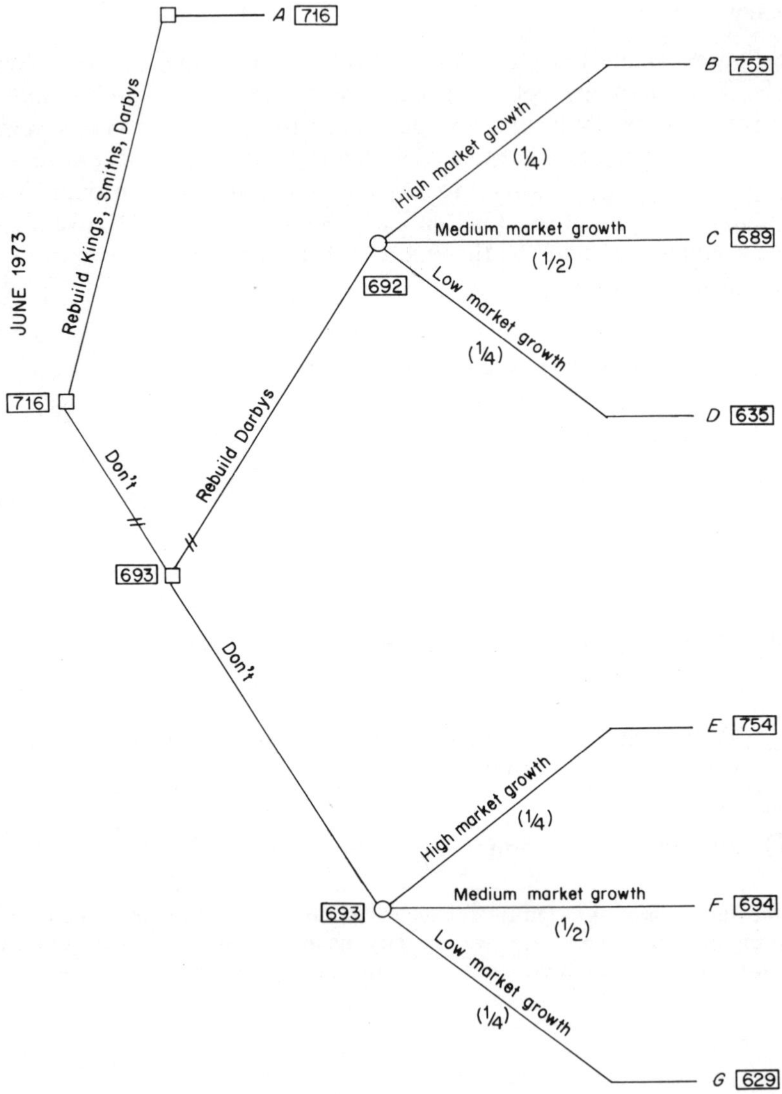


Figure 3A.1 Summarized decision tree analysis of options for discount rate 11%

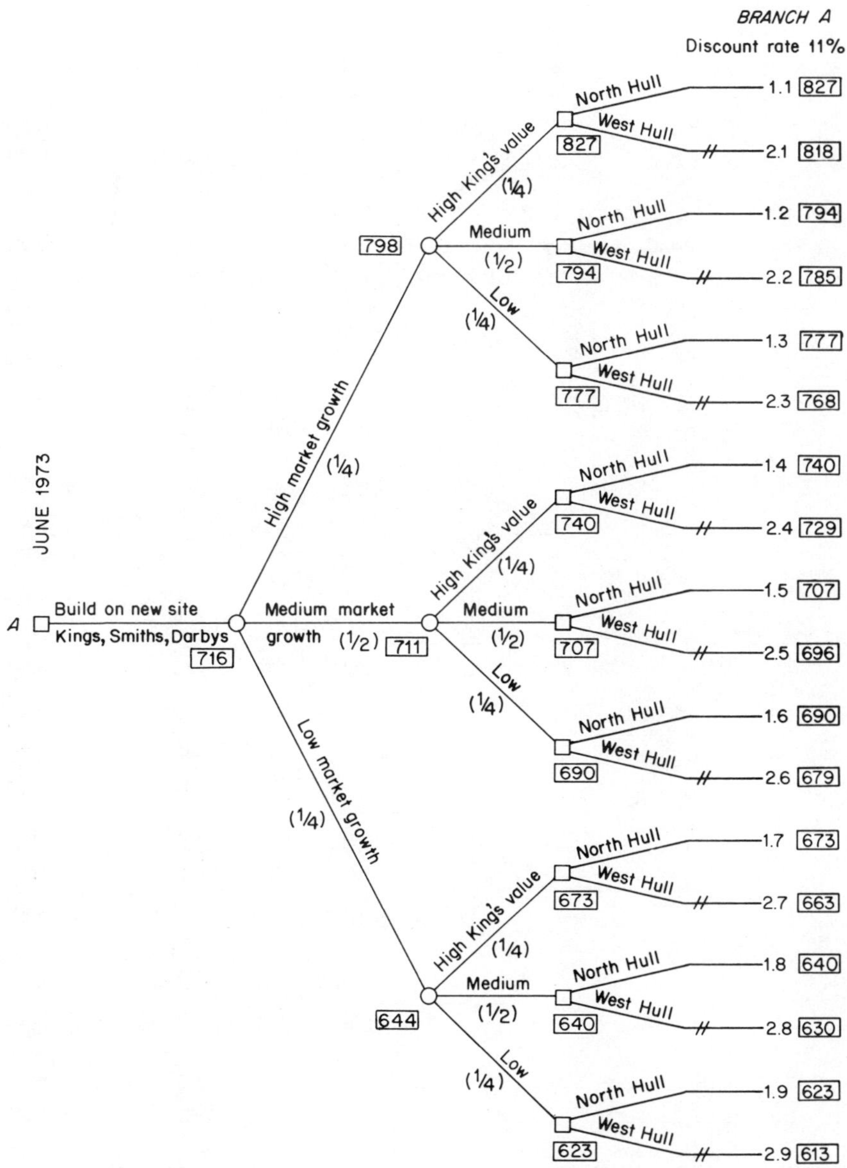


Figure 3A.2 Analysis of Branch A, discount rate 11%

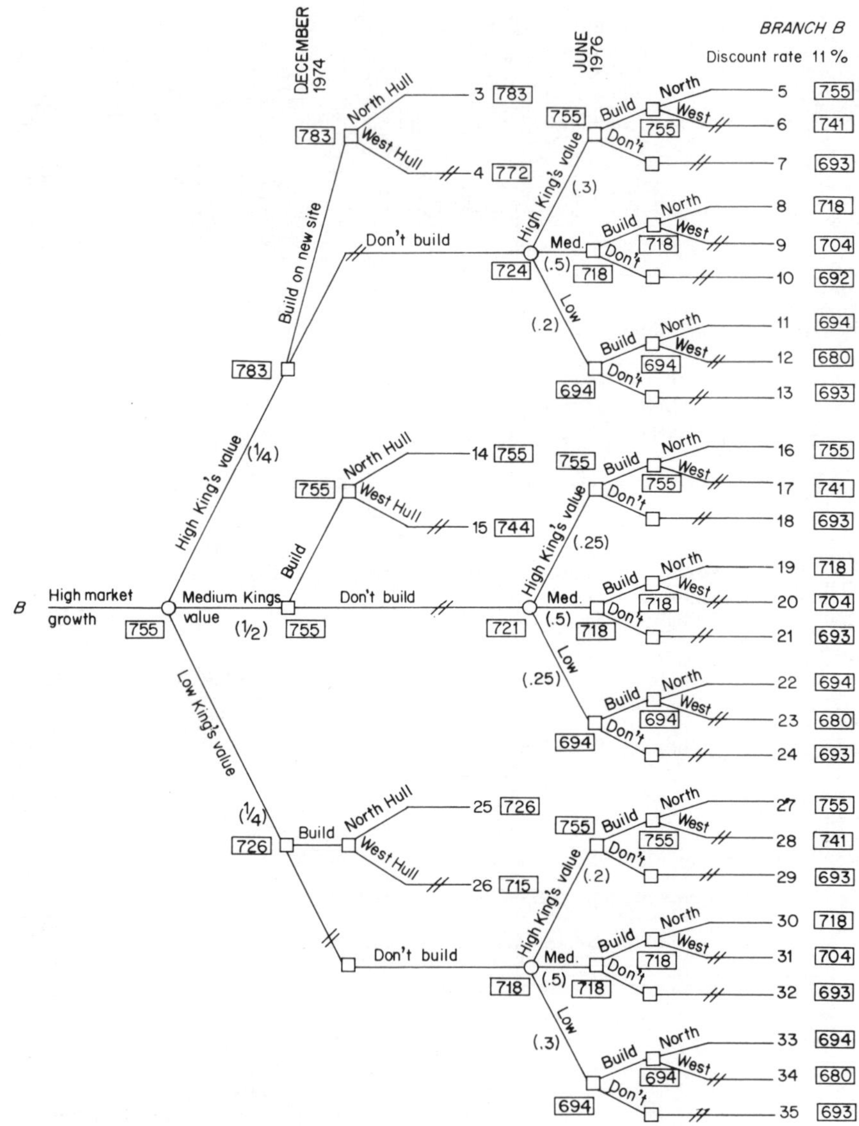


Figure 3A.3 Analysis of Branch B, discount rate 11%

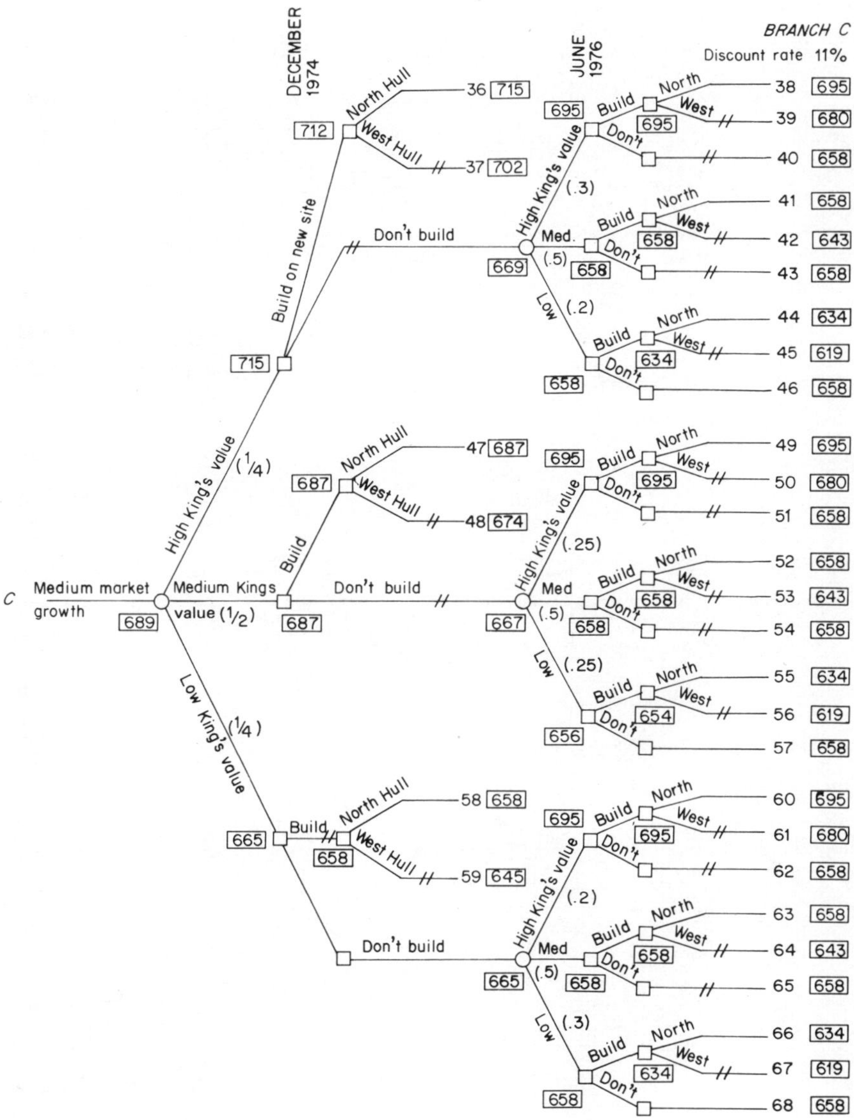


Figure 3A.4 Analysis of Branch C, discount rate 11%

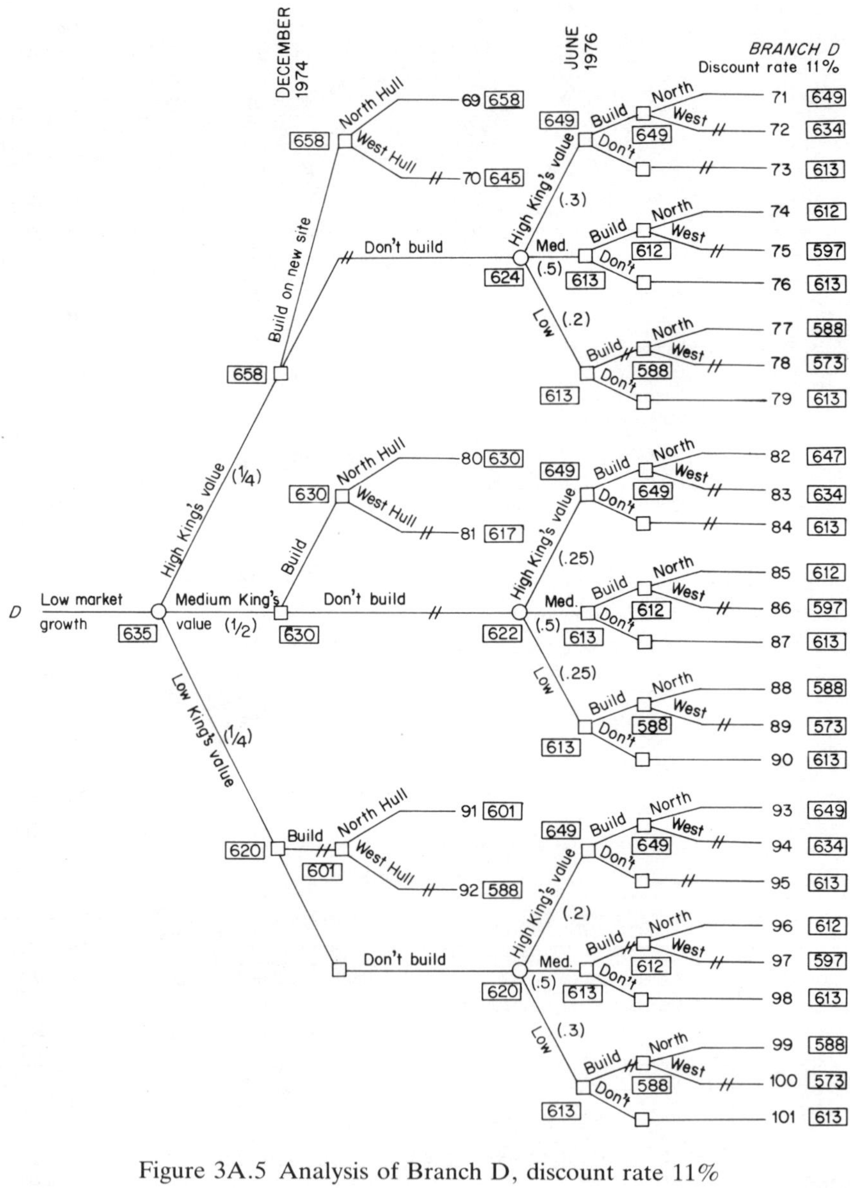


Figure 3A.5 Analysis of Branch D, discount rate 11%

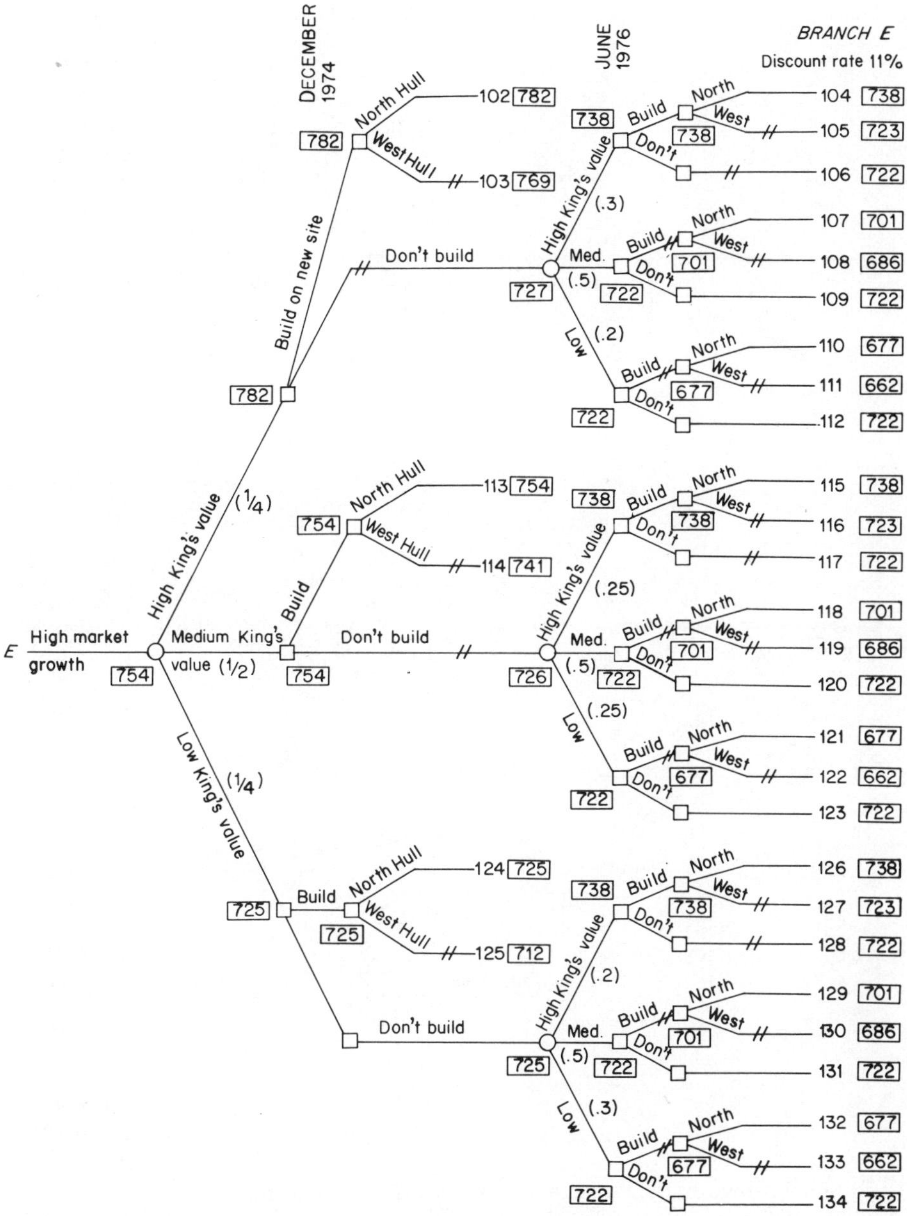


Figure 3A.6 Analysis of Branch E, discount rate 11%

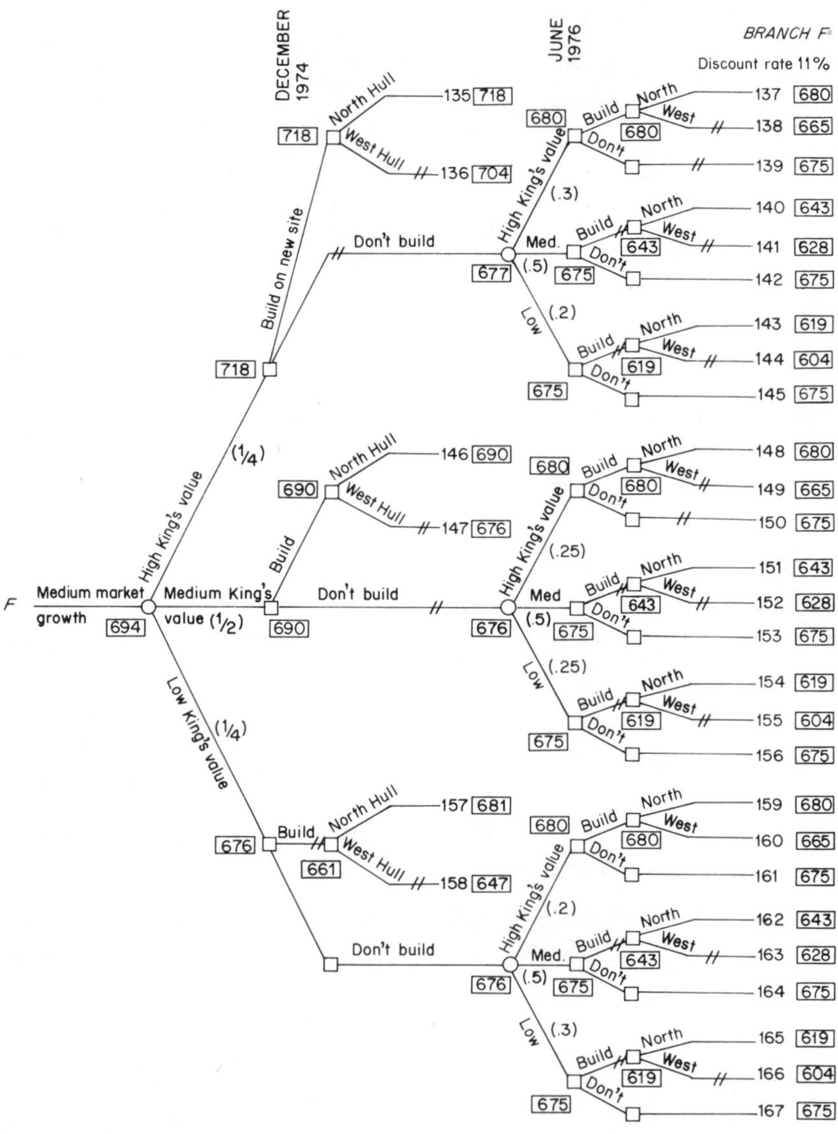


Figure 3A.7 Analysis of Branch F, discount rate 11%

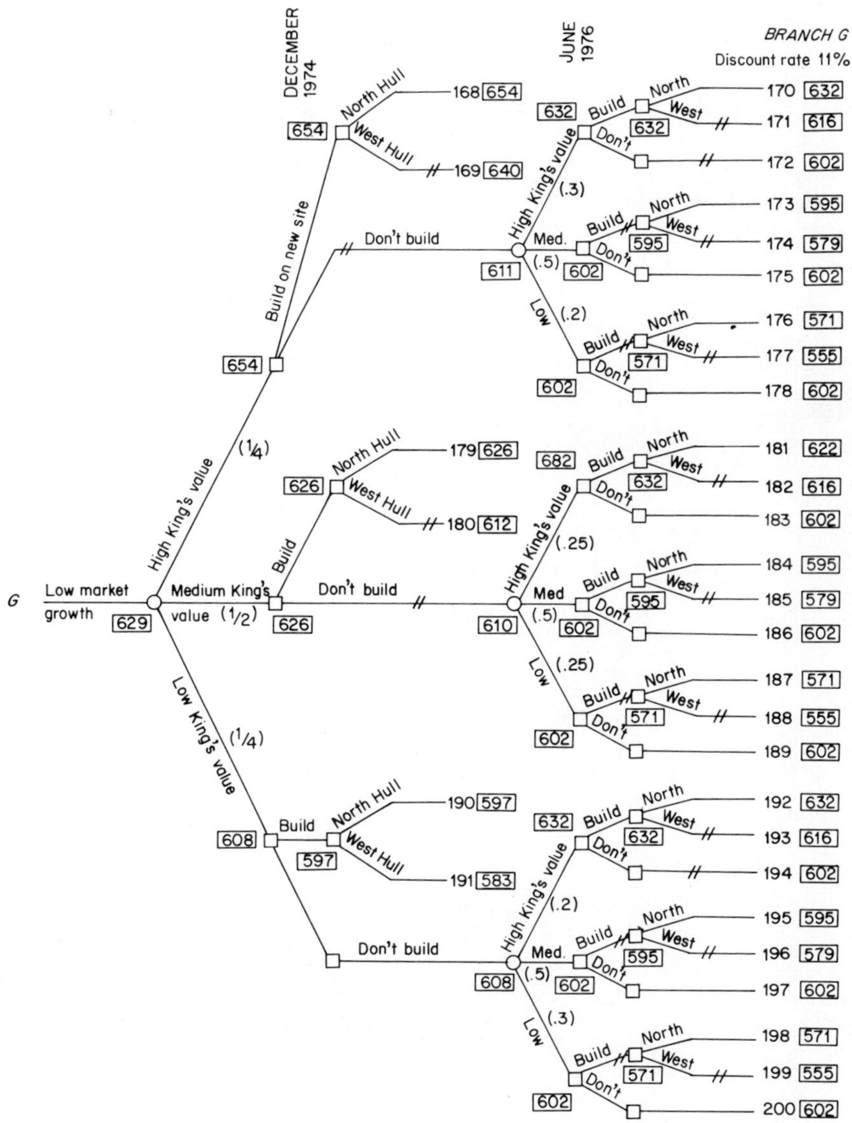


Figure 3A.8 Analysis of Branch G, discount rate 11%

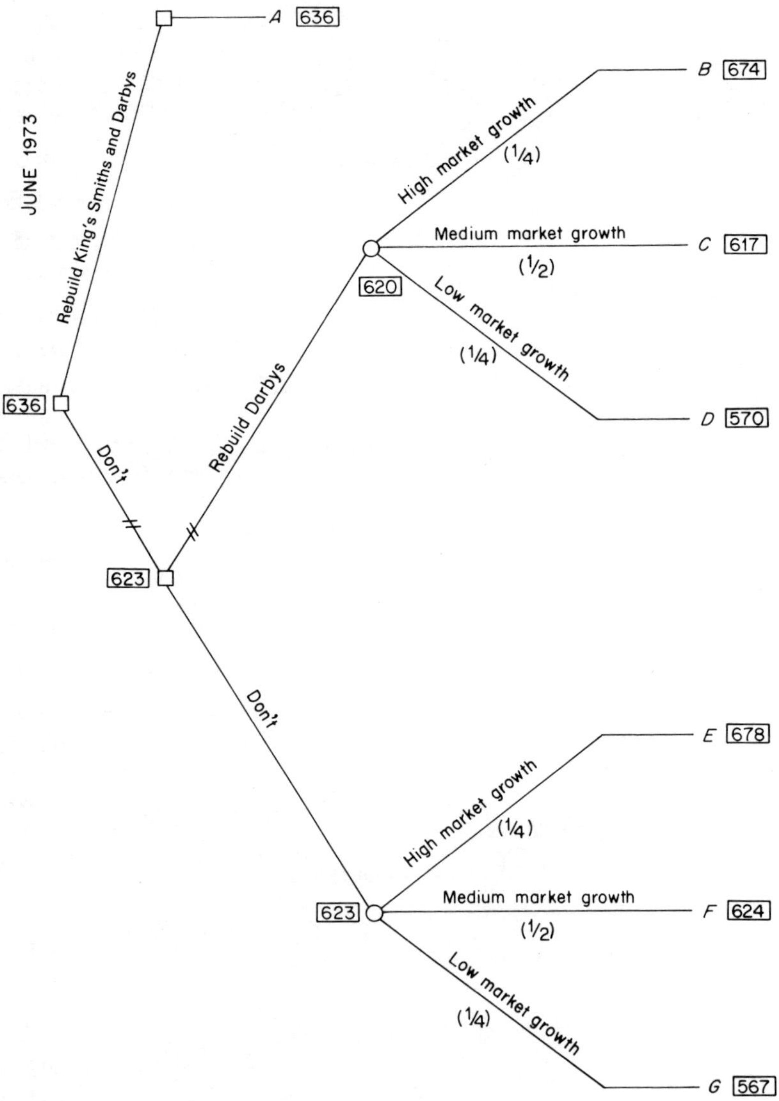


Figure 3A.9 Summarized decision tree analysis of options for discount rate 13%

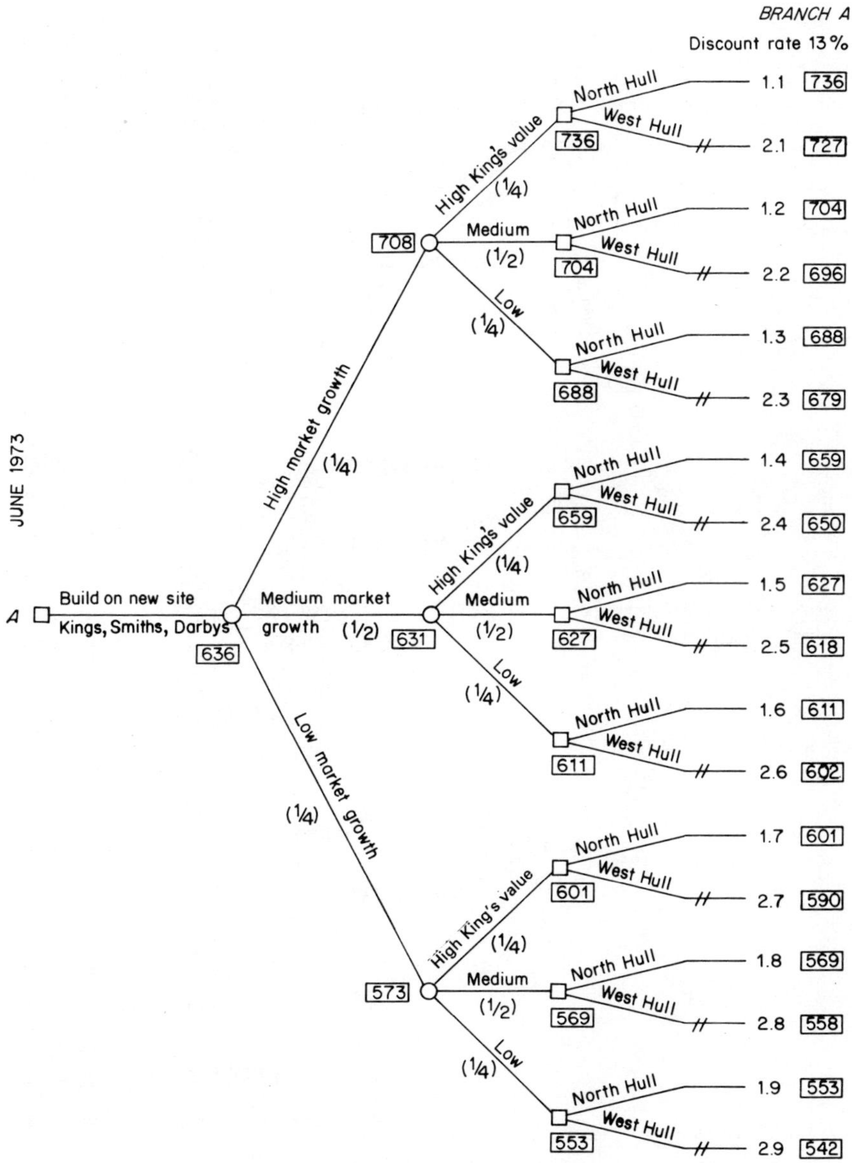


Figure 3A.10 Analysis of Branch A, discount rate 13%

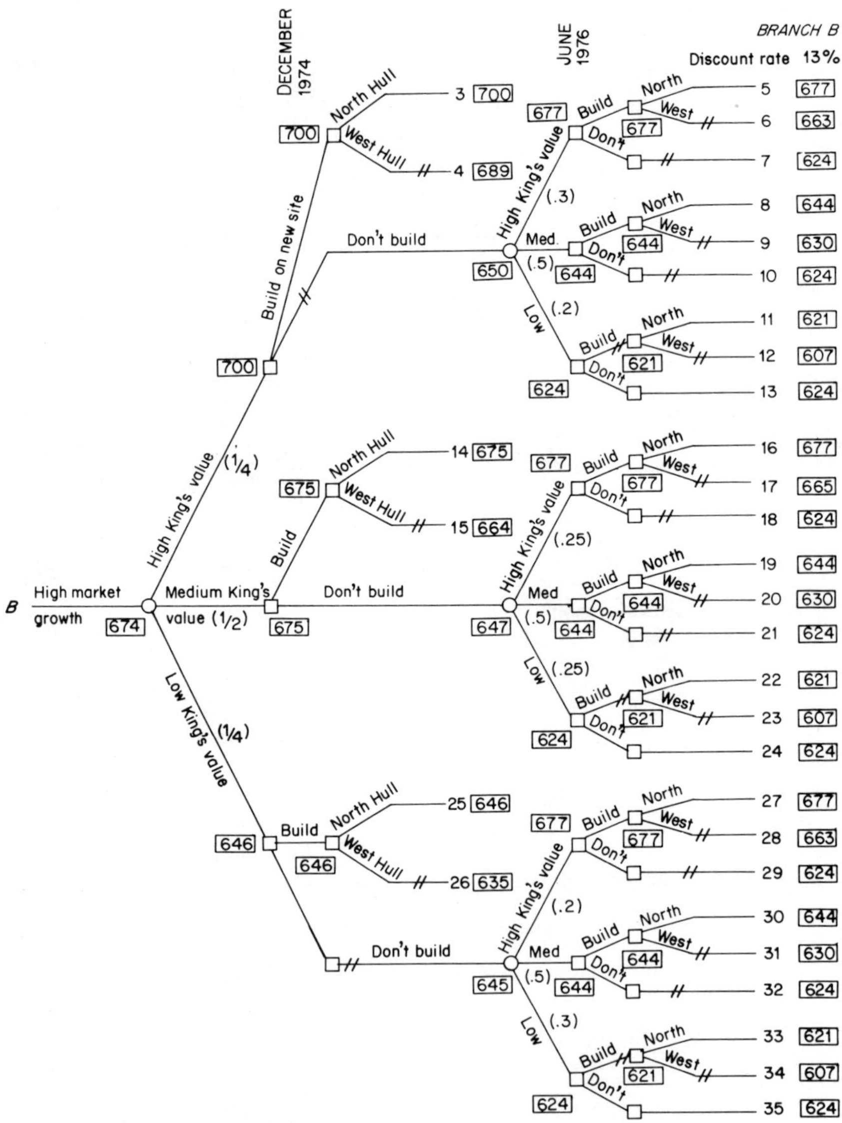


Figure 3A.11 Analysis of Branch B, discount rate 13%

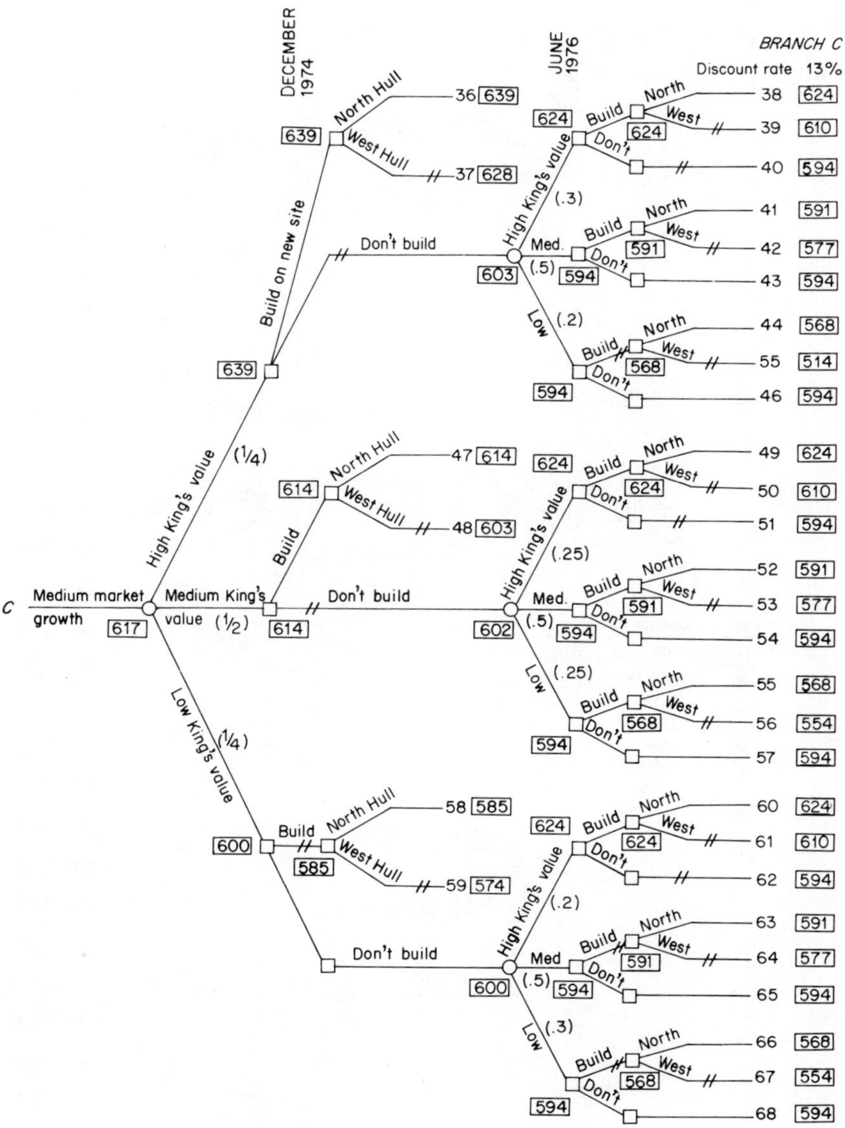


Figure 3A.12 Analysis of Branch C, discount rate 13%

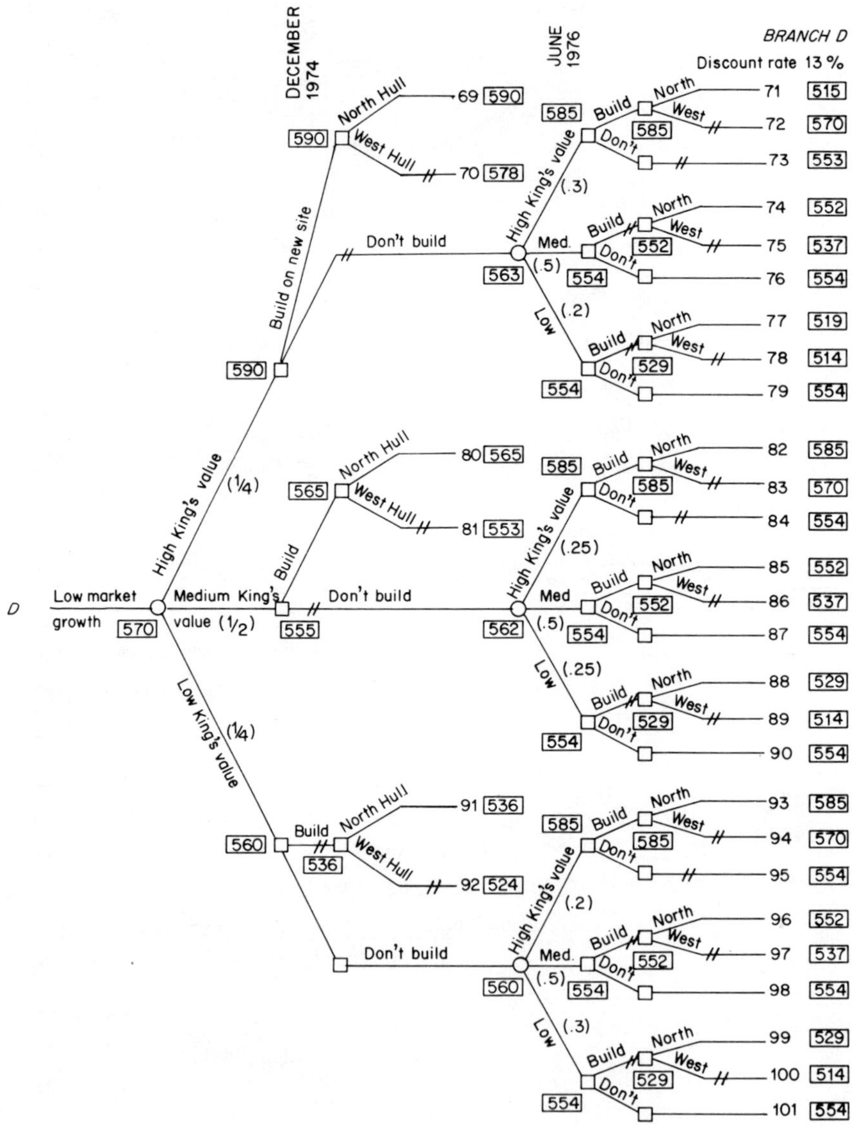

Figure 3A.13 Analysis of Branch D, discount rate 13%

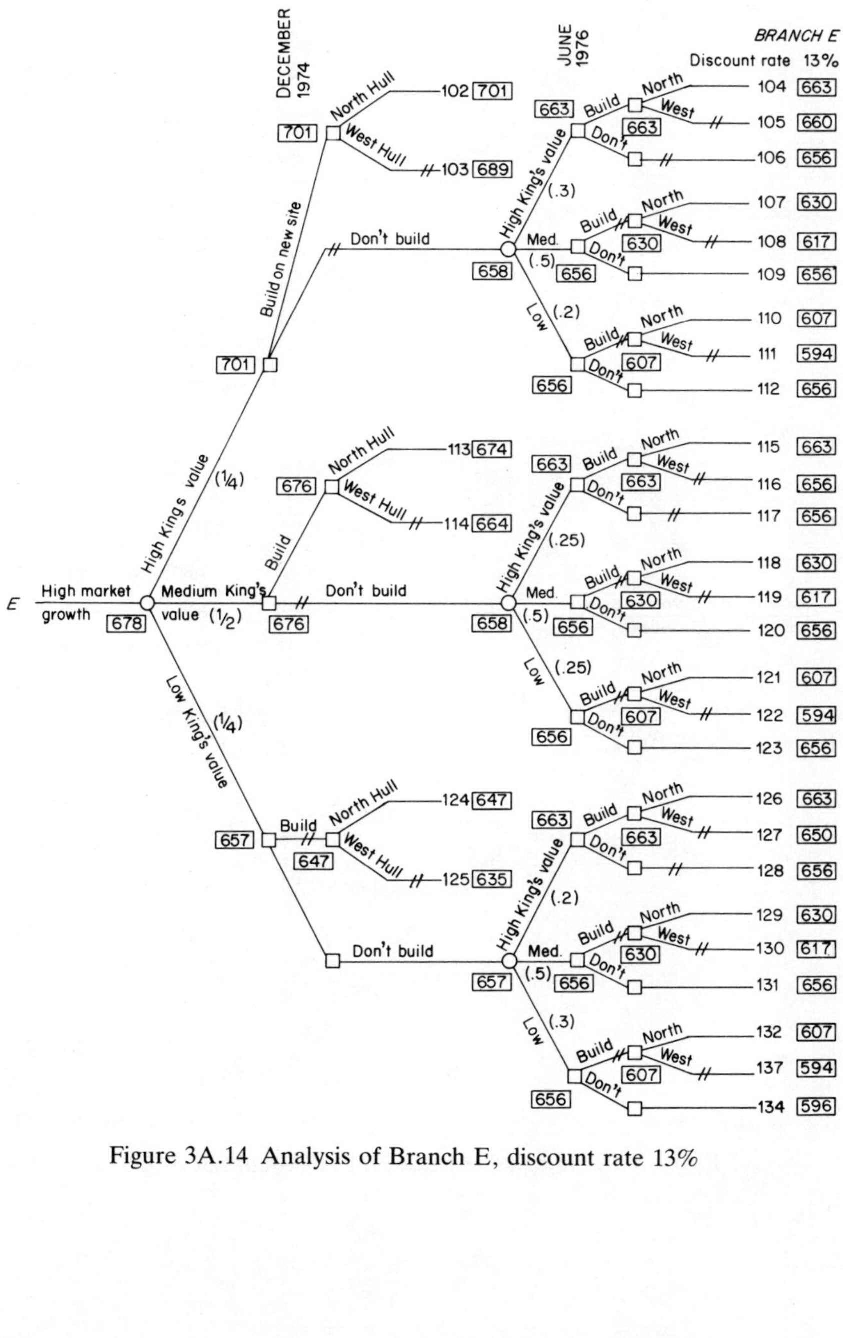


Figure 3A.14 Analysis of Branch E, discount rate 13%

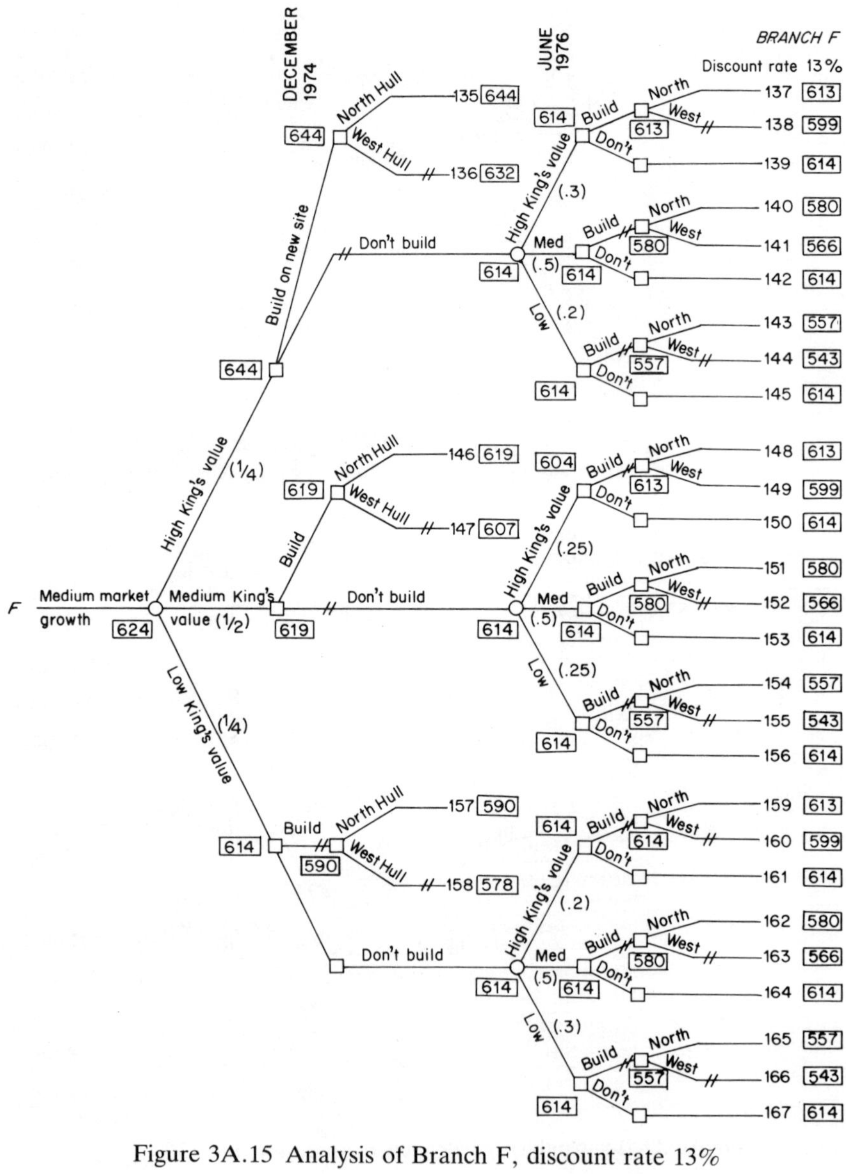


Figure 3A.15 Analysis of Branch F, discount rate 13%

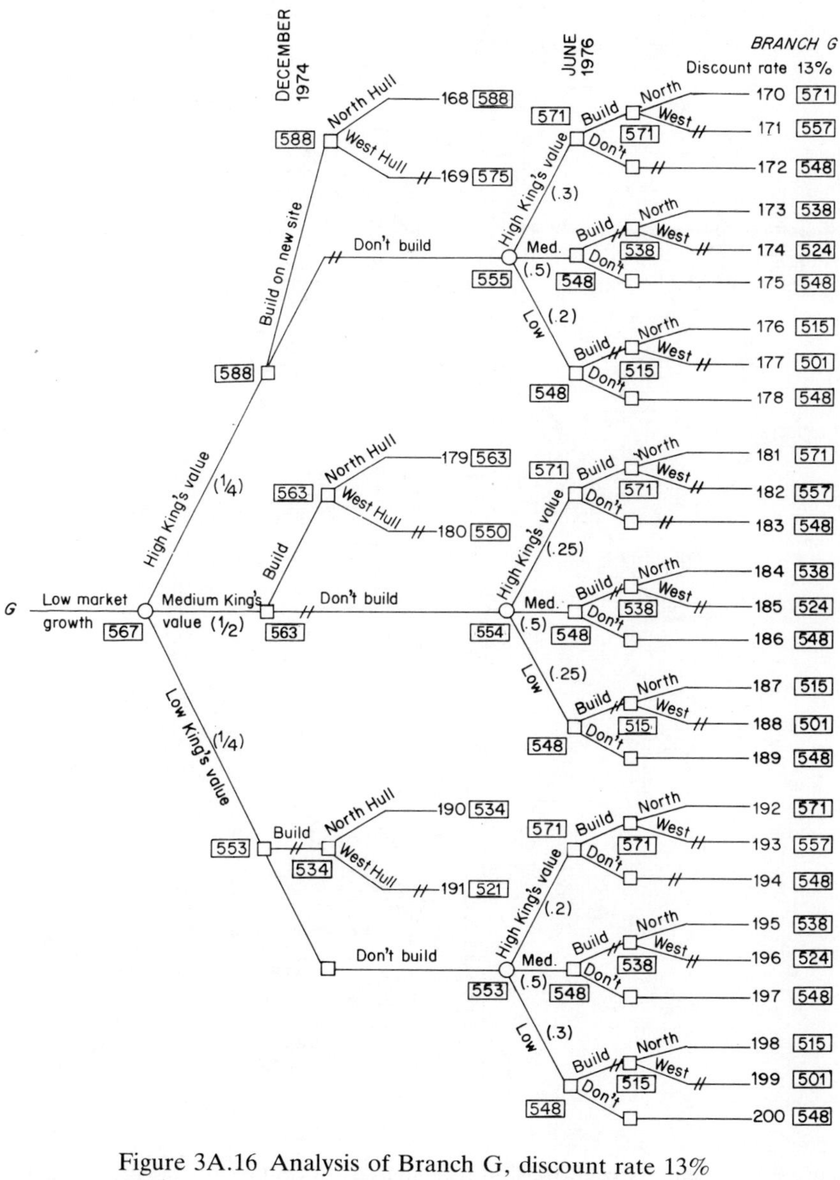


Figure 3A.16 Analysis of Branch G, discount rate 13%

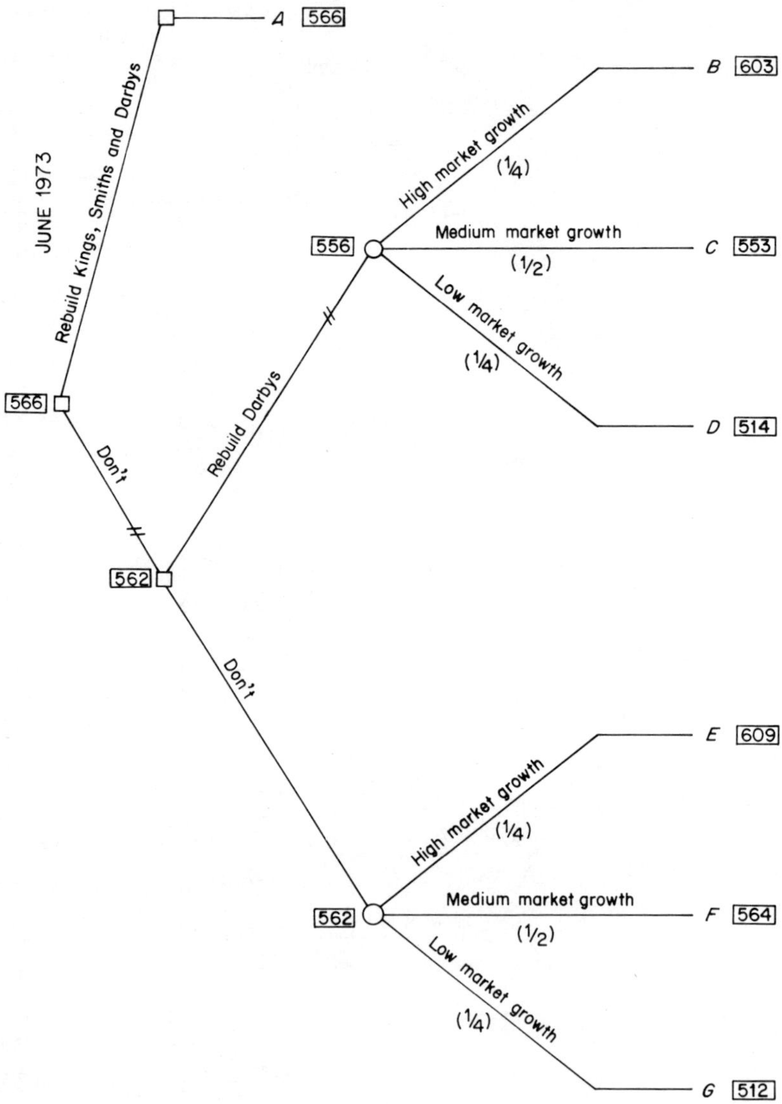


Figure 3A.17 Summarized decision tree analysis of options for discount rate 15%

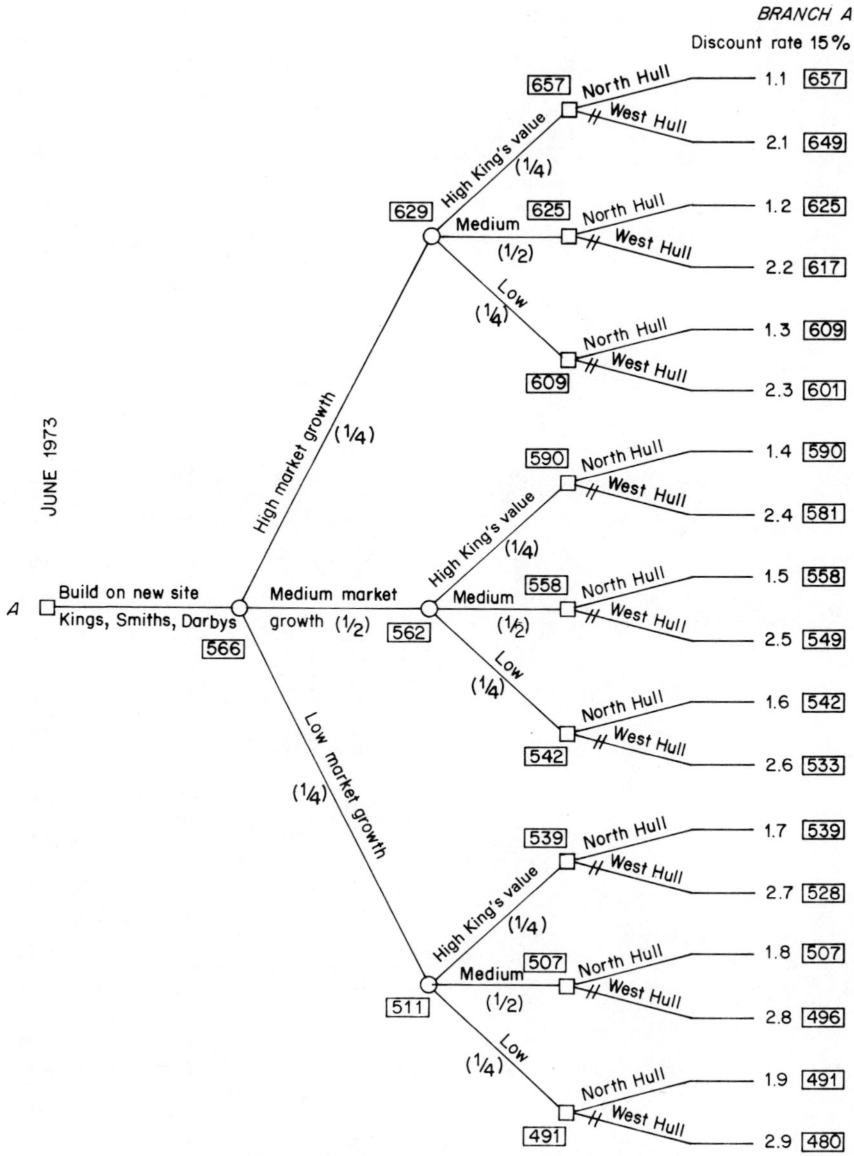


Figure 3A.18 Analysis of Branch A, discount rate 15%

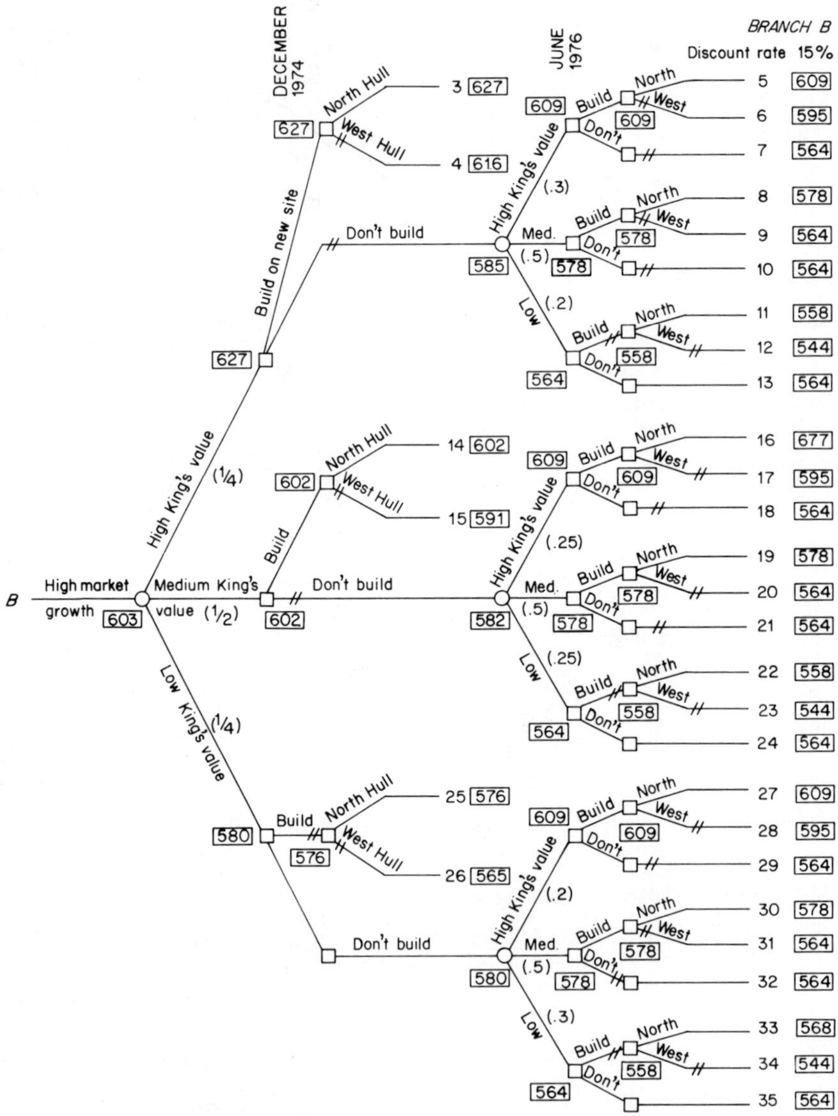


Figure 3A.19 Analysis of Branch B, discount rate 15%

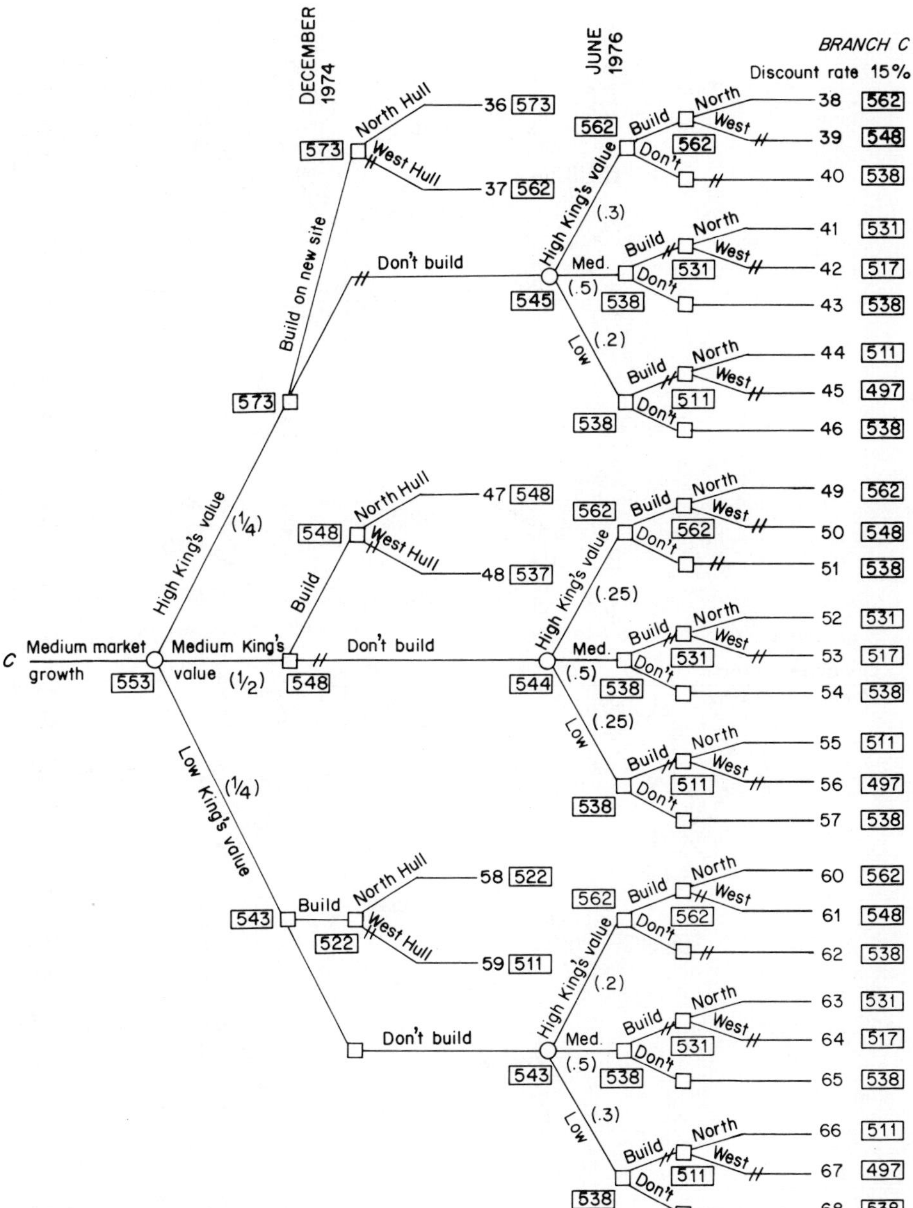


Figure 3A.20 Analysis of Branch C, discount rate 15%

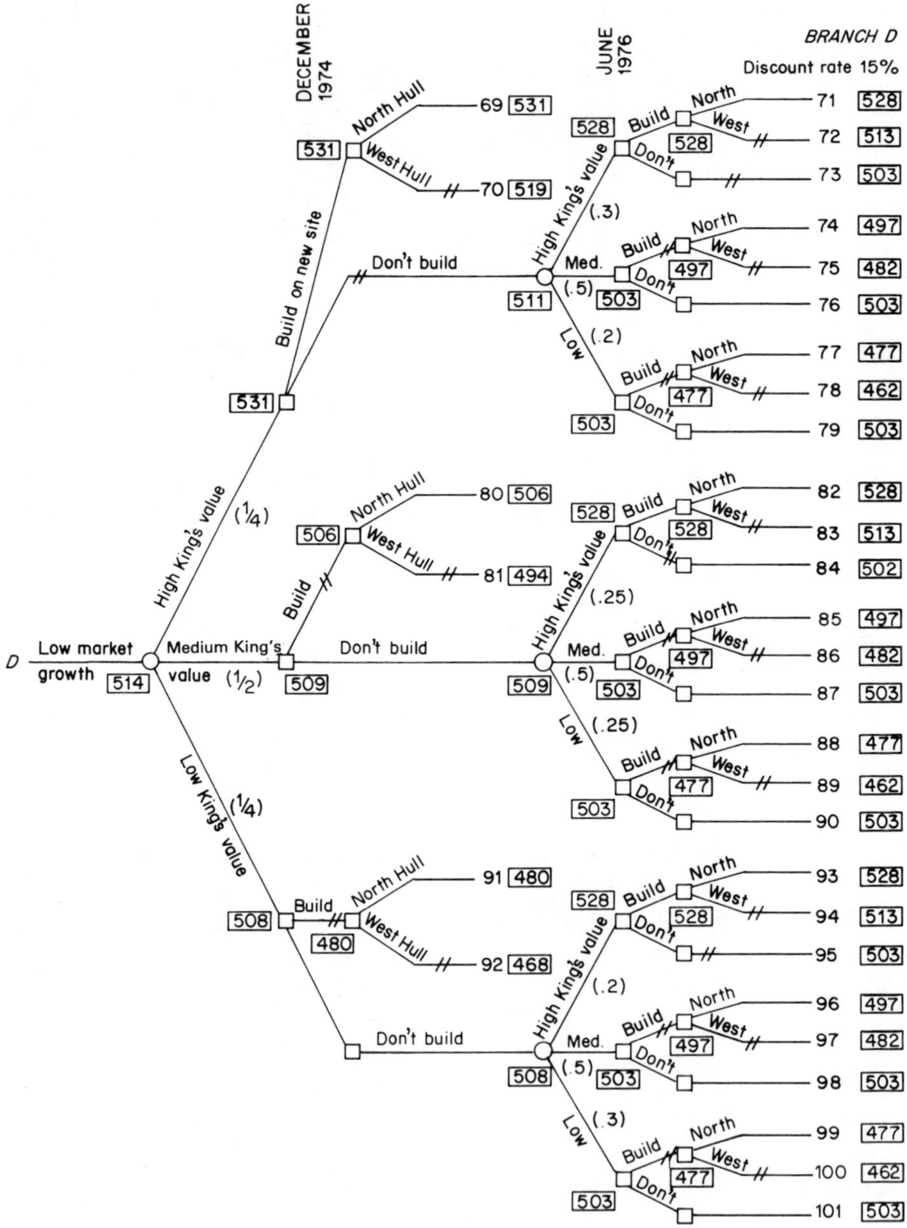


Figure 3A.21 Analysis of Branch D, discount rate 15%

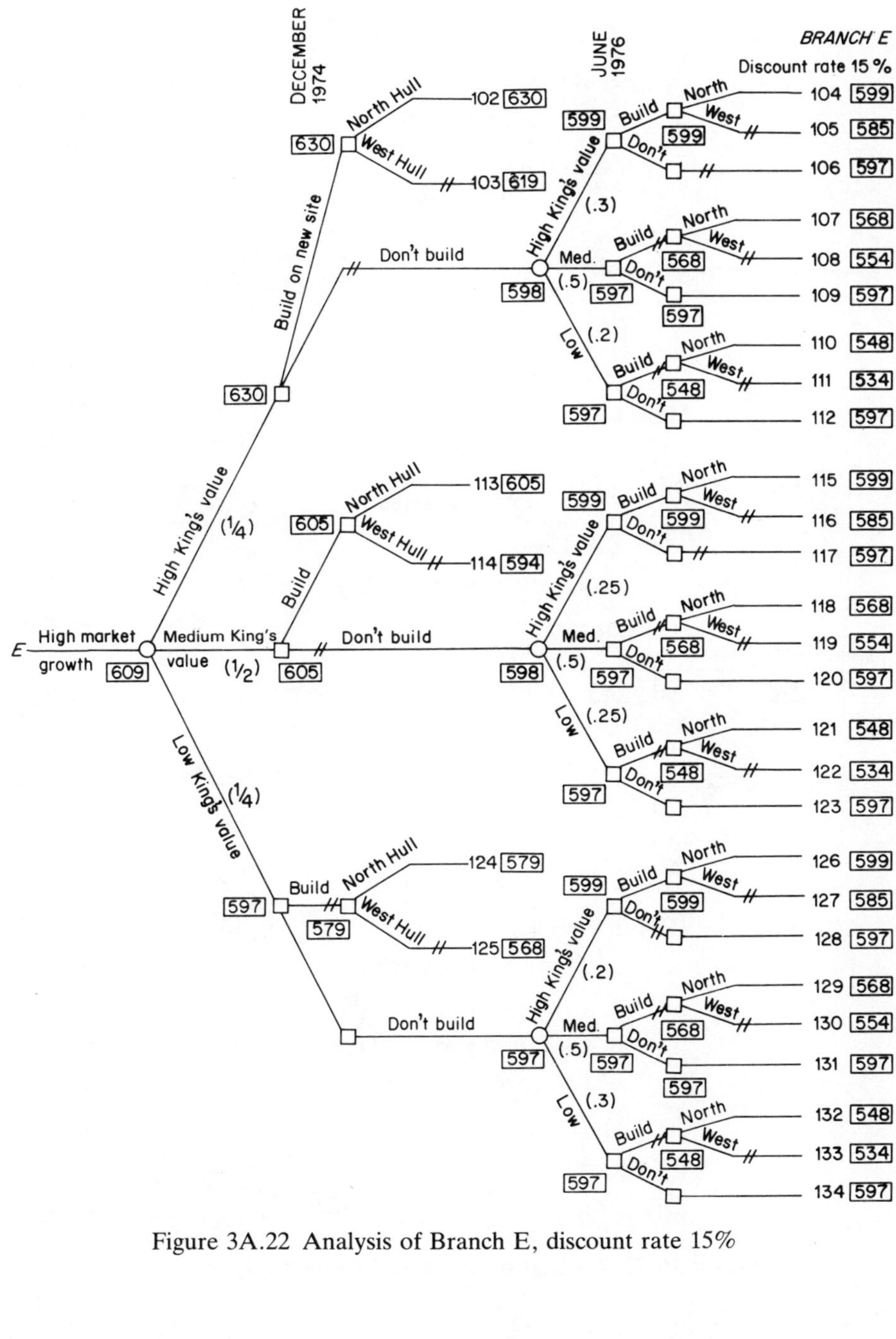


Figure 3A.22 Analysis of Branch E, discount rate 15%

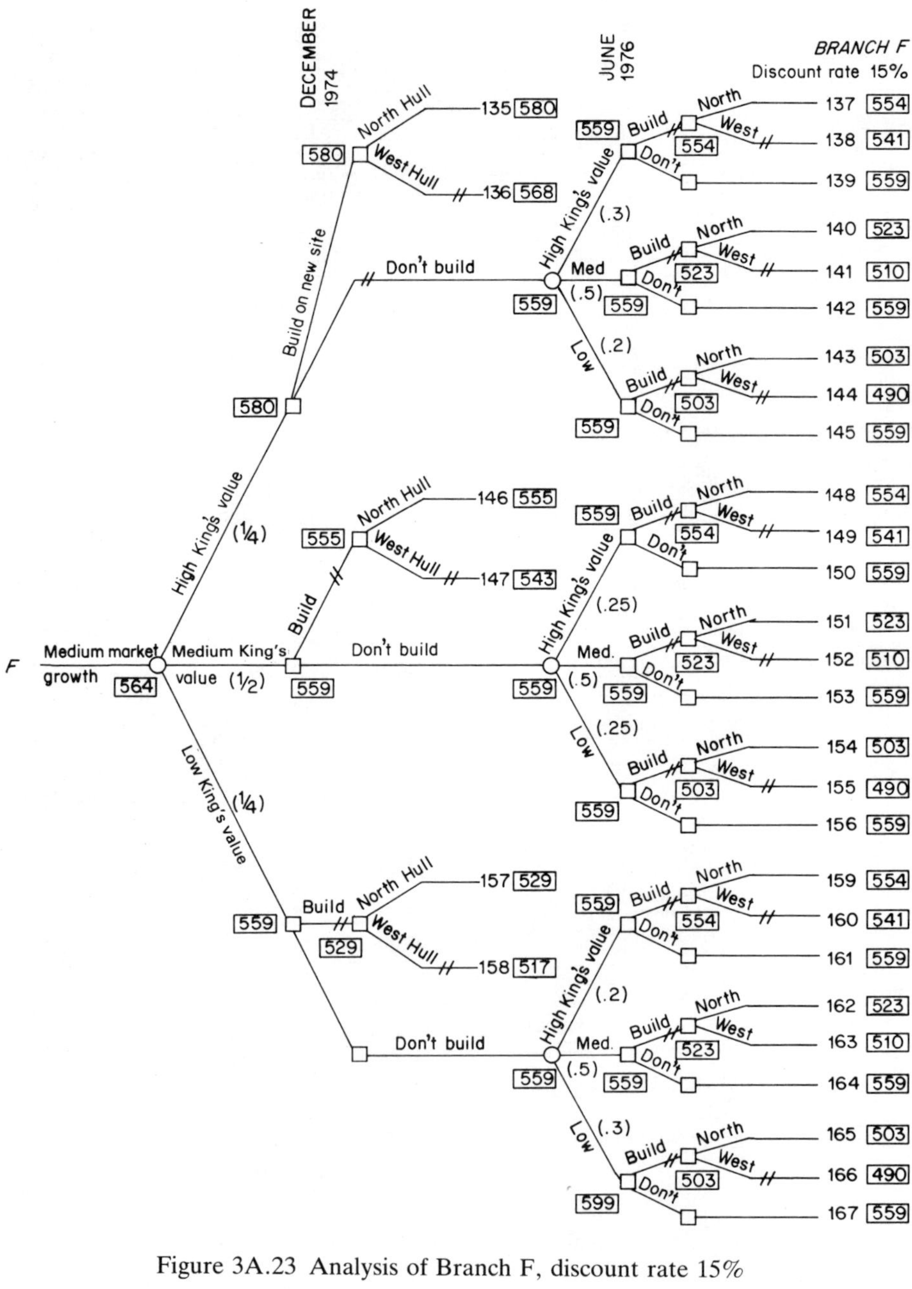


Figure 3A.23 Analysis of Branch F, discount rate 15%

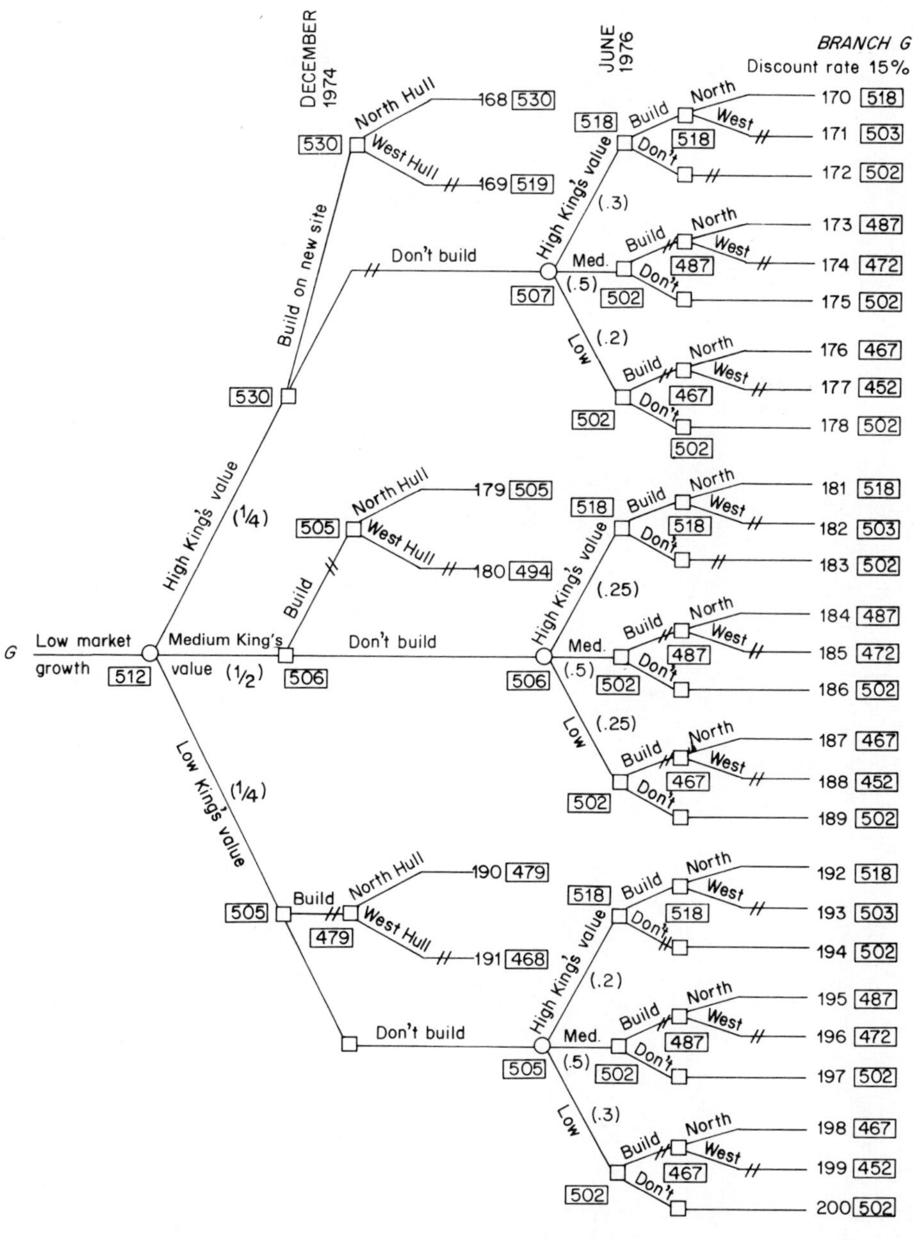


Figure 3A.24 Analysis of Branch G, discount rate 15%

# Appendix II. Cost Data for this Project

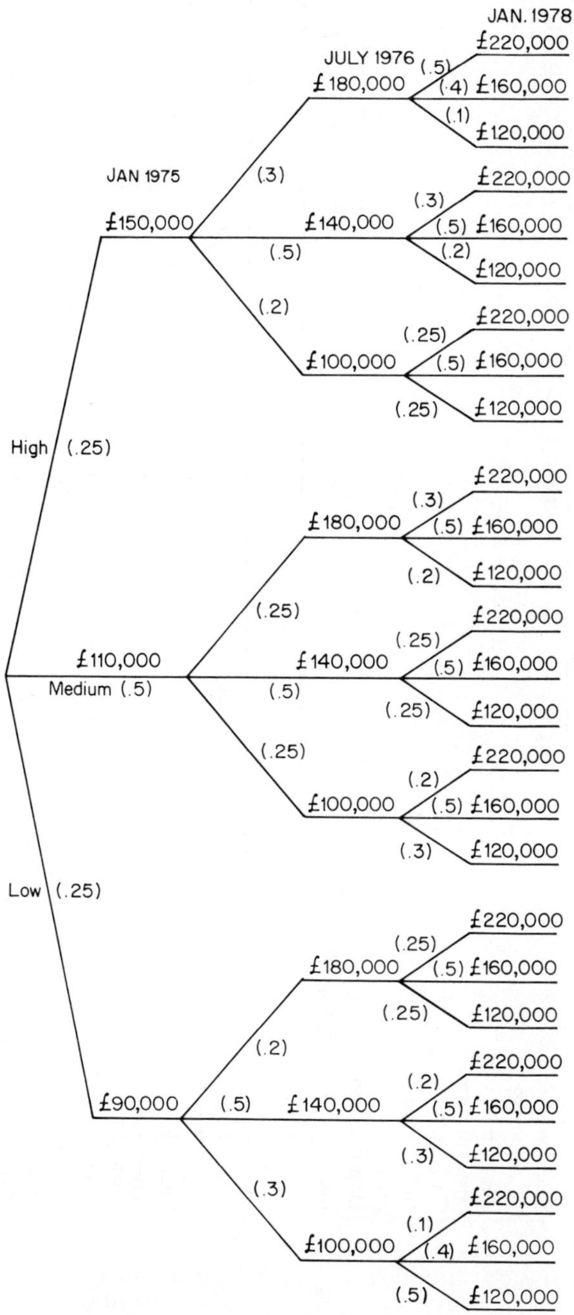


| | Discount rates 11% | 13% | 15% |
|---|---|---|---|
| JAN 1975 | | | |
| 150 | 125 | 121 | 113 |
| 110 | 92 | 89 | 86 |
| 90 | 75 | 73 | 70 |
| JULY 1976 | | | |
| 180 | 123 | 121 | 114 |
| 140 | 100 | 96 | 89 |
| 100 | 71 | 67 | 63 |
| JAN 1978 | | | |
| 220 | 134 | 123 | 113 |
| 160 | 97 | 90 | 82 |
| 120 | 73 | 67 | 62 |
| TERMINAL VALUE 200 | 96 | 85 | 75 |

Table showing present values of King's site at alternative discount rates (units £'000)

Figure 3A.25 King and Co's value: probabilistic scenarios

Table 3A.1
Cash flow table (Kings, Smiths, Darbys on existing sites)

| | (£'000) | Sept 1973 | Sept 1974 | Oct 1974 | Jan 1975 | Sept 1975 | July 1976 | Sept 1976 | Sept 1977 | Jan 1978 | Sept 1978 | Sept 1979 | |
|---|---|---|---|---|---|---|---|---|---|---|---|---|---|
| HIGH MARKET GROWTH | Sales: West | 1514 | 1717 | — | — | 1950 | — | 2214 | 2515 | — | 2858 | 3250 | |
| | North | | | — | — | | — | | | — | | | |
| | Lost sales | | | — | — | | — | | | — | | | |
| | Gross margin % | 23.0 | 22.6 | — | — | 22.4 | — | 22.1 | 21.8 | — | 21.4 | 21.2 | I |
| | Costs % | 14.7 | 14.1 | — | — | 13.7 | — | 13.6 | 13.5 | — | 13.6 | 13.7 | |
| | Net margin % | 8.3 | 8.5 | — | — | 8.7 | — | 8.5 | 8.3 | — | 7.8 | 7.5 | |
| | Profits | 126 | 146 | — | — | 170 | — | 188 | 209 | — | 223 | 244 | |
| | Depreciation | 6 | 7 | — | — | 8 | — | 9 | 10 | — | 11 | 13 | |
| | Increased working capital | 28 | 32 | — | — | 38 | — | 42 | 48 | — | 56 | −244 | |
| MEDIUM MARKET GROWTH | Sales: West | 1476 | 1630 | — | — | 1799 | — | 1986 | 2193 | — | 2423 | 2679 | |
| | North | | | — | — | | — | | | — | | | |
| | Lost sales | | | — | — | | — | | | — | | | |
| | Gross margin % | 23.0 | 22.6 | — | — | 22.4 | — | 22.1 | 21.8 | — | 21.4 | 21.2 | |
| | Costs % | 14.8 | 14.2 | — | — | 13.8 | — | 13.7 | 13.6 | — | 13.7 | 13.8 | I |
| | Net margin % | 8.2 | 8.4 | — | — | 8.6 | — | 8.4 | 8.2 | — | 7.7 | 7.4 | |
| | Profits | 121 | 137 | — | — | 155 | — | 163 | 184 | — | 187 | 198 | |
| | Depreciation | 6 | 7 | — | — | 8 | — | 8 | 9 | — | 9 | 11 | |
| | Increased working capital | 24 | 27 | — | — | 30 | — | 33 | 36 | — | 41 | −191 | |

| | | | | | | | | | | | | | |
|---|---|---|---|---|---|---|---|---|---|---|---|---|---|
| LOW MARKET GROWTH | Sales: West | 1427 | 1527 | — | — | 1633 | — | 1746 | 1867 | — | 1996 | 2136 | |
| | North | | | — | — | | — | | | — | | | |
| | Lost sales | | | — | — | | — | | | — | | | |
| | Gross margin | 23.0 | 22.6 | — | — | 22.4 | — | 22.1 | 21.8 | — | 21.4 | 21.2 | |
| | Costs | 14.9 | 14.3 | — | — | 13.9 | — | 13.8 | 13.7 | — | 13.8 | 13.9 | I |
| | Net margin | 8.1 | 8.3 | — | — | 8.5 | — | 8.3 | 8.1 | — | 7.6 | 7.3 | |
| | Profits | 116 | 127 | — | — | 139 | — | 145 | 133 | — | 152 | 156 | |
| | Depreciation | 6 | 6 | — | — | 7 | — | 7 | 7 | — | 8 | 9 | |
| | Increased working capital | 19 | 20 | — | — | 22 | — | 24 | 26 | — | 29 | −140 | |
| CAPITAL 'CASH FLOWS' | Sale of Smiths | | | | | | | | | | | 60 | |
| | Cost of land | | | | | | | | | | | | |
| | Cost of buildings, etc. | | | | | | | | | | | | II |
| | Value of buildings, etc. | | | | | | | | | | | 293 | |

| | DISCOUNT RATE 11% | | | 13% | | | 15% | | |
|---|---|---|---|---|---|---|---|---|---|
| | High N W | Med. N W | Low N W | High N W | Med. N W | Low N W | High N W | Med. N W | Low N W |
| $NPV_I$ | 308 | 296 | 293 | 290 | 279 | 258 | 274 | 263 | 245 |
| $NPV_{II}$ +WC | 318 | 283 | 283 | 281 | 250 | 205 | 248 | 221 | 182 |
| $NPV_{TOT}$ | 626 | 579 | 506 | 57 | 529 | 463 | 522 | 484 | 427 |

Table 3A.2 Cash Flow Table
(Kings, Smiths on Existing Site; Darbys Move October 1974)

| | (£'000) | Sept 1973 | Sept 1974 | Oct 1974 | Jan 1975 | Sept 1975 | July 1976 | Sept 1976 | Sept 1977 | Jan 1978 | Sept 1978 | Sept 1979 |
|---|---|---|---|---|---|---|---|---|---|---|---|---|
| HIGH MARKET GROWTH | Sales: West | 1514 | 1002 | 721 | — | 1954 | — | 2532 | 2553 | — | 2922 | 3346 |
| | North | — | — | — | — | — | — | — | — | — | — | — |
| | Lost sales | | | 5 | | 7 | | | | | | |
| | Gross margin % | 23.0 | 22.6 | 22.6 | — | 22.4 | — | 22.1 | 21.8 | — | 21.4 | 21.2 |
| | Costs % | 14.7 | 14.2 | 14.1 | — | 13.5 | — | 13.4 | 13.4 | — | 13.5 | 13.6 |
| | Net margin % | 8.3 | 8.5 | 8.5 | | 8.9 | | 8.7 | 8.4 | | 7.9 | 7.6 |
| | Profits | 126 | 85 | 61 | — | 173 | — | 194 | 214 | — | 231 | 254 |
| | Depreciation | 6 | 4 | 3 | — | 8 | — | 9 | 10 | — | 12 | 13 |
| | Increased working capital | 29 | 33 | 0 | — | 37 | — | 47 | 51 | — | 59 | −250 |
| MEDIUM MARKET GROWTH | Sales: West | 1476 | 954 | 679 | — | 1803 | — | 2003 | 2226 | — | 2476 | 2753 |
| | North | — | — | — | — | — | — | — | — | — | — | — |
| | Lost sales | | | 5 | | 6 | | | | | | |
| | Gross margin % | 23.0 | 22.6 | 22.6 | — | 22.4 | — | 22.1 | 21.8 | — | 21.4 | 21.2 |
| | Costs % | 14.8 | 14.2 | 14.2 | — | 13.6 | — | 13.5 | 13.5 | — | 13.6 | 13.7 |
| | Net margin % | 8.2 | 8.4 | 8.4 | — | 8.8 | — | 8.6 | 8.3 | — | 7.8 | 7.5 |
| | Profits | 121 | 80 | 57 | — | 159 | — | 172 | 185 | — | 193 | 206 |
| | Deprecitation | 6 | 4 | 3 | — | 7 | — | 8 | 9 | — | 10 | 11 |
| | Increased working capital | 22 | 25 | 0 | — | 28 | — | 33 | 38 | — | 42 | −188 |

| | | | | | | | | | | | | | |
|---|---|---|---|---|---|---|---|---|---|---|---|---|---|
| LOW MARKET GROWTH | Sales: West | 1427 | 891 | 640 | — | 1645 | — | 1770 | 1906 | — | 2053 | 2213 | |
| | North | — | — | — | — | — | — | — | — | — | — | — | |
| | Lost sales | | | 4 | | 6 | | | | | | | |
| | Gross margin % | 23.0 | 22.6 | 22.6 | — | 22.4 | — | 22.1 | 21.8 | — | 21.4 | 21.2 | |
| | Costs % | 14.9 | 14.3 | 14.3 | — | 13.7 | — | 13.6 | 13.6 | — | 13.7 | 13.8 | I |
| | Net margin % | 8.1 | 8.3 | 8.3 | — | 8.7 | — | 8.5 | 8.2 | — | 7.7 | 7.4 | |
| | Profits | 116 | 74 | 53 | — | 143 | — | 150 | 156 | — | 158 | 164 | |
| | Depreciation | 6 | 4 | 3 | — | 7 | — | 7 | 8 | — | 8 | 9 | |
| | Increased working capital | 15 | 16 | 0 | — | 18 | — | 20 | 22 | — | 24 | −115 | |
| CAPITAL 'CASH FLOWS' | Sale of Smiths | | | | | | | | | | | 60 | |
| | Cost of land | 1 | 2 | — | — | 2 | — | 2 | 2 | — | 3 | 3 | II |
| | Cost of buildings etc | | 40 | 20 | | | | | | | | | |
| | Value of buildings, etc ex Kings | | | | | | | | | | | 360 | |

DISCOUNT RATE

| | 11% | | | 13% | | | 15% | | |
|---|---|---|---|---|---|---|---|---|---|
| | High N W | Med N W | Low N W | High N W | Med N W | Low N W | High N W | Med N W | Low N W |
| $NPV_I$ | 307 | 307 | 313 | 289 | 290 | 295 | 273 | 274 | 279 |
| $NPV_{II}$+WC | 290 | 255 | 204 | 250 | 219 | 174 | 216 | 139 | 149 |
| $NPV_{TOT}$ | 597 | 562 | 517 | 539 | 509 | 469 | 489 | 463 | 428 |

Table 3A.3 Cash flow table
(Kings, Smiths, Darbys. Move January 1975)

| | | Sept 1973 | Sept 1974 | Oct 1974 | Jan 1975 | Sept 1975 | July 1976 | Sept 1976 | Sept 1977 | Jan 1978 | Sept 1978 | Sept 1979 | |
|---|---|---|---|---|---|---|---|---|---|---|---|---|---|
| HIGH MARKET GROWTH | Sales: West | 1514 | 1432 | — | 273 | 2016 | — | 2477 | 2928 | — | 3463 | 4093 | |
| | North | 1514 | 1432 | — | 272 | 1986 | — | 2440 | 2884 | — | 3411 | 4032 | |
| | Lost sales | | | — | 25 | 90 | — | | | — | | | |
| | Gross margin % | 23.0 | 22.6 | — | 22.4 | 22.2 | — | 22.0 | 21.7 | — | 21.3 | 21.1 | I |
| | Costs % | 14.7 | 14.1 | — | 13.9 | 11.5 | — | 11.0 | 10.7 | — | 10.4 | 10.4 | |
| | Net margin % | 8.3 | 8.5 | — | 8.5 | 10.7 | — | 11.0 | 11.0 | — | 10.9 | 10.7 | |
| | Profits (West) | 126 | 122 | — | 23 | 216 | — | 272 | 32 | — | 377 | 438 | |
| | Depreciation | 6 | 6 | — | 1 | 8 | — | 10 | 12 | — | 14 | 16 | |
| | Increased working capital | 27 | 30 | — | 0 | 50 | — | 74 | 72 | — | 86 | −359 | |
| MEDIUM MARKET GROWTH | Sales: West | 1476 | 1363 | — | 250 | 1824 | — | 2151 | 2448 | — | 2785 | 3169 | |
| | North | 1476 | 1363 | — | 249 | 1773 | — | 2119 | 2411 | — | 2743 | 3121 | |
| | Lost sales | | | — | 23 | 82 | — | | | — | | | |
| | Gross margin % | 23.0 | 22.6 | — | 22.4 | 22.2 | — | 22.0 | 21.7 | — | 21.3 | 21.1 | |
| | Costs % | 14.8 | 14.2 | — | 14.0 | 11.6 | — | 11.1 | 10.8 | — | 10.5 | 10.5 | I |
| | Net margin % | 8.2 | 8.4 | — | 8.4 | 10.6 | — | 10.9 | 10.9 | — | 10.8 | 10.6 | |
| | Profits (West) | 121 | 114 | — | 21 | 193 | — | 234 | 267 | — | 301 | 336 | |
| | Depreciation | 6 | 5 | — | 1 | 7 | — | 8 | 10 | — | 12 | 13 | |
| | Increased working capital | 20 | 16 | — | 0 | 35 | — | 55 | 50 | — | 59 | −225 | |

| | | | | | | | | | | | | |
|---|---|---|---|---|---|---|---|---|---|---|---|---|
| LOW MARKET GROWTH | Sales: West | 1427 | 1271 | — | 238 | 1633 | — | 1857 | 2032 | — | 2225 | 2434 |
| | North | 1427 | 1271 | — | 238 | 1609 | — | 1829 | 2002 | — | 2192 | 2397 |
| | Lost sales | | | — | 22 | 75 | — | | | — | | |
| | Gross margin % | 23.0 | 22.6 | — | 22.4 | 22.2 | — | 22.0 | 21.7 | — | 21.3 | 21.1 |
| | Costs % | 14.9 | 14.3 | — | 14.1 | 11.7 | — | 11.2 | 10.9 | — | 10.6 | 10.6 |
| | Net margin % | 8.1 | 8.3 | — | 8.3 | 10.5 | — | 10.8 | 10.8 | — | 10.7 | 10.5 |
| | Profits (West) | 116 | 105 | — | 20 | 171 | — | 201 | 219 | — | 238 | 256 |
| | Depreciation | 6 | 6 | — | 1 | 7 | — | 7 | 8 | — | 9 | 10 |
| | Increasēd working capital | 13 | 13 | — | 0 | 20 | — | 36 | 28 | — | 31 | −141 |

I

| | | | | | | | | | | | | |
|---|---|---|---|---|---|---|---|---|---|---|---|---|
| CAPITAL 'CASH FLOWS' | Sale of Smiths | | | 35 | | | | | | | | |
| | Cost of land W(N) | 3(5) | 6(10) | — | — | 6(10) | — | 6(10) | 6(10) | — | 10(14) | 10(14) |
| | Cost of buildings, etc. | | 267 | 89 | | | | | | | | |
| | Value of buildings, etc. ex Kings | | | | | | | | | | | 783 |

II

DISCOUNT RATE

| | 11% | | | | | | 13% | | | | | | 15% | | | | | |
|---|---|---|---|---|---|---|---|---|---|---|---|---|---|---|---|---|---|---|
| | High | | Med. | | Low | | High | | Med. | | Low | | High | | Med. | | Low | |
| | N | W | N | W | N | W | N | W | N | W | N | W | N | W | N | W | N | W |
| $NPV_I$ | 415 | 423 | 399 | 406 | 389 | 396 | 387 | 395 | 373 | 380 | 365 | 371 | 362 | 370 | 351 | 357 | 344 | 349 |
| $NPV_{II}$ | 287 | 270 | 216 | 198 | 159 | 142 | 228 | 211 | 165 | 149 | 115 | 98 | 177 | 161 | 121 | 106 | 77 | 61 |
| $NPV_{TOT}$ | 702 | 693 | 615 | 604 | 548 | 538 | 615 | 606 | 538 | 529 | 480 | 469 | 539 | 531 | 472 | 463 | 421 | 410 |

Table 3A.4 Cash flow table
(Kings, Smiths, Darbys. Move July 1976)

| | | Sept 1973 | Sept 1974 | Oct 1974 | Jan 1975 | Sept 1975 | July 1976 | Sept 1976 | Sept 1977 | Jan 1978 | Sept 1978 | Sept 1979 |
|---|---|---|---|---|---|---|---|---|---|---|---|---|
| HIGH MARKET GROWTH | Sales: West | 1514 | 1717 | — | — | 1950 | 738 | 1404 | 2619 | — | 3207 | 3792 |
| | North | 1514 | 1717 | — | — | 1950 | 738 | 1383 | 2580 | — | 3159 | 3735 |
| | Lost sales | | | | | | | 133 | 93 | | | |
| | Gross margin % | 23.0 | 22.6 | — | — | 22.4 | 22.1 | 22.1 | 21.7 | — | 21.4 | 21.2 |
| | Costs % | 14.7 | 14.1 | — | — | 13.7 | 13.6 | 11.7 | 11.1 | — | 10.9 | 10.8 |
| | Net margin % | 8.9 | 8.5 | — | — | 8.7 | 8.5 | 10.4 | 10.6 | — | 10.5 | 10.4 |
| | Profits (West) | 126 | 146 | — | — | 170 | 63 | 146 | 278 | — | 337 | 394 |
| | Depreciation | 6 | 7 | — | — | 8 | 3 | 6 | 10 | — | 13 | 15 |
| | Increased working capital | 27 | 32 | — | — | 37 | 31 | 0 | 76 | — | 94 | −297 |
| MEDIUM MARKET GROWTH | Sales: West | 1476 | 1630 | — | — | 1799 | 662 | 1246 | 2248 | — | 2650 | 3015 |
| | North | 1476 | 1630 | — | — | 1799 | 662 | 1227 | 2214 | — | 2610 | 2970 |
| | Lost sales | | | | | | | 118 | 80 | | | |
| | Gross margin % | 23.0 | 22.6 | — | — | 22.4 | 22.1 | 22.1 | 21.7 | — | 21.4 | 21.2 |
| | Costs % | 14.8 | 14.2 | — | — | 13.8 | 13.7 | 11.8 | 11.2 | — | 11.0 | 10.9 |
| | Net margin % | 8.2 | 8.4 | — | — | 8.6 | 8.4 | 10.3 | 10.5 | — | 10.4 | 10.3 |
| | Profits (West) | 121 | 137 | — | — | 155 | 56 | 128 | 236 | — | 276 | 311 |
| | Depreciation | 6 | 6 | — | — | 7 | 2 | 5 | 9 | — | 11 | 12 |
| | Increased working capital | 20 | 24 | — | — | 27 | 22 | 0 | 56 | — | 67 | −215 |

| | | | | | | | | | | | | | |
|---|---|---|---|---|---|---|---|---|---|---|---|---|---|
| LOW MARKET GROWTH | Sales: West | 1427 | 1527 | — | — | 1633 | 582 | 1088 | 1878 | — | 2129 | 2329 | |
| | North | 1427 | 1527 | — | — | 1633 | 582 | 1072 | 1850 | — | 2097 | 2294 | |
| | Lost sales | | | | | | | 103 | 67 | | | | |
| | Gross margin % | 23.0 | 22.6 | — | — | 22.4 | 22.1 | 22.1 | 21.7 | — | 21.4 | 21.2 | |
| | Costs % | 14.9 | 14.3 | — | — | 13.9 | 13.8 | 11.9 | 11.3 | — | 11.1 | 11.0 | I |
| | Net margin % | 8.1 | 8.3 | — | — | 8.5 | 8.3 | 10.2 | 10.4 | — | 10.3 | 10.2 | |
| | Profits (West) | 116 | 127 | — | — | 139 | 48 | 111 | 195 | — | 219 | 238 | |
| | Depreciation | 6 | 6 | — | — | 7 | 2 | 4 | 8 | — | 9 | 9 | |
| | Increased working capital | 13 | 16 | — | — | 17 | 12 | 0 | 33 | — | 40 | −125 | |
| CAPITAL 'CASH FLOWS' | Sale of Smiths | | | | | | 40 | | | | | | |
| | Cost of land W(N) | 3(5) | 6(10) | — | — | 6(10) | | 6(10) | 6(10) | — | 10(14) | 10(14) | |
| | Cost of buildings, etc. | | | | | 288 | 96 | | | | | | II |
| | Value of buildings, etc. ex Kings | | | | | | | | | | | 783 | |

DISCOUNT RATE

| | 11% | | | | | | 13% | | | | | | 15% | | | | | |
|---|---|---|---|---|---|---|---|---|---|---|---|---|---|---|---|---|---|---|
| | High | | Med. | | Low | | High | | Med. | | Low | | High | | Med. | | Low | |
| | N | W | N | W | N | W | N | W | N | W | N | W | N | W | N | W | N | W |
| $NPV_I$ | 368 | 373 | 358 | 362 | 352 | 356 | 345 | 349 | 336 | 340 | 331 | 334 | 324 | 328 | 316 | 320 | 312 | 315 |
| $NPV_{II}$+WC | 286 | 268 | 232 | 214 | 174 | 156 | 235 | 219 | 187 | 171 | 136 | 120 | 192 | 177 | 150 | 134 | 104 | 89 |
| $NPV_{TOT}$ | 654 | 641 | 590 | 576 | 526 | 512 | 580 | 568 | 523 | 511 | 467 | 454 | 516 | 505 | 466 | 454 | 416 | 405 |

Table 3A.5 Cash flow table
(Kings, Smiths, Darbys. Move January 1978)

| | | Sept 1973 | Sept 1974 | Oct 1974 | Jan 1975 | Sept 1975 | July 1976 | Sept 1976 | Sept 1977 | Jan 1978 | Sept 1978 | Sept 1979 | |
|---|---|---|---|---|---|---|---|---|---|---|---|---|---|
| HIGH MARKET GROWTH | Sales: West | 1514 | 1717 | — | — | 1950 | — | 2214 | 2096 | 404 | 2940 | 3614 | |
| | North | 1514 | 1717 | — | — | 1950 | — | 2214 | 2096 | 402 | 2896 | 3560 | |
| | Lost sales | | | | | | | | | 48 | 118 | 50 | |
| | Gross margin % | 23.0 | 22.6 | — | — | 22.4 | — | 22.1 | 21.8 | 21.8 | 21.3 | 21.1 | |
| | Costs % | 14.7 | 14.1 | — | — | 13.7 | — | 13.6 | 13.5 | 13.5 | 11.3 | 11.2 | I |
| | Net margin % | 8.3 | 8.5 | — | — | 8.7 | — | 8.5 | 8.3 | 8.3 | 10.0 | 9.9 | |
| | Profits (West) | 126 | 146 | — | — | 170 | — | 188 | 174 | 84 | 294 | 358 | |
| | Depreciation | 6 | 7 | — | — | 8 | — | 9 | 8 | 2 | 12 | 14 | |
| | Increased working capital | 27 | 32 | — | — | 37 | — | 42 | 46 | 0 | 70 | −256 | |
| MEDIUM MARKET GROWTH | Sales: West | 1476 | 1630 | — | — | 1799 | — | 1986 | 1828 | 350 | 2398 | 2842 | |
| | North | 1476 | 1630 | — | — | 1799 | — | 1986 | 1828 | 347 | 2362 | 2799 | |
| | Lost sales | | | | | | | | | 37 | 110 | 40 | |
| | Gross margin % | 23.0 | 22.6 | — | — | 22.4 | — | 22.1 | 21.8 | 21.8 | 21.3 | 21.1 | |
| | Costs % | 14.8 | 14.2 | — | — | 13.8 | — | 13.7 | 13.6 | 13.6 | 11.4 | 11.3 | I |
| | Net margin % | 8.2 | 8.4 | — | — | 8.6 | — | 8.4 | 8.2 | 8.2 | 9.9 | 9.8 | |
| | Profits (West) | 121 | 137 | — | — | 155 | — | 161 | 150 | 29 | 237 | 279 | |
| | Depreciation | 6 | 6 | — | — | 7 | — | 8 | 7 | 1 | 10 | 16 | |
| | Increased working capital | 20 | 24 | — | — | 27 | — | 30 | 32 | 0 | 47 | −180 | |

| | | | | | | | | | | | | |
|---|---|---|---|---|---|---|---|---|---|---|---|---|
| LOW MARKET GROWTH | Sales: West | 1427 | 1527 | — | — | 1633 | — | 1746 | 1556 | 295 | 2000 | 2275 |
| | North | 1427 | 1527 | — | — | 1633 | — | 1746 | 1556 | 293 | 1970 | 2241 |
| | Lost sales | | | | | | | | | 31 | 97 | 35 |
| | Gross margin % | 23.0 | 22.6 | — | — | 22.4 | — | 22.1 | 21.8 | 21.8 | 21.3 | 21.1 |
| | Costs % | 14.9 | 14.3 | — | — | 13.9 | — | 13.8 | 13.7 | 13.7 | 11.5 | 11.4 |
| | Net margin % | 8.1 | 8.3 | — | — | 8.5 | — | 8.3 | 8.1 | 8.1 | 9.8 | 9.7 |
| | Profits (West) | 116 | 127 | — | — | 139 | — | 145 | 126 | 24 | 196 | 221 |
| | Depreciation | 6 | 6 | — | — | 7 | — | 7 | 6 | 1 | 8 | 9 |
| | Increased working capital | 13 | 16 | — | — | 17 | — | 18 | 17 | 0 | 24 | −105 |

I

| | | | | | | | | | | | | |
|---|---|---|---|---|---|---|---|---|---|---|---|---|
| CAPITAL 'CASH FLOWS' | Sale of Smiths | | | | | | | | | 46 | | |
| | Cost of land (W(N)) | 3(5) | 6(10) | — | — | 6(10) | — | 6(10) | 6(10) | — | 10(14) | 10(14) |
| | Cost of buildings, etc. | | | | | | | | 318 | 106 | | |
| | Value of buildings, etc. ex. Kings | | | | | | | | | | | 783 |

II

DISCOUNT RATE

| | 11% | | | | | | 13% | | | | | | 15% | | | | | |
|---|---|---|---|---|---|---|---|---|---|---|---|---|---|---|---|---|---|---|
| | High | | Med. | | Low | | High | | Med. | | Low | | High | | Med. | | Low | |
| | N | W | N | W | N | W | N | W | N | W | N | W | N | W | N | W | N | W |
| $NPV_I$ | 331 | 333 | 325 | 327 | 328 | 330 | 310 | 313 | 306 | 308 | 309 | 311 | 292 | 294 | 288 | 290 | 292 | 293 |
| $NPV_{II}$+WC | 273 | 256 | 221 | 204 | 170 | 152 | 230 | 214 | 184 | 168 | 139 | 123 | 194 | 178 | 153 | 138 | 113 | 97 |
| $NPV_{TOT}$ | 604 | 589 | 546 | 531 | 498 | 482 | 540 | 527 | 490 | 476 | 448 | 434 | 486 | 472 | 441 | 428 | 405 | 390 |

Table 3A.6 Cash flow table
(Kings, Smiths move July 1976, Darbys move 1974)

| | | Sept 1973 | Sept 1974 | Oct 1974 | Jan 1975 | Sept 1975 | July 1976 | Sept 1976 | Sept 1977 | Jan 1978 | Sept 1978 | Sept 1979 |
|---|---|---|---|---|---|---|---|---|---|---|---|---|
| HIGH MARKET GROWTH | Sales: West | 1514 | 1718 | — | — | 1947 | 744 | 1416 | 2622 | — | 3230 | 3819 |
| | North | 1514 | 1718 | — | — | 1947 | 744 | 1395 | 2583 | — | 3182 | 3762 |
| | Lost sales | | | | | | | 124 | 109 | | | |
| | Gross margin % | 23.0 | 22.6 | — | — | 22.3 | 22.2 | 22.1 | 21.8 | — | 21.4 | 21.2 |
| | Costs % | 14.7 | 14.2 | — | — | 13.5 | 13.5 | 11.4 | 10.9 | — | 10.8 | 10.8 |
| | Net margin % | 8.3 | 8.5 | — | — | 8.8 | 8.8 | 10.7 | 10.9 | — | 10.6 | 10.4 |
| | Profits (West) | 126 | 146 | — | — | 171 | 65 | 152 | 286 | — | 342 | 397 |
| | Depreciation | 6 | 7 | — | — | 8 | 3 | 6 | 10 | — | 13 | 15 |
| | Increased working capital | 27 | 33 | — | — | 37 | 34 | 0 | 74 | — | 97 | −302 |
| MEDIUM MARKET GROWTH | Sales: West | 1476 | 1630 | — | — | 1803 | 667 | 1255 | 2235 | — | 2651 | 3016 |
| | North | 1476 | 1630 | — | — | 1803 | 667 | 1236 | 2201 | — | 2611 | 2971 |
| | Lost sales | | | | | | | 110 | 94 | | | |
| | Gross margin % | 23.0 | 22.6 | — | — | 22.3 | 22.2 | 22.1 | 21.8 | — | 21.4 | 21.2 |
| | Costs % | 14.8 | 14.2 | — | — | 13.6 | 13.5 | 11.5 | 11.0 | — | 10.9 | 10.9 |
| | Net margin % | 8.2 | 8.4 | — | — | 8.7 | 8.7 | 10.6 | 10.8 | — | 10.5 | 10.3 |
| | Profits (West) | 121 | 137 | — | — | 157 | 58 | 133 | 241 | — | 278 | 311 |
| | Depreciation | 6 | 6 | — | — | 7 | 2 | 5 | 9 | — | 11 | 12 |
| | Increased working capital | 20 | 25 | — | — | 28 | 23 | 0 | 53 | — | 70 | −219 |

| | | | | | | | | | | | | | |
|---|---|---|---|---|---|---|---|---|---|---|---|---|---|
| LOW MARKET GROWTH | Sales: West | 1427 | 1527 | — | — | 1639 | 590 | 1104 | 1891 | — | 2156 | 2359 | I |
| | North | 1427 | 1527 | — | — | 1639 | 590 | 1087 | 1863 | — | 2124 | 2324 | |
| | Lost sales | | | | | | | 96 | 78 | | | | |
| | Gross margin % | 23.0 | 22.6 | — | — | 22.3 | 22.2 | 22.1 | 21.8 | — | 21.4 | 21.2 | |
| | Costs % | 14.9 | 14.3 | — | — | 13.7 | 13.6 | 11.6 | 11.1 | — | 11.0 | 11.0 | |
| | Net margin % | 8.1 | 8.3 | — | — | 8.6 | 8.6 | 10.5 | 10.7 | — | 10.4 | 10.2 | |
| | Profits (West) | 116 | 127 | — | — | 141 | 51 | 116 | 202 | — | 224 | 252 | |
| | Depreciation | 6 | 6 | — | — | 7 | 2 | 4 | 8 | — | 9 | 9 | |
| | Increased working capital | 13 | 16 | — | — | 18 | 12 | 0 | 82 | — | 42 | −130 | |

| | | | | | | | | | | | | | |
|---|---|---|---|---|---|---|---|---|---|---|---|---|---|
| CAPITAL 'CASH FLOWS' | Sale of Smiths | | | | | | 40 | | | | | | II |
| | Cost of land W(N) | 3(5) | 6(10) | — | — | 6(10) | — | 6(10) | 6(10) | — | 10(14) | 10(14) | |
| | Cost of buildings, etc. | | 40 | 20 | | 246 | 82 | | | | | | |
| | Value of buildings, etc. ex Kings | | | | | | | | | | | 742 | |

DISCOUNT RATE

| | 11% | | | | | | 13% | | | | | | 15% | | | | | |
|---|---|---|---|---|---|---|---|---|---|---|---|---|---|---|---|---|---|---|
| | High | | Med. | | Low | | High | | Med. | | Low | | High | | Med. | | Low | |
| | N | W | N | W | N | W | N | W | N | W | N | W | N | W | N | W | N | W |
| $NPV_I$ | 375 | 381 | 362 | 366 | 363 | 367 | 351 | 356 | 339 | 344 | 341 | 345 | 330 | 334 | 319 | 323 | 322 | 325 |
| $NPV_{II}+WC$ | 280 | 263 | 225 | 208 | 167 | 150 | 228 | 212 | 179 | 163 | 128 | 112 | 183 | 168 | 140 | 125 | 95 | 80 |
| $NPV_{TOT}$ | 655 | 644 | 587 | 574 | 530 | 517 | 579 | 568 | 518 | 507 | 469 | 457 | 513 | 502 | 459 | 448 | 417 | 405 |

Table 3A.7 Cash flow table
(Kings, Smiths move January 1978, Darbys move 1974)

| | | Sept 1973 | Sept 1974 | Oct 1974 | Jan 1975 | Sept 1975 | July 1976 | Sept 1976 | Sept 1977 | Jan 1978 | Sept 1978 | Sept 1979 | |
|---|---|---|---|---|---|---|---|---|---|---|---|---|---|
| HIGH MARKET GROWTH | Sales: West | 1514 | 1718 | — | — | 1947 | — | 2232 | 2128 | 404 | 2924 | 3621 | |
| | North | 1514 | 1718 | — | — | 1947 | — | 2232 | 2128 | 400 | 2880 | 3567 | |
| | Lost sales | | 5 | | | 7 | | | | 36 | 198 | 70 | |
| | Gross margin % | 23.0 | 22.6 | — | — | 22.3 | — | 22.2 | 21.9 | 21.7 | 21.5 | 21.1 | I |
| | Costs % | 14.7 | 14.1 | — | — | 13.5 | — | 13.4 | 13.4 | 13.4 | 11.3 | 11.2 | |
| | Net margin % | 8.3 | 8.5 | — | — | 8.8 | — | 8.8 | 8.5 | 8.3 | 10.2 | 9.9 | |
| | Profits (West) | 126 | 146 | — | — | 171 | — | 196 | 181 | 34 | 298 | 358 | |
| | Depreciation | 6 | 7 | — | — | 8 | — | 9 | 9 | 2 | 12 | 15 | |
| | Increased working capital | 27 | 33 | — | — | 37 | — | 46 | 48 | 0 | 63 | −254 | |
| MEDIUM MARKET GROWTH | Sales: West | 1476 | 1630 | — | — | 1803 | — | 2003 | 1856 | 349 | 2368 | 2827 | |
| | North | 1476 | 1630 | — | — | 1803 | — | 2003 | 1856 | 346 | 2332 | 2785 | |
| | Lost sales | | 5 | | | 6 | — | — | | 31 | 166 | 57 | |
| | Gross margin % | 23.0 | 22.6 | — | — | 22.3 | — | 22.2 | 21.9 | 21.7 | 21.5 | 21.1 | |
| | Costs % | 14.8 | 14.2 | — | — | 13.6 | — | 13.5 | 13.5 | 13.5 | 11.4 | 11.3 | I |
| | Net margin % | 8.2 | 8.4 | — | — | 8.7 | — | 8.7 | 8.4 | 8.2 | 10.1 | 9.8 | |
| | Profits (West) | 121 | 137 | — | — | 157 | — | 174 | 156 | 29 | 239 | 277 | |
| | Depreciation | 6 | 6 | — | — | 7 | — | 8 | 8 | 1 | 10 | 12 | |
| | Increased working capital | 20 | 25 | — | — | 28 | — | 34 | 33 | 0 | 40 | −180 | |

| | | | | | | | | | | | | | |
|---|---|---|---|---|---|---|---|---|---|---|---|---|---|
| LOW MARKET GROWTH | Sales: West | 1427 | 1527 | — | — | 1639 | — | 1770 | 1588 | 297 | 1987 | 2277 | |
| | North | 1427 | 1527 | — | — | 1639 | — | 1770 | 1588 | 295 | 1957 | 2243 | |
| | Lost sales | | 4 | | | 6 | | | | 26 | 134 | 144 | |
| | Gross margin % | 23.0 | 22.6 | — | — | 22.3 | — | 22.2 | 21.9 | 21.7 | 21.5 | 21.1 | |
| | Costs % | 14.9 | 14.3 | — | — | 13.7 | — | 13.6 | 13.6 | 13.6 | 11.5 | 11.4 | I |
| | Net margin % | 8.1 | 8.3 | — | — | 8.6 | — | 8.6 | 8.3 | 8.1 | 10.0 | 9.7 | |
| | Profits (West) | 116 | 127 | — | — | 141 | — | 152 | 132 | 24 | 199 | 221 | |
| | Depreciation | 6 | 6 | — | — | 7 | — | 7 | 6 | 1 | 8 | 9 | |
| | Increased working capital | 13 | 16 | — | — | 18 | — | 21 | 18 | 0 | 16 | −102 | |

| | | | | | | | | | | | | | |
|---|---|---|---|---|---|---|---|---|---|---|---|---|---|
| CAPITAL 'CASH FLOWS' | Sale of Smiths | | | | | | | | | 46 | | | |
| | Cost of land (W(N)) | 3(5) | 6(10) | | | 6(10) | | 6(10) | 6(10) | 6(10) | 10(14) | 10(14) | II |
| | Cost of buildings, etc. | | 40 | 20 | | | | | 267 | 89 | | | |
| | Value of buildings, etc. ex. Kings | | | | | | | | | | | 742 | |

DISCOUNT RATE

| | 11% | | | 13% | | | 15% | | |
|---|---|---|---|---|---|---|---|---|---|
| | High N W | Med. N W | Low N W | High N W | Med. N W | Low N W | High N W | Med. N W | Low N W |
| $NPV_{II}$ | 336 339 | 327 330 | 335 337 | 315 318 | 308 310 | 316 317 | 297 299 | 290 292 | 298 299 |
| $NPV_{II}+WC$ | 285 268 | 234 216 | 180 163 | 239 222 | 193 177 | 146 130 | 199 183 | 159 143 | 117 101 |
| $NPV_{TOT}$ | 621 607 | 561 546 | 515 500 | 554 540 | 501 487 | 462 447 | 496 482 | 449 435 | 415 400 |

Table 3A.8 Cost data for decision tree
(Numbers refer to branches on tree; figures in £'000)

| | 11% | 13% | 15% | | 11% | 13% | 15% | | 11% | 13% | 15% | | 11% | 13% | 15% |
|---|---|---|---|---|---|---|---|---|---|---|---|---|---|---|---|
| 1.1 | 827 | 736 | 657 | 39 | 680 | 610 | 548 | 93 | 649 | 585 | 528 | 147 | 676 | 607 | 543 |
| 1.2 | 794 | 704 | 625 | 40 | 658 | 594 | 538 | 94 | 634 | 570 | 513 | 148 | 680 | 613 | 554 |
| 1.3 | 777 | 688 | 609 | 41 | 658 | 591 | 531 | 95 | 613 | 554 | 503 | 149 | 665 | 599 | 541 |
| 1.4 | 740 | 659 | 590 | 42 | 643 | 577 | 517 | 96 | 612 | 552 | 497 | 150 | 675 | 614 | 559 |
| 1.5 | 707 | 627 | 558 | 43 | 658 | 594 | 538 | 97 | 597 | 537 | 482 | 151 | 643 | 580 | 523 |
| 1.6 | 690 | 611 | 542 | 44 | 634 | 568 | 511 | 98 | 613 | 554 | 503 | 152 | 628 | 566 | 510 |
| 1.7 | 673 | 601 | 539 | 45 | 619 | 554 | 497 | 99 | 588 | 529 | 477 | 153 | 675 | 614 | 559 |
| 1.8 | 640 | 569 | 507 | 46 | 658 | 594 | 538 | 100 | 573 | 514 | 462 | 154 | 619 | 557 | 503 |
| 1.9 | 623 | 553 | 491 | 47 | 687 | 614 | 548 | 101 | 613 | 554 | 503 | 155 | 604 | 543 | 490 |
| 2.1 | 818 | 727 | 649 | 48 | 674 | 603 | 537 | 102 | 782 | 701 | 630 | 156 | 675 | 614 | 559 |
| 2.2 | 785 | 696 | 617 | 49 | 695 | 624 | 562 | 103 | 769 | 689 | 619 | 157 | 661 | 590 | 529 |
| 2.3 | 768 | 679 | 601 | 50 | 680 | 610 | 548 | 104 | 738 | 663 | 599 | 158 | 647 | 578 | 517 |
| 2.4 | 729 | 650 | 581 | 51 | 658 | 594 | 538 | 105 | 723 | 650 | 585 | 159 | 680 | 613 | 554 |
| 2.5 | 696 | 618 | 549 | 52 | 658 | 591 | 531 | 106 | 722 | 656 | 597 | 160 | 665 | 599 | 541 |
| 2.6 | 679 | 602 | 533 | 53 | 643 | 577 | 517 | 107 | 701 | 630 | 568 | 161 | 675 | 614 | 559 |
| 2.7 | 663 | 590 | 528 | 54 | 658 | 594 | 538 | 108 | 686 | 617 | 554 | 162 | 643 | 580 | 523 |
| 2.8 | 630 | 558 | 496 | 55 | 634 | 568 | 511 | 109 | 722 | 656 | 597 | 163 | 628 | 566 | 510 |
| 2.9 | 613 | 542 | 480 | 56 | 619 | 554 | 497 | 110 | 677 | 607 | 548 | 164 | 675 | 614 | 559 |
| 3 | 783 | 700 | 627 | 57 | 658 | 594 | 538 | 111 | 662 | 594 | 534 | 165 | 619 | 557 | 503 |
| 4 | 772 | 689 | 616 | 58 | 658 | 585 | 522 | 112 | 722 | 656 | 597 | 166 | 604 | 543 | 490 |
| 5 | 755 | 677 | 609 | 59 | 645 | 574 | 511 | 113 | 754 | 676 | 605 | 167 | 675 | 614 | 559 |
| 6 | 741 | 663 | 595 | 60 | 695 | 624 | 562 | 114 | 741 | 664 | 594 | 168 | 654 | 588 | 530 |
| 7 | 693 | 624 | 564 | 61 | 680 | 610 | 548 | 115 | 738 | 663 | 599 | 169 | 640 | 575 | 519 |
| 8 | 718 | 644 | 578 | 62 | 658 | 594 | 538 | 116 | 723 | 650 | 585 | 170 | 632 | 571 | 518 |
| 9 | 704 | 630 | 564 | 63 | 658 | 691 | 531 | 117 | 722 | 656 | 597 | 171 | 616 | 557 | 503 |
| 10 | 693 | 624 | 564 | 64 | 643 | 577 | 517 | 118 | 701 | 630 | 568 | 172 | 602 | 548 | 502 |

| | | | | | | | | | | | | | | | |
|---|---|---|---|---|---|---|---|---|---|---|---|---|---|---|---|
| 11 | 694 | 621 | 558 | 65 | 658 | 594 | 538 | 119 | 686 | 617 | 554 | 173 | 595 | 538 | 487 |
| 12 | 680 | 607 | 544 | 66 | 634 | 568 | 511 | 120 | 722 | 656 | 597 | 174 | 579 | 524 | 472 |
| 13 | 693 | 624 | 564 | 67 | 619 | 554 | 497 | 121 | 677 | 607 | 548 | 175 | 602 | 548 | 502 |
| 14 | 755 | 675 | 602 | 68 | 658 | 594 | 538 | 122 | 662 | 594 | 534 | 176 | 571 | 515 | 467 |
| 15 | 744 | 664 | 591 | 69 | 658 | 590 | 531 | 123 | 722 | 656 | 597 | 177 | 555 | 501 | 452 |
| 16 | 755 | 677 | 609 | 70 | 645 | 578 | 519 | 124 | 725 | 647 | 579 | 178 | 602 | 548 | 502 |
| 17 | 741 | 663 | 595 | 71 | 649 | 585 | 528 | 125 | 712 | 635 | 568 | 179 | 626 | 563 | 505 |
| 18 | 693 | 624 | 564 | 72 | 634 | 570 | 513 | 126 | 738 | 663 | 599 | 180 | 612 | 550 | 494 |
| 19 | 718 | 644 | 578 | 73 | 613 | 554 | 503 | 127 | 723 | 650 | 585 | 181 | 632 | 571 | 518 |
| 20 | 704 | 630 | 564 | 74 | 612 | 552 | 497 | 128 | 722 | 656 | 597 | 182 | 616 | 557 | 503 |
| 21 | 693 | 624 | 564 | 75 | 597 | 537 | 482 | 129 | 701 | 630 | 568 | 183 | 602 | 548 | 502 |
| 22 | 694 | 621 | 558 | 76 | 613 | 554 | 503 | 130 | 686 | 617 | 554 | 184 | 595 | 538 | 487 |
| 23 | 680 | 607 | 544 | 77 | 588 | 529 | 477 | 131 | 722 | 656 | 597 | 185 | 579 | 524 | 472 |
| 24 | 693 | 624 | 564 | 78 | 573 | 514 | 462 | 132 | 677 | 607 | 548 | 186 | 602 | 548 | 502 |
| 25 | 726 | 646 | 576 | 79 | 613 | 554 | 503 | 133 | 662 | 594 | 534 | 187 | 571 | 515 | 467 |
| 26 | 715 | 635 | 565 | 80 | 630 | 565 | 506 | 134 | 722 | 556 | 597 | 188 | 555 | 501 | 452 |
| 27 | 755 | 677 | 609 | 81 | 617 | 553 | 494 | 135 | 718 | 644 | 580 | 189 | 602 | 548 | 502 |
| 28 | 741 | 663 | 595 | 82 | 649 | 585 | 528 | 136 | 704 | 632 | 568 | 190 | 597 | 534 | 479 |
| 29 | 693 | 624 | 564 | 83 | 634 | 570 | 513 | 137 | 680 | 613 | 554 | 191 | 583 | 521 | 468 |
| 30 | 718 | 644 | 578 | 84 | 613 | 554 | 503 | 138 | 665 | 599 | 541 | 192 | 632 | 571 | 518 |
| 31 | 704 | 630 | 564 | 85 | 612 | 552 | 497 | 139 | 675 | 614 | 559 | 193 | 616 | 557 | 503 |
| 32 | 693 | 624 | 564 | 86 | 597 | 537 | 482 | 140 | 643 | 580 | 523 | 194 | 602 | 548 | 502 |
| 33 | 694 | 621 | 558 | 87 | 613 | 554 | 503 | 141 | 628 | 566 | 510 | 195 | 595 | 538 | 487 |
| 34 | 680 | 607 | 544 | 88 | 588 | 529 | 477 | 142 | 675 | 614 | 559 | 196 | 577 | 524 | 472 |
| 35 | 693 | 624 | 564 | 89 | 573 | 514 | 462 | 143 | 619 | 557 | 503 | 197 | 602 | 548 | 502 |
| 36 | 715 | 639 | 573 | 90 | 613 | 554 | 503 | 144 | 604 | 543 | 490 | 198 | 571 | 515 | 467 |
| 37 | 702 | 628 | 562 | 91 | 601 | 536 | 480 | 145 | 675 | 614 | 559 | 199 | 555 | 501 | 452 |
| 38 | 695 | 624 | 562 | 92 | 588 | 524 | 468 | 146 | 690 | 619 | 555 | 200 | 692 | 548 | 502 |
| | 11% | 13% | 15% | | 11% | 13% | 15% | | 11% | 13% | 15% | | 11% | 13% | 15% |

# Appendix III. Maps and Development Sites for the Hull Project

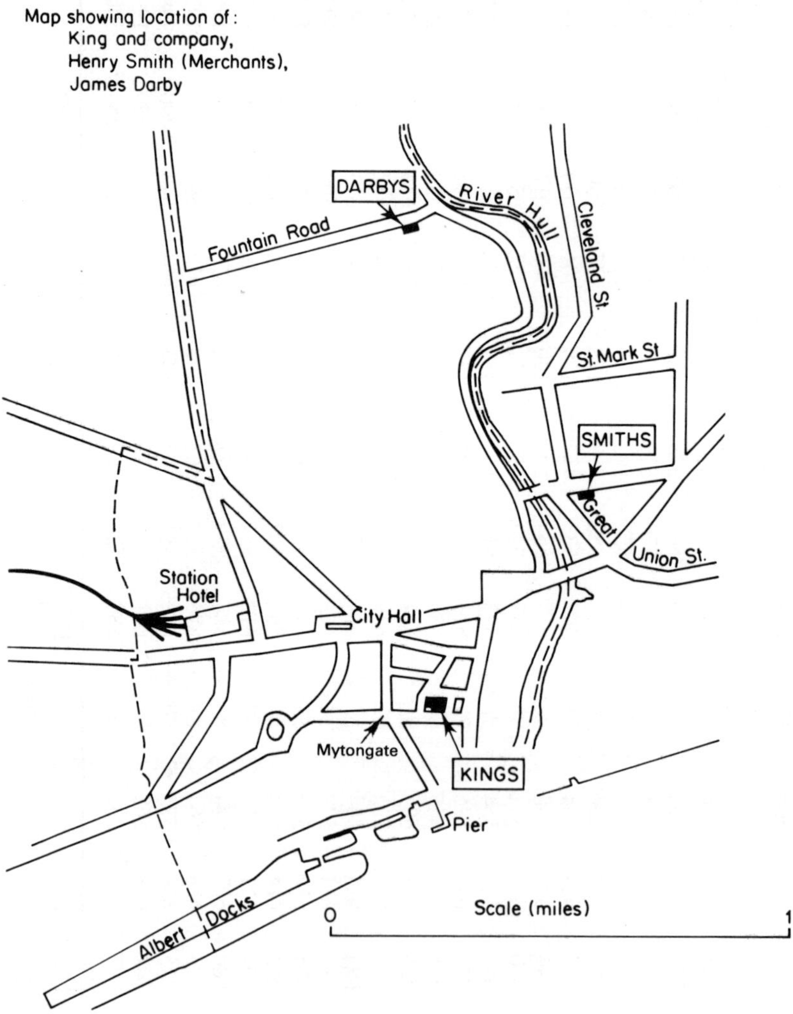


Figure 3A.26 Map showing the location of: King and Company; Henry Smith (Merchants); James Darby

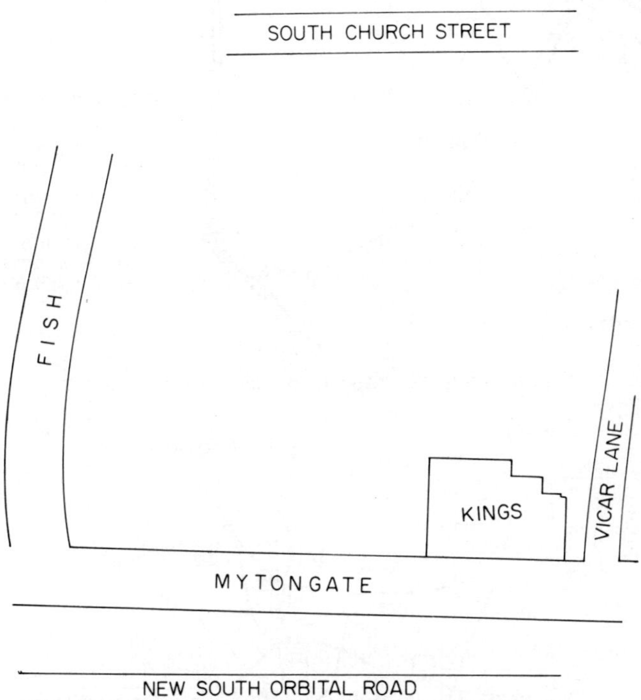


Figure 3A.27 Map showing Kings existing site

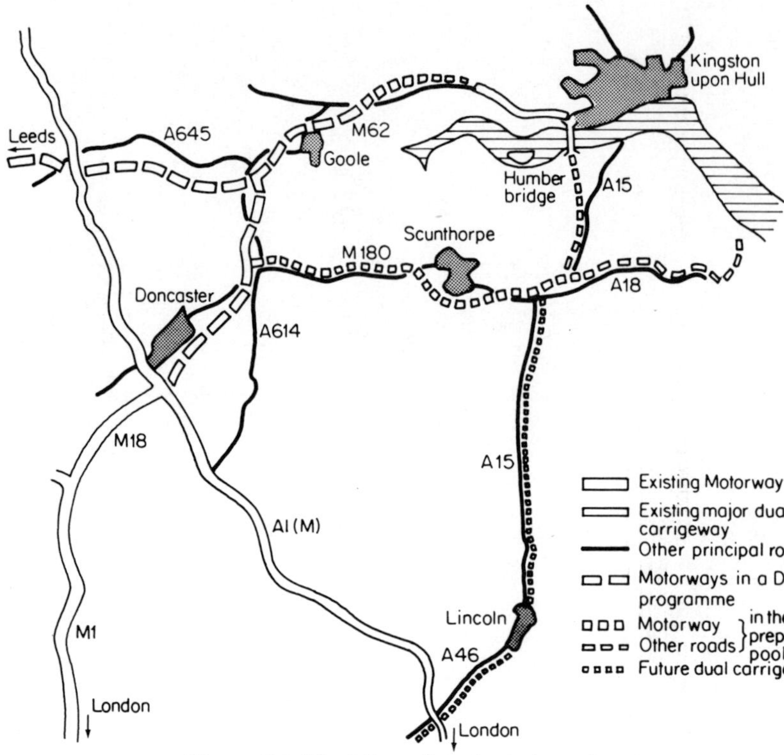


Figure 3A.28 Map of projected road system

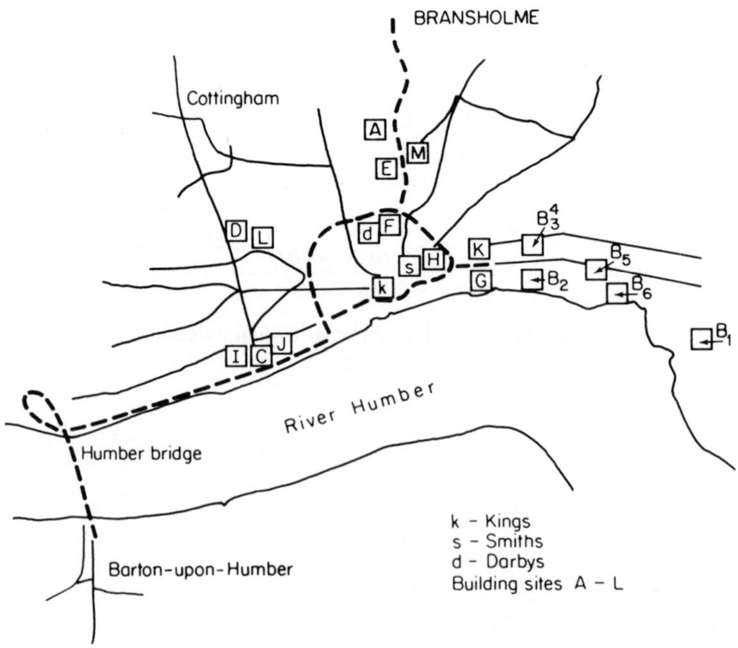


Figure 3A.29 Map of Hull area showing existing sites and potential building sites

From: Director of Industrial Development,
Guildhall,
Kingston-upon-Hull.

29th January 1973

## LAND AND BUILDINGS FOR REDEVELOPMENT

*Kingston-upon-Hull*

A. *SUTTON FIELDS INDUSTRIAL ESTATE* – (Hull Corporation) – comprising 255 acres. Land available in lots of between half an acre and 50 acres or more if needed. Fully serviced sites available for manufacturing and light industries for immediate development.

B. *BRITISH TRANSPORT DOCKS BOARD LANE*

2. 500 acres adjacent to BP Chemicals at Salt End. 200 acres available with planning permission for heavy process industry. (300 acres waiting for Government decision on potential use.)
2. 35-acre site (ex-timber yard) with riverside frontage (no riverside wharfage), available for manufacturing industry, or warehousing/storage.
3. 8-to-10-acre site adjacent to King George V Docks, with frontage to Hedon Road, available for manufacturing industry or warehousing/storage.
4. 17-acre, light-industry estate adjacent to King George V docks.
5. 23 acres to the East of the new entrance to King George V and Queen Elizabeth Docks, available for manufacturing industry or warehousing/storage.
6. 100 acres approximately on King George V and Queen Elizabeth docks extension, available for manufacturing industry or warehousing/-
storage.

For further details contact:
Estates Surveyor,
British Transport Docks Board,
Kingston House North,
Bond Street,
Kingston upon Hull. (Telephone 26431)

C. Land owned by *British Railways*, to be cleared for further development, extending to about 60 acres to the east of St Andrew's Dock; expected to have a frontage to the South Docks Road when built.

For further details contact:

District Estates Surveyor,
British Railways,
Aire Street,
Leeds, LS1 4PR.

D. Land at *Ideal Standard*, National Avenue, available in various lots for light industry. Total site approximately 30 acres net of roads, with building of 70,000 7,500 and 28,000 square feet available for early use.

For further details contact:

Company Secretary,
Ideal Standard Ltd.,
National Avenue,
Kingston upon Hull. (Telephone 46551)

E. Land and buildings owned by *Rushbrook Properties Ltd.*, on Bankside, ex-Sissons paint factory. Land extending to some 15 acres and buildings of 103,000 square feet. Some buildings and land for early development in small lots.

For further details contact:

Lander Bedells & Stuart Edwards, 36 Lambs Conduit Street, London, WC1N 3LL. (Telephone 01-405-4881)

F. Land and buildings at *Wilmington* (formerly Blue Circle Cement Works). 10 acres available for industrial redevelopment.

For further details contact:

Estates Surveyor,
Blue Circle Cement Co. Ltd.,
Portland House,
Stag Place,
London SW1.

G. Land and buildings occupied on medium-term lease by Unilever – ex-BOCM works, frontage to River Humber.

For further details contact:

Estate Surveyor,
Unilever Ltd.,
P.O. Box 31,
8 Salisbury Square,
London EC4P 4AN.

H. Land and buildings, Priestmans Ltd., extending to some 40,000 square feet. Being converted into smaller units.

For further details contact:

Wykeland Property Co.,
48 High Street,
Kingston upon Hull. (Telephone 20968)

I. Land at Gypsyville (Reckitts old works) owned by Wykeland Limited, 5 acres of open development land for light manufacturing industry.

For further details contact:

Wykeland Property Co.,
48 High Street,
Kingston upon Hull. (Telephone 20968)

J. Scarborough Street industrial area (Hull Corporation).

K. Crowle Street/Lee Smith Street industrial area (Hull Corporation)

L. National Avenue/Harpings Road industrial area (Hull Corporation).

M. 5-acre site, Leads Road, for light industrial purposes (Hull Corporation).

# Appendix IV: Fire at Henry Smith, 12 April 1973

DECISION: REBUILD OR NOT?

### The Situation

(1) The fire destroyed c. 30 percent of Henry Smith's buildings.
(2) Insurance cover should provide:
  (a) 30 percent of £61,600 = £18,500 to rebuild
  (b) 30 percent of c. 0.9 × £61,600 = £16,600 if it is decided to rebuild on another site.
(3) At present Henry Smith's collect trade is being operated from the remaining warehouse at Witham. The rest of Henry Smith's trade is being moved to Kings.

### Alternatives

(1) Not to rebuild, but to wait until Ferguson Humberside is formed outside Hull in say:
  (i) January 1975;
  (ii) July 1976;
  (iii) January 1978.
(2) To rebuild a permanent prefabricated building:
  (i) cost £26,000,
  (ii) time 20 weeks,
  before deciding on eventual amalgamation.
(3) To rebuild a temporary prefabricated building;
  (i) cost c. £20,000,
  (ii) time c. 15 weeks,
  just to tide over until Ferguson Humberside is formed.

### The Analysis

There are both quantitative and intangible or non-quantitative factors that affect the decision. The quantitative analysis consists of estimating the costs and revenues that will result from the three alternatives, and then calculating the Net Present Value of the differences between the alternative courses of action. These differences can then be traded-off against the non-quantitative factors. It is felt that this can best be done by the directors.

### Non-quantitative factors

As we see it, the non-quantitative factors, some of which favour rebuilding and some of which do not, are largely as follows:

(i) Rebuilding the burnt-out warehouse will enable Smiths to return to the status quo fairly rapidly. Smith's trading from Kings will only be temporary and, what is perhaps more important, will be seen to be only temporary. Both companies will retain their identities. Possible management and personnel difficulties may be avoided and problems over the profit-sharing scheme minimized.

(ii) Rebuilding will mean that the directors will not be pressurized into taking a decision over the eventual resiting and amalgamation of the companies.

(iii) If the eventual resiting and amalgamation is only a question of when, the problems of bringing Smiths and Kings together will have to be faced at some stage. The fire may be a suitable trigger for this purpose.

**Cost Considerations**

The following costs were considered in the analysis (Table 3A.9).

Table 3A.9

| | | Alternatives 1 | 2 | 3 |
|---|---|---|---|---|
| (1) | Cash from insurance – building | £16,600 | £18,500 | £18,500 |
| | – stocks, fixtures, fittings, etc. | √ | √ | √ |
| (2) | Cost of rebuilding | — | £26,000 | £20,000 |
| (3) | Loss of profits | | | |
| | (a) During the initial 3 weeks, due to stocks difficulties | √ | √ | √ |
| | (b) During the next 12 weeks, without either of the building possibilities | √ | √ | √ |
| | (c) During the next 5 weeks, without the 'permanent' building (2) | £1,900 | £1,900 | — |
| | (d) During the next few months or years if rebuilding does not occur. This depends on whether the eventual move to the new site is in: | | | |
| | (i) January 1975 (15 months) | £6,700 | — | — |
| | or (ii) July 1976 (34 months) | £16,000 | — | N.A. |
| | or (iii) January 1978 (52 months) | £26,100 | — | N.A. |
| (4) | Final selling cost of H. Smith's premises | √ | √ | √ |

NB 'Ticks' means the costs are the same for each alternative and can thus be ignored for comparison purposes.
It assumes that, on sale, it is Henry Smith's site, not the buildings, which will be of value. Rebuilding will not therefore affect the site value.

**Conclusion**

The following table (Table 3A.10) shows the maximum amount that should be paid for rebuilding the burnt-out warehouse under various assumptions of lost sales and eventual move date.

Table 3A.10

| | Eventual move | Lost sales | | | Building type |
|---|---|---|---|---|---|
| | | 5% | 10% | 20% | |
| | Jan. 1975 | 3.79 | 7.59 | 15.18 | Temporary |
| Figures in £'000 discounted at 13% p.a. | | 2.90 | 5.80 | 11.60 | Permanent |
| | July 1976 | 6.23 | 12.46 | 24.92 | Permanent |
| | Jan. 1978 | 9.41 | 18.81 | 37.62 | Permanent |

The relative* costs of rebuilding are: (i) permanent £24,100, (ii) temporary £18,000. Thus, on financial grounds the building should not be replaced, *especially* if an early start to the major rebuilding is anticipated and if sales are not expected to fall more than 10 percent below previous estimates. The major report recommends an early start to rebuilding.

NOTES

**Calculation of loss in profits** (see Table 3A.11, Figure 3A.30)

(1) Net profit before tax = sales × gross margin − fixed costs − variable costs,
i.e. $P = S.Gm - Fc - Vc$
but, $Vc = \alpha \times S$
so, $P = (\mathrm{Gm} - \alpha) \times S - Fc$
and $\Delta P = (Gm - \alpha) \times \Delta S$.
Thus a reduction in sales of $\Delta S$ means a reduction in profits of $(Gm - \alpha) \times \Delta S$

(2) It is estimated that for Henry Smiths:

(a) Gross margin $\simeq$ 18 percent.
(b) Most costs, such as salaries, are fixed, so since total costs are 11 percent of sales, '$\alpha$' is taken as 1½ percent. This means $\Delta P = 0.165\Delta S$ or for every £1000 of lost sales, profits before tax are down £165.

(3) Without rebuilding the lost sales are 'estimated' to be about 10 percent, although they will be higher than this initially.

*Relative to the £16,000 obtainable if rebuilding does *not* go ahead.

(4) Tax. The lost profits should be calculated after corporation tax (paid about a year in arrears) in order to be on a comparable basis with the capital cash flows.

$$\text{PAT} = \text{PBT}.\quad \left(\frac{1 - (\text{tax rate})}{1 + (\text{discount rate})}\right)$$

A tax rate of 50 percent is assumed.

Table 3A.11 Profits lost under the various alternatives (Discount rate 8%[a])

| | | | | (£'000) | |
|---|---|---|---|---|---|
| | | | Sales per annum | Initial lost profits | Final lost profits |
| *Quarter* | | | | | |
| May–July | 1973 | | 670 | | |
| Aug–Oct | 1973 | | 686 | 1.84 | |
| Nov–Jan | 1973/4 | | 700 | | 1.25 |
| Feb–Apr | 1974 | | 717 | | 1.28 |
| May–July | 1974 | | 733 | | 1.31 |
| Aug–Oct | 1974 | | 748 | | 1.33 |
| Nov–Jan | 1974/5 → | move? | 764 | | 1.36 |
| Feb–Apr | 1975 | | 782 | | 1.39 |
| May–July | 1975 | | 799 | | 1.42 |
| Aug–Oct | 1975 | | 817 | | 1.46 |
| Nov–Jan | 1975/6 | | 834 | | 1.49 |
| Feb–Apr | 1976 | | 849 | | 1.51 |
| May–July | 1976 → | move? | 868 | | 1.55 |
| Aug–Oct | 1976 | | 886 | | 1.58 |
| Nov–Jan | 1976/7 | | 906 | | 1.61 |
| Feb–Apr | 1977 | | 926 | | 1.65 |
| May–July | 1977 | | 946 | | 1.68 |
| Aug–Oct | 1977 | | 970 | | 1.73 |
| Nov–Jan | 1977/8 → | move? | 996 | | 1.77 |

[a]The 'discounting' factor only accounts for the fact that corporation tax is paid about a year in arrears. It does not discount back to the present, this is done at a later stage.

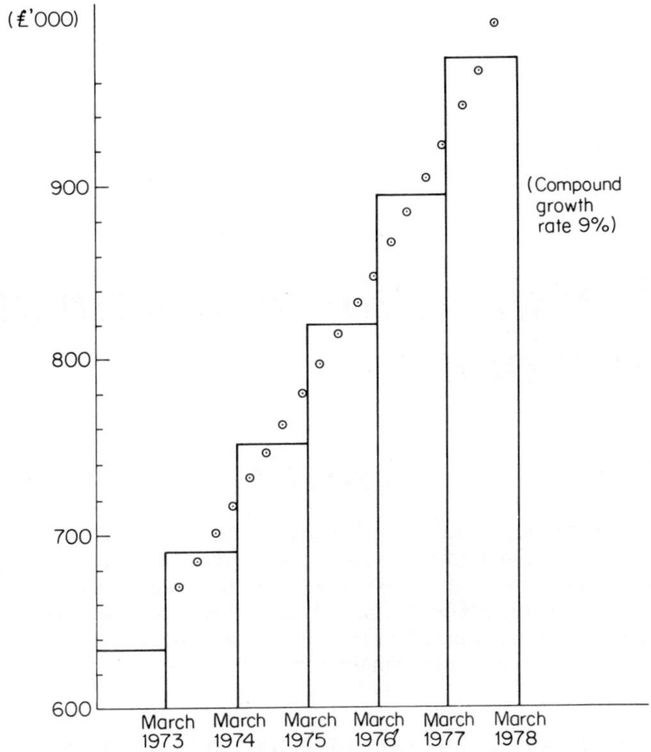


Figure 3A.30 Likely growth in sales, 1971–1978[a] H. Smith and Sons pre-fire

[a]It is felt that, given inflation, Henry Smith's current budget for 1973/4 is rather cautious.

## REFERENCE

Hertz, D. B. and H. Thomas. *Risk Analysis and its Applications*. Chichester: John Wiley, 1983.

## QUESTIONS FOR DISCUSSION

1. Provide a critical evaluation of the analytic approach described in the case.
2. How would you amend the analysis?
3. Do you feel that the approach is sensitive to the measurement of, for example, subjective probabilities or problem formulation assumptions?

*Chapter 4*

# *A Diversification Problem at Egg n' Foam**

SUMMARY

In this chapter we develop a strategic risk analysis approach in relation to the evaluation by Egg n' Foam of the potential acquisition of Pethow Ltd. The approach includes thorough treatment of forecasting cash flows, sensitivity analysis to identify uncertain variables, and the identification of required rates of return for acquisition candidates. The detailed form of the risk model is presented in an Appendix but the essential details of the approach are presented in the main body of the Chapter.

## 4.1 EGG N' FOAM/PETHOW ACQUISITION

This case considers the appraisal by Egg n' Foam of a proposed acquisition of a company (Pethow Ltd.) which was primarily in the field of egg producing, packaging and marketing but with subsidiary interests in poultry products and feedstuffs. Such an acquisition was seen by Egg n' Foam to represent an expansion into a *related* business area which would make use of Egg n' Foam's packaging and production-oriented set of skills.

The initial checklist appraisal by managers envisaged the acquisition as being beneficial in terms of, first, the quality and specialist skills of Pethow's management; second, the existence of rationalization benefits and savings from more efficient packaging and marketing of eggs; third, the development of a base from which to expand into other agricultural business areas, i.e. to develop an agribusiness-type strategy. Some other lesser advantages were mentioned but the real issue was to evaluate the acquisition's potential worth and fit with Egg n' Foam's operations over, say, a five-year horizon. Such a horizon was thought to be reasonable, particularly for forecasting purposes, and would also allow different but sensible assumptions about the acquisition's residual value at the end of the horizon to be thoroughly tested.

*This case was developed by Howard Thomas through risk analysis seminars in London Business School and the Australian Graduate School of Management, Sydney.

## 4.2 DECISION STRUCTURING AND CASH FLOW MODELING

### Cash Flow, Financial Model

Prior to evaluating the main decision options for Egg n' Foam, it was decided that the need to forecast cash flows would require the construction of a financial model of Pethow's operations. This would develop the relevant cost and revenue variables, e.g. capacity costs, egg prices and margins as a prelude to cash flow equations of the 'revenue minus cost' type. The detail of the model is not presented here (for further detail see Appendix) as the nature of accounting relationships, working capital, tax and depreciation policies, etc. is beyond the scope of the present discussion and specific to the firm. The key lesson for implementation, however, is that a financial model must be developed for any potential acquisition.

In this particular case the capital requirements for the model were assessed in single-valued terms. This was because not enough was known about Pethow and it was, therefore, felt that the uncertainty on the capital side (e.g. acquisition price, further investment in the processing and rearing areas, etc.) would be better treated in terms of *ex-post* sensitivity analysis rather than *ex-ante* assessment of rather 'soft' subjective distributions for capital investments.

Assessments in probabilistic terms were made for the more sensitive and uncertain variables such as hen productivity, egg selling price, stock costs, feeding costs, margin per chicken, margin per case of eggs on packing and marketing and margin per ton for feedstuff production. If the assessments were in the form of symmetric distributions then a normality assumption was made. Otherwise asymmetry was treated by using beta distributions with appropriate parameters. These assessments were necessary in order to assess the cash flow arising from the egg production, egg marketing and feedstuff operations respectively. Other assessments were made in single-valued terms because a crude prior sensitivity analysis had shown that the uncertainty in those other variables was much tighter in range and distributional terms.

### Decision Structuring

Much of the prior discussion on financial modeling and evaluation was found to be a necessary input into the strategy formulation process. It was thought, for example, that the risk-simulation model would have to be structured so that each executive affected would be willing to accept the structure, provide input evaluations and accept the relevance of the model's output in terms of the judgment, review and choice phases of the decision process. As a consequence, it was clear that dialogue about strategic assumptions and problem content was so valuable and important that a series of 'decision-making' group discussions were regularly scheduled.

The basic structuring reduced to the decision tree structure shown in Figure 4.1. It should be noted that the initial tree was much larger and reduced to the current form after heated discussion, communication and a degree of conceptual

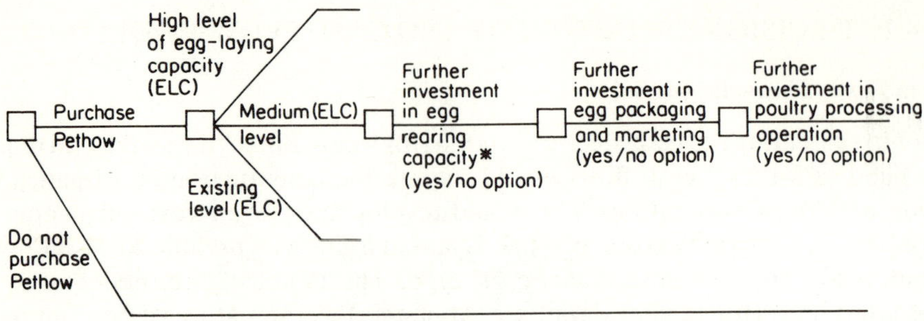


Figure 4.1 Decision tree for Pethow acquisition
*This means supply of egg-laying chickens from own farms

realism apparent in the consensus decision process. Consensus was, in fact, achieved through a 'whirling' type of process in which decision trees (initially often much too complex) provided the focus for communication and discussion both about the nature of the problem and the set of assumptions on which the structuring should be based. The 'whirling' took the form of successive 'pruning' of the series of decision trees until something like Figure 4.1 became a sensible compromise. It should be pointed out, however, that consensus did not appear to be arrived at through either the role of a leader in the decision-making group or a so-called devil's advocate.

The skeletal structure shown in Figure 4.1 in effect defines the $3 \times 2 \times 2 \times 2 = 24$ possible decision combinations highlighted by the acquisition study, i.e. that there might be a need to invest further in various aspects of Pethow's business, e.g. in the poultry processing section *B* and in the marketing operation *A*, depending upon the various uncertain events which might occur over the five-year time-horizon. Thus, the structure suggested that a Hertz-type risk simulation should be carried for each of the 24 possible strategy options, thus producing a probability distribution of the return measure. We used the model in one other way in order to test its internal consistency and validity. By using expected values for all variables we projected the balance sheet and profits for the current year and also made one-year-ahead projections. This proved to be really 'spot-on' (in the current-year case), and gave confidence in the specification and structure of the model in spite of the attendant complications of the unknown impact of uncertainty on future model projections.
[*Note*: The reader who is interested in the detail of the model, the assumptions, etc. should refer to the Appendix.]

**Output: The Best Option**

There was one option which dominated all the 23 others in a mean, standard deviation sense. This was probably because of such things as the absence of non-linearities in the model, the dominance of one option (in a mean/standard deviation sense) at each of the four decision stages and the presence of monotonic relationships between the decision variables.

The option that was clearly preferable in dominance terms was the path involving the greatest expansion of all phases of the business — the risk profile of that option is shown in Figure 4.2.

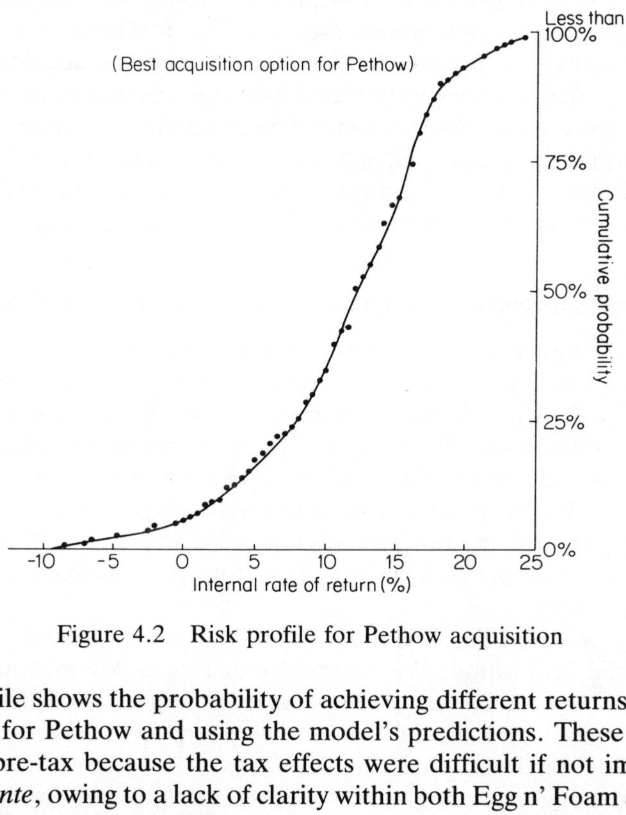


Figure 4.2 Risk profile for Pethow acquisition

This profile shows the probability of achieving different returns assuming a given price for Pethow and using the model's predictions. These returns are calculated pre-tax because the tax effects were difficult if not impossible to model, *ex-ante*, owing to a lack of clarity within both Egg n' Foam and Pethow about tax effects and tax policies.

The range can be seen to be approximately 2–18 percent and with a median value of 11.5 percent (probably reasonably close to the mean since the distribution is approximately symmetrical).

Some sensitivity testing was carried out as follows. Each variable was changed in turn and the results are as shown in the table below:

| *Variable* | *Change* % | *Change in Rate of Return* % |
|---|---|---|
| Egg price | +10 | Up by 70, i.e. median 19.5 |
| Hen productivity | + 2 | Up by 25, i.e. median 14.5 |
| Acquisition price | −33 | Up by 35, i.e. median 15.5 |

Those variables shown in the table have the most dramatic effect on rate of return. Indeed the acquisition price would have to come down about 60 percent of the anticipated price in order to obtain a 20 percent pre-tax rate of return.

At the current acquisition price the acquisition has both an extremely low pre-tax return and a high risk measured in terms of the standard deviation surrogate. This therefore looks a weak proposition and would look even weaker if financing considerations required Egg n' Foam to raise debt to finance the takeover — it would be 'on the cards' that the acquisition returns would not be sufficient to meet the interest obligations thus incurred.

Perhaps a more useful approach might be to tie the acquisition price to the future performance of the company, i.e. to try to substantially reduce and renegotiate Pethow's current acquisition price if Egg n' Foam would deem the acquisition worthwhile on longer-term strategic or synergistic grounds.

**Possible Other Approaches to Acquisition Appraisal for Egg n' Foam**

Research in the financial area has shown that the *after tax* return on equities for the time period during which this acquisition appraisal was undertaken was in the range 11–13 percent, say 12 percent. Now, if we were to assume a corporate tax rate of, say, 40–45 percent for the same period, then this would give an average return on equity of 20–22 percent *before tax*. Also, if we were to assume that the risk-free rate of return (such as the return on a bond of equivalent duration to the project) was 6 percent after tax or 10 percent, say, before tax, we could develop another 'lens' for the acquisition's worth using asset-pricing theory.

Therefore, we used the CAPM, capital asset-pricing model to assess the viability of the acquisition. We assumed that Egg n' Foam would evaluate acquisitions on a pre-tax basis (which was certainly consistent with their current financial practice) and would continue a policy of keeping an absolute minimum of debt in the capital structure. From asset-pricing data the CAPM beta for similar egg-producing companies (at the acquisition time horizon) was around 1, in fact about 0.96. Assuming $R_f$, the risk-free rate, = 10 percent pre-tax, $R_m$, the market return, = 20 percent pre-tax, using the formula derived from asset-pricing theory we calculated the expected return on investment (more strictly, the company's cost of equity capital) as shown below:

$$
\begin{aligned}
E(\text{Return on Investment}) &= R_f + \beta(E(R_m) - R_f) \\
&= 10 + 0.96(20 - 10) \\
&= 19.6
\end{aligned}
$$

The Hertz-type total risk profile (Figure 4.2) for the acquisition shown earlier indicates that there is only a projected 7.5 percent probability that acquisition returns would exceed 19.6 percent. The expected return from the acquisition pre-tax of around 12 percent (Figure 4.2) looks well below average compared with the industry expectation of around 20 percent (19.6 percent exactly), measured in terms of the cost of equity capital.

This analysis confirms and reinforces the fact that on current acquisition terms the project is probably not worthwhile. If conditions were to change, or if significant operating or financial synergies were to become evident, then this conclusion might change however unlikely this may seem at the current point.

# Appendix: Construction of the Model

## 1 SUMMARY OF EGG MODEL

There were 6 options for eggs (the product of 3 laying capacities and 2 options for rearing) (see the Decision Tree Structure, Figure 4.1). The capital requirements of these are outlined (see the Decision Tree Structure, Figure 4.1) below. Revenue per animal is determined from hen productivity, and the selling price for eggs. Costs per animal were separated into stock costs (dependent upon the nature of the rearing option) and feed costs plus other direct costs. The resultant margin (gross of depreciation and administration) per animal was multiplied by the number of animals implicit in the particular rearing option being studied.

In each of the succeeding paragraphs the essence of each of the model's basic elements is discussed in a more detailed manner.

### Egg Capital

Apart from $3m potential initial acquisition outlay, the main investment requirements are likely to arise in egg farms. The options we have explored consist of different elements of Pethow's current plans. Incremental investments beyond this scale are not really part of the appraisal of the Pethow acquisition —they will be so large as to constitute an entirely different and much more complex decision process. The options are: (i) to cut back expansion to the existing laying farm's total capacity; (ii) to add one further site to laying capacity; (iii) to add two further sites to laying capacity. These three options could be further extended by the addition of 'own rearing' capacity in order to provide as much stock supply to the laying farms as economic unit size will permit, i.e. (iv) existing laying capacity plus existing rearing *capacity*; (v) medium laying capacity (modest expansion) with existing *rearing capacity*; and (vi) high laying capacity, with additions to 'own rearing capacity.'

By making some assessments of necessary investment levels and assuming (i) that working capital requirements are $40,000 for a laying farm and $20,000 for a rearing farm; (ii) that farm land can be sold at cost; and (iii) that contract penalties of about 10 percent must be paid on the cancellation of firm building commitments, then the following capital requirements emerge (all for Year 1):

| *Option* | *Net cash flows ($000s)* |
|---|---|
| (i) | +48.0 |
| (ii) | −98.0 |
| (iii) | −120.0 |
| (iv) | −240.0 |
| (v) | −280.0 |
| (vi) | −504.0 |

**Egg Price**

It is assumed that the price secured by Pethow would be the same as that prevailing in the market as a whole. It is further assumed that only by owning a captive packing station and marketing organization will that price be obtainable. For this reason, we include the acquisition of Site A as a compulsory investment. (An extra 2 cents a dozen on the price obtained represents $20,000 of contribution to Pethow at the 320,000-layer level compared to a site A acquisition price of $300,000.)

The price model was based on industry and expert opinion about price levels for the years after acquisition, and on the historical movement of prices for the years up to the potential acquisition appraisal date.

From a historical graph pattern, we developed a simple price predictor, that is that next year's average price would be the same as this year's within a range limited by 1 cent if the change is in the same direction as the previous year, and 2 cents if the change is in a different direction. A floor of 27 cents per dozen is assumed to operate in normal conditions.

The next year's price was thus forecast as most likely around 26–27 cents per dozen with a range 25 cents to 31 cents. A graph is shown in Figure 4.3.

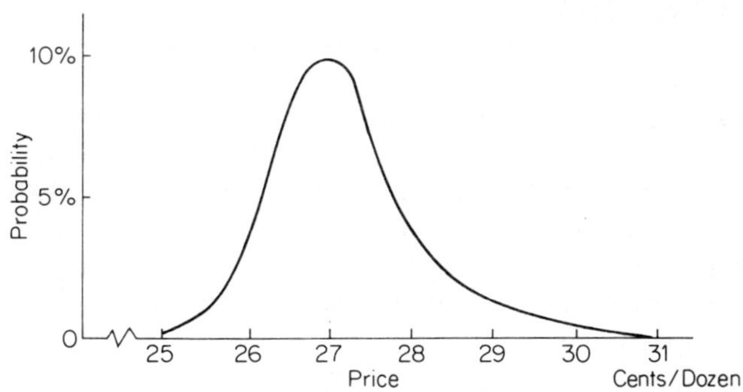


Figure 4.3 Price forecast graph

The above, however, represents average annual prices. For each subsequent year prices were assumed to change in a range 5–15 percent of the existing price with a mean of 7 percent.

**Hen Productivity**

It was assumed that hens would lay an average of about 240 eggs a year within a range 220 to 260, but that this level would probably improve over time, say by 2–4 percent (mean 3 percent) p.a. to allow for industry developments in husbandry, medicine, etc.

**Egg Costs**

The basic measure of egg costs involved calculating the expected cost of maintaining one laying animal for a year. Its main elements are feed, labor, direct costs and stock.

Feed cost per animal is assessed by fixing annual consumption at around 95–100 lbs and by then assuming an expected feed price of between $70 and $80 per hen.

Labor and direct costs are assumed to be fixed at 30 cents and 20 cents, respectively, per animal.

Stock costs depend on whether day-old chicks are purchased outside or reared on own farms. From industry investigation it was found that the relevant outside price/internal transfer price was $1.50 and $1.20 respectively with a 10-cent range either side. Further, an addition of 10 cents was made for unavoidable deaths (representing about 8–10 percent mortality) and an allowance of 30 cents for carcass value.

The expected value of the resultant model was as follows:

| | | |
|---|---|---|
| Feed | | $3.30 |
| Labor | | .30 |
| Direct | | .20 |
| Stock | $1.00 or | 1.30 |
| Total | $4.80 or | 5.10 |

Actual costs in the two most recent years were estimated to be $4.90 and $4.78, both with a high proportion of 'own rearers.' Pethow, however, seemed from investigation to have a somewhat different mix of direct and stock costs so that direct comparisons could not be made.

[*Note*: The proportion of the different stock cost used depends on which option is being evaluated, i.e. there will be differing egg-laying, and 'own egg-rearing' capacities.]

## 2 SITE A (PACKAGING AND MARKETING SITE)

It was assumed that site A must be purchased, but that it would require necessary renovations costing $100,000, which would serve to increase both its capacity and cost effectiveness.

From the industry margins prevailing in the most recent year (30 cents per case), the actual volume (approximately 210,000 cases), their variable costs and other factors and the assumed profits of $50,000, it was estimated that overhead was around $30,000. By a similar process it was estimated that for the expansion proposal, Site A could expect packers' margins to equal 25 cents per case, with a range of 24 to 32 cents. These margins were later considered optimistic and the range altered to 15–20 cents per case.

Site A was currently operating at less than capacity. Without the expansion, it was assumed that the capacity would gradually be filled if Pethow were to expand its laying flock and make the necessary adjustments for transferring both formerly non-site A Pethow eggs and lost customers on takeover.

## 3 FEED

The feed mills owned by Pethow produce approximately 33,000 tons of feed each year. About 40 percent of this production represents internal use charged on the basis of an arbitrary transfer price (the details of the determination of this price were difficult to assess). For the purpose of the acquisition exercise, it was assumed that Egg n' Foam would take the profit at the feed stage by transferring at market price to internal operations. The average net margin prevailing at the time of the acquisition appraisal was about $5.00 per ton, i.e. about $170,000 a year, after allowance for depreciation. For each subsequent year, we have taken $5.00 as the mean margin and varied it within the range $4.00 to $5.50 per ton. In the appraisal future capital investment plans for the feed business were not considered even though these might prove to be profitable. It was felt that the simplicity of the feed-mixing process, the existence of large-size producers reaping substantial scale economies and the relatively low industry rates of return currently prevailing would make such potential investments unattractive.

## 4 SITE B (POULTRY PROCESSING PLANT)

Pethow currently owned site B for which annual throughput was around $1.65m per year. It was assumed that an animal was worth, in terms of revenue after processing, about 50 cents and, thus, by assuming a 10 percent sale margin, annual net profit could be estimated at a current value of around $80,000.

It was felt that the operation was highly successful and that, with additional capital expenditure, it could provide useful future returns. It was estimated that further potential diversification into cold storage (about $150,000 cost) would probably add about $50,000 p.a. profits to the current stream. Net profits for Site B were thus estimated at $130,000 but in a range of $120,000 to $170,000.

## 5 BROILERS

Given the buoyant state of the broiler market and the sort of margins available to producers who get their animal size and conversion ratios right, it was somewhat disappointing to discover that industry observers and experts felt that Pethow's broiler unit was definitely unprofitable. The alternative would be to sell for $60,000 but experts felt that another option, namely investigating the possibility of jointly developing processing and breeding capacity in order to form an integrated unit, would be worth some further study. It was felt that a production capacity of 55,000 animals at around six cycles a year should generate earnings of about $60,000 a year under this integration possibility.

Given Pethow's own feed-mill processing units and chick-buying capacity, in addition to its inherent breeding knowledge, investment of at least $100,000 in such integrated facilities would be worthwhile in order to be able to obtain the earnings capacity estimated above.

The *base* assumption in the model was, however, the sale of the facility at around $60,000.

## 6 OTHER PETHOW BUSINESS AND METHODS OF APPRAISAL

### Pigs and Pig Production

The current herd is of around 150 sows, each producing a possible 15 piglets a year, with general gross profits of about $8,000 to $10,000 per annum. It was felt that any plans to double capacity would have little effect on total earnings. Although development capabilities may well be large, it was felt that the market niche provided by the current investment was very small and better vehicles for pig development doubtless existed. Thus it was assumed that returns from pig production would remain at their current level.

### Sheep Production (Intensive Sheep Housing)

The economics of intensive sheep housing were thought to be doubtful in relation to the geographic terrain and the overall economic environment for sheep production. A flock of 640 ewes, each producing say 1–3 lambs per year on average, currently brings in about $5,000–$10,000 p.a. (dependent on lamb margin). It was felt that there would have to be some dramatic developments and some heavy investment for such a project to make a significant contribution.

### Arable

The existence of around 500 acres of cereal probably earns next to nothing. There would seem to be little likelihood of any significant change and as a result it was assumed that a profit contribution of $2,000 could be assumed (i.e. a level to cover overhead).

Despite the CEO's claims of the benefits that might accrue to Egg n' Foam from Pethow's wide range of products (the agribusiness type of strategic argument) Egg n' Foam is basically contemplating the purchase of an egg company, with feed mills and processing plant attached at each end and with very minor additional farming interests. Further diversification into agriculture or agribusiness on a wider scale would require either further acquisitions or an aggressive internal growth path as Pethow provides only a poultry expansion base.

As a result the model adds a total profit of around \$15,000 p.a. for pigs, sheep and arable farming and makes adjustments to this figure for a series of returns resulting from further investment in these products.

## 7 DEPRECIATION ASSUMPTIONS

The profit figures for A, B, Broilers and Feed were all calculated to be net of depreciation charges. The Egg cost model is gross of depreciation and of administration.

As a result depreciation has been added back (apart from the egg case) in order to get a valid cash flow picture. However, an allowance (of \$60,000 p.a.) has been made for the cost of maintaining fixed assets, which would probably not require substantial replacement over the next five years and this has been deducted from net cash flow. Whilst the concept of economic depreciation is one fraught with practical difficulties it is felt that the figure of \$60,000 fairly represents the current situation. Pethow's depreciation in the last financial year totalled \$160,000. Depreciation of existing assets should decline as follows:

| | *Year 0* | *Year 1* | *Year 2* | *Year 3* | *Year 4* | *Year 5* | |
|---|---|---|---|---|---|---|---|
| Eggs | 40 | 40 | 30 | 20 | 20 | 20 | |
| Others | 120 | 100 | 80 | 60 | 40 | 20 | |
| TOTAL | 160 | 140 | 110 | 80 | 60 | 40 | (\$000s) |

Depreciation at 10 percent straight-line on the proposed capital expenditure is as follows:

| | | *Investment* | *Depreciation* | |
|---|---|---|---|---|
| Eggs: option | (i) | 0 | 0 | \$000s |
| | (ii) | 100 | 10 | |
| | (iii) | 80 | 8 | |
| | (iv) | 180 | 18 | |
| | (v) | 200 | 20 | |
| | (vi) | 360 | 36 | |
| B expansion | | 160 | 16 | |
| A acquisition | | — | say 20 | |
| | | 100 | 10 | |

For example, year 2 depreciation with option (vi) would be: 110 + 36 + 16 + 20 + 10 = 192. But only 126 would be added back for DCF purposes (80 + 16 + 20 + 10 = 126) as the egg model is gross of depreciation.

## 8 ADMINISTRATION EXPENSES

Deductions for administration charges were made for other businesses and some of the egg business. A figure of a mean value of $30,000 p.a. was assumed.

Head Office expenses were assumed to be $40,000 p.a.

## 9 PROJECT LIFE AND TERMINAL VALUE ASSUMPTIONS

We have chosen a project life of 5 years. In so doing, we not only reach the limit of reasonable forecasting, but avoid the potential inclusion of reinvestment decisions on the assumption that the fixed assets will be in sufficient shape to be still earning around the level of profit predicted by the model.

We propose to place a value on the company at the end of year 5 by multiplying that year's after-tax profits by a P/E ratio of a mean value of 16 (range 10–20). This ratio is probably too high given the limited growth potential of the company and the likely earnings requirements of any potential buyers. It is, however, the current P/E and can be viewed as representing the current value of the company.

On the basis of expected profits for year 5 of $400,000 and a notional tax rate of 40 percent, terminal value works out at about $3.8m.

Alternative assumptions about P/E values were tested in order to assess sensitivity.

## 10 FURTHER ASSUMPTIONS

(1) Calculations assumed *year-end* cash flows, except for the initial investment outlay which was assumed to occur at the beginning of year 1. All further investment is assumed to occur at the end of year 1 and to show immediate returns.

(2) The IRR criterion has been used because it conforms to Egg n' Foam's appraisal format. [Note: calculations for NPV and other criteria were also carried out.]

(3) Except in terminal value calculations *taxation* has been ignored. Egg n' Foam had a pre-tax appraisal policy and the analysis conformed to this policy. Such a policy might, however, lead to invalid conclusions especially when comparing investments offering different tax depreciation packages (e.g. in terms of size). Further, investment grants and accelerated depreciated provisions have also been ignored. However, as the alternative with the highest capital commitment is also the most preferred before tax, it will almost certainly be so after tax.

(4) It was assumed that there was very little scope in the assets here to allow for any early *liquidation* without affecting the profit performance of the company. It was felt that even the land was not particularly undervalued in balance sheet terms.

(5) Inflation effects were assumed to be allowed for by the process of using 'real' cash flow assessments.
(6) As a 'realism' test on the model we tried to use it to predict Pethow's last reported figure. The prediction estimate was within 5 percent of the reported figure.

## QUESTIONS FOR DISCUSSION

1. How useful is risk analysis in the formulation of diversification/acquisition strategies?
2. In cost/benefit terms, what is the usefulness of this approach in comparison to alternative approaches?

*Chapter 5*

# *Strategic Sensitivity Analysis: The Case of an Electricity Generation Project**


## SUMMARY

This chapter examines the role of sensitivity analysis in relation to a major capacity expansion decision. This analysis seeks to identify the key uncertain variables and problem assumptions by a process of elimination. Through the subsequent discussion process, managers can amend their structuring of the problem prior to a more extensive and thorough strategic risk analysis of the capacity decision. Data and graphs are given to demonstrate and reinforce the manner in which this strategic sensitivity analysis process works.


## 5.1 INTRODUCTION

In a recent article, Singhvi (1980) argues for sensitivity analysis as an adjunct and supplement to risk analysis. However, most of the literature (e.g. Rappaport, 1967; Hertz, 1979) suggests that sensitivity analysis is a logical adjunct to deterministic capital budgeting, particularly as a means of developing a better initial understanding of the nature and impact of risk. Typically, it is designed to answer recurring questions of the 'What If ...?' type in relation to costs, prices and revenues.

Risk analysis, with its development of a project system model and a thorough measurement of subjective probability distributions for uncertain variables, should be regarded as a much more comprehensive form of uncertainty appraisal following an initial sensitivity analysis in which uncertain variables are identified.

In this chapter we present, by means of a case example involving a large-scale electric utility project, a systematic sensitivity analysis aimed at developing the crucial system variables. This sensitivity analysis, which is presented in tabular form, points to possible project weaknesses, and indicates 'first-pass'

*This case was developed by Jean-Roch Dubourdieu and Howard Thomas at the Australian Graduate School of Management.

sensitivity analysis results which further improve the policy dialogue and strategic thinking about the nature of the project.

## 5.2 ENERGY UTILITY INVESTMENT SITUATION

An Australian Electicity Commission is at present evaluating the viability of a project involving the potential investment in new generation plant to produce electricity from coal mined at a specially developed 'open-cut' mine nearby.

The evaluation of the project is based on certain assumptions about inflation and other factors that will influence the viability of the whole project. Consequently, the objective of the following study is to establish the sensitivity of the project's viability in relation to the factors of relevance such as those outlined in the next section.

## 5.3 INPUT DATA

### Costs

For this project three types of costs were considered: two types of capital costs (namely, electrical and mechanical as one category and all other capital costs as the other category) and the maintenance costs. It should be noted that these categories of expense are dependent upon the timely completion of the plant and are subject to escalation as a result of material and labor cost increases.

### Revenues

Revenues in each year are provided by the combination of electricity sales and price variables, both of which are uncertain. Income is furthermore subject to variations in the energy 'sent out' as a result of variations in the so-called 'energy balance,' i.e. the available capacity (and efficiency) in the system which can be affected by breakdowns or early plant retirements.

### Base Year

The base year for the estimates was January 1980; this condition holds true for costs as well as prices.

### Machinery

In discussions with staff it was indicated that machinery installation could be subject to delays – the information supplied was, however, too sketchy and ill-structured to determine the effect of the timing of any particular installation on capital cost and capacity, and consequently it has been ignored in the following analysis. This particular aspect of the approach will be

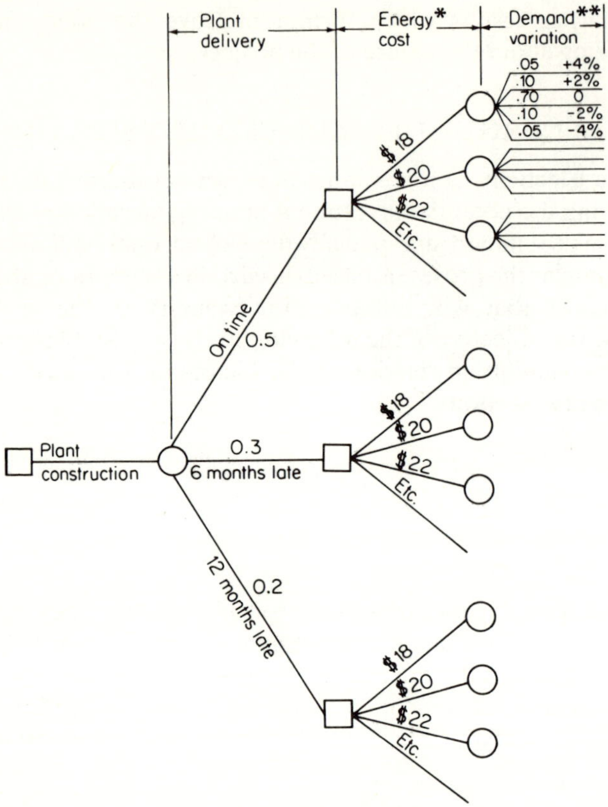


Figure 5.1 Problem structure
(*Measured in $\$ \times 10^6$/TWh.
**Measured as percentage variations about an expected value)

commented upon in the discussion of the impact of plant timing on the project's viability.

## 5.4 SENSITIVITY ANALYSIS

### Objective

The object of this analysis is to determine how sensitive the profitability of the project is to the various variables considered as a prelude to policy dialogue and a more extensive risk analysis simulation, see Hertz (1979). The plant construction problem is shown in the decision tree in Figure 5.1.

### Relevant factors

Many potentially uncertain factors have to be considered in this analysis – the most important ones include:

Price of energy (measured in $\$ \times 10^6$/TWh (terawatt hour));
Capital investment;
Maintenance costs;
Energy output;
Discount rate;
Energy demand variations;
Timing of plant completion;
CPI (consumer price index) increases;
Labor cost increases;
Material cost increases;
Implicit deflator (an internal company index) value;

and finally

Company objectives;
Government policies.

**Approach**

The approach followed here is to determine the most sensitive factors by a process of elimination. It is obviously not possible, nor indeed practical, to consider all of the above factors at once in a 'first-pass' type of sensitivity analysis. Furthermore, as we shall see, some of the above factors have a negligible impact and can therefore be safely ignored.

**Output data and program**

All the data used in this analysis came as a by-product of a conventional NPV analysis of the project, on the basis of several assumptions about the project's completion time (i.e. 0 months, 6 months and 12 months later). [Note that the project's time horizon was assumed to be twenty years at which time it was assumed that the project would be fully depreciated and have no further useful economic life.]

*Sensitivity analysis*

In a step-by-step fashion an examination of the project's sensitivity to various factors was carried out. For each variable considered relevant we have indicated below what type of approach was taken in the analysis and the nature of the results obtained.

*Capital investment*

The original NPV analysis was based upon most likely values for capital investment, given different completion times. The capital investment values were varied both by constant positive and negative percentages and by the use of different assumptions concerning cost escalation factors.

*Maintenance costs*

The same approach as detailed above for capital investment was applied to the most likely values for maintenance costs.

*Energy output*

The output was varied from the projected value using historical 'energy balance' variation data which showed that a range of ± 4 percent around the norm would typically cover any eventuality arising from strikes or mechanical failures.

*Energy demand variations*

The initial NPV analysis calculated the NPVs if energy demand is always 4 percent, 2 percent below; on target; or 2 percent, 4 percent above expectations for the given plant completion times and for the given values for CPI (etc...). When these NPVs are weighted by their respective probabilities, it can be seen that the variations in NPVs as a result of anticipated demand fluctuations, for a given energy price, are fairly small. Furthermore, varying the probabilities for the variations in demand so that $P(0\%\text{ var}) \geqslant P(\pm 2\%\text{ var}) \geqslant P(\pm 4\%\text{ var})$ has a negligible effect.

The values and probabilities given for energy demand variations were the result of the 'smoothing' of many years of actual time series observations and consequently were used as given.

*Plant timing*

The plant, it was indicated, could be up to 12 months late on completion, assuming a 'worst case' scenario. The probabilities given for 0, 6 and 12 months delays were 0.5, 0.3 and 0.2 respectively.

For the purpose of the analysis it was assumed that $P$ (0 mths delay) $\geqslant P$(6 mths delay) $\geqslant P$(12 mths delay). Using increments of 0.1 then all the possible combinations are as given below:

| | | | | | | | | |
|---|---|---|---|---|---|---|---|---|
| $P$ (no delay) | 0.4 | 0.4 | 0.5 | 0.5 | 0.6 | 0.6 | 0.7 | 0.8 |
| $P$ (6 mths delay) | 0.3 | 0.4 | 0.4 | 0.3 | 0.2 | 0.3 | 0.2 | 0.1 |
| $P$ (12 mths delay) | 0.3 | 0.2 | 0.1 | 0.2 | 0.2 | 0.1 | 0.1 | 0.1 |

From the analytic results, it was concluded that the variations in NPVs as a result of changes in plant timing, for a given energy price, are very small.

At this stage, therefore, it can be said that the variations in energy demand considered and the plant completion delays have little effect on the NPVs. Moreover, once these variations are weighted by their respective probabilities, the resultant effect is even less significant. Finally, varying the given probabilities has no significant effect on the NPVs.

The above results demonstrate that it is very unlikely that delays in machinery installation will have any significant effect *unless* these are large and more than occasional. From the information provided, it is unfortunately not possible to test this hypothesis. However, in view of what can reasonably be expected, there should be no problem in this area.

**Standard values defined**

For the remainder of this analysis we will concentrate on the factors that have not yet been examined. To test the relevance of each factor, it is necessary to vary the particular factor under study, keeping all others constant.

To avoid numerous repetitions a set of *Standard Values* was defined as follows. This set of standard values is none other than the most likely values the Electricity Commission is considering using for the analysis of this project. Therefore, notwithstanding the variable under consideration, the other 'fixed' variables will have the following values:

| | | | | | | |
|---|---|---|---|---|---|---|
| 1. | Energy demand variations | −4% | −2% | 0 | 2% | 4% |
| 2. | Probabilities for the above | 0.05 | 0.10 | 0.70 | 0.10 | 0.05 |
| 3. | Plant completion delays | 0 mths | | 6 mths | | 12 mths |
| 4. | Probabilities for the above | 0.5 | | 0.3 | | 0.2 |
| 5. | Discount rate | | | 8.5% | | |
| 6. | Average earning index | | | 7.1% | | |
| 7. | Materials price index | | | 5.8% | | |
| 8. | Implicit deflator | | | 4.6% | | |
| 9. | CPI | | | 4.5% | | |

[Note: the indices in 6 through 9 were obtained from official sources and econometric forecasts over the 20-year horizon.]

The first four variables have been discussed above and will remain at those given values for the remainder of the analysis.

**Need for adjustments**

The first question that arises is whether we should make corrections in the analysis for such things as material price increases. In other words should we worry about the last four quantities listed in the table of Standard Values?

Before answering this question, let us look at the effect of adjusting the analysis for the standard values 6 through 9.

Table 5.1 shows how the NPV of the project varies with the discount rate considered and the price of energy, all other variables being standard. The thick line merely shows where the changeover occurs, from negative to positive NPVs.

Table 5.2 shows how the NPV of the project varies with the discount rate considered and the price of energy, when *no* adjustment is provided for inflation indices such as the CPI and the other indices shown in the Standard Values earlier. The thick line shown here serves the same purpose as previously.

Table 5.3 is obtained by subtracting the values of Table 5.2 from the corresponding values of Table 5.1. The two original thick lines are reproduced to show the shift caused by introducing the inflation adjustments.

To appreciate better the effect of the adjustments let us look at a particular case, say the \$20 case (i.e. energy is valued at \$20 × $10^6$TWh) which is the price of energy considered lately by the Electricity Commission. Figure 5.2 shows the NPVs for the given price and for the various discount rates, with and without correction for the other variables (such as CPI etc...).

It can be seen from Figure 5.2 that the standard corrections considered have no effect on the analysis if the appropriate discount rate happens to be exactly 19 percent. Above 19 percent, not making any corrections for CPI (etc...) would result in a conservative estimate.

The conclusion is therefore that the significance of the corrections depends on their magnitude and the discount rate used.

**Discount Rate**

The effect of the discount rate can be seen by inspecting Table 5.1. For the purpose of this discussion, let us consider again the case where energy is valued at \$20 × $10^6$/Twh as shown on Figure 5.2. This time however we concentrate on the dotted line as we are interested only in the changes in NPVs due to changes in discount rate, for the given energy price, (all other variables being at their standard values).

It can readily be seen that the impact of a change in discount rate very much depends on the base value. For example, increasing the discount rate from 5 percent to 6 percent reduces the NPV by almost \$1,500m whereas increasing the discount rate from 16 percent to 17 percent causes a barely noticeable change in NPV.

Table 5.1 NPVs for different combinations of discount rate and energy price
(All other variables standard)
($ × $10^6$)

| | | Discount rate % | | | | | | | | | | | |
|---|---|---|---|---|---|---|---|---|---|---|---|---|---|
| | $ | 5 | 6 | 7 | 8 | 8.5 | 9 | 10 | 11 | 12 | 13 | 14 | 15 |
| | 15 | 2250 | 1440 | 837 | 380 | 195 | 34 | −226 | −421 | −566 | −673 | −751 | −807 |
| | 16 | 2787 | 1874 | 1184 | 662 | 450 | 266 | −33 | −260 | −431 | −559 | −653 | −723 |
| E | 17 | 3324 | 2303 | 1531 | 944 | 706 | 498 | 159 | −99 | −295 | −444 | −556 | −639 |
| N | 18 | 3862 | 2733 | 1877 | 1227 | 962 | 731 | 351 | 61 | −160 | −329 | −458 | −555 |
| E | 19 | 4399 | 3162 | 2224 | 1509 | 1218 | 963 | 544 | 222 | −25 | −215 | −360 | −471 |
| R | 20 | 4936 | 3592 | 2571 | 1791 | 1473 | 1195 | 736 | 383 | 110 | −100 | −262 | −387 |
| G | 21 | 5474 | 4021 | 2917 | 2074 | 1729 | 1427 | 928 | 544 | 246 | 15 | −164 | −303 |
| Y | 22 | 6011 | 4451 | 3264 | 2356 | 1985 | 1659 | 1121 | 704 | 381 | 129 | −66 | −219 |
| | 23 | 6548 | 4880 | 3610 | 2639 | 2240 | 1891 | 1313 | 865 | 516 | 244 | 31 | −135 |
| P | 24 | 7085 | 5310 | 3957 | 2921 | 2496 | 2123 | 1505 | 1026 | 651 | 359 | 129 | −51 |
| R | 25 | 7623 | 5739 | 4304 | 3203 | 2752 | 2355 | 1698 | 1186 | 787 | 473 | 227 | 33 |
| I | 26 | 8160 | 6164 | 4650 | 3486 | 3008 | 2587 | 1890 | 1347 | 922 | 588 | 325 | 117 |
| C | 27 | 8697 | 6598 | 4997 | 3768 | 3263 | 2814 | 2082 | 1508 | 1057 | 703 | 423 | 201 |
| E | 28 | 9235 | 7028 | 5344 | 4050 | 3519 | 3051 | 2275 | 1668 | 1192 | 817 | 521 | 285 |
| | 29 | 9772 | 7457 | 5690 | 4333 | 3775 | 3283 | 2467 | 1829 | 1325 | 932 | 618 | 369 |
| | 30 | 10309 | 7887 | 6037 | 4615 | 4030 | 3515 | 2659 | 1990 | 1963 | 1047 | 716 | 453 |

Table 5.2 NPVs for different combinations of discount rate and energy price
(*No* adjustments for other variables)
($ $\times 10^6$)

| | Discount rate | | | | | | | | | | |
|---|---|---|---|---|---|---|---|---|---|---|---|
| ENERGY PRICE $ | % 5 | 6 | 7 | 8 | 8.5 | 9 | 10 | 11 | 12 | 13 | 14 | 15 |
| 15 | 459 | 124 | −129 | −321 | −398 | −465 | −573 | −653 | −711 | −752 | −781 | −799 |
| 16 | 688 | 315 | 30 | −186 | −274 | −351 | −475 | −569 | −638 | −689 | −726 | −751 |
| 17 | 918 | 505 | 190 | −52 | −150 | −236 | −377 | −485 | −566 | −626 | −670 | −702 |
| 18 | 1147 | 696 | 344 | 83 | −26 | −122 | −280 | −401 | −493 | −563 | −615 | −653 |
| 19 | 1376 | 886 | 509 | 218 | 98 | −8 | −152 | −316 | −420 | −499 | −560 | −605 |
| 20 | 1605 | 1076 | 668 | 352 | 222 | 107 | −84 | −232 | −347 | −436 | −504 | −556 |
| 21 | 1834 | 1267 | 828 | 487 | 345 | 221 | 14 | −148 | −275 | −373 | −449 | −508 |
| 22 | 2063 | 1457 | 987 | 621 | 469 | 335 | 111 | −64 | −202 | −310 | −394 | −459 |
| 23 | 2292 | 1648 | 1147 | 756 | 593 | 449 | 209 | 20 | −129 | −246 | −338 | −410 |
| 24 | 2522 | 1838 | 1306 | 890 | 717 | 564 | 307 | 104 | −56 | −183 | −283 | −362 |
| 25 | 2751 | 2028 | 1466 | 1025 | 841 | 678 | 404 | 188 | 16 | −120 | −228 | −313 |
| 26 | 2980 | 2219 | 1625 | 1159 | 965 | 792 | 502 | 272 | 89 | −56 | −172 | −265 |
| 27 | 3209 | 2409 | 1784 | 1294 | 1089 | 907 | 600 | 356 | 162 | 7 | −117 | −216 |
| 28 | 3438 | 2600 | 1944 | 1428 | 1213 | 1021 | 698 | 440 | 235 | 70 | −62 | −167 |
| 29 | 3667 | 2790 | 2103 | 1563 | 1337 | 1135 | 795 | 524 | 307 | 133 | −6 | −119 |
| 30 | 3896 | 2981 | 2263 | 1691 | 1460 | 1244 | 893 | 608 | 380 | 197 | 49 | −70 |

Table 5.3 NPVs for different combinations of discount rate and energy price (Demonstrates *shift* due to adjustments) ($ $\times 10^6$)

| | | Discount rate | | | | | | | | | | | |
|---|---|---|---|---|---|---|---|---|---|---|---|---|---|
| | $ | % 5 | 6 | 7 | 8 | 8.5 | 9 | 10 | 11 | 12 | 13 | 14 | 15 |
| | 15 | 1791 | 1316 | 966 | 701 | 593 | 499 | 347 | 232 | 145 | 79 | 30 | −8 |
| | 16 | 2094 | 1559 | 1154 | 848 | 724 | 617 | 442 | 309 | 207 | 130 | 73 | 28 |
| E | 17 | 2406 | 1798 | 1341 | 996 | 856 | 734 | 536 | 386 | 271 | 182 | 114 | 63 |
| N | 18 | 2715 | 2037 | 1528 | 1144 | 988 | 853 | 631 | 462 | 333 | 234 | 157 | 98 |
| E | 19 | 3023 | 2276 | 1715 | 1291 | 1120 | 971 | 726 | 538 | 395 | 284 | 200 | 134 |
| R | 20 | 3331 | 2516 | 1903 | 1439 | 1251 | 1088 | 820 | 615 | 457 | 336 | 242 | 169 |
| G | 21 | 3640 | 2754 | 2089 | 1587 | 1384 | 1206 | 914 | 692 | 521 | 388 | 285 | 205 |
| Y | 22 | 3948 | 2994 | 2277 | 1735 | 1516 | 1324 | 1010 | 768 | 583 | 439 | 328 | 240 |
| | 23 | 4256 | 3232 | 2463 | 1883 | 1647 | 1442 | 1104 | 845 | 645 | 490 | 369 | 275 |
| P | 24 | 4563 | 3472 | 2651 | 2031 | 1779 | 1559 | 1198 | 922 | 707 | 542 | 412 | 311 |
| R | 25 | 4782 | 3711 | 2838 | 2178 | 1911 | 1677 | 1294 | 998 | 771 | 593 | 455 | 346 |
| I | 26 | 5180 | 3950 | 3025 | 2327 | 2043 | 1795 | 1388 | 1075 | 833 | 644 | 497 | 382 |
| C | 27 | 5488 | 4189 | 3213 | 2474 | 2174 | 1912 | 1475 | 1152 | 895 | 696 | 540 | 417 |
| E | 28 | 5797 | 4428 | 3400 | 2622 | 2306 | 2030 | 1517 | 1228 | 957 | 747 | 583 | 452 |
| | 29 | 6105 | 4667 | 3587 | 2710 | 2438 | 2148 | 1612 | 1308 | 1021 | 799 | 624 | 488 |
| | 30 | 6413 | 4906 | 3774 | 2918 | 2570 | 2266 | 1706 | 1382 | 1083 | 850 | 667 | 523 |

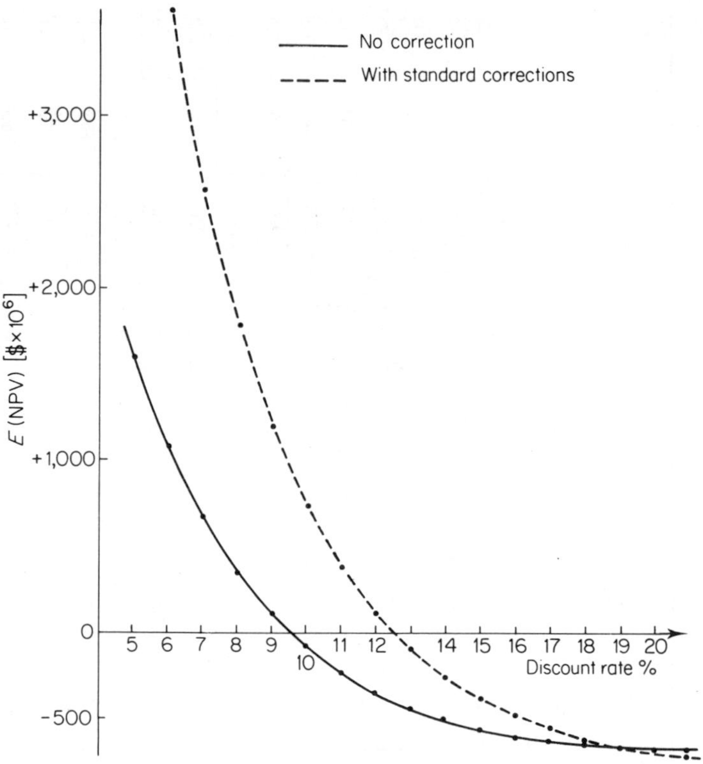


Figure 5.2 Graph of NPV against discount rate (Energy price at $20 × 10^6$TWh)

For the range of interest rates now considered by the Commission (about 8.5 percent) a change in discount rate from 8 percent to 9 percent (say) causes an appreciable change in NPV of about $600m.

However, the appropriateness of the assumption of an 8.5 percent discount rate can be questioned. In view of the prevailing economic conditions it appears that the present discount rate is underestimated. Possibly a discount rate between 10 and 15 percent would be more appropriate. Because no information on the capital structure of the firm was given other than that gleaned from regulatory hearings, it is not possible to use values other than the one given. However, it is interesting to note than an error in estimating the 'true' discount rate will have less and less effect on the analysis as we move towards the 15 percent mark and this should influence the more detailed problem structuring at the risk analysis stage. An error of 1 percent around the 15 percent level (say using 14 percent instead of 15 percent) causes an error of $100m on the NPV which is a fairly small value when we consider the time frame of the project and its sensitivity in relation to other variables.

The 8.5 percent was presented as 'company policy', meaning that it should not be changed. However, we would suggest that the appropriateness of the discount rate used should be thoroughly investigated.

**Materials price index and average earning index**

These indices were used to take into account the effects of inflationary increases in capital investment and maintenance costs using as a basis a number of correction formulas developed within the Commission. The values recommended were:

(i) Material price index 5.8 percent;
(ii) Average earning index 7.1 percent

These values were based on econometric forecasts for the period covering the span of the project and were developed by a local economic consulting firm.

For the sensitivity analysis both indices were varied at the same time because of their relationship. Obviously, if labor costs go up then material costs will go up too, but to a lesser extent than one would expect. The difference between the two indices was set arbitrarily to 1 percent simply because it is roughly that shown by the recommended values. In other words, when the Average Earning index is X percent, then the Material Price index is set at (X–1 percent).

The results obtained using this approach are shown in Table 5.4. The table shows the effect of changing the above indices for the different energy prices, all other variables being fixed at their standard values.

Once again let us consider a particular case, that where energy is valued at $\$20 \times 10^6$/TWh. This case is shown by Figure 5.3. It can be seen that changing both indices by say 1 percent causes the NPV to change by different amounts depending on the section of the range we are looking at. The graph shows that for the standard values of the indices, a change of 1 percent for both indices, either way, causes the NPV to vary by about \$400m. This change in NPV is very similar to that obtained by changing the discount rate by 1 percent from the recommended 8.5 percent value.

**Implicit deflator**

The implicit deflator is a device which is used to remove the effects of price increases to isolate those due to productivity increases. Table 5.5 shows the effect on NPV resulting from changes in the value of the implicit deflator, for the various energy prices considered, all other variables being kept at their standard values.

Here again we propose to look at a particular case, namely the $\$20 \times 10^6$/TWh case shown by Figure 5.4.

Table 5.4 Changes in NPV for different combinations of MPI, AEI and energy price (All other variables at standard values) ($ × $10^6$)

| | MPI | 3 | 5 | 7 | 9 | 10 | 7.1 |
|---|---|---|---|---|---|---|---|
| | AEI | | | | | | |
| | $ | 2 | 4 | 6 | 8 | 9 | 5.8 |
| | 15 | 1220 | 794 | 207 | −638 | −1202 | 195 |
| | 16 | 1476 | 1050 | 462 | −382 | −947 | 450 |
| E | 17 | 1732 | 1306 | 718 | −126 | −691 | 706 |
| N | 18 | 1988 | 1561 | 974 | 130 | −435 | 962 |
| E | 19 | 2243 | 1817 | 1229 | 385 | −180 | 1218 |
| R | 20 | 2499 | 2073 | 1485 | 641 | 76 | 1473 |
| G | 21 | 2755 | 2324 | 1741 | 897 | 332 | 1729 |
| Y | 22 | 3010 | 2584 | 1997 | 1152 | 588 | 1985 |
| | 23 | 3266 | 2840 | 2252 | 1408 | 843 | 2240 |
| P | 24 | 3522 | 3096 | 2508 | 1664 | 1099 | 2496 |
| R | 25 | 3778 | 3351 | 2764 | 1920 | 1355 | 2752 |
| I | 26 | 4033 | 3607 | 3020 | 2175 | 1610 | 3008 |
| C | 27 | 4289 | 3863 | 3275 | 2431 | 1866 | 3263 |
| E | 28 | 4545 | 4119 | 3531 | 2681 | 2122 | 3519 |
| | 29 | 4800 | 4314 | 3787 | 2942 | 2378 | 3775 |
| | 30 | 5056 | 4630 | 4048 | 3198 | 2633 | 4030 |

MPI = Materials price index
AEI = Average earning index

It can readily be seen that the changes in NPV are small (about $50m) for constant changes (1 percent) in the implicit deflator, for a given price, all other variables being kept at their standard values.

## CPI

The CPI (consumer price index) usually indicates by how much the Electricity Commission is allowed to increase its prices every year, as determined by the regulatory authorities. The Commission's stated objective here is to keep increases below CPI increase levels.

Table 5.6 shows the changes in NPV that occur as a result of the changes in CPI, for the different energy prices, all other variables being kept at their standard values.

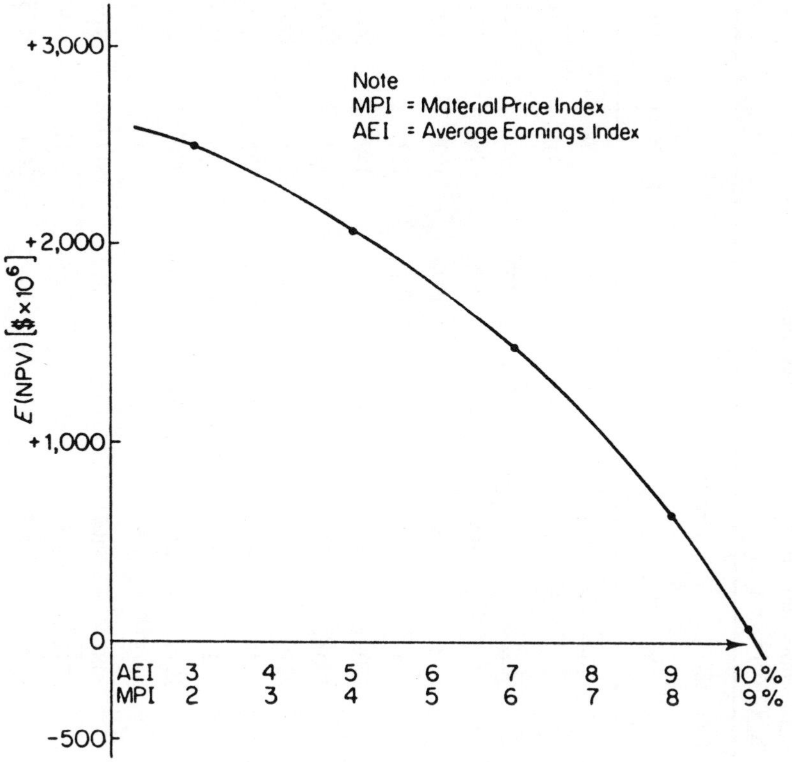


Figure 5.3 Graph of NPV against MPI, AEI
(Energy price at $20 × 10^6TWh)

Again we propose to consider the $20 × 10^6/TWh case that is shown by Figure 5.5. It can easily be seen that the analysis is very sensitive to the CPI increases allowed. For example, increasing the CPI value by 1 percent from 4.5 percent to 5.5 percent causes an increase in NPV of $100m. A decrease of 1 percent from 4.5 percent to 3.5 percent reduces the NPV by $900m. This variable (essentially a surrogate for price increases), has by far the greatest impact on the NPV.

## Energy Price

The sensitivity analysis to energy prices is a by-product of the other studies. Figures 5.6 and 5.7, for example, show how much the NPV increases when we increase the price by $1 × 10^6/TWh for either a given discount rate (Figure 5.6) or a given CPI value (Figure 5.7), all other variables being kept at their standard values.

Table 5.5 Changes in NPV for different combinations of price and implicit deflator ($\$ \times 10^6$)

| | | Deflator | | | | | | | | |
|---|---|---|---|---|---|---|---|---|---|---|
| | $ \ % | 3 | 4 | 4.6 | 5 | 6 | 7 | 8 | 9 | 10 |
| | 15 | 240 | 212 | 195 | 184 | 156 | 129 | 103 | 78 | 53 |
| | 16 | 503 | 470 | 450 | 438 | 406 | 376 | 346 | 316 | 288 |
| E | 17 | 765 | 728 | 706 | 692 | 656 | 622 | 588 | 555 | 522 |
| N | 18 | 1027 | 986 | 962 | 946 | 906 | 868 | 830 | 793 | 757 |
| E | 19 | 1290 | 1244 | 1218 | 1200 | 1157 | 1114 | 1073 | 1032 | 992 |
| R | 20 | 1552 | 1503 | 1473 | 1454 | 1407 | 1360 | 1315 | 1270 | 1227 |
| G | 21 | 1814 | 1761 | 1729 | 1708 | 1657 | 1606 | 1557 | 1509 | 1462 |
| Y | 22 | 2077 | 2019 | 1985 | 1962 | 1907 | 1853 | 1799 | 1747 | 1696 |
| | 23 | 2339 | 2277 | 2240 | 2216 | 2157 | 2094 | 2042 | 1986 | 1931 |
| P | 24 | 2601 | 2535 | 2496 | 2470 | 2407 | 2345 | 2284 | 2224 | 2166 |
| R | 25 | 2864 | 2793 | 2752 | 2725 | 2657 | 2591 | 2526 | 2463 | 2401 |
| I | 26 | 3126 | 3052 | 3008 | 2979 | 2907 | 2837 | 2769 | 2702 | 2636 |
| C | 27 | 3388 | 3310 | 3263 | 3233 | 3157 | 3083 | 3011 | 2940 | 2871 |
| E | 28 | 3651 | 3568 | 3519 | 3487 | 3407 | 3330 | 3253 | 3179 | 3105 |
| | 29 | 3913 | 3826 | 3775 | 3741 | 3657 | 3576 | 3496 | 3417 | 3340 |
| | 30 | 4175 | 4084 | 4030 | 3995 | 3908 | 3822 | 3738 | 3656 | 3575 |

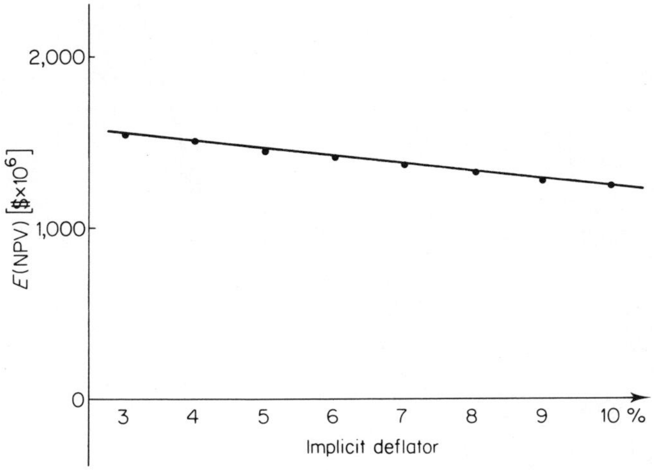


Figure 5.4 Graph of NPV against implicit deflator
(Energy price at $20 × $10^6$TWh)

Table 5.6 Changes in NPV for different combinations of CPI and energy price
($ × $10^6$)

| | $ | CPI % 3.0 | 3.5 | 4.0 | 4.5 | 5.0 | 5.5 | 6.0 |
|---|---|---|---|---|---|---|---|---|
| | 15 | −723 | −448 | −144 | 195 | 571 | 990 | 1456 |
| E | 16 | −528 | −235 | 90 | 450 | 852 | 1298 | 1796 |
| N | 17 | −333 | −22 | 323 | 706 | 1133 | 1607 | 2136 |
| E | 18 | −139 | 191 | 556 | 962 | 1413 | 1916 | 2476 |
| R | 19 | 56 | 403 | 784 | 1218 | 1694 | 2225 | 2816 |
| G | 20 | 250 | 616 | 1022 | 1473 | 1975 | 2533 | 3155 |
| Y | 21 | 445 | 829 | 1255 | 1729 | 2256 | 2842 | 3495 |
| | 22 | 639 | 1042 | 1489 | 1985 | 2536 | 3151 | 3835 |
| P | 23 | 834 | 1255 | 1722 | 2240 | 2817 | 3459 | 4175 |
| R | 24 | 1029 | 1468 | 1955 | 2496 | 3048 | 3768 | 4515 |
| I | 25 | 1223 | 1681 | 2188 | 2752 | 3379 | 4077 | 4855 |
| C | 26 | 1418 | 1893 | 2421 | 3008 | 3660 | 4385 | 5194 |
| E | 27 | 1612 | 2106 | 2654 | 3263 | 3940 | 4694 | 5534 |
| | 28 | 1807 | 2319 | 2888 | 3519 | 4221 | 5003 | 5874 |
| | 29 | 2001 | 2532 | 3121 | 3775 | 4502 | 5312 | 6214 |
| | 30 | 2196 | 2745 | 3354 | 4030 | 4783 | 5620 | 6554 |

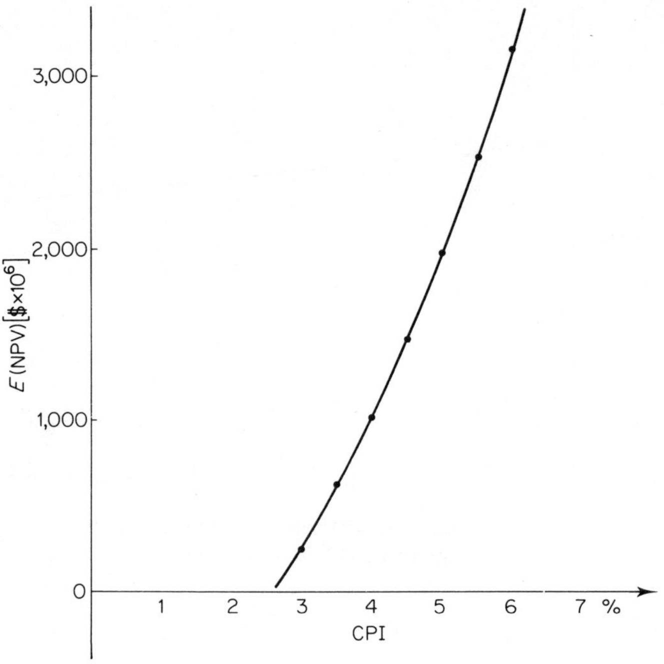


Figure 5.5 Graph of NPV against CPI
(Energy price at \$20 × $10^6$TWh)

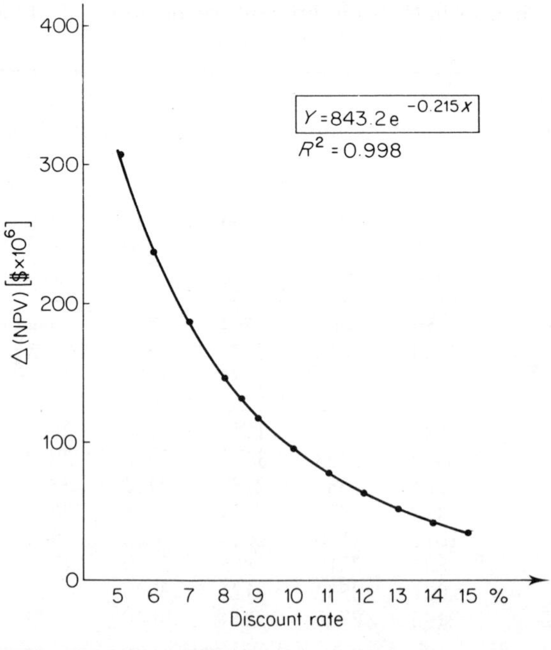


Figure 5.6 Change in NPV/\$ price change against discount rate

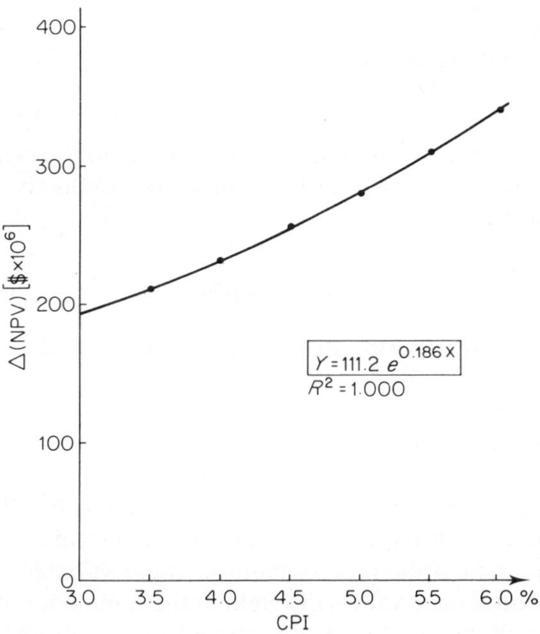


Figure 5.7 Change in NPV/$ price change against CPI

## 5.5 DISCUSSION

Many factors had to be considered in this analysis, the most important were:

Price of energy;
Capital investment;
Maintenance costs;
Energy output;
Discount rate;
Energy demand variations;
Timing of plant completion;
Timing of machinery installation;
CPI increases;
Labor cost increases;
Material cost increases;
Implicit deflator value;

and finally

Company objectives;
Government policies.

Mainly due to a lack of information, the following data were used substantially as given:

Maintenance costs;
Capital investment expenditure;
Energy output values.

The effects of machinery-installation timing could not be evaluated because of lack of information, however this aspect is not likely to change the following conclusions.

## CONCLUSIONS

The effects of the following were found to have little impact:

Energy demand variations;
Timing of plant completion.

Moreover when these variations were weighted by their respective probabilities, the overall impact was found to be insignificant, and furthermore insensitive to changes in probabilities. These variables were therefore used at their recommended values throughout the remainder of the analysis.

Next in order of magnitude is the impact of variations in the implicit deflator. The impact was found constant for constant variations in the implicit deflator. For example, a change of about \$50m in NPV was experienced for every 1 percent change in the deflator, in the case where energy is valued at $\$20 \times 10^6$TWh, all other variables being kept at their standard values.

Changes in the Materials Price Index (MPI) and the Average Earning Index (AEI) caused variations of NPV of about \$300–\$400m for each 1 percent variation, in the region of interest (6 to 7 percent). It should be noted that as explained in the analysis, both indices are assumed to change in the same direction, by the same amount with a given gap of 1 percent between the two indices.

The next two variables are put in a category of their own because their impact, unlike that of the above variables, is greatly dependent on the conditions considered.

A change of 1 percent in discount rate for example could cause a change in NPV of \$100m (i.e. from 6 percent to 7 percent) or a change as small as \$50m (i.e. from 18 percent to 19 percent), with the energy valued at $\$20 \times 10^6$/TWh. However, over the range of interest to the Electricity Commission at this stage (8.5 percent), a change of 1 percent in discount rate would result in a change in NPV of about \$600m, when energy is valued at $\$20 \times 10^6$/TWh, all other variables being kept constant at their standard values.

It was also suggested that the appropriateness of the discount rate used be investigated. If the appropriate discount rate happened to be in the 10–12 percent region (as we are led to believe), then a change of 1 percent in discount rate would cause an impact of the same order of magnitude as that due to similar variations in the MPI and AEI.

The other variable to fall in this category is the energy price. Changing the price of energy by $1 × 10⁶/TWh can result in an NPV change as large as $500m or as small as $50m depending on the values of the other variables (i.e. CPI, discount rate, etc.). At the given recommended values, changing the price by $1 × 10⁶/TWh causes a change in NPV of just under $300m.

The last variable considered is the CPI which was really used as an indicator of future allowable price increases. The analysis was found to be extremely sensitive to the CPI values used. The impact on the NPV due to a change in CPI was always found to be significant and sometimes very large.

## 5.6 SUGGESTED STRATEGY

The results of this analysis indicate that, subject to the limited information given, the following approach would probably be most adequate for the present problem in designing the structure of the subsequent risk analysis/policy dialogue model and in suggesting the direction of the Commission's strategy with respect to this project.

The Commission should not worry about:

energy demand variations,
timing of plant completion,
timing of machinery installation,

*if and only if* the values suggested are representative.

However, the Commission's discount rate should be chosen carefully for three reasons:

(i) the impact of the discount rate in the region of interest is non-negligible although not large in view of the span of the project;
(ii) the discount rate should as a matter of principle reflect the cost of capital to the Commission;
(iii) and additionally because the effectiveness of the pricing policy will very much depend on the discount rate used.

The greatest difficulty with the analysis occurs in the process of 'balancing' the analytic results against the Company's objectives, the interaction between those objectives and Government policies and the predictability of the future demand for energy.

It was assumed that the Commission wants to provide energy at the cheapest possible cost, and still recover its investment. The Government on the other side has made it known that price increases in excess of CPI will not be allowed. So the project must be viable within the constraints imposed on the Commission. It should be obvious also that planning for increases below CPI would be advantageous for two reasons:

(i) this would create goodwill from the Government as a result of the 'responsible' attitude of the Commission; and

(ii) this would leave room for the Commission to have price increases up to the CPI, should the need arise later. Many values used in the analysis depend on forecasts many years in the future and consequently these cannot be considered very reliable.

In summary, therefore, it appears that the Commission will have to balance its strategy according to what it can charge for the energy it supplies, how much it will be allowed to increase its price every year to keep this project profitable and how cleverly and strategically it can operate with respect to the externally imposed regulatory constraints.

Finally, it should be pointed out that this 'first-pass' analysis generated considerable discussion about the strategic nature of the project and the strategic assumptions underlying the results. It was clearly agreed that the key system variables already evident needed to be examined more carefully in a more detailed risk analysis approach. Thus, further dialogue could be generated concerning the policy options, project assumptions and the structuring of the Commission's future posture in its dealings with the regulatory and governmental authorities which had the responsibility for policing the Commission's activities. It is interesting to note that managers put forward a range of environmental and demand scenarios which they wanted to be examined as part of the continuing conduct of the strategic management process. Further, their final 'go' decision for the project was based upon extensive discussion of the 'second-pass' risk analyses of the alternative strategic scenarios and assumption bases which are not reported here.

## REFERENCES

Hertz, D. B. (1979). 'Risk Analysis in Capital Investment,' *Harvard Business Review*, **57** (Sept./Oct.) 169–181.

Rappaport, A. (1967). 'Sensitivity Analysis in Decision Making,' *Accounting Review*, (July) 441–456.

Singhvi, S. S. (1980). 'A Practical Approach to Risk and Sensitivity Analysis,' *Long Range Planning,* **13** (February) 12–19.

## QUESTIONS FOR DISCUSSION

1. What is the role of sensitivity analysis in relation to risk analysis? What insight, if any, does it throw upon the nature of the project?
2. What implications does the use of sensitivity analysis have for model-building and problem-solving?
3. How would you design an extended risk analysis model to better manage the uncertainty associated with this project?

*Chapter 6*

# *XYZ Limited: A Risk Management Scenario**


## SUMMARY

The case in this chapter describes the risk management processes suggested by consultants for implementation by a major trading bank. An assessment of risks is undertaken and a range of options for managing those risks are identified.

This chapter, therefore, provides an introduction to concepts of risk management which are becoming increasingly common managerial practices in modern corporations.


## 6.1 INTRODUCTION

Risk management consultants were called in to help XYZ Ltd. in the identification, analysis and measurement of areas of corporate risk which could involve XYZ in significant direct and indirect losses as a result of:

(a) exposure of the company's physical assets to risk of loss or damage;
(b) injury to or illness of Group employees; and
(c) legal liability to other parties.

The study was intended to aid XYZ Ltd. in assessing the best methods of dealing with their risks, both insured and uninsured. It would pay particular attention to the structure, strategy and cost effectiveness of the existing program and would present alternative and future considerations that would be of benefit to XYZ Ltd.

XYZ is a major trading bank operating in Australia with its head office in Sydney but with branches dispersed throughout Australia. It was felt that with the centralization of management and information systems in a head office block of sixteen storeys in Sydney, it would be appropriate to undertake the pilot risk management study at that location.

*This case was developed by Howard Thomas whilst a Foundation Professor at the Australian Graduate School of Management in Sydney.

The brief for the risk management consultants was the development of a recommended strategy for the handling of those risks identified as significant for XYZ Ltd.

## 6.2 RISK MANAGEMENT

The consultants asked for an immediate appointment with the senior manager in XYZ with prime responsibility for security. The purpose of the interview was to make some assessment of issues such as:

(i) the potential security problems in XYZ;
(ii) the vulnerability of the organization to possible breaches of security;
(iii) the chances of the particular types of vulnerability occurring within XYZ;
(iv) the potential losses which might occur with each type of security breach;
(v) the valuation in monetary terms of potential security risks.

Subsequently a meeting was arranged at which the senior organizational development executive and a number of colleagues met with two consultants.

The two consultants returned from this preliminary meeting and set their thoughts down on paper. XYZ was a fairly large banking operation with assets of $1,500m. XYZ had adopted computer systems extensively for recording and storing information, details of accounts, financial calculations, banking and exchange control transactions and many other things – most of these systems were centralized with land-line links to branches. It had achieved an adequate rate of return on assets employed in the business but was obviously concerned about the safety of deposits and cash and possible threats to its employees as a result of theft or terrorist attack on the head office.

The consultants decided that they would have to do two things in relation to the security problems at XYZ. First, they would have to identify the sources of threats to physical assets, people, etc., i.e. *scenarios* by which events leading to security breaches would occur. Second, they would have to classify these security risks in terms of potential *severity* and *probability*. The basis of this classification follows from definitions of severity as an estimate of loss of assets and earnings as a result of an undesirable event and probability as an estimate of the likelihood of that undesirable event.

Their preliminary thoughts about the risks faced by XYZ are summarized in the classification of exposures shown in Table 6.1.

The sources of risk identified were:

(1) *Fire*
The risk of fire arising from electrical failure, human error or some other assignable clause.

Table 6.1 Classification of exposures

| | Source of risk | | | | | | | | | | | | | | | |
|---|---|---|---|---|---|---|---|---|---|---|---|---|---|---|---|---|
| | Fire | | Water damage | | Computer Equipment failure | | Computer fraud | | Theft of cash | | Political sabotage, bomb damage | | Theft of information | | Employee and personal liability | |
| Head Office | F | S | F | S | F | S | F | S | F | S | F | S | F | S | F | S |
| | L | M | L | L | L | L | L | H | M | M | L | H | L | M | L | M |

*Notes*:

(1) F denotes frequency

*Frequency classification*
L – Possible, but likelihood remote
M – Likely to happen from time to time
H – Likely to be commonplace

(2) S denotes severity

*Severity classification*
L – Envisaged loss likely to be less than $250,000
M – Envisaged loss likely to be in the range of $250,000 to $2.5m
H – Envisaged loss likely to exceed $2.5m

(2) *Water damage*
The risk of flood.

(3) *Computer equipment failure*
The risk of the computer system being down and causing administrative and other delays. This risk might be reduced by having some back-up facilities available – e.g. a company-owned time-sharing system and a reserve electrical generator.
Another source of computer failure might be human error, e.g. error causing the erasure of tapes, the incorrect specification of programs, etc.

(4) *Computer fraud*
The risk of fraudulent conversion of XYZ's assets by an individual or the risk of theft of information from the system. This may be reduced by closely monitoring the access of computer and other key personnel to the system and setting up some reasonably regular random audit procedure for checking the status of individual accounts.

(5) *Theft of cash*
The risk of robbery at head office. Risk-reduction measures could be closed-circuit television (CCTV), bullet-proof glass, etc.

(6) *Political sabotage; bomb damage*
The risk to XYZ of deliberate acts of sabotage by extremist groups such as the Red Brigade. This again may be reduced by a combination of adequate security checks and limiting people access at key points of XYZ's building.

(7) *Theft of information*
The risk of loss of sensitive information about a client's banking and exchange control records and the possible use of such information in the media.

(8) *Employee and personal liability*
The risk of injury or illness to a bank employee or innocent bystander as a result of any breach of security risk.

The consultants realized that the classification of exposures analysis shown in Table 6.1 was a 'first-pass' at the problem. They knew that there were going to be difficulties in getting managers to assess the probabilities to be attached to the occurrence of the various risk sources. This was largely because they were all felt to be 'rare events', i.e. have an extremely low probability of occurrence.

However, the consultants felt that Table 6.1. gave the opportunity for the managers in XYZ to structure their security problem more clearly. It was felt that the managers in XYZ had, at least, three strategies open to them in determining XYZ's attitude towards risk:

(i) XYZ could 'self-insure', i.e. bear the losses associated with the risks itself;

(ii) XYZ could insure against all risks in the insurance market; or
(ii) XYZ could buy insurance against some risks in the market and 'self-insure' against other risk sources.

The consultants also felt that the risks identified in Table 6.1 would expose XYZ to losses which could be unnecessarily severe. They decided that they would subsequently have to submit a series of risk prevention and control recommendations in order to try to reduce the incidence of some of these risks. In particular, they felt that there was a somewhat cavalier attitude to the access of individuals to key areas in head office other than the banking floor. There seemed to be very little security and policing of individuals in relation to visits to computer facilities, offices, etc.

Initially, however, they felt that they should have a further discussion with senior managers at XYZ to determine what directions the study should now take.

## QUESTIONS FOR DISCUSSION

Take the stance of the senior management group with responsibility for security questions in XYZ and examine the following issues.

1. What do you feel about the risk management approach put forward by the consultants?
2. In what areas of the study would you like to see more work undertaken?
3. Do you feel that the consultants have identified the range of possible alternative strategies for XYZ?
4. What risk reduction and control measures would you suggest?
5. How would you judge the cost-effectiveness of a security program given that it is probably impossible to obtain 100 percent security and even if it were possible the cost would probably be prohibitively high?

*Chapter 7*

# *The FINCOMSOC Case:* Computer Security Assessment*


## SUMMARY

The case in this chapter reinforces some of the issues about risk management introduced in the previous chapter. In particular, it addresses risks associated with fraud and employee dishonesty in a financial services company and considers the possibilities of insurance against these risks by the use of the mechanism of fidelity-guarantee insurance.


## 7.1 INTRODUCTION

This case considers some of the basic issues involved in the problem of policing computer security in business firms and organizations. Many breaches of computer security, e.g. computer fraud, have come to light in recent years, the most notable amongst which is the notorious Equity Funding Corporation of America (EFCA) case, which involved insurance company fraud in the United States. What are the risks involved in such breaches of security? How should the manager assess the vulnerability of his organization with respect to such security breaches? Should he insure against such breaches through the formal insurance market? These are some of the relevant questions in this area.

It is equally clear from legal authorities and sources that criminal law offers some protection against fraud of this type but does not necessarily guarantee redress because of the possibility of different interpretations of the law. Thus, compensation is not guaranteed and court actions themselves tend to be very costly. The manager in such a situation would have to assemble all the expert advice and decide whether the expected gain from legal action would be sufficient to balance the expected costs of the action. Alternatively, he could decide to transfer the risk from the law courts to the unconditional guarantee of redress afforded by the insurance market.

The Equity Funding Case points out some major reasons why computer fraud can be so successful and why its existence is often difficult either to

*This case was developed by Howard Thomas whilst a faculty member at London Business School.

predict or detect. First, because the computer is very often a substitute for a manual system, e.g. for recording and updating details of insurance policies or bank records, it is very often the data that is the object of fraudulent intent. Second, the integrity of the computer system in the Equity Case was not questioned, even though a large number of bogus policies had been added to it, because consistent insurance-policy activity seemed to be taking place. In other words, it seemed that premiums were being paid, commissions paid and policy lapses, for whatever reason, recorded. Third, Equity Funding's auditors seemed to be deceived by the apparent accuracy of the computer output and, therefore, did not question closely the nature of the input (containing as we know a significant proportion of bogus policies!).

Equity Funding thus highlights the range of security problems which a financial service organization may face. FINCOMSOC develops these issues more fully.

## 7.2 FINCOMSOC

The underwriting manager of the GENINSEX company had been asked by the administrative manager of FINCOMSOC, a savings and loan company, to quote him a premium for insurance (including fidelity guarantee, see Appendix), cover for the company's computer facility which was used largely to process savings accounts. He indicated that he would like both computer and a number of other key personnel to be named in the policy. He preferred that a limit of indemnity should be set overall at £1m for fidelity guarantee (with a deductible of say £25,000–£150,000) and that such a limit should apply to any single named employee and the policy as a whole.

The underwriting manager stated that he was willing to quote, but needed to make a visit to the computer site in order to judge the insurance needs of FINCOMSOC and make some assesssment of issues such as:

- (i) the potential security problems in FINCOMSOC;
- (ii) the vulnerability of the organization to the possible breaches of security;
- (iii) the chances of the particular types of vulnerability occurring within the firm;
- (iv) the potential losses which might occur with each type of security breach;
- (v) the valuation in monetary terms of potential computer security risks.

The administrative manager agreed to GENINSEX's request and suggested that the underwriter might wish to come along to lunch and in the first instance meet with some of his key staff. The underwriting manager also felt that this meeting would be useful as it would enable him to structure his decision problem in a meaningful way by talking through the potential problems with Fincomsoc's staff.

He returned from this meeting and collected his thoughts. His immediate impression of Fincomsoc was that it was a pleasant, medium-sized (funds under management approximately £100m) company which seemed to operate fairly efficiently. Computer systems had been set up to record and update savings accounts and calculate necessary interest payments. In essence, the computer had taken over the functions of what had in the past been a completely manual system.

He assessed that there could be computer problems as a result of a series of factors detailed below and also noted how he might check on the company's precautions in attempting to avoid these problems:

(1) *Physical hazard*
The risk of fire or flood. This risk could perhaps be alleviated if computing resources were spread over a number of sites rather than just one central facility.

(2) *Equipment failure*
The risk of the system being down and causing administrative and other delays. This problem again could perhaps be improved if some back-up facility were available – such as a service bureau or company-owned time-sharing system.

(3) *Human error*
The risk of error causing the erasure of tapes, the incorrect specification of programs, etc. He decided that he would look for evidence of sensible training and checking procedures in assessing the likely extent of this risk factor.

(4) *Personnel/labor relations problems*
The risk of delay in processing records, etc. as a result of industrial action by computer personnel.

(5) *Fraud and theft*
The risk of fraudulent conversion of Fincomsoc's assets by an individual or the risk of theft of information from the system. This could be reduced by closely monitoring the access of computer and other key personnel to the system and setting up a random audit procedure for checking the status of individual accounts.

(6) *Interference*
The risk of deliberate act of sabotage by an employee or outside organization. This again could be reduced by a combination of adequate security checks and limiting access of all personnel to the system.

From these notes the underwriter determined his strategy for his next visit to Fincomsoc and decided that he would try to assess the extent of the incidence of computer security problems. The results are shown in Table 7.1. This table clearly provides no more than a rough, crude screening of the extent of the problem and indicates that the fraud and theft potential was very high.

Table 7.1
Computer Security Problem

| Potential extent of incidence of problem | Physical hazard | Equipment failure | Human error | Personnel | Fraud and theft | Inter-ference |
|---|---|---|---|---|---|---|
| Large | | | | | √ | |
| Medium | | √ | | | | √ |
| Small | √ | | √ | √ | | |

Note: √ denotes likely extent of incidence of a given security problem

Table 7.2
Computer Security Problem: Probability and Severity Estimates

| Range of loss / Probability | $\left(P_1 = \frac{1}{100,000}\right)$ Hazard | $\left(P_2 = \frac{1}{10,000}\right)$ Equipment failure | $\left(P_3 = \frac{1}{1,000,000}\right)$ Human error | $\left(P_4 = \frac{1}{10,000,000}\right)$ Personnel | $\left(P_5 = \frac{1}{1000}\right)$ Fraud and theft | $\left(P_6 = \frac{1}{50,000}\right)$ Interference |
|---|---|---|---|---|---|---|
| High | £7.5m | £0.1m | £0.05m | £0.2m | £10m | £2.5m |
| Medium | £3.5m | £0.05m | £0.03m | £0.1m | £6m | £1.5m |
| Low | £0.5m | £0.02m | £0.02m | £0.02m | £4m | £1m |

The underwriter felt that he now needed only to assess the chances of each source of computer security breach occurring and the resultant extent of organizational loss if such a breach did occur.

He collected as much information as possible on the probable circumstances of the various types of loss and then faced the task of estimating the probabilities of occurrence of each event. He realized that this task was not a straightforward one because unlike the more commonly insured risks (e.g. life insurance) he had no hard historical data on which to base his estimates.

The underwriter also knew that an accurate set of probabilities for the events was essential because the probabilities would directly affect the premiums to be quoted. Whilst overestimation of the probabilities might cause the loss of Fincomsoc's business, underestimation of the probabilities might cause overall long-term underwriting losses. The method used for estimating the probabilities was one which involved three steps:

(1) Description of the type of loss.
(2) Calibration of the uncertainty.
(3) Assigning a numerical value to the probability.

The underwriter treated each category of loss separately and he systematically recorded everything that he knew about each type of risk. In cases where he felt that there was scope for obtaining additional information by research, he ensured that this was done.

Having clearly defined and described each type of risk, he passed on to the calibration stage. Calibration involves the expression of relative relationships of uncertainty between different events and bringing one's past experience to bear on judgments about the rare event under consideration. The calibration technique used in this instance was to compare the events and their probabilities of occurrence with standard rare events such as the probability of flipping a coin 10 times and turning up 10 'heads' $\left(\frac{1}{1024}\right)$ or the probability of an airliner crashing.

As an example, the underwriter was able to compare the probability of 'fraud and theft' with the probability of a number of other rare events and then decide:

(1) Whether the fraud or theft had, in his opinion, a higher or lower probability of occurrence than the other event.
(2) How much more or less (as a ratio) he estimated the 'fraud or theft' event was likely to occur compared to the various standard events (whose probabilities were known).

In estimating the final figures for the probability for each event, the underwriter realized that he was dealing with cases where possible loss was a continuously distributed random variable. To define the loss probability fully he could either define a relationship between loss and probability for each event or discretize the losses for each event and estimate a probability for each loss class. The underwriter felt that he was not in a position to do either of these things because of his lack of hard data and accurate information.

The procedure he adopted was to translate his calibration statements into single-figure probability estimates for each event (results are in Table 7.2) and to estimate values of the severity of loss for each type of loss which might define the distribution of loss severity.

He estimated three figures for each type of loss:

(1) Probable maximum loss. This amount represents the highest expected loss under ordinary circumstances. Only in rare and exceptional cases would losses greater than the PML occur.
(2) Possible maximum loss. This figure represents the amount which is roughly the average loss expected (if a loss occurs).
(3) Minimum loss. This figure represents the value of loss which would be the lowest probable loss value (given that a loss occurs).

He evaluated figures for (1), (2) and (3) as defined above for each type of loss and classified these losses as High, Medium or Low, respectively (results are in Table 7.2).

Having obtained the preliminary analysis shown in Table 7.2 the underwriter recognized that it was a 'first-stab' at the problem. He had found difficulties in getting company experts to assess the probabilities to be attached to the various risk sources, largely because the managers regarded them as being extremely small – a common comment being 'what's the difference between $\frac{1}{50,000}$ and $\frac{1}{100,000}$? They are still both extremely unlikely events.'

The underwriter decided, however, that Table 7.2 did provide a basis for getting closer to a premium calculation. It seemed clear to him that the administrative director of FINCOMSOC had at least three strategies open to him in determining the firm's attitude towards risk:

(i) the firm could self-insure, i.e. bear the losses associated with the risks itself;
(ii) the firm could buy insurance from GENINSEX, or some other company, to safeguard against the occurrence of all types of risk;
(iii) the firm could buy insurance for some risk sources and 'self-insure' against other risk sources.

The underwriter decided, therefore, that he would go back to the administrative director and his colleagues and ask them a number of questions. First, he asked them to answer questions of the following type. If

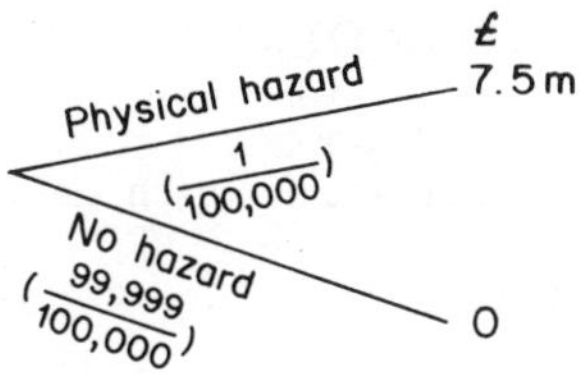


Figure 7.1

you were offered the wager shown in Figure 7.1, what is your minimum selling price for this wager? Or, alternatively, the question could be framed as follows:

'How much money would you trade this wager for?'

Suppose for the moment that the answer were £20,000. The expected value for the wager is

$$\frac{1}{100.000} \times 7{,}500{,}000 + \frac{99{,}999}{100{,}000} \times 0 = £75$$

The difference of £20,000 – £75 can be interpreted as the additional risk premium that FINCOMSOC would be willing to pay over and above the actuarial value of the gamble, i.e. the expected loss. In addition, it points clearly to the fact that in this instance FINCOMSOC would wish to transfer such a risk from itself to the insurance company.

After a similar series of wagers the underwriter was able to construct some evidence in the form of Table 7.3. He felt, at this stage, that he could do no more to refine his analysis of the problem even though he recognized that he could do more research into computer fraud and suggest improvements to the computer system which, if effected and implemented, would reduce the cost of insurance to FINCOMSOC.

Table 7.3
Risk premiums

| Security problem | Risk premium |
|---|---|
| Hazard | £1925 |
| Equipment failure | £100 |
| Human error | Almost zero |
| Personnel | 0 |
| Fraud or theft | £7500 |
| Interference | £700 |

## QUESTIONS FOR DISCUSSION

1. What should FINCOMSOC do about insurance?
2. What premiums should GENINSEX charge for each class of risk or for fidelity guarantee separately?
3. Should any further analysis be undertaken?

# Appendix: Fidelity Guarantee Insurance

The British insurance market does considerable insurance business in the area of physical hazard. Most of the other sources of risk can be insured against (generally in terms of the fidelity type of policy) but the evidence indicates that very little business is done in these areas in the UK compared with the United States. Currently UK experience suggests that there is considerable inertia in the market to take up the business because it is claimed that premiums are unacceptably low and claims are relatively large in size. An attitudinal change is necessary to persuade company management to accept that a fidelity policy (covering indemnity against staff risks, e.g. fraud, theft, dishonesty, etc.) is as necessary as a fire policy since either set of circumstances would be damaging to the continued existence of the company. Unless there is a greater spread of fidelity business in the UK it will become difficult for insurance companies to be able to offer insurance on meaningful, competitive terms. In the US, however, there is a great deal of fidelity guarantee business and many offices seek to write such business.

*Chapter 8*

# *Globair Limited:* Insurance Premium Setting*


## SUMMARY

This case presents a disguised version of an insurance decision problem faced by underwriters within a major British insurance company. The purpose of the case is to demonstrate how the employers' liability risk of an airline Globair Ltd. can be assessed and valued by underwriters prior to the process of premium setting.


## 8.1 INTRODUCTION

The Chief Liability Underwriter of an insurance company (and his Assistant) were considering whether to insure the employer's liability risk of Globair, an Australian-based independent airline providing regular and charter services to Australia, New Zealand and South East Asia.

Globair had an annual wage roll of $25m. Although there were employees under contract in Australia who were stationed abroad, no overseas local labor was hired. It was established that routine non-catastrophe claims experience – such as normal industrial accidents to ground staff or crew members – justified a premium rate of 0.17 percent overall, yielding a premium of $42,500 on the total salary and wage roll of $25m projected for the coming year; this rate included a build-up for commission and expenses. So far there had been no flying accidents in the company's history.

However, as the Chief pointed out to his Assistant, large claims occur when there is a serious aircraft accident. Indeed, this prospect could make the $140,000 premium received for their share of some of the other insurances written for Globair look less attractive in spite of the currently profitable experience. The aircraft hull risk was placed elsewhere and not on offer for insurance underwriting.

Their attention was thus focussed on the employers' liability (EL) risk

*This case was originally written by Roger Miller and Barrie West of Commercial Union Insurance, London Head Office. It is reproduced here with permission and grateful thanks. It was adapted for use in Australia by Howard Thomas whilst at the Australian Graduate School of Management.

presented by the flight deck and cabin crews. It appeared that the fleet consisted of eight DC-9s, each with three flight deck personnel and four cabin crew, and two 747s (on the longer runs) each carrying three flight deck personnel and seven cabin crew. 'Jump' or 'dead-heading' crews were from time to time carried on company aircraft on their way to or from active crew duty (that is, 747 jump crews on 747s and DC-9 jump crews on DC-9s); normally they would travel as passengers and be issued with passenger tickets, but the underwriters knew from experience that this would not necessarily rule out the possibility of an EL claim in all circumstances. Standards of safety and maintenance were acknowledged to be first-class, but the Company was prospering and the aircraft heavily employed.

'Let's do some analysis ana structuring of the probabilities here', said the Chief. 'Accidents will happen sooner or later and we must look at the likely cost of flying accidents on an annualized basis. Therefore, let's have a realistic basis for making our rate, before the meeting you have set up with the brokers tomorrow. We will try and analyze the problem first, so that we can more clearly see what further information we need about the flying risk.'

## 8.2 PRELIMINARY RISK ASSESSMENT OF EMPLOYER'S LIABILITY RISK

The following exhibits show some of the parts of the preliminary information-gathering and analysis phase. Exhibit 8.1 shows the composition of Globair's fleet and crew operations.

(a) 2 × Boeing 747
    (3 flight deck personnel)
    (7 cabin crew)
(b) 8 × Douglas DC-9
    (3 flight deck personnel)
    (4 cabin crew)
(c) On average a jump crew is present on 50% of 747 flights
(d) On average a jump crew is present on 10% of DC-9 flights

Exhibit 8.1 Globair fleet

Exhibit 8.2 shows the underwriter's estimation of the average maximum monetary exposure per head on EL claims where 100 percent liability is subsequently established.

| | | (NB If crew single and without dependants average minimum monetary exposure per capita) |
|---|---|---|
| Flight deck | $210,000 | |
| Cabin crew | $ 70,000 | $2,500 |

Exhibit 8.2 Maximum monetary exposure per head

(Note: These estimates were based on a fifteen-year time horizon and allow for tax effects.)

Exhibit 8.3 shows the underwriter's further analysis of five possible scenarios by which claims could arise.

| *Scenario* | | | | *Value of claim* $ |
|---|---|---|---|---|
| 1 | (a) | Policy decision of management leads directly to lack of maintenance and disaster: 100% liability occurs | | |
| | | If plane were: | | |
| | | (i) 747 all crew 6 + 14 killed | | 2,240,000 |
| | | (ii) DC-9 all crew 6 + 8 killed | | 1,820,000 |
| 2 | As (a) above but: | | | |
| | (i) | only one crew on board – | 747 | 1,120,000 |
| | | | DC-9 | 910,000 |
| | | OR | | |
| | (ii) | both crews on board but 'jump' crew have passenger tickets which are held to be effective | | |
| 3 | Pilot error held to be 100% responsible: | | | |
| | (i) | both crews killed | 747 | 2,030,000 |
| | | | DC-9 | 1,610,000 |
| | (ii) | as 2(i) above | 747 | 910,000 |
| | | | DC-9 | 700,000 |
| | (iii) | as 2(ii) above | 747 | 910,000 |
| | | | DC-9 | 700,000 |
| 4 | Combination of two men's errors on flight deck (each should have checked the other): | | | |
| | (i) | both crews killed | 747 | 1,820,00 |
| | | | DC-9 | 1,400,000 |
| | (ii) | as 2(i) above | 747 | 700,000 |
| | | | DC-9 | 490,000 |
| | (iii) | as 2 (ii) above | 747 | 700,000 |
| | | | DC-9 | 490,000 |
| 5 | All crew single: | | | |
| | (a) | as Situation 1 | 747 | 50,000 |
| | | | DC-9 | 35,000 |
| | | 2(i) | 747 | 25,000 |
| | | | DC-9 | 17,500 |
| | | 2(ii) | 747 | 25,000 |
| | | | DC-9 | 17,500 |

Exhibit 8.3 Possible scenarios

The analysts have also derived probabilty estimates for various uncertain events as shown in Exhibit 8.4.

(a) Probability of flying accident:
One aircraft lost per 500,000 hours flown
Each aircraft flies –
Maximum of 2500 hours per year
Therefore, one loss per 200 years
Therefore, with 10 aircraft we could expect one loss every 20 years

(b) Probability of liability attaching for total loss situation:

| | |
|---|---|
| 100% liability | 60% |
| Nil liability | 40% |

(c) Possible levels of claims (including costs):

| | *Low* ($m) | *Medium* ($m) | *High* ($m) |
|---|---|---|---|
| Small crew plus jump | 0.06 | 0.7 | 1.8 |
| Small crew ex jump* | 0.04 | 0.35 | 0.9 |
| Large crew plus jump | 0.08 | 0.9 | 2.2 |
| Large crew ex jump* | 0.05 | 0.45 | 1.1 |

(* or jump crew as *bona fide* passengers)

(d) Probability of level of claim:

| | | |
|---|---|---|
| low | – | 5% |
| medium | – | 35% |
| high | – | 60% |

Exhibit 8.4 Probability estimates

The analysts further argued that the estimated cost of successfully contesting claims arising from an accident (where no liability attaches) would be around $30,000.

## QUESTION FOR DISCUSSION

Analyze the chief underwriter's problem, using the decision tree approach. In so doing, you should be able to estimate the 'burning cost' (the expected value) for the EL risk and you then use this 'burning cost' figure to estimate the reasonableness of the premium.

*Chapter 9*

# *Austrans Limited:* Determination of Risk Management Policies*

## SUMMARY

This short case examines questions of risk management faced by an Australian road-haulage company. The intention is to alert the reader to the processes of risk identification, assessment and measurement in a business context. A consultant's very preliminary attempt at risk identification is presented as a basis for generating dialogue about alternative risk management approaches.

## 9.1 INTRODUCTION

Austrans Ltd. is a company which was incorporated in Victoria, Australia, in 1953. It has since become a fairly large transport and haulage company specializing in the transportation of goods around the East Coast of Australia.

Austrans has a fleet of road-trains (large road-haulage vehicles) as well as a smaller number of trucks and service vehicles. In April 1978, the General Manager of Austrans decided to call in a risk management consultant to see whether Austrans' existing risk management policies were reasonable and whether they could be improved upon.

The consultant began by interviewing a number of people, including the general manager, the sales manager, the scheduling manager and a sample of drivers. By this process, the risk consultant and his associates wished to determine what risks the company faced, and what was the likelihood of their occurrence. He also intended to investigate Austrans range of exposure to potential losses from its diverse operations and how this exposure to risk could be reduced and handled efficiently.

The General Manager (GM) of Austrans had recently read a paper by Haines in the *Insurance Monitor* (January 1977, p.7) in which it was stated that damage or losses had three dimensions:

*This case was developed by D. A. Samson and Howard Thomas as a basis for classroom discussion of risk management issues at the Australian Graduate School of Management.

(1) frequency with which the threat occurs;
(2) probability of loss or damage occurring; and
(3) severity of its effect.

The GM of Austrans had taken out comprehensive insurance on all its vehicles and had installed fire extinguishers on board all road-trains, but apart from these measures very little consideration had been given in the past to risk management. He therefore asked the risk consultant to undertake two main tasks:

(1) to identify the range of possible risks faced by Austrans; and
(2) to look more closely at whether Austrans was getting value for its insurance dollar.

The consultant decided to study the problem in stages as follows:

(1) Evaluation of existing insurance arrangements.
(2) Identification of risks faced by Austrans.
(3) Evaluation and recommendation of risk-reduction procedures.

## 9.2 COMPREHENSIVE VEHICLE INSURANCE

The consultant found that for the 64 road-trains and other vehicles involved in the fleet policy, Austrans was liable for the first $200 of any event resulting in a claim (i.e. a $200 deductible). In addition, the policy conditions stated that for any claim there were limits on maximum claim size of $300,000 for vehicle damage, and $750,000 for public liability. Further, a deductible of $500 was imposed on liability claims.

The consultant decided to question Austrans' management to see whether these limits reflected the risk attitudes of the company. He also obtained quotes from three further insurance companies for Austrans' insurance coverage. Details of the cheapest quotes are in Table 9.1. (See policies 2, 3 and 4).

When this data was presented to management, it was thought that the extra $11,000 cost of policy 4 over policy 1 was worthwhile because of the extra cover

Table 9.1 (Figures in $)

| | Deductible | | Max. claim limit | | |
|---|---|---|---|---|---|
| Policy no. | Damage | Liability | Damage | Liability | Premium |
| 1 | 200 | 500 | 300,000 | 750,000 | 181,000 |
| 2 | 300 | 600 | 300,000 | 750,000 | 180,000 |
| 3 | 500 | 1,000 | 300,000 | 750,000 | 176,000 |
| 4 | 500 | 1,000 | 500,000 | 1,000,000 | 192,000 |

provided. However, the risk consultant suggested that the actual most recent loss distribution experience should be examined closely to determine the range of risks faced by Austrans. This analysis would then allow him to design a policy which would be better suited to the current needs of Austrans. The General Manager, (GM) of Austrans said that this was not necessary because policy 4 seemed to fit the company's needs very well. He said that the past three years experience (since the original policy had been taken out) had been marked by two main factors:

(2) growth of Austrans' fleet; and
(2) inflation of costs.

These factors were judged to have changed the risk attitude of Austrans. It was now felt that the company could bear the higher deductible since it was spread over a larger financial and operating base. Further, since operating costs had risen and liability claims were becoming ever larger, it was thought that an increase in the claim limits was necessary and prudent.

The consultant also mentioned to management that several insurance companies had suggested that significantly lower premiums might be charged if the drivers had compulsory rests during long hauls. For example, rests of two hours for every six hours of driving were suggested. Mr Jones, the scheduling manager of Austrans, suggested that the idea was preposterous and highly inflationary, but the GM instructed the consultant to investigate the possibility.

## 9.3 OTHER RISKS

The consultant suggested that Austrans consider taking out insurance against loss of profit due to consequential losses. He identified some possible sources of such a loss:

(1) Since Austrans supplied a number of inland centers with supplies ranging from petrol to beer and agricultural products, etc., it was usual for the transport contracts to have a stipulated delivery date. If Austrans failed to deliver by the due date, the company was liable to pay fairly large sums in damages. The GM suggested that one or two late loads were tolerable but that events like a major flood could significantly affect deliveries and result in catastrophic and unwelcome losses.
(2) If spare parts and maintenance service for trucks became difficult to obtain, Austrans might lose business because of its reduced transport capacity. It appeared that this was a real probability because the type of truck used by Austrans was being superseded. In addition, some of Austrans routes traversed difficult and isolated terrain which had few specialized service facilities readily available.

(3) Strikes could have a crippling effect on Austrans' profit. Austrans was not only vulnerable to losses from internal strikes (it employed members of at least six different unions) but would be seriously affected by a petrol strike. The current climate of instability in the Australian oil industry made this factor a real threat. Strikes involving production of the goods which Austrans was contracted to carry would also have an adverse effect, but probably not of the same severity as a petrol strike.

## QUESTIONS FOR DISCUSSION

1. Evaluate the quality of the study done by the consultant.
2. Were there any facets of the situation that the consultant may not have accounted for?
3. What other options were open to Austrans and what risk-reduction control and transfer measures could be undertaken?
4. How would you improve the risk assessment and measurement process?

*Chapter 10*

# *Smith, Tyne and Georges:* Simulating Alternative Premium Structures*

SUMMARY

This disguised case provides data to enable the reader to carry out a risk analysis of the potential accident, crash and damage risks faced by an airline. This risk analysis could then be used as one basis for the evaluation of a number of alternative aircraft hull insurance packages suggested to the company by the insurance brokers Smith, Tyne and George and their underwriters.

Smith, Tyne and Georges (STG) are a firm of insurance brokers who act as consultants and insurance/reinsurance brokers. They have offices in five capital cities of states in Australia.

In August 1978, Leonard Tyne of STG began an investigation of the insurance package held by one of STG's clients which was one of Australia's major internal airlines. He was particularly concerned with his client's aircraft hull insurance. Losses resulting in insurance claims could be classified into one of two types:

(1) Partial damage to a hull resulting in relatively small claims.
(2) Complete losses where the hull insurance would pay for a replacement aircraft.

The current insurance cover held by the airline for hull damage was a policy whereby the annual premium paid was equal to 150 percent of the actual losses incurred within that year, subject to an annual minimum of \$0.4 per \$100 insured and an annual maximum of \$2.1 per \$100 insured.

The group of underwriters who held the hull insurance approached Mr Tyne with a suggestion of a modified hull insurance policy. They suggested that the modified policy conditions would be more suitable both to the insurer and the insured and they asked Mr Tyne to put the suggestion to the airline. The

*This case was developed by D. A. Samson and Howard Thomas at the Australian Graduate School of Management.

modified policy would have a premium set equal to losses, with a minimum of \$0.6 per \$100 insured and a maximum premium of \$1.3 per \$100 insured.

Mr Tyne suggested that the client should view the opportunity as a chance to arrange for a modified type of insurance which might well work out to be significantly cheaper. Mr Alan Jones, who was considered the airlines' 'statistical expert', was commissioned to study and investigate the possibility.

He began by gathering necessary data. A reasonably large amount of data was available in claims resulting in partial hull damage. Partial hull damage usually occurred during take-off and landing and experience allowed Mr Jones to predict that partial hull damage resulted in insurance claims of between \$150,000 and \$300,000 per annum. On the question of total hull destruction Mr Jones was less confident of being able to assess the risk because of the very small amount of data available on Australian cases.

He knew that most serious accidents and failures occurred near airports and that taking-off and landing were the most dangerous parts of flying. He needed to estimate the risk of a crash occurring and therefore decided to begin with a point estimate figure based on combined European and American data of past years. The probability of an aircraft crashing in a one-year period was found to be 0.005 and he decided to use this figure in his initial calculations.

Data on fleet size and value were also collected (see Table 10.1).

Table 10.1
Fleet Size and Value Data

| Aircraft | Number | Book value | | Insured value | |
|---|---|---|---|---|---|
| | | Plane | Fleet | Plane | Fleet |
| 727/200 | 8 | \$5.5m | \$44m | \$5.7m | \$45.6m |
| 727/100 | 2 | 4.9m | 9.8m | 5.0m | 10.0m |
| DC9 | 12 | 3.6m | 43.2m | 3.8m | 45.6m |
| Fokker Friendship | 12 | 1.2m | 14.4m | 1.3m | 15.6m |
| Twin Otter | 6 | 0.6m | 3.6m | 0.65m | 3.9m |
| TOTAL | 40 | | \$111.4m | | \$120.7m |

## QUESTIONS FOR DISCUSSION

1. What is the meaning of the premium structures being considered by STG? Construct a graph for each premium structure showing the relationship between premium and losses. Explain these relationships.
2. How would you go about using a Monte-Carlo simulation procedure to analyze the risk? What would be the input variables, output variables, distribution forms, etc.? What sensitivity analysis could be of use to management in their decision?
3. What might be an alternative form of analysis to Monte-Carlo techniques and how might such an alternative be implemented?
4. What is the expected total loss and what would be the corresponding premium in each premium structure?

*Chapter 11*

# *Cassida Ltd:* New Product Marketing*


## SUMMARY

The Cassida case illustrates some of the difficulties involved in problem formulation for decision and risk analysis. An initial 'framing' of a new product packaging problem is presented which involves three main strategy alternatives ranging from 'national launch' to 'hire further market research'. The reader is encouraged to structure this new product decision (perhaps in decision tree terms) and to critique the set of strategy alternatives suggested in the case. The aim is to stimulate dialogue about alternative options and to discuss the role of analysis in this dialogue process.


## 11.1 INTRODUCTION

The marketing manager of Cassida, a ground-coffee and coffee-equipment manufacturing division of a multi-national corporation, was considering what to do following notification from Alumicans Ltd. that they had developed a new type of packaging can for ground coffee. Cassida had initially made their name as manufacturers of filter-coffee equipment but had diversified over the last three years into producing their own brand of ground coffee to compete with such existing brands as Africo, Cohens and Aromatic. Demand for their coffee had been extremely satisfactory and they were currently working their coffee manufacturing plants at full capacity as a result of receiving sizeable orders from supermarkets and wholesalers who had not previously taken as much of their product. Management felt that there was currently a major and continuing shift in consumer taste. Indeed, it appeared that the 'delicatessen', somewhat upper-class image of ground-coffee drinking was now disappearing from the UK market. Recent market research figures indicated that ground coffee sales were increasing significantly relative to instant coffee sales. Further, the increased sales of ground coffee were distributed across the range of social class levels.

*This case was developed by Howard Thomas at the London Business School in 1976. It is based upon the early stages (problem formulation) of a real-life decision analysis in the consumer product area.

Taking into account the shift in demand patterns, the success of their brand name and the communication from Alumicans, the marketing management in Cassida felt that they should review their marketing strategy. They were certain from market research that the Cassida name brand (with drip-grind, regular-grind, etc. variants) provided an image of a quality product which could be priced at premium levels, and that there was no need to diversify their product lines from blends that had for some years proved to be extremely acceptable. However, they felt that two issues needed careful attention. First, a review of their marketing operations (i.e. the sales force organization) and, second, a review of product packaging including a discussion of issues of pack size. It was also agreed that sales-force matters would be reviewed initially by a subcommittee of the main board, but that there was much more immediacy about the packaging issue.

There were a number of existing packaging methods in use in the ground-coffee market either by Cassida or by competitors. First, there were brands which used either a plastic opaque heavy-duty paper bag or a transparent heavy-duty polythene bag. The advantages of such bags were cheapness and convenience, given that they could maintain reasonable standards of freshness for an average shelf-life of several months on a supermarket counter. Second, vacuum cans had been used by some brands employing normal screw-can opening, either with keys of the type found on sardine cans, or without keys but with a removeable polythene lid for purposes of reclosure. Cans were more expensive than bags, but had the additional advantage that they could, with a reclosing polythene lid, provide a means for the consumer to store and keep the coffee acceptably fresh after initial use. Cans also had a much longer shelf-life than the plastic bag.

Experience within Cassida over the last three years had led to a complete packaging switch, from a mix of bags and cans to an almost total dependence on the can as a package (save for a very small output of the bagged product for the loyal delicatessen market). Indeed, Cassida had about a year ago adopted the keyless can with a recloseable lid as themost satisfactory package for its product. The 'quick-strip-can' with a reclosable polythene lid had just been developed by Alumicans Ltd. and Cassida had been offered first refusal on its use and exclusivity of the product for a period of one year. The advantage was that the consumer could open the can without a screw-opener or key and still keep the can as a storage medium for the coffee. Unfortunately, the 'quick-strip' facility would result in a slightly more expensive can and this cost would have to be largely borne by the consumer. Would the consumer want the quick-strip can given the higher price? Should the company accept the option of the initial batch of quick-strip cans or pass the opportunity and thus convey any subsequent competitive advantage to its immediate competitors?

## 11.2 MARKETING CONSIDERATIONS

It was accepted by the marketing director and his team that any change in package and/or pack size must be influenced by cost considerations, scenarios of likely competitive action and by the anticipated effect on the firm's market share position and profitability. They felt that the immediate question of what to do with the Alumicans offer was important because they were optimistic in regard to consumer potential of the new can. However, they were uncertain about its effect on demand and cautious about doing anything which might lead to a decrease in Cassida's currently healthy market share position. The marketing director felt that the appropriate time period for reviewing the possible packaging change should be long enough to permit consideration of all possible influences (e.g. consumer reaction, competitive action) on Cassida's market share position. Since marketing strategy in Cassida was normally appraised annually, it was decided initially that one year would be a sufficiently long planning horizon. Cost data showed that the quick-opening can was likely to cost 0.10p more for a ¼lb size can than the existing keyless can, and about 0.20p more for the same size than for the plasticated bag variants. This implied that Cassida's costs would go up by only slightly more than an average of 0.10p per can, allowing for the company's current mix of almost 100 percent canned ground coffee.

Cassida was the leading brand of ground coffee in the UK with a market share of approximately 20 percent and a sales volume of 1,000,000 lbs of coffee annually at an average price of £1.20 per lb. Cassida was much stronger in the South-East and the wealthier areas in the UK and had a very loyal following in such markets. It had recently been pursuing a cautious expansionary strategy in new areas and according to the most recent market research data was making satisfactory progress.

## 11.3 THE OPTIONS AVAILABLE

The marketing team felt that there were a range of possible options which Cassida should discuss in considering a packaging change. First, they could go ahead immediately and introduce the new can across the entire market area, perhaps at a slightly higher price than the existing keyless can. Second, they could delay immediate action in order to find out whether they would face competition from other manufacturers who might adopt the new can. Alternatively they could take a third option, that is to delay a national launch in favour of a limited regional market test of the quick-strip can. The purpose of this strategy would be to collect further information about likely market reaction before making an irrevocable commitment to the new can.

### National Launch

If they went ahead with the change immediately and launched the rapid-opening can nationally, the team decided to consider two launching strategies, namely, by pricing at 4p/lb above existing price levels or by maintaining the status quo. In either case they felt that the only real source of uncertainty concerned the likely change in market share. They decided to categorize such changes as positive (range +1 to +5 percent), stays roughly the same (range −1 to +1 percent) or negative (−1 to −5 percent). In the case of a quick-strip can priced at existing levels, the director felt that the odds were in favour of a positive change, say 3 to 2 on a positive change. At the same time he felt that the odds against staying the same and falling negative were approximately 4 to 1 in each case. On the other hand, the director felt that if prices were raised 4p per lb, the odds for a positive change would be evens, and approximately 3 to 1 odds against staying the same or becoming negative. The change in net profit figures for each possible outcome calculated on a present value basis is shown in Table 11.1.

Table 11.1 Immediate National Launch of New Can: Change in Net Profits (£ thousand) (Over a one-year horizon)

| Strategy | Change in share of market: Positive | Same | Negative |
|---|---|---|---|
| Same price | 39 | −1 | −41 |
| 4p/lb price rise | 46 | 6 | −40 |

**Delayed Launch**

At the same time Cassida believed that if they decided to keep the keyless can for the time being, then Alumicans would almost certainly offer the new can on a non-exclusive basis to one of Cassida's major competitors. Cassida's executives reasoned that any competitors's marketing strategy would be somewhat similar to Cassida's since they had access to roughly the same information about the product area. Therefore, if a competitor took up the offer from Alumicans, it was assumed that they would also offer the new product priced either at 4p per lb above existing prices or at the current level. Cassida could then assess, through marketing intelligence over a six-month period, the direction of the change in market share (i.e. positive, no change or negative) which the competitor might achieve through adoption of the new can. At that stage Cassida could make a decision on whether to adopt the new can on a non-exclusive basis or stay with the keyless can. Cassida's marketing team felt that any such decision would depend heavily upon their perception of the likely changes in market share which might occur. It was felt currently that some preliminary odds statements about the change in market share over the initial six-month period (if a competitor used the new can) could be made. These would be 3 to 2 on 'positive', 4 to 1 against 'no change' and 4 to 1 against 'negative' for the scenario of *no price change*. However, these would alter to evens odds for 'positive' and 3:1 against 'no change' and 'negative' respectively in the situation of a *4p per lb price change*. Any further assessment of the second six-month change in market share was, in fact, dependent upon the outcomes which might result from the first six-month's experience of a competitor using the new can. If the initial competitive change was 'positive', then it was reasoned that the odds on a positive change in the second six months would be 4:1 on with a chance of 9:1 against each of the scenarios of 'stays the same' and a 'negative' change. If the initial change indicated a scenario of 'no change' then the odds statements would become about 2:1 against each of the possible outcomes. Finally, if the initial change were 'negative' then the subsequent odds on a negative change would be 3:2 with odds against the 'no change' and 'positive' scenarios being 4 to 1 in each case. It was felt that these odds statements for the second six months would not be changed significantly if Cassida launched after six months at either premium or existing price levels.

One of the team raised the possibility that no competitor would take up the offer from Alumicans because of caution about market conditions. In that situation Alumicans might be forced to quote a lower price for the quick-opening can, or to listen very closely to arguments that Cassida might make about a possible reduction in the offered can price. It was felt that Alumicans would contact Cassida within a month given an initial refusal of the offer by Cassida and a lack of interest from competitors. It was reasoned that they might then bargain about the offer price for the quick-opening can. If they were willing to sell at roughly the same price as a keyless can the executives reasoned that it might then be worthwhile for Cassida or a competitor to launch. Again if Cassida or a competitor launched at this stage the odds would be the same for an immediate launch. It would still be possible for Cassida not to use the quick-strip can for a six-month period and launch later under the assumption that the odds statements at this stage would be the same as those assessed for the second six-month period earlier. The change in net profits associated with this set of options is shown in Table 11.2.

**Market Research**

Cassida reasoned that they could buy further information in the form of specific commissioned market research (MR) before making a decision about launch or rejection of the new can. Such a survey might be a limited regional test with the new can for a three-month period (at a cost of, say, £2,500) and would result in a 'positive' indication of change in market share, a 'constant' indication or a 'negative' indication. The odds for such results given by the MR company (which has worked with this type of product for over three years) are given in Table 11.3 together with odds values for the change in market share that would result if an eventual national market launch were to take place. Table 11.4 indicates the changes in net profits estimated to result from each of the possible outcomes in this situation.

The team realized that pack-size considerations could not be isolated from the total packaging mix but recognized that some answer must be given to Alumicans in a matter of a week or so.

Table 11.2 Influence of Competition on Decision – Change in Net Profits

| | | Change in market share Positive | Stays the same | Negative |
|---|---|---|---|---|
| I | *Competitor uses new can (4p/lb more)* | | | |
| (a) → | If positive reaction Cassida then launches at 4p/lb more | 30 | −10 | −55 |
| (b) → | If reaction is 'stays same' Cassida then either: | | | |
| | (i) launches at existing prices | 25 | −15 | −55 |
| | (ii) stays keyless | 10 | 4 | − 2 |
| (c) → | If negative reaction, Cassida then stays keyless | 10 | 4 | − 2 |
| II | *Competitor uses new can (at same price)* | | | |
| (a) → | If positive reaction Cassida then launches at existing price | 25 | −15 | −55 |
| (b) → | If 'stays same' reaction Cassida then either: | | | |
| | (i) launches at existing prices, or | 25 | −15 | −55 |
| | (ii) stays keyless | 5 | − 1 | − 4 |
| (c) → | If 'negative' Cassida stays keyless | 5 | − 1 | − 4 |
| III | *Competitor stays keyless but subsequently Alumicans lowers price* | | | |
| (a) → | Cassida then launches at existing prices – no competition | 35 | 0 | −35 |
| (b) → | Cassida stays keyless but competitor uses new can at existing price allowing Cassida after 6 months to either launch | 25 | −15 | −55 |
| → | or stay keyless | 5 | − 1 | − 4 |
| (c) → | Cassida and competitors stay keyless | 0 | 0 | 0 |
| IV | Alumicans holds price, competitors and Cassida stay keyless | 0 | 0 | 0 |

Table 11.3 Market Regional Test

| | | | |
|---|---|---|---|
| (a) | | *Odds relating to market test* | |
| | | Positive indication: | Evens |
| | | Constant indication: | 7:3 against |
| | | Negative indication: | 4:1 against |
| (b) | | *Odds relating to change in market share given test market indications* | |
| | (i) | *If positive test market indication* | |
| | | Positive change: | 9:1 on |
| | | Stays same: | 19:1 against |
| | | Negative change: | 19:1 against |
| | (ii) | *If constant test market indication* | |
| | | Positive change: | 4:1 against |
| | | Stays same: | 7:3 on |
| | | Negative change: | 9:1 against |
| | (iii) | *If negative test market indication* | |
| | | Positive change: | 19:1 against |
| | | Stays same: | 3:1 against |
| | | Negative change: | 7:3 on |

Table 11.4 Change in Net Profits (£ thousand): Regional Test Market Option

| | Market share change | | |
|---|---|---|---|
| | Positive | Stays same | Negative |
| New can<br>Launch: 4p per lb Premium | 35 | 4 | −30 |
| New can<br>Launch: Same price | 30 | −1 | −31 |
| Keyless can | 0 | 0 | 0 |

Cost of market research: £2,500

## QUESTIONS FOR DISCUSSION

1. Assuming that you were the marketing director of Cassida seeking to determine the best course of action in relation to the new can:
   (i) What alternative strategies would you have considered?
   (ii) What course of action would you take on the basis of the information presented?

2. Comment upon your analysis, indicating features of the problem you would wish to reconsider, and whether you would recommend any additional information-gathering.

## FURTHER READING

Readers may wish to consult the following:

Brown, R. V., A. S. Kahr and C. R. Peterson (1974). *Decision Analysis for the Manager*. New York: Holt, Rinehart and Winston.

Pessemier, E. A. (1966), *New Product Decisions: An Analytical Approach* New York: McGraw-Hill.

Newman, J. W. (1971). *Management Applications of Decision Theory* New York: Harper and Row.

*Chapter 12*

# *J. Sainsbury:* Bidding*


## SUMMARY

This chapter provides an example of a complex competitive bidding situation faced by a major British supermarket company. The company was invited to tender for the purchase of a cargo of butter confiscated by British Customs for contravening regulations regarding butter import quotas. The cargo had been disguised as sweetfat (a 'near butter' not subject to import quotas) although there was believed to be a significant proportion of real butter in the cargo. The case describes a decision analysis of this tender bidding situation and details the assumptions necessarily made in order to arrive at an acceptable formulation of the problem and, hence, a final bid price.


## 12.1 INTRODUCTION

J. Sainsbury Ltd. were invited to tender for a consignment of butter which had been impounded by H.M. Customs & Excise at the Port of London. At that time, butter imports were restricted under a quota scheme and this particularly unfortunate consignment had attempted to evade the Customs, being packaged as sweetfat. The ratio of butter to sweetfat in the consignment was unknown. The future market prices for similar imported butter and sweetfat pertaining at that time when they would receive the consignment (if the bid were successful) were not easily predictable. Not only was there such considerable uncertainty in the value of the consignment, but also, being a relatively unusual business opportunity, Sainsbury could only speculate on the number of competitors coming into the running and the sort of bidding strategies they might employ. The problem which faced Sainsbury is clearly an example of what is conventionally described as a non-cooperative, competitive sealed bidding game. Christenson (1965), although finding that a game-theoretic model described the bidding pattern for US Government Bonds quite well, argued that, for prescriptive purposes, the game-theoretic model was unsatisfactory because of its weak equilibrium solutions: there seemed little incentive for a protagonist to adopt policies of low profitability. The weakness

*This case was originally developed by D. W. Bunn and Howard Thomas whilst both were faculty members at London Business School. Thanks are due to J. Sainsbury Ltd. for permission to present the case in a disguised form. This version is based upon a presentation made at a conference on 'Decision Theory and its Applications' Paris, 1975.

of these early models was partly due to the strong assumptions made about the information bases of the participants. More recent formulations of the problem, such as those of Wilson (1967), Lavalle (1967) and Rothkopf (1969) have incorporated the uncertainty each competitor has on the value of the tender and have thereby obtained 'stronger' solutions, though with still far from attractive profitability. Lavalle (1967) and Rothkopf (1969) also take a Bayesian approach by allowing the protagonist to assign subjective probabilities on the competitors' strategies. The probabilities are based upon judgment rather than mixed strategies obtained from the Minimax approach of von-Neumann & Morgenstern (1944) or the more general Equilibrium Principle of Nash (1951).

For such a non-repetitive game as that confronting Sainsbury, a Bayesian approach would appear quite attractive. It is pragmatic, based upon a less pessimistic decision criterion and avoids the contrivance of using artificial randomization in the once-only situation. Friedman (1956) formulated a Bayesian, decision analytic model which has been a basis for much of the applied prescriptive work in competitive bidding. However, in considering only the optimality of the protagonist, insufficient account has been taken of the 'interestedness' of the competitors. They would not behave as Natural Uncertainty, but would try to out-think the protagonist by simultaneously optimizing their own behavior. The protagonist's need is for an explicit consideration of out-thinking probabilities in contrast to the purely Bayesian argument that out-thinking should implicitly have been taken into account in arriving at one's final subjective distribution. The minimax criterion, recognizing the theoretically infinite regress inherent in attempting to incorporate out-thinking behavior in a decision criterion, deliberately avoids the problem by refusing to speculate on the opponent's strategies and considers only the worst that could happen. As we have mentioned, such approaches yield unacceptably (at least for prescriptive purposes) weak solutions. A simple way which we have found useful is to conceive of the final 'reassured' probability measure on the opponents' strategies to be the sum of a probability measure on typical behavior and a probability measure on out-thinking behavior. Typical behavior is that behavior generally expected of your opponent and which he would be conscious of being characteristic of himself. Out-thinking behavior is the extent to which he will depart for the typical in order to win the tender. Clearly this is no more than a structuring device to explicitly consider out-thinking – the distinction between typical and out-thinking behavior is suggested only as a conceptual device. Lavalle (1967) talks of the 'order of out-guessing' to reflect the extent to which an opponent will try to out-think what you think he thinks you think, etc. However one must also distinguish the extent to which each order shifts the distribution. For this reason, and in an attempt to deal with the problem in a reasonably practical way, we modified the 'typical behaviour' subjective distribution with a distribution over the possible 'shift' in typical behavior due to out-thinking.

## 12.2 DECISION ANALYSIS OF SAINSBURY'S PROBLEM

In considering the uncertainty in the value of the tender, three uncertain variables had to be taken into account: the proportion of butter in the haul and the future market prices of butter and sweetfat pertaining at the time when Sainsbury would receive it, if the bid were successful. Subjective distributions over the possible future market prices were easily assessed by the Chief Buyer, but there was very little satisfactory indication of the proportion of butter in the consignment.

Representatives of any of the companies invited to tender were allowed, if they wished, to inspect a sample of the haul chosen by a Customs Officer at random from the deep freeze, prior to submitting their bid. 250 of the 20,000 cartons had already been withdrawn from the deep freeze and when Sainsbury's Chief Buyer arrived, he was given 10 of these, without choice, to inspect. From a laboratory analysis, the sample was found to contain 8 cartons of butter and 2 of sweetfat, and was of satisfactory quality. However, it was considered that because of the small size of the sample, very little could be said about the proportion of butter in the full 500-ton haul, and furthermore, nothing could be gleaned from the markings on the cartons.

Some inspired reasoning on the part of the Chief Buyer was able to provide a more compelling indication. He argued that one could subjectively infer the proportion of butter by considering the geometry of the way in which the cartons were packed into the hold of the ship. If the hold contained both butter and sweetfat, then either the sweetfat would be separated on a pallet above the butter, or it would be separated by pallets on all sides. Given the rough dimensions of the hold and the assumption that such an importer would not conceivably take such risks if the butter proportion were less than 50 percent, the Chief Buyer was able subjectively to assess a probability distribution over the proportion of butter in the consignment.

Hence the subjective probability distributions, Tables 12.1, 12.2 and 12.3 were obtained.

Table 12.1
Probability distribution for butter proportion

| | | | | | | | |
|---|---|---|---|---|---|---|---|
| % Butter | 85 | 80 | 75 | 70 | 65 | 60 | 55 |
| Probability | 0.05 | 0.2 | 0.4 | 0.2 | 0.05 | 0.05 | 0.05 |

Table 12.2
Probability distribution for butter price

| | | | | | | |
|---|---|---|---|---|---|---|
| Butter price (£/ton) | 200 | 220 | 240 | 260 | 260 | 300 |
| Probability | 0.05 | 0.1 | 0.1 | 0.2 | 0.5 | 0.05 |

Table 12.3
Probability distribution for sweetfat price

| | | | | | | |
|---|---|---|---|---|---|---|
| Sweetfat price (£/ton) | 110 | 130 | 150 | 170 | 190 | 210 |
| Probability | 0.05 | 0.4 | 0.2 | 0.2 | 0.1 | 0.05 |

The value ($V$) of the consignment is clearly given by

$$V = fb + (1\text{-}f)s$$

where $f$, $b$ and $s$ are the uncertain quantities, assumed independent

$f$ = the proportion of butter in the haul
$b$ = Sainsbury's future buying price of butter
$s$ = Sainsbury's future buying price of sweetfat.

The probabilities over the range of $V$ were evaluated from the possible combinations of $f$, $b$ and $s$, and the resulting histogram is shown in Figure 12.1.

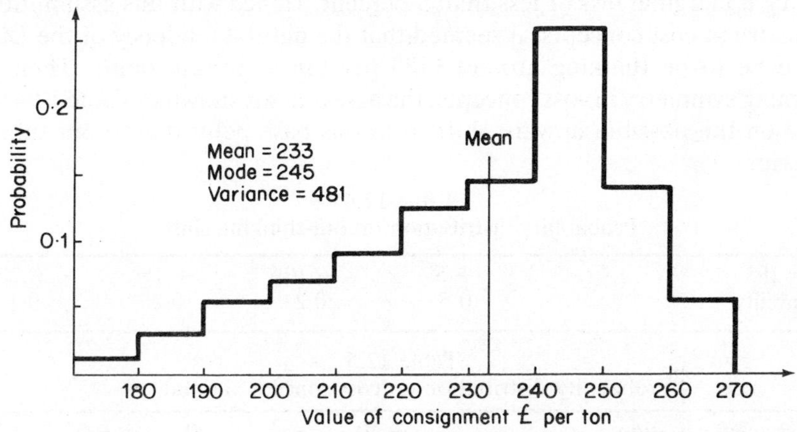


Figure 12.1 Probability distribution for Value of Consignment

Since this was effectively an opportunity to obtain raw materials at a discount, only the marginal costs of stockholding and administration were considered relevant and these amounted to some £8 per ton. Hence the expected value of the tender was evaluated at £225 per ton.

The Chief Buyer then had to face probably the most complex aspect of the whole problem: that of considering his pricing strategy in relation to the competitive nature of the tender. Through his contacts in the trade, he knew that there were four or five other large companies like Sainsburys in the running, who would have similar costs and who would most likely be thinking along the same lines. Also, there would doubtless be a larger number of smaller companies appearing, but who, it was recognized, generally have higher marginal costs, and with smaller weekly demands they would not be expected to bid for the whole tender.

Accordingly, the competition was divided into two sets, the large company set and the small company set. It was generally recognized that the small companies would have their best chance of success if they each were to bid only for their weekly demand (and hence avoid marginal stockholding costs) and hope that there would be a sufficient number to make up a composite bid which would be attractive enough for the Customs & Excise to split up the consignment. But from the fact that the Customs & Excise only set aside 150 cartons (10 being given out to each prospective bidder for examination) it was possible to infer roughly the number of companies invited to bid and with the marginal stockholding costs for the LC set not really being considered significant compared with the overall within set variability of the bid, the possibility of a composite SC set bid winning the tender was dismissed as very unlikely. With no indication of how the other LC competitors assessed the value for the consignment, an assumption of symmetry was made to start with.

Thus, Sainsbury's estimate of $V$ is also their best estimate of how the others were evaluating its value. It was suggested that the LC set of competitors would typically expect a 20 percent margin on this sort of business, with a risk of making a marginal loss of less than 5 percent. Hence with this assumption of symmetry in cost concepts, it seemed that the natural tendency of the LC set would be to be thinking around £185 per ton as a base point. Then, still assuming symmetry in cost concepts, the assessments shown in Table 12.4 were made on the possible upward shift from this base point due to out-thinking behavior.

Table 12.4
Probability distribution on out-thinking shift

| | | | | |
|---|---|---|---|---|
| Bid = 185 | + 5 | + 10 | + 15 | + 20 |
| Probability | 0.5 | 0.2 | 0.2 | 0.1 |

Table 12.5
Probability distribution on cost concept variability

| | | | | | |
|---|---|---|---|---|---|
| Cost concept variation | − 10 | − 5 | 0 | + 5 | + 10 |
| Probability | 0.05 | 0.2 | 0.5 | 0.2 | 0.05 |

Finally, relaxing the symmetry assumption to take account of the uncertainty in the postulated average £185 per ton base point, it was thought that the LC set average cost concept might be distributed about Sainsbury's estimate as shown in Table 12.5

Hence the average LC bid was conceived as being made up of the natural tendency base point, an out-thinking shift and cost-concept variability evaluated as in Table 12.6.

Table 12.6
Procedure for Determination of Average LC Bids

| | | | Out-thinking shift | | | |
|---|---|---|---|---|---|---|
| | | | .5 | .2 | .2 | .1 |
| | | 185 | + 5 | + 10 | + 15 | + 20 |
| Cost concept variation | .05 | − 10 | .025 | .01 | .01 | .005 |
| | .2 | − 5 | .1 | .04 | .04 | .02 |
| | .5 | 0 | .25 | .1 | .1 | .05 |
| | .2 | + 5 | .1 | .04 | .04 | .02 |
| | .05 | + 10 | .025 | .01 | .01 | .005 |

Table 12.7
CDF of Average LC Bids

| Average LC bid | $\leqslant 190$ | $\leqslant 195$ | $\leqslant 200$ | $\leqslant 205$ | $\leqslant 210$ |
|---|---|---|---|---|---|
| Probability | 0.435 | 0.680 | 0.865 | 0.965 | 0.995 |

Table 12.7 gives the average LC bid subjective probability distribution in cumulative form. The number of LC set competitors coming into the running was assumed to be adequately represented as a Poisson process, parameter 3. The distribution approximated to subjective judgment on the number of LC set competitors, and was moreover theoretically reasonable in view of the large number of potential competitors who could come into the bidding (although only three were expected), in the same way as a queuing system develops with Poisson arrivals.

If Sainsbury were to bid at '$i$', and $p_i$ is the probability of an average LC competitor bidding higher, then Sainsbury's probability of winning is exp ($-3p_i$). Hence that value of $i$ which maximized the expected marginal profit (EMP) was identified as in Table 12.8, where EMP = (225-$i$) (exp ($-3p_i$)).

Table 12.8
Calculation of EMP for Different Bids

| Bid '$i$' | 190 | 195 | 200 | 205 | 210 |
|---|---|---|---|---|---|
| $p_i$ | 0.565 | 0.320 | 0.135 | 0.035 | 0.005 |
| $\exp(-3p_i)$ | 0.19 | 0.39 | 0.77 | 0.90 | 0.99 |
| (225-$i$) | 35 | 30 | 25 | 20 | 15 |
| EMP | 6.6 | 11.7 | 19.2 | 18 | 14.8 |

Such an analysis prescribed a bid of £203 per ton, and J. Sainsbury Ltd. were subsequently awarded the consignment, profiting to the extent of some £40 per ton.

## DISCUSSION

The success of the model in this particular instance is a vindication but not a justification. The essential feature of the analysis is that of providing a 'thinking structure' with which the protagonist can build up his subjective probability distribution on competitive strategies. There is considerable psychological evidence (c.f. Kahneman and Tversky, 1973) to show that individuals do not aggregate probabilistic information at all well and that they need such algorithms to help structure their thinking. The algorithm we propose here is a simple additive model which was intuitively reasonable. Intuitive acceptability must be a necessary prerequisite for any thinking algorithm.

It was postulated that a competitor's bid ($x$) is the sum

$$x = b + e + s$$

where

$b$ = base point under the assumption of symmetry of cost-concepts to represent conventional norms of behavior.

$e$ = cost concept variability to take into account asymmetry of cost-concepts (i.e. different information bases).

$s$ = out-thinking shift to represent the extent to which the competitor will trade-off expected gain against a higher probability of winning.

$b$, $e$ and $s$ are subjectively assessed distributions (although in the Sainsbury case, $b$ was a point estimate) and are assumed to be cognitively independent. Thus we assume that whether or not a competitor underestimates the value of the tender, it will not affect his out-thinking behavior.

It is a feature of non-repetitive competitive bidding that such a highly subjective analysis needs to be carried out. In repetitive bidding, distributions on mark-up and errors in cost-estimation can be empirically constructed on the basis of past data. However, it is suggested that even these frequency distributions will require subjective modification in any particular instance, and that the model presented could provide a simple acceptable procedure in the more general case.

## REFERENCES


Christenson, C. (1965) *Strategic Aspects of Competitive Bidding for Corporate Securities*, Harvard.

Friedman, L. (1956) 'A Competitive Bidding Strategy', *Ops. Res.* **4**.

Kahneman, D. & Tversky, A. (1973) 'Judgement under Uncertainty', a paper presented at the Fourth Research Conference on Subjective Probability, Utility and Decision Making, Rome. Reprinted in G. M. Kaufman and H. Thomas *Modern Decision Analysis*, Penguin, 1977.

Lavalle, I. (1967) 'A Bayesian Approach to an Individual Player's Choice of Bid in a Competitive Sealed Auction.' *Mgt Sci. B.*

Nash, J. F. (1951) 'Non-cooperative Games,' *Annals of Mathematics,* **54**.

Rothkopf, M. (1969) 'A Model of Rational Competitive Bidding,' *Mgt. Sci.* **15**.

Von Neumann, J. & Morgenstern O. (1944) *The Theory of Games and Economic Behaviour*, Princeton.

Wilson, R. (1967) 'Competitive bidding with asymmetric information', *Mgt. Sci.* **13B**


## QUESTIONS FOR DISCUSSION

1. Critically evaluate the analytical approach adopted within the case.
2. Suggest alternative approaches which either make different problem assumptions or use alternative solution procedures.

*Chapter 13*

# *Quantock Plastics Ltd;* A Case Study of a Decision Problem in the Plastics Industry*


## SUMMARY

Quantock Plastics is involved in a facilities planning and capital investment decision in relation to the acquisition of additional plastics extrusion equipment. The dialogue between members of the evaluation team represents closely the events which took place in the actual decision situation. Owing to the need for a quick decision, a relatively straightforward 'first-pass' decision and risk analysis was carried out. This initial analysis demonstrated the need to address the strategy alternatives such as the acquisition of a custom-built, special-purpose machine.


## 13.1 INTRODUCTION

On 8 April 1970, Mr John Chisholm, Managing Director of Quantock Plastics Ltd., received a telephone call from his immediate superior, Mr Edward Kendall, Chief Executive of the Plastics Division of Finar International Ltd. After the usual preliminaries Mr Kendall said: 'John, I've just had a call from Charles Beywood of Purfleet Paper and Packaging. It seems that they installed a coextrusion casting machine a couple of months ago and now they find they can't operate it properly. On top of this they have cash flow problems and Charles was ringing me to offer Finar the first refusal to purchase the machine.

It seems to me that this might be a very profitable deal for either Quantock or the Australian company since the negotiating price is fairly low, around £50,000. The main problem is that Charles wants to know our answer in 10 days, that is by 17 April. Do you think we can get together a reasonable case by then?'

*This case was originally developed by Geoff Easton (now at Lancaster University) and Howard Thomas whilst at the London Business School.

John Chisholm replied, ‘Well, as you know, Edward, I am in Germany and the States from Monday for about 3 weeks so I will ask Don Edwards to get a team together to tackle it and come up with some specific recommendations to discuss with you by, say, the 15th.’

‘OK, John, that sounds fine. Tell Don he is free to contact Purfleet himself and ask him to ring me if he has any problems. Have a good trip.’

## 13.2 BACKGROUND

Finar International Ltd. is a large London-based chemical paper and plastics company. The original company, Finar Ltd., was engaged in the manufacture of heavy and speciality chemicals and diversified by buying a large paper company and several small plastics convertors. There are three main divisions; chemicals, paper and plastics, each with a chief executive sitting on the main board. The international aspects of Finar’s operations are mainly confined to the old British Commonwealth countries and Europe. The geographical distribution had been largely determined by the location of the overseas subsidiaries of the acquired companies.

The plastics division comprises seven companies of varying size and technical sophistication, concentrating on converting plastic resins by different processes to a variety of end products. The main processes involved are blow and injection moulding, thermoforming and blowing and casting films. There is also a plastic adhesives company. Finar International Ltd. manufactures little or no plastic resins and there is no question of vertical integration.

Quantock Plastics Ltd. is situated in the West Country and is the only producer of plastic films in the division. The two main production processes are blowing and casting.

Blown film is produced by melting a plastic resin such as polyethylene or nylon and extruding it vertically through a thin annular ring through the centre of which cooled compressed air is blown. The result is a large vertical sausage-shaped balloon of rapidly cooling plastic which is deflated over a series of rollers and finally round into a reel. This reel of doubled material is subsequently slit along one edge to produce a wide (120 inch), thin (around 1/1000 inch) film. The process is relatively slow but the equipment is inexpensive and easy to run.

Quantock Plastics produced only blown film until 1967. Late in 1965 a team of managers from the company visited the Canadian company and a number of US convertors. They were impressed by the market possibilities for coextruded films and decided to study the situation more closely when they returned to the UK.

Coextrusion is a process by which two molten plastic films are united at the moment of extrusion. The main advantage of two-ply films is that the properties of the individual components can complement each other. For example, a film with good oxygen barrier properties could be married to one with high mechanical strength. The process is often used to provide an economic method of utilizing high-cost plastic films with interesting properties. A thin film of the expensive resin can be coextruded with a thick film of a cheaper 'carrier' film. Two-ply films were already being produced in large quantities by the process of lacquer lamination. This consists of 'glueing' together two films which had previously been produced on blow extrusion machines. The process is expensive both because it is slow, to allow the lacquer 'glue' to dry, and because the films laminated in this way have to be thick enough to withstand mechanical handling.

The main process used for coextrusion in 1965 in the United States was a patented blowing process. The machine was not expensive but was even slower than existing monoextrusion blowing machines. The main reason for its popularity was that it was the first process which employed a method of guaranteeing the adhesion of the two films. It did this by introducing ozone into the space between two annular rings on a blowing unit. This gas reacted with most of the common blowing plastics and virtually guaranteed a good bond.

More recently a number of US convertors had commissioned coextrusion casting machines with the express intention of getting round the tight patent coverage on the blowing process. Casting films is carried out by melting a plastic resin and forcing it through a narrow slit in a steel barrel so as to form a curtain of molten plastic which falls onto an ice-water-cooled chill roller. The plastic cools and sets and is then wound up into a reel. Coextrusion is achieved by using two extrusion barrels and nipping the semi-molten films beteen two chill rollers. The adhesion is promoted by the use of an arc discharge tube situated between the films. While this is not as good as the ozone system convertors, they found in practice that by paying attention to the running conditions and controlling the machines to within fine limits, they could obtain films that were satisfactory for most purposes.

After several months study of coextrusion film technology and likely markets, Quantock Plastics Ltd. entered into a knowhow agreement with an American convertor, Albany Packaging Inc., to build a coextrusion casting machine. The decision was largely a technical one. It appeared that the range of films that could be produced by blowing and casting was fairly similar, though more operating expertise was required in the case of the casting machine. The capital cost of a casting machine was higher, but it operated at higher speeds and the royalties required for the blowing machine were not small. Finally, casting produced a better film surface and more even thickness and this was likely to be an important factor in the markets Quantock Plastics Ltd. was about to enter. With the active cooperation of a machine manufacturer Quantock were able to design and build a coextrusion casting machine (C1) in under a year. However, it took another 6 months, some redesign work and intensive operator training before the machine could be handed over to the production department late in 1966.

In the early 1960s Quantock had concentrated mainly on the heavy end of the plastic film business. The main products were heavy-duty colored polyethylene films for agricultural building and industrial uses. However, interchange of personnel within the Finar International Group meant that a number of people in Quantock Plastics Ltd. had gained experience of more sophisticated up-stream markets. The appointment of a new Commercial Director with experience of speciality chemical marketing also led the company to question its marketing policies, or lack of them. The major effect was to lead Quantock Plastics to develop expertise in thinner gauge films and more esoteric resins to serve the packaging films market. The new customers tended to be mainly traditional flexible packaging convertors who laminated the films to paper or aluminium foil, printed them and then sold them to pharmaceutical, detergent, toiletries and confectionery manufacturers. However, a few contracts were obtained with end-use manufacturers who printed the plain films that Quantock Plastics supplied.

The decision to install coextrusion capacity was probably influenced by the success achieved by the company in this new field and by the prospect of the continuing expansion of the market for packaged goods and therefore packaging films.

Quantock Plastics was the first UK firm to install coextrusion casting capacity, although several blowing units using the patented US system had been installed in the UK in the previous two years. With a small price advantage over the blown films and a large price advantage over laminated films, Quantock Plastics quickly captured a major share of the available market. The revitalized commercial department pioneered new uses and developed new customers and within 2 years C1 was operating to 3-shift capacity.

In late 1968 Mr John Chisholm was appointed Managing Director. His first task was to set up a study group to decide whether or not to buy a second coextrusion machine. The study group reported early in 1969 and the result was a foregone conclusion. The main problem was seen to be how to contain demand until the new machine could be installed. The Finar board agreed the capital requisition in March 1969. C2, a bigger, faster machine than CI, was scheduled to be installed in June/July 1970 and become fully operational during the next year. The study group further recommended that the position be reviewed midway through 1971 since the market forecasts indicated that another new machine might be required in 1972.

Immediately after receiving the telephone call from Mr Kendall, Mr John Chisholm called Mr Don Edwards (Production Director) and Mr Alan Osborne (Coextrusion Department Manager) into his office and explained the situation. Mr Edwards' immediate reaction was that it would not be possible to complete the study in 10 days. The C2 study group of which he had been a member took 3 months to report. Mr Osborne said that in any case he would have to run trials on the machine before he could give any opinion about its usefulness. He suggested that this could be used as a very good excuse to push back the decision date a week or two. Mr Chisholm decided to contact Purfleet Paper and Packaging direct and after talking to Charles Beywood managed to arrange for trials to be run on Monday 20 April and a final decision postponed until the 30th. He also obtained permission for Mr Osborne to contact the

Technical Manager at Purfleet by telephone to obtain some details about the machine.

Mr Edwards suggested that a team be chosen immediately to work exclusively on this project for the next 3 weeks. The following people were agreed on: Mr Edwards, Mr Osborne, Mr Phillip Artis (Engineering Manager), Mr Vernon Ould (Marketing Analyst), Mr Michael Ryan (Chief Accountant) and Mr Peter Sadler (Corporate Planner) (see Table 13.1). The first meeting was scheduled for the next day.

Table 13.1 Quantock Plastics Ltd. Organization Chart

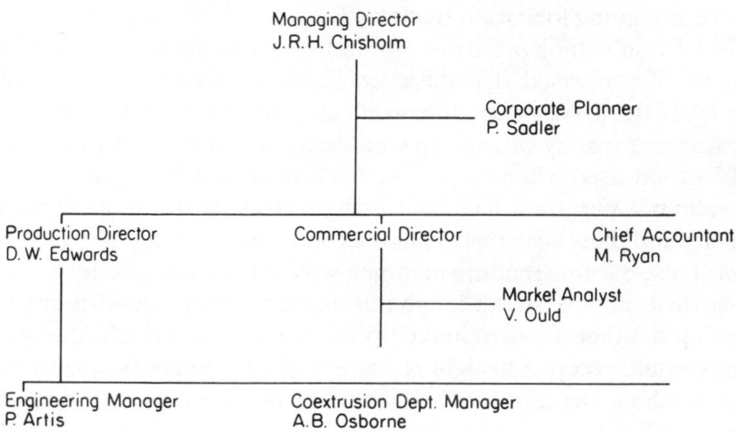


## 13.3 FIRST MEETING, THURSDAY, 10 APRIL 1970

Mr Edwards explained the situation to the group and went on:

*Edwards*: I think we should treat this like the normal capital requisition we have to make to the Group. Only in this case we have about two weeks to complete all the work. Peter, do you think we will have enough time to get all the information we need?

*Sadler*: Normally I would say not, but since we did the C2 case about a year ago, I would think that all we have to do is to update the information. The most critical element will be the market forecasts but we know the sources now so it shouldn't be too difficult to see if any new trends have emerged. It will also be interesting to see how close we were with our forecasts for 1969. Vernon should be able to get the figures within a week.

*Ould*: One thing that will affect the share we are likely to get of the coextruded film market is the range of films we can produce. Do you know, Alan, if the Purfleet machine will be able to handle the same range of films as say C1 and C2?

*Osborne*: It's designed to produce the same range but I won't know for certain until I see it. All I have at the moment is secondhand information

from the Technical Manager at Purfleet. Since they can't operate the machine I'm not sure how much that is worth. As far as I can judge a useful approximation would be to say that it is very similar to C1. It's designed by the same firm as well.
*Sadler*: We'll work on that basis, at least in the first instance. It won't be too difficult to change the figures if you find out that they are likely to be wrong.
*Ryan*: I had better look out my working papers in the C2 case and update the cost forecasts. Are we going to handle the price/value added problem in the same way? You remember that with so many slightly different raw material costs we used an average value added figure per ton of throughput. Are we still going to work it that way?
*Sadler*: I don't think we have any option particularly in view of the time element. We assumed that the average value added would gradually drop, didn't we? Resin costs probably won't change very much but prices are likely to soften as capacity catches up with demand. That was the key assumption that Vernon used when he did the C2 forecasts. I think that assumption is still valid but Vernon will in any case have to check on competitors' installed capacity and their investment plans as far as that is possible.
*Ryan*: I also assume that the manning will be the same as C1.
*Edwards*: I suppose so, although this might be a good opportunity to reduce manning in other areas to make up the new crews. I doubt though that the unions would accept a straight reduction. We may make some progress but I think we should assume that any labor will be additional to the current labor force.
*Ryan*: I presume we can continue to forecast that wage awards are likely to be 8 percent? This will be the main factor in the additional burden.
*Edwards*: I'm afraid so.
*Artis*: I think that space might well be a problem. Although we have room in the extension we built to house C2, we have got to find somewhere to put the, additional slitting and rewinding machines as well as the increased work in progress (WIP). The present WIP store will only just handle the expected output of C2. We may have to convert the existing resin store and build a new one somewhere else on the factory site. I'll have to get an estimate from the Group Architect's department on what that might cost.
*Sadler*: Alan has already arranged to go to Purfleet on Monday to get an idea of what reinstallation costs are likely to be. Perhaps Phillip ought to go along too and check on the space problem.
*Edwards*: That sounds reasonable. Peter, you will have to do the DCF calculations for the capital requisition. I presume you will do the usual optimistic, most likely, and pessimistic format? Do you know now who is to give you the different items of information?
*Sadler*: Yes, I think so.
*Edwards*: Good. If I wanted a first rough outline of the case by next Friday when would you require your figures by?
*Sadler*: Next Wednesday, hopefully before lunch.

*Edwards*: Right. Everybody agree? The next meeting will be Friday 17th in my office at 9.30 a.m.

## 13.4 SECOND MEETING, FRIDAY 17 APRIL 1970

Mr Don Edwards opened the meeting.

*Edwards*: Have you managed to do the DCF calculations, Peter?

*Sadler*: Yes. I'm sorry that I couldn't circulate them before the meeting but they were only typed this morning. Perhaps we could look at them for a moment and then I can explain each item in detail (Table 13.2).

*Edwards*: This looks very promising, Peter.

*Sadler*: Yes, but I would like to caution the group about making a decision before we have had a chance to review and discuss the assumptions made in this preliminary analysis of our problem. First of all I have taken a 10-year period but starting from 1971. Alan and Phillip are convinced we are not going to have the engineering staff to enable us to get the machine installed until mid-1971. It will all depend on the commissioning period of C2, which should end around Christmas.

*Osborne*: It may be even later than that. In any case I don't think we could get as much as a half-year's production from the Purfleet machine in 1971.

*Sadler*: Vernon has checked through the market forecasts and we can see no reason to change them very much from those used in the C2 case (Table 13.3). In fact the actual figure for 1969 was above the most likely estimate we made in 1968. The mix of films has changed somewhat and this is reflected in the reduced figure we have used for value added per ton. We have assumed a 25 percent market share throughout. This is probably a reasonable long-term figure. We realize that when we have excess capacity we could increase this figure and when our capacity is below 25 percent of the market we could reduce demand by putting prices up. But the short-term strategy in a particular situation is also governed by other factors so we feel the use of a straight 25 percent across the board is justifiable. The actual sales in any year are indicated by underlining. For example, the most likely case sales are below capacity until 1974, and at capacity thereafter. I think it is important to realize that even in the pessimistic case the total market is forecast to increase by around 6 percent a year. For the most part industry capacity should be in balance with demand.

*Artis*: The sales figures here aren't the same as those in the DCF calculations.

*Sadler*: No, because in fact we are only interested in the additional sales that buying the Purfleet machine will enable us to get. All the figures given in the DCF calculations are additional to those we would have if we were only operating C1 and C2.

*Edwards*: What rather worries me is the amount of capital involved. The final figure is nearly 3 times the cost of the machine. Also why is the pessimistic figure different from the most likely and optimistic?

Table 13.2 Case for the Purchase of Coextrusion Machine from Purfleet Paper and Packaging

1. *Most Likely*

| | | | | | | | | | |
|---|---|---|---|---|---|---|---|---|---|
| Additional sales (tons) | 700 | 1200 | 1580 | 1870 | 2100 | 2100 | 2100 | 2100 | 2100 |
| Additional value added (£000) | 147 | 247 | 319 | 370 | 407 | 399 | 390 | 382 | 374 |
| Additional overhead (£000) | −110 | −119 | −130 | −141 | −152 | −164 | −177 | −191 | −206 |
| Additional tax (£000) | −9 | −45 | −70 | −86 | −96 | −88 | −79 | −70 | −121 |
| Additional fixed capital (£000) | −170 | | | | | | | | |
| Additional grants (£000) | | +20 | | | | | | | |
| Additional working capital (£000) | −73 | −50 | −36 | −25 | −18 | +4 | +4 | +4 | +150 |
| Additional cash flow (£000) | −215 | 53 | 83 | 118 | 141 | 151 | 138 | 125 | 197 |

Net Present Value = £189,000

2. *Optimistic*

| | | | | | | | | | |
|---|---|---|---|---|---|---|---|---|---|
| Additional sales (tons) | 800 | 2100 | 2100 | 2100 | 2100 | 2100 | 2100 | 2100 | 2100 |
| Additional value added (£000) | 168 | 432 | 424 | 416 | 407 | 399 | 390 | 382 | 374 |
| Additional overhead (£000) | −110 | −119 | −130 | −141 | −152 | −164 | −177 | −191 | −206 |
| Additional tax (£000) | −17 | −119 | −112 | −104 | −96 | −88 | −80 | −71 | −121 |
| Additional fixed capital (£000) | −170 | | | | | | | | |
| Additional grant (£000) | | +20 | | | | | | | |
| Additional working capital (£000) | −84 | −132 | 4 | 4 | 4 | 4 | 4 | 4 | 150 |
| Additional cash flow (£000) | −213 | 82 | 186 | 175 | 164 | 152 | 139 | 125 | 197 |

Net Present Value = £445,000

3. *Pessimistic*

| | | | | | | | | | |
|---|---|---|---|---|---|---|---|---|---|
| Additional sales (tons) | 130 | 580 | 950 | 1080 | 1360 | 1580 | 1810 | 2010 | 2100 |
| Additional value added (£000) | 27 | 120 | 192 | 214 | 264 | 300 | 336 | 366 | 374 |
| Additional overhead (£000) | −110 | −119 | −130 | −141 | −152 | −164 | −177 | −191 | −206 |
| Additional tax (£000) | 41 | 5 | −17 | −21 | −37 | −46 | −56 | −62 | −119 |
| Additional fixed capital (£000) | −230 | | | | | | | | |
| Additional grant (£000) | | 30 | | | | | | | |
| Additional working capital (£000) | −13 | −47 | −36 | −11 | −25 | −18 | −18 | −15 | −150 |
| Additional cash flow (£000) | −285 | −11 | 9 | 41 | 50 | 72 | 85 | 98 | 199 |

Net Present Value = £60,000

Table 13.3 Market Forecasts for Coextruded Plastic Films. 1970–1979 (tons)

| | | | 1967 | 1968 | 1969 | 1970 | 1971 | 1972 | 1973 | 1974 | 1975 | 1976 | 1977 | 1978 | 1979 |
|---|---|---|---|---|---|---|---|---|---|---|---|---|---|---|---|
| Total market | : | Actual | 4800 | 9200 | 15000 | | | | | | | | | | |
| Quantock sales | : | Actual | 1200 | 1800 | 1800 | | | | | | | | | | |
| *Most likely* | | | | | | | | | | | | | | | |
| Total market | : | Forecast | | | | 21000 | 24100 | 26200 | 27500 | 28700 | 29800 | 30500 | 31000 | 32000 | 32500 |
| Quantock | : | Forecast | | | | 5250 | 6000 | 6500 | 6880 | 7170 | 7450 | 7630 | 7760 | 8000 | 8130 |
| Quantock | : | Capacity | | | | 3100 | 6100 | 7400 | 7400 | 7400 | 7400 | 7400 | 7400 | 7400 | 7400 |
| *Optimistic* | | | | | | | | | | | | | | | |
| Total market | : | Forecast | | | | 24300 | 28400 | 31400 | 33000 | 34300 | 35000 | 35000 | 35000 | 35000 | 35000 |
| Quantock | : | Forecast | | | | 6080 | 7100 | 7850 | 8260 | 8590 | 8750 | 8750 | 8750 | 8750 | 8750 |
| Quantock | : | Capacity | | | | 3100 | 6100 | 7400 | 7400 | 7400 | 7400 | 7400 | 7400 | 7400 | 7400 |
| *Pessimistic* | | | | | | | | | | | | | | | |
| Total market | : | Forecast | | | | 19300 | 21700 | 23500 | 25000 | 25500 | 26600 | 27500 | 28400 | 29200 | 30000 |
| Quantock | : | Forecast | | | | 4830 | 5430 | 5880 | 6250 | 6380 | 6660 | 6880 | 7110 | 7310 | 7500 |
| Quantock | : | Capacity | | | | 3100 | 6100 | 7400 | 7400 | 7400 | 7400 | 7400 | 7400 | 7400 | 7400 |

Table 13.4 Capital Outlay on Purfleet Project

| | £ |
|---|---|
| Purchase price | 50,000 |
| Uplift, transport, reinstallation | 25,000 |
| Essential modifications and additions | 25,000 |
| Slitting machine | 20,000 |
| Rewinding machines (2) | 35,000 |
| Additional resin silo | 10,000 |
| Contingency | 5,000 |
| | 170,000 |
| Conversion of resin store to work in progress | 15,000 |
| New resin store | 45,000 |
| | 60,000 |

*Osborne*: There's a breakdown of the capital costs on the next page. (Table 13.4). The main thing we tend to forget is that we need ancilliary equipment for slitting and rewinding whenever we install increased extruder capacity. The minimum we could get away with would be 1 slitter and 2 rewinders. This affects overheads too since we need extra crew on 3 shifts for these machines. The modifications involved are mainly instrumentation and controls. Peter and Phillip decided that we could probably rearrange the WIP store and only in the pessimistic case would it be necessary to build the new resin store.

*Edwards*: That's another point, Peter. Why not have 3 sets of figures for capital, overheads, etc? I'm sure we are not particularly certain about any of the figures. Why only optimistic, most likely and pessimistic figures for the market forecasts?

*Sadler*: The main reasons are the amount of work involved and interpretation. If we used 3 figures for each variable we would have to work out over 100 possible answers. That means several weeks' work and what would the figures mean anyway when we got them? The market is in any case the most important element and the one least under our control. However, another aspect which has worried me about the group's use of 3 figures is that different people mean different things by optimistic, most likely and pessimistic. For example, Vernon and I talked about the market estimates and tried to agree on the probability of each forecast being about right. We finally agreed on the figures 0.2 for optimistic, 0.45 for most likely and 0.35 for pessimistic. I think it might be useful to develop this sort of analysis further.

*Edwards*: I agree, but only for our own use. The group will want the figures in the traditional format. Wouldn't it be better in any case to define the probabilities first to, say, 0.25, 0.5 and 0.25 and change the estimates to match the probabilities?

*Sadler*: That was more or less my thought. I'll write a note on it when we have finished this project. I might even have some idea about how to incorporate 3 values for each variable. Anyway there are still some other points to clear up in the present case. Michael, was there anything special about the overhead increase?

*Ryan*: No. It was larger than I first thought because of the additional machines. It is mostly labor costs together with consumables, spares, power services etc. I don't think we will be far out in these figures. I calculated tax on the basis of 40 percent and you may notice that the grant is fairly low. This is because there is no grant on second-hand machines or buildings. Working capital was calculated at 50 percent of value added. The present figure is around 46 percent so I think this is a justifiable figure. I assumed that the scrap value of the machine would be zero after 10 years but that we would recover 80 percent of working capital. That about covers my areas.

*Sadler*: The discount rate was the usual 17 percent after tax that the group requires on new capacity projects and as you can see we meet that in the mostly likely and optimistic cases but not the pessimistic.

*Edwards*: Well, even if the machine is not quite such a bargain as I first thought it still looks a good bet. I suggest we recommend purchase subject to the trials being successful and after checking back on the detailed calculations.

*Sadler*: As I said earlier I'm not so sure we should make a decision yet. What we are really deciding is how to meet the estimated demand. There might be a more profitable way of doing it by, for example, buying another machine like C2. Shouldn't we judge the decision about the Purfleet machine against the alternatives open to us? Alan, looking at the market forecasts, what kind of machine would you suggest as an alternative to the Purfleet one?

*Osborne*: Well, if I had the choice I would certainly prefer to design our own machine like C2 rather than try to adapt someone else's ideas. In fact I think a machine like C2 would be about the right capacity, although even before we have installed it I know some modifications I would make. The main problem would be timing. Redesign would take some time but delivery would be the main problem. It could easily take a year.

*Edwards*: I think I see your point, Peter. Can you and Alan get together and make some estimates of capital cost, etc? I assume most of the other factors would remain the same. We can compare the results with the case for the Purfleet machine and see which alternative looks most profitable.

*Artis*: If we have time to consider other alternatives, then Alan and I have been discussing another two uses for the Purfleet machine. Firstly, the drive on the Purfleet machine and the rollers are engineered to produce at speeds near that of C2 but it's limited by the barrels and screw capacity.

We could cannabalize it and with chunks of C1 we could probably produce a machine of the same capacity as C2. It wouldn't be a particularly elegant piece of design but it would work. The second use also involves taking C1 apart but to obtain a machine capable of triple extrusion. I know they are doing this in the States now. I'm not sure what markets they intend to use the films in but Vernon could probably find out by ringing the Canadian company. There would be a tremendous amount of design work but I can't see in principle why it can't be done.

*Edwards*: OK, we had better add those two to the list if you and Alan are reasonably confident that the engineering is possible. Peter, you had better work fairly closely with Phillip and Alan over the next week because I want us to be able to come up with a firm decision after our next meeting today week. That's the 24th. I have to see Mr Kendall on the Monday in London.

## 13.5 THIRD MEETING, FRIDAY 24 APRIL 1970

*Edwards*: I assume that you all have copies of the DCF calculations for the purchase of C3 and the modification of C1 using the Purfleet machine (Tables 13.5 and 13.6). I see that you haven't got any figures for the triple extrusion alternative, Peter. Couldn't you get the figures in time?

*Sadler*: We got enough to realize that it was a non-starter.

*Osborne*: The basic problem is operating speed. With the makeshift design we would have to use, we would be operating at half the normal speed. The value added would be of course higher than for double-ply films but not 50 percent higher. So the more multiple-ply film business we obtained the less money we would make.

*Ould*: I've had a quick look at the markets involved and I suggest that we should perhaps look into the possibility of buying a purpose-built machine. I'm convinced that, particularly in the medical market, there are many opportunities.

*Edwards*: OK, but let's just concentrate on the job in hand. We can tie up the loose ends later. Peter, have you got a detailed breakdown of the capital cost for C3? Five hundred thousand is £100,000 up on C2 and in only two years.

*Sadler*: The extra costs are due to increased prices, modifications and additions and the inclusion of the new resin store. I can let you have the details if you want them. The £120,000 for modification of C1 includes 1 extra slitting machine for operation on 2 shifts. We have checked with the machine manufacturers and this would be about 60 percent of the cost of doing it from scratch without using the Purfleet machine.

*Osborne*: Incidentally, the trials on the machine were OK in the sense that everything worked. The main problem was operator inexperience. They certainly never got anywhere near acceptable quality while we were there. I don't know what possessed them to try this line of business. They haven't even any ordinary extrusion experience.

Table 13.5 Purchase of a new coextrusion machine C3

| | 1971 | 1972 | 1973 | 1974 | 1975 | 1976 | 1977 | 1978 | 1979 |
|---|---|---|---|---|---|---|---|---|---|
| 1. *Most likely* | | | | | | | | | |
| Additional sales (tons) | | 1200 | 1580 | 1870 | 2150 | 2330 | 2460 | 2700 | 2830 |
| Additional value added (£000) | | 247 | 319 | 370 | 417 | 443 | 458 | 492 | 504 |
| Additional overheads (£000) | | −119 | −130 | −141 | −152 | −164 | −177 | −191 | −206 |
| Additional tax (£000) | | −35 | −60 | −76 | −90 | −96 | −97 | −104 | −274 |
| Additional fixed capital (£000) | | −500 | | | | | | | |
| Additional grants (£000) | | | 100 | | | | | | |
| Additional working capital (£000) | | −123 | −36 | −25 | −24 | −13 | −7 | −17 | 200 |
| Additional cash flow (£000) | | −530 | 193 | 128 | 151 | 170 | 177 | 180 | 430 |
| Net Present Value = £131,000 | | | | | | | | | |
| 2. *Optimistic* | | | | | | | | | |
| Additional sales (tons) | | 1200 | 2960 | 3290 | 3450 | 3450 | 3450 | 3450 | 3450 |
| Additional value added (£000) | | 247 | 598 | 652 | 670 | 655 | 643 | 628 | 614 |
| Additional overheads (£000) | | −119 | −130 | −141 | −152 | −164 | −177 | −191 | −206 |
| Additional tax (£000) | | −35 | −171 | −188 | −191 | −180 | −170 | −159 | −203 |
| Additional fixed capital (£000) | | −500 | | | | | | | |
| Additional grants (£000) | | | +100 | | | | | | |
| Additional working capital (£000) | | −123 | −175 | −27 | −9 | 7 | 12 | 15 | 240 |
| Additional cash flow (£000) | | −530 | 222 | 296 | 318 | 318 | 308 | 293 | 345 |
| Net Present Value = £384,000 | | | | | | | | | |
| 3. *Pessimistic* | | | | | | | | | |
| Additional sales (tons) | | 580 | 950 | 1080 | 1360 | 1580 | 1810 | 2010 | 2200 |
| Additional value added (£000) | | 119 | 192 | 214 | 264 | 300 | 337 | 366 | 392 |
| Additional overheads (£000) | | −119 | −130 | −141 | −152 | −164 | −177 | −191 | −206 |
| Additional tax (£000) | | 16 | −9 | −13 | −29 | −39 | −48 | −54 | −122 |
| Additional fixed capital (£000) | | −500 | | | | | | | |
| Additional grants (£000) | | | 100 | | | | | | |
| Additional working capital (£000) | | −59 | −36 | −11 | −25 | −18 | −18 | −15 | 160 |
| Additional cash flow (£000) | | −425 | 118 | 49 | 58 | 79 | 94 | 106 | 224 |
| Net Present Value = −£33,000 | | | | | | | | | |

Table 13.6 Modification of existing C1 to C2 standards

| | 1971 | 1972 | 1973 | 1974 | 1975 | 1976 | 1977 | 1978 | 1979 |
|---|---|---|---|---|---|---|---|---|---|
| 1. *Most likely* | | | | | | | | | |
| Additional sales (tons) | −500 | 1100 | 1100 | 1100 | 1100 | 1100 | 1100 | 1100 | 1100 |
| Additional value added (£000) | −105 | 227 | 222 | 218 | 213 | 209 | 205 | 200 | 196 |
| Additional overhead (£000) | −5 | −10 | −11 | −12 | −13 | −14 | −15 | −17 | −19 |
| Additional tax (£000) | 47 | −84 | −81 | −79 | −77 | −75 | −73 | −70 | −100 |
| Additional fixed capital (£000) | −120 | | | | | | | | |
| Additional grants (£000) | | 10 | | | | | | | |
| Additional working capital (£000) | −52 | −61 | 2 | 2 | 2 | 2 | 2 | 2 | 80 |
| Additional cash flow (£000) | −235 | 82 | 132 | 129 | 125 | 122 | 119 | 115 | 147 |
| | | | Net Present Value = £192,000 | | | | | | |
| 2. *Optimistic* | | | | | | | | | |
| Additional sales (tons) | −500 | 1100 | 1100 | 1100 | 1100 | 1100 | 1100 | 1100 | 1100 |
| Additional value added (£000) | −105 | 227 | 222 | 218 | 213 | 209 | 205 | 200 | 196 |
| Additional overhead (£000) | −5 | −10 | −11 | −12 | −13 | −14 | −15 | −17 | −19 |
| Additional tax (£000) | 47 | −84 | −81 | −79 | −77 | −75 | −73 | −70 | −100 |
| Additional fixed capital (£000) | −120 | | | | | | | | |
| Additional grants (£000) | | 10 | | | | | | | |
| Additional working capital (£000) | −52 | −61 | 2 | 2 | 2 | 2 | 2 | 2 | 80 |
| Additional cash flow (£000) | −235 | 82 | 132 | 129 | 125 | 122 | 119 | 115 | 147 |
| | | | Net Present Value = £192,000 | | | | | | |
| 3. *Pessimistic* | | | | | | | | | |
| Additional sales (tons) | −500 | 580 | 950 | 1080 | 1100 | 1100 | 1100 | 1100 | 1100 |
| Additional value added (£000) | −105 | 119 | 192 | 214 | 213 | 209 | 205 | 200 | 196 |
| Additional overhead (£000) | −5 | −10 | −11 | −12 | −13 | −14 | −15 | −17 | −19 |
| Additional tax (£000) | 47 | −40 | −69 | −79 | −77 | −75 | −13 | −70 | −100 |
| Additional fixed capital (£000) | −120 | | | | | | | | |
| Additional grants (£000) | −52 | −7 | −36 | −11 | | 2 | 2 | 2 | 80 |
| Additional working capital (£000) | | 10 | | | | | | | |
| Additional cash flow (£000) | −235 | 72 | 76 | 112 | 123 | 122 | 119 | 115 | 147 |
| | | | Net Present Value = £137,000 | | | | | | |

*Edwards*: Good. All we have to decide now is whether we want to buy it at all! It seems to me that the case is pretty clear. The return is best if we buy it and put into production as an additional production machine. Agreed?
*Osborne*: No, I don't really agree. The return is highest for the most likely and optimistic cases but the return is negative for the pessimistic case. As Peter and Vernon have said, there is a higher probability of the pessimistic forecast coming true. I am even less convinced than they are. I have seen too many rose-colored market forecasts in the past. It seems to me the best option is cannabalization. We may not make a fortune if the market takes off but at least we won't make a loss if the market drops below the pessimistic level.
*Edwards*: As I understand it, we can't start installation until after Christmas anyway and the actual figures for 1970 should be available then. So we don't have to make any decision until we have more information and are in a better position to see the long-term trends. I assume everyone agrees that we buy the Purfleet machine regardless of what we do with it anyway.
*Sadler*: I'm not sure. The main reason the C3 return is lower than that for the Purfleet machine is that we can't install it until mid-1972. But if we look at it another way, that means we could have two extra years before we commit ourselves irreversibly. We would probably have to start some design work before the second set of actual figures are out, but that shouldn't be too expensive. Vernon and I have been looking at this aspect using probabilities and I have some estimates here (Table 13.7) of how certain we would be of the long term given that certain sales had occurred in the next two years. For example, if we get an actual figure in 1970 in line with our optimistic forecast we think this will increase the probability that this will be correct, in the long term, to 0.6. Two in a row would make us 0.9 certain. What we thought would be of interest is how quickly we felt we could be fairly certain one way or the other. In other words after two years, most of the probabilities, 17 out of 27, are either above 0.75 or below 0.25. Vernon and I agree that the next two years will be critical in this market and we really feel that the difference in return between the Purfleet machine and C3 is not too big a price to pay to be more certain about the outcome.
*Edwards*: I'm not sure I understand all the details but I can see what you are getting at. I'm sorry but I just can't agree with you. We will certainly have a better idea of the long-term trends in the market in two years, but I'm sure that when you get there you won't be nearly so certain as you think you will be. We will be back in the same position as we are now. You can carry on this sort of analysis and figure juggling forever. My feeling is that we can't afford to hold off any longer. I've come to realize during our investigations that the main virtue of the Purfleet machine is not that it is cheap but that it's available. We need to get in now and tie up the market before the competitors get in. I'm convinced we should buy this machine; that is unless Peter and Vernon want to change their market forecasts in the light of their later analyses.

Table 13.7

| | Now | After 1970 actual figures | After 1970/71 actual figures |
|---|---|---|---|
| 1. | *Probability of optimistic forecast being correct* | | |
| | 0.2 | H 0.6 | HH 0.9 |
| | | | HM 0.7 |
| | | | HL 0.5 |
| | | M 0.3 | MH 0.4 |
| | | | MM 0.05 |
| | | | ML 0.0 |
| | | L 0.1 | LH 0.3 |
| | | | LM 0.0 |
| | | | LL 0.0 |
| 2. | *Probability of most likely forecast being correct* | | |
| | 0.45 | H 0.1 | HH 0.1 |
| | | | HM 0.2 |
| | | | HL 0.3 |
| | | M 0.8 | MH 0.5 |
| | | | MM 0.9 |
| | | | ML 0.7 |
| | | L 0.1 | LH 0.4 |
| | | | LM 0.2 |
| | | | LL 0.0 |
| 3 | *Probability of pessimistic forecast being correct* | | |
| | 0.35 | H 0.1 | HH 0.0 |
| | | | HM 0.1 |
| | | | HL 0.2 |
| | | M 0.2 | MH 0.1 |
| | | | MM 0.05 |
| | | | ML 0.3 |
| | | L 0.7 | LH 0.3 |
| | | | LM 0.8 |
| | | | LL 1.0 |

Note: H denotes high (optimistic)
M denotes most likely
L denotes low (pessimistic)

*Sadler*: No, we still think that the figures are the best available. It's just that we feel we are being stampeded because of the availability of this machine. Waiting a year or two for developments won't cost us very much but it could save us from making a costly error.

*Edwards*: I know that both Alan and Phillip are eager to buy this machine so clearly we can't reach a unanimous decision. I was going to suggest anyway that you accompany me on Monday, Peter, when I meet Mr Kendall to make the final decision. I think it is even more essential that you do so now that we can't agree on a recommendation. We'll both have to put our viewpoints and let Mr Kendall make the final decision.

Thank you for your help, gentlemen. I'll let you know the outcome of Monday's meeting sometime on Tuesday.

## QUESTIONS FOR DISCUSSION

1. Figure 13.1 gives an initial, 'first-pass' decision tree analysis of Quantock's problem. Critically evaluate this approach.
2. What alternative approaches would you suggest?
3. Design a risk analysis simulation approach and use it to throw further light upon the problem. (Hint: for example, consider such issues as cash flow analysis and sensitivity analysis.)

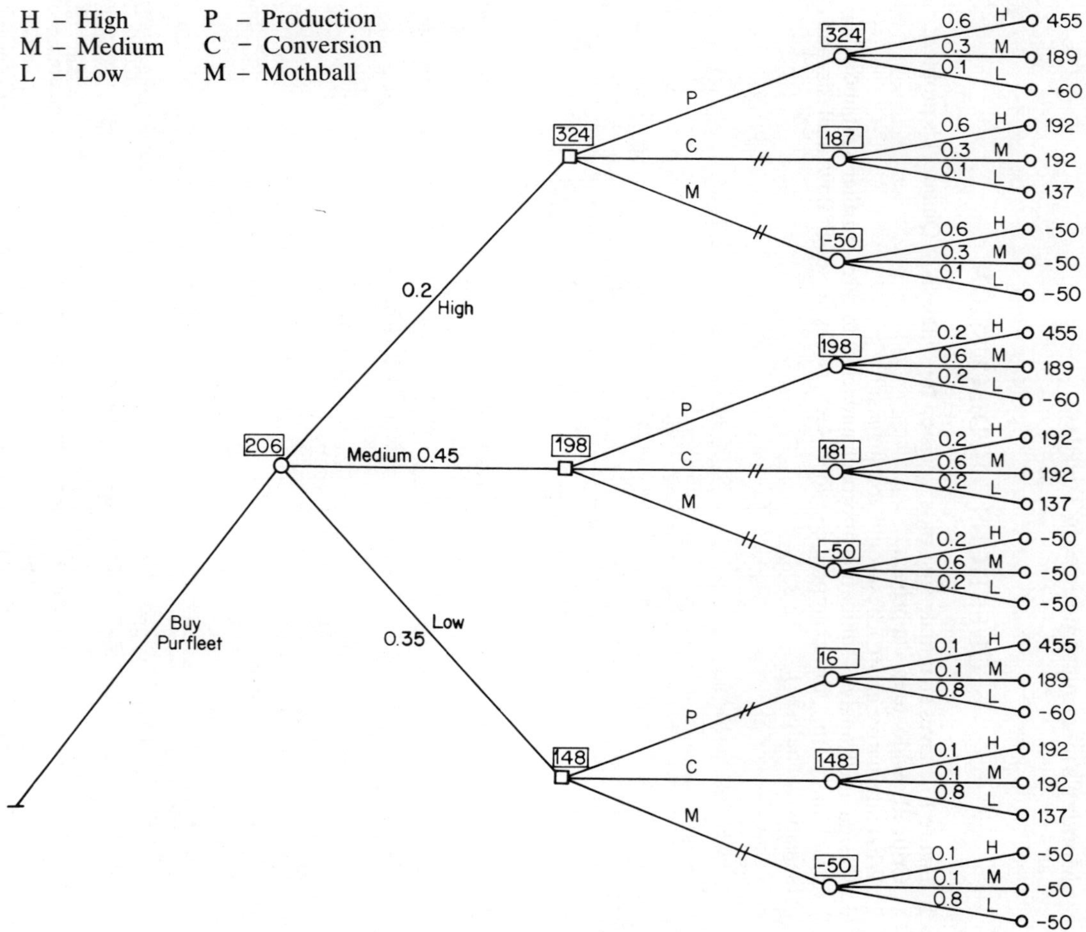
H – High
M – Medium
L – Low
P – Production
C – Conversion
M – Mothball
Buy Purfleet
206
0.2 High
Medium 0.45
0.35 Low
324
198
148
P
C
M
324
187
-50
198
181
-50
16
148
-50
0.6
0.3
0.1
0.2
0.6
0.2
0.1
0.1
0.8
H
M
L
455
189
-60
192
192
137
-50
-50
-50

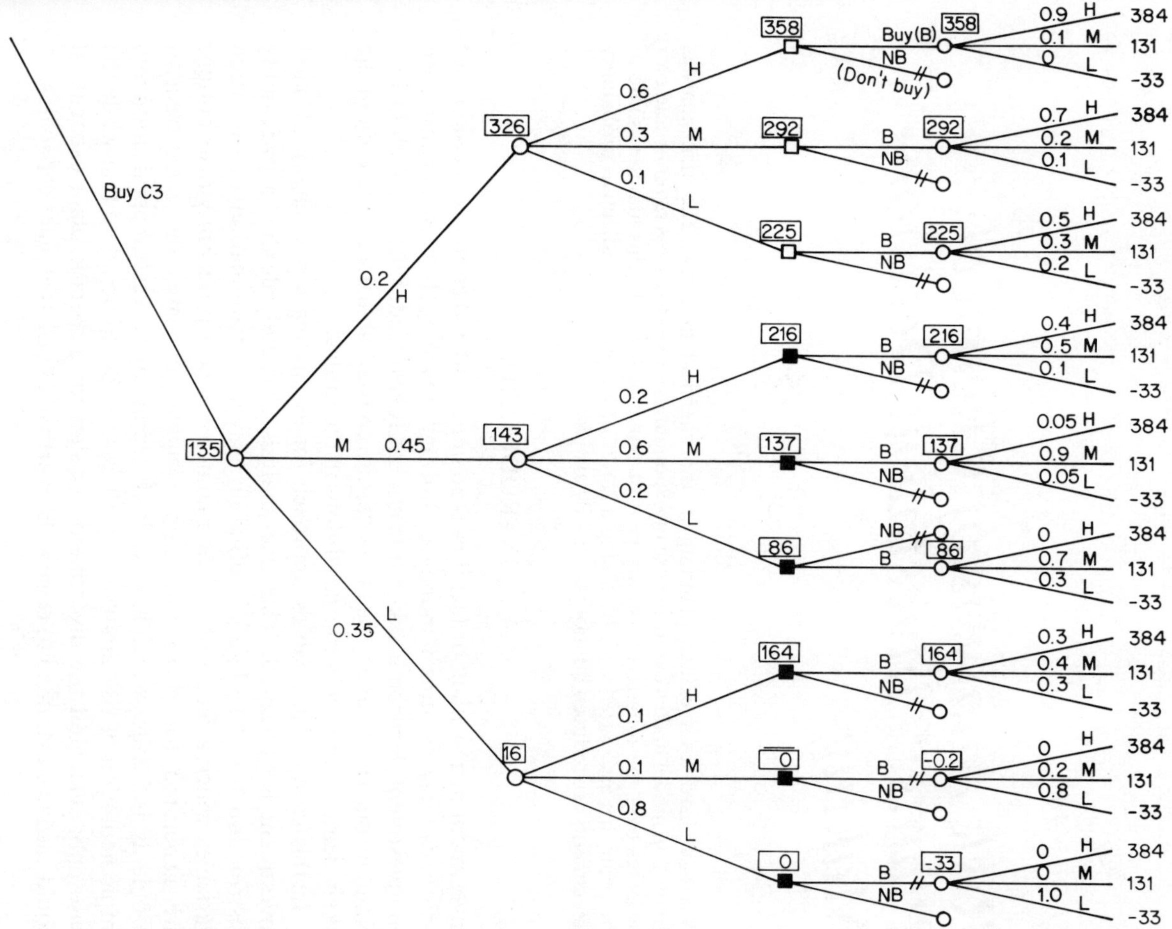
Buy C3
135
0.2 H
M 0.45
0.35 L
326
143
16
0.6 H
0.3 M
0.1 L
0.2 H
0.6 M
0.2 L
0.1 H
0.1 M
0.8 L
358
292
225
216
137
86
164
0
0
Buy(B)
NB
(Don't buy)
B
NB
358
292
225
216
137
86
164
-0.2
-33
0.9 H
0.1 M
0 L
0.7 H
0.2 M
0.1 L
0.5 H
0.3 M
0.2 L
0.4 H
0.5 M
0.1 L
0.05 H
0.9 M
0.05 L
0 H
0.7 M
0.3 L
0.3 H
0.4 M
0.3 L
0 H
0.2 M
0.8 L
0 H
0 M
1.0 L
384
131
-33

Figure 13.1

*Chapter 14*

# *Risk Analysis of Chemical Plants:* Investment Decision-Making*


## SUMMARY

This case involves facilities planning in the chemical industry. The risk analysis simulation model makes extensive use of exponential curves to assess revenue and cost variables over the long-term, twenty-year planning horizon. In this manner, some of the problems associated with obtaining a series of longer term subjective probability assessments are reduced but not necessarily avoided.


## 14.1 INTRODUCTION

Investment in new plant or facilities is an important and complex decision, not only because large sums of money are normally involved, but also because once an investment decision is taken it is not easily reversed. Further, such facility planning decisions have to be taken despite considerable uncertainty about the likely demand and economic conditions in the future.

In this case a risk analysis approach for evaluating a new chemical plant investment is presented. This risk analysis ultimately defines a probability distribution for the plant's profitability given a combination of uncertain variables which affect profits. The manner in which probability distributions are generated for these uncertain variables indicates the measurement problems and issues which have to be faced in any successful application and implementation of risk analysis procedures. It should be noted that while the case only evaluated the investment decision for a specific plant capacity, it could easily be extended to review the worth of alternative plant capacities.

## 14.2 PROJECT MODEL

In this model, the potential plant's present worth (net present value)

*Parts of this case study are adapted from an application-oriented article reporting work in Amoco and Standard Oil: J. B. Malloy 'Risk Analysis of Chemical Plants' *Chemical Engineering Progress*, **67**, October 1971, p. 65.

distribution was evaluated using the now familiar 'Hertz-simulation' risk analysis approach.

In order to obtain this net present value distribution, subjective probability distributions were first evaluated for the series of broad categories of *revenue* variables, *cost* variables and *project life* as outlined below:

*Revenue Variables*
Price
Market demand
Market share
Price-market demand interaction

*Cost Variables and Project Life*
Investment cost
Operating cost – production learning curve
Project life

These variables, and the cost of capital, were the set of input variables required in order to define the NPV (net present value) output variable.

In subsequent paragraphs we shall show the detail of the uncertainty assessment process for each uncertain quantity. The logic of the risk analysis plant evaluation process is shown in the flow diagram.

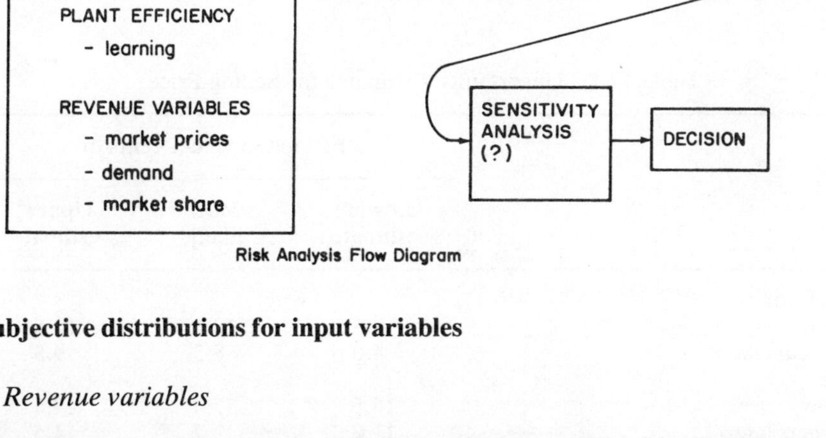


Risk Analysis Flow Diagram

## Subjective distributions for input variables

### *A Revenue variables*

*(i) Selling price*. The main problem in estimating subjective distributions for the price variable results from the 10 to 20-year life cycle of the chemical plant

project. Somehow or other a realistic and meaningful projection of chemical prices has to be obtained over this time horizon.

A number of methods were considered, including the approach of giving the manager a piece of graph paper (with time on the horizontal axis and price on the vertical axis) and asking him to assess directly a pessimistic, a most likely and an optimistic scenario for price (see Alderson and Green (1964) for an example of this approach). This graphical approach was rejected on the grounds that some managers have found it cognitively difficult in previous applications.

However, the assessment approach adopted was an attempt to break down and simplify the assessment task. First, a mathematical model for projecting chemical prices was postulated as follows:

$$P = M_0 e^{-K_M t} + F_0 e^{-K_F t}$$

where $P$ is price;
$M_0$ is the initial margin over a price floor (defined as the minimum price required by an efficient producer with a modern plant);
$K_M$ is the rate of decay of this margin due to competitive pressure;
$F_0$ is the initial price floor at time zero (0);
$K_F$ is the rate of decline in the price floor as a result of technological improvements and larger plants.

Such a model is an example of the use of exponential-curve techniques to describe growth and decline situations. These have been used widely in the area of time-series forecasting.

In order to estimate the parameters $K_M$ and $K_F$ of this relationship, managers were asked to estimate prices and price floors (i.e. lowest possible prices) at two points in time and their assessments are shown in Table 14.1. The critical estimate is the future price because this estimate establishes how rapidly price will decay. This estimate was made for year 5 as this horizon was thought

Table 14.1 Uncertainty Estimates for Selling Price

| | Estimated value, cents/lb | | |
|---|---|---|---|
| | Lower[a] estimate | Most likely | Upper[a] estimate |
| Price floor | | | |
| Now | 9.5 | 10.0 | 10.5 |
| 15 years later | 8.0 | 8.5 | 9.5 |
| Price | | | |
| Now | 16.5 | 17.0 | 17.5 |
| 5 years later | 11.0 | 12.7 | 14.5 |

[a]10% chance of actual value outside estimated value.

to be cognitively feasible for the managers concerned and would result in meaningful price assessments. On the other hand, the price floors were conceived as prices calculated to yield a 10 percent return to a large producer now and to a producer with somewhat bigger plant 15 years from now.

These price distributions (assessed as 3-branch chance event distributions) enable the parameters $K_M$ and $K_F$ to be estimated for each set of prices simulated randomly from the distributions given in Table 14.1. As a result, one possible price projection can be obtained from the price equation on each iteration of the simulation which will in turn lead to a price projection distribution over time given a large number of iterations (500). The price distribution obtained from 500 simulated trials is shown in Figure 14.1.

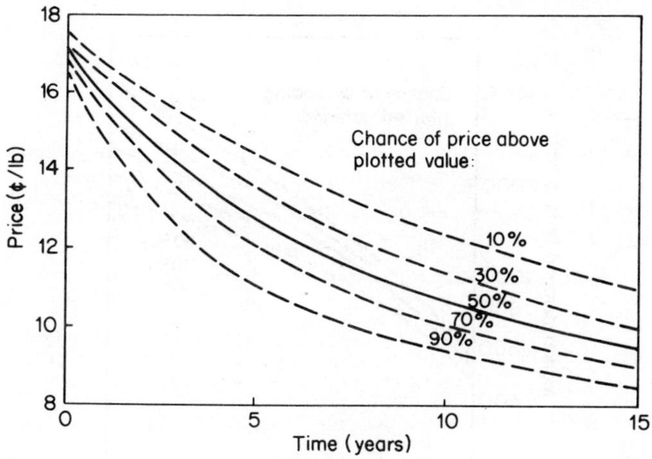


Figure 14.1 Uncertainty in projected prices

*(ii) Market Demand*. The process of obtaining market demand projections was broken down in a similar manner to the approach adopted in the price projection case. First, a demand model (of the exponential-growth type) in relation to time was specified as shown below:

$$D = D_0 \exp[r_\infty t + (r_0 - r_\infty)(1 - e^{-k_D t})|(k_D)]$$

where $D$ is demand;
$D_0$ is demand now at time zero (0)
$r_0$ is growth rate at time zero (0)
$r_\infty$ is growth rate at time $\infty$ (i.e. long run);
$k_D$ is decay rate in demand over time.

Certain subjective probabilities of demand in years 0, 3 and 6 of the plant's life were then assessed in order to obtain estimates of the parameters of the demand projection equation. It was felt that managers could make meaningful demand estimates for the short to medium term (i.e. up to 5 or 6 years) and this

Table 14.2 Uncertainty Estimates for Market Demand

| | Estimated Value | | |
|---|---|---|---|
| | Lower[a] estimate | Most likely | Upper[a] estimate |
| Demand, million lb/yr. | | | |
| At Year 0 | 460 | 500 | 540 |
| 3 | 730 | 830 | 950 |
| 6 | 1,000 | 1,200 | 1,500 |
| Long-run Growth, %/yr. | 2 | 4 | 6 |

[a]10% chance of actual value outside estimated value.

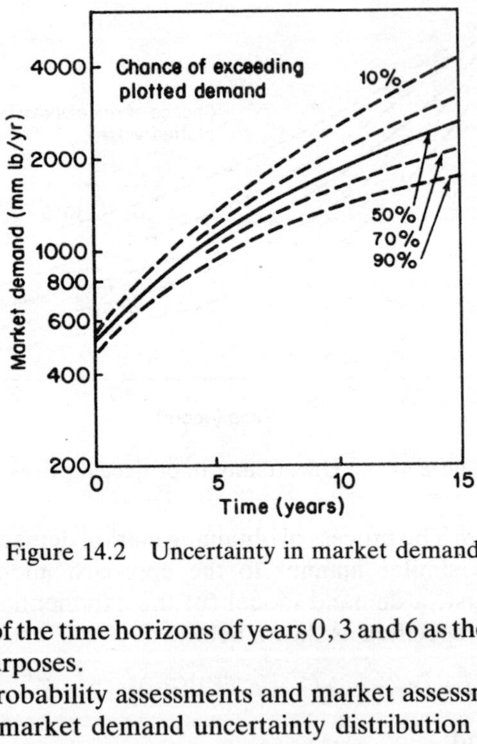


Figure 14.2 Uncertainty in market demand

led to the choice of the time horizons of years 0, 3 and 6 as the appropriate years for assessment purposes.

The demand probability assessments and market assessments are shown in Table 14.2. The market demand uncertainty distribution was then obtained from application of estimates above, the demand projection equation and a simulation run of 500 trials. A graph plot of this market demand is shown in Figure 14.2. Not surprisingly the demand distribution is tighter in terms of the short-run situation but fans out gradually the further demand is projected in time.

*(iii) Market Share*. Market share was assumed to change gradually from an initial level, $f_0$, towards some long-run limit $f_\infty$ as specified by the exponential-type relationship shown in the following equation for $f$, the market share.

$$f = f_0 + (f_\infty - f_0)(1 - e^{-k_f t})$$

where $f$ is market share;
$f_0$ is initial market share;
$f_\infty$ is long-run market share;
$k_f$ is a decay parameter.

The assessment procedure involves estimating 3-point distributions for initial and long-run shares and at an intermediate point, year 5, which was thought to be feasible in assessment terms for the appropriate managers. The set of estimates is shown in Table 14.3.

Table 14.3 Uncertainty Estimates for Market Share

| | Estimated share, % | | |
|---|---|---|---|
| | Lower[a] estimate | Most likely | Upper[a] estimate |
| Initial share | 3.5 | 4 | 4.5 |
| Share at year 5 | 5.5 | 7 | 7.5 |
| Long-run share | 7.0 | 10 | 11.0 |

[a]10% chance of actual value outside estimated value.

If a randomly generated set of these three market share estimates is produced then the value for the parameter $k_f$ can be estimated from the market share equation and thus, one market share projection is obtained. By repetition of this random selection process 500 times, the uncertainty in market share graph is obtained as shown in Figure 14.3.

*(iv) Sales projection*. It should by now be clear that we have already obtained the inputs from earlier analyses to enable a projection for sales to be derived. In particular, by combining in a multiplicative fashion a randomly selected market demand projection from the demand distribution with a randomly selected value from the market share distribution, a single value for likely sales would be produced. Repetition of this process, say 500 times, would enable the sales distribution to be obtained and the resulting distribution is plotted on the graph of Figure 14.4.

Finally, on the revenue side of the model it should be noted that an allowance was made for a possible price–market demand interaction. The simulation model regarded a low price as being likely to be associated with high demand and vice versa. The degree of interaction was not formally assessed in correlation terms but a pattern of possible dependence was

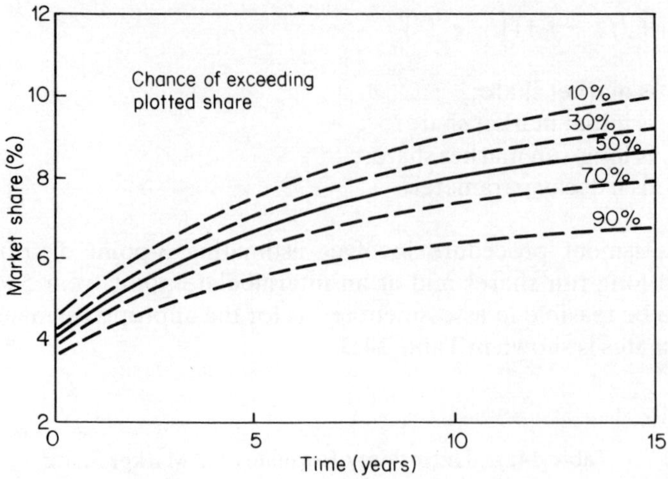


Figure 14.3 Uncertainty in market share

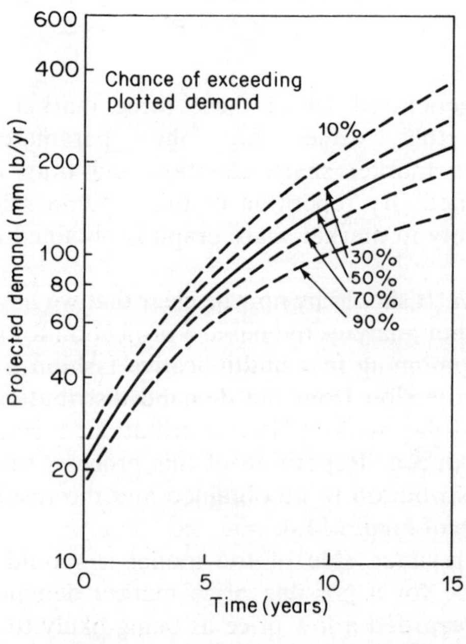


Figure 14.4 Uncertainty in the firm's demand

Table 14.4 Uncertainty Estimates for Risk Analysis

| 75 million lb/yr. chemical plant | Estimated values | | |
|---|---|---|---|
| | Lower[a] estimate | Most likely | Upper[a] estimate |
| *Investment* | | | |
| Initial investment, millions $ | 9.3 | 10 | 11.8 |
| Sustaining investment, % of initial invest./yr. | 0.5 | 1.0 | 1.5 |
| Debottlenecking cost, % of initial invest./annual lb | 20 | 33 | 60 |
| SYD depreciation period, yr. | — | 11 | — |
| *Operating cost* | | | |
| Variable cost, ¢/lb | | | |
| Initially | 5.60 | 5.75 | 5.95 |
| At year 15 | 5.30 | 5.45 | 5.65 |
| Maintenance, % of investment/yr. | 3 | 4 | 5 |
| Insurance and taxes, % of investment/yr. | .75 | 1 | 1.5 |
| Other fixed cost, million $/yr. | 0.8 | 1 | 1.2 |
| Startup cost, millions $ | 0.25 | 0.5 | 1.0 |
| Inflation of fixed costs, %/yr. | 2 | 3 | 4 |
| *Working capital* | | | |
| Receivables, months | 0.8 | 1 | 2 |
| Inventories, months | | | |
| Feed | 0.5 | 0.7 | 1.0 |
| Product | 0.7 | 1 | 1.5 |
| Cash, months cost, ex-raw material | 0.7 | 1 | 1.5 |
| Spares, % of Investment | 1.5 | 2 | 2.5 |
| Payables, months processing cost | 0.8 | 1 | 1.2 |
| Federal tax rate, % | 48 | 50 | 52 |
| Project life, yr. | 12 | 15 | 18 |

[a]10% chance of actual value outside estimated value.

hypothesized and translated in heuristic form into the simulation program.

## B *Cost and Accounting Variables*

The uncertainty estimates for the set of cost variables, i.e. investment and operating costs and likely working capital requirements, are shown in Table 14.4.

[Please note that assumptions about tax rates and project lives are also made. Investment costs are assessed for the initial investment, for an annual sustaining investment to maintain a competitive product and for 'debottlenecking' investment to raise the plant's capacity and take advantage of possible production-learning curve effects.]

Variable costs are assessed for two points in time so that gradual changes in cost can be allowed for as given by the following equation

$$C = C_0 e^{\pm k_c t}$$

(where $C_0$ represents the initial value).

The assumption made in this analysis would be for a declining trend in raw material costs. This results in a decline in variable costs of above 0.4 percent per year.

Fixed costs were also assumed to vary in accordance with the type of cost equation shown above based upon estimates of initial costs and of likely inflation rates.

### C *Learning Curve Effects*

Operations management literature and concepts of accumulated experience tend to suggest that the production capacity of chemical plants often grows beyond the original design capacity because of the 'learning curve' effect. One way of taking account of this is to postulate a growth relationship for $R$, the ratio of actual to design capacity, over time. $R$ is hypothesized to grow, hopefully, from an initial value of 1 towards a long-run limit $R_\infty$ as given by the following equation:

$$R = 1 + (R_\infty - 1)(1 - e^{-k_L t})$$

In order to estimate $R_\infty$ and $k_L$, the decay rate, estimates of $R$ for years 5 and 10 were made as shown in Table 14.5. These estimates were based on previous engineering and managerial experience of the operation of similar plants.

Table 14.5 Uncertainty Estimates for Learning

| | Estimated ratio, Actual/design capacity | | |
|---|---|---|---|
| | Lower[a] estimate | Most likely | Upper[a] estimate |
| At year 5 | 1.20 | 1.32 | 1.35 |
| At year 10 | 1.30 | 1.43 | 1.50 |

[a]10% chance of actual value outside estimated value.

The assessment process involves random selection of one set of values of the capacity ratios at years 5 and 10 in order to fix $R_\infty$ and $k_L$. Thus, one possible learning curve is obtained. By repeating the simulation process 500

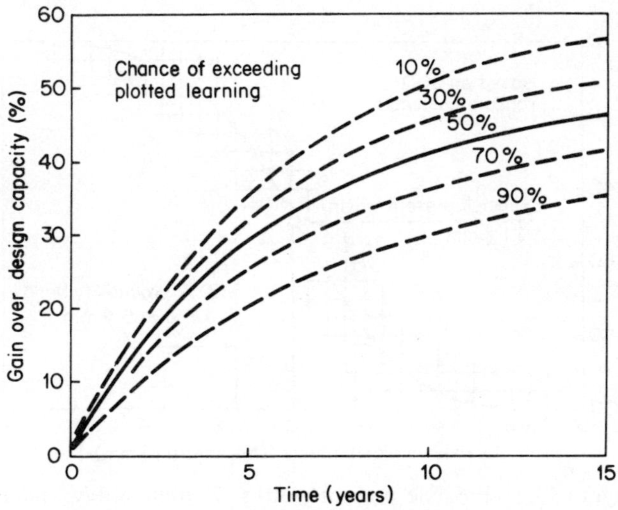


Figure 14.5 Uncertainty in projected learning

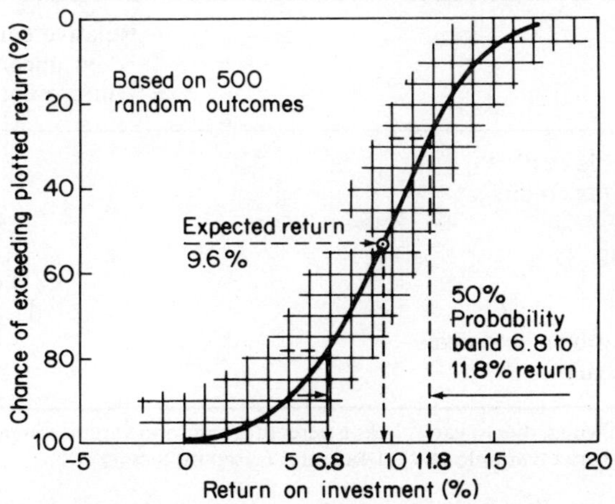


Figure 14.6 Possible rates of return, 75 million lb/yr. plant

times the uncertainty plot for the learning curve is derived and the plot is reproduced in Figure 14.5. The possible productivity gains would be reflected both in unit cost reductions and revenue gains and would hence change the rate of return values in the final model output.

## *D Results*

500 simulation runs of the overall profitability model were carried out and yield and present-worth plots derived as shown in Figures 14.6 and 14.7. A further

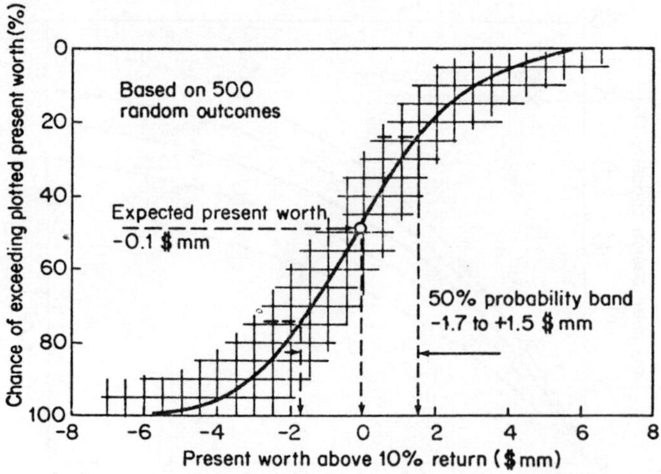


Figure 14.7 Possible present worths, 75 million lb/yr. plant

Table 14.6 Relative Importance of Sources of Risk

| Source | Relative contribution to uncertainty in present worth[a] |
|---|---|
| Margin over variable cost[b] | 96 |
| Investment, after tax credits | |
| Initial | 7.9 |
| Debottlenecking | 1.1 |
| Sustaining | 0.6 |
| Fixed costs | 11.8 |
| Maintenance, insurance, and taxes | 3.6 |
| Working capital charge | 1.5 |

[a]Variance in present worth due to variable as a percentage of total variance in present worth.
[b]Margin = $\int_0^t$ (sales) (price-variable cost) (1-tax rate) (discount factor) *dt*.

table, Table 14.6, shows the relative contribution to uncertainty in present value given by the various sources of risk. It can be seen very clearly that the variables which contribute to margin, i.e. price, demand, market share, learning curve and variable cost projections, are of crucial importance in determining present worth, suggesting that greater effort should be made in making assessments of these uncertain quantities.

## 14.3 CONCLUSIONS

The process of risk analysis clearly highlights the impact of uncertainty on facilities planning decisions. In particular, the major contributors to uncertainty about project worth are the price and demand projections, suggesting that concentrated effort should be directed towards the development of meaningful forecasting methods for sales and market-oriented variables.

As a postscript, perhaps the planning process should also include the consideration of some further decision options such as do nothing; or install smaller plant and 'buy-in' surplus capacity. Such policies of efficient investment and asset management are being stressed in more recent strategic planning literature.

## REFERENCES

Alderson, W. and P. E. Green (1964). *Planning and Problem Solving in Marketing*, Homewood, Ill.: Richard D. Irwin Inc.

Hertz, D. B., and H. Thomas (1983). 'Decision and risk analysis in a new product and facilities planning problem'. *Sloan Management Review,* **24**(2), 17–31.

## QUESTIONS FOR DISCUSSION

1. How does the parent company's financial position affect the analysis? Do you think that the approach adopted is generally applicable?
2. The various variables considered in the model are just some of the more obvious and important variables. Would you say that those used are the most relevant ones? For example, how sensitive might the analysis be to technological breakthrough? Chemical plants are generally high-risk ventures. How should this aspect be included in the analysis? (e.g. insurance costs).
3. What do you think of the flow diagram? Is it really explicit? (For example, how should sensitivity analysis be used to refine the rate of return distribution).
4. How useful are the exponential-type models postulated in this analysis?
5. A 10 percent ROR is used in this case on pp. 206. The chemical industry has traditionally been very competitive, relying almost invariably on small margins and large outputs for its viability. In view of these facts, do you have any comment about the ROR used?
6. Managers' expectations were quantified for the short term (about 5 years) because 'this horizon was thought to be cognitively feasible for the managers concerned and would result in meaningful ... assessments.' Table 14.1 nevertheless shows estimates for 15 years. Other tables (e.g. Table 14.3) show assessments for even longer horizons. What are your comments on the approach?
7. The case considers the generation of sales projections by 'combining in a multiplicative fashion' demand and market share projections. What is your understanding of the process? Do you think that 500 repetitions are necessary? In particular, critically examine the analytic treatment of correlation effects.
8. The relative contribution figures in Table 14.6 add up to more than 100 percent. What does that tell you about the variables? Would you like to see the analysis expanded in this particular area? Why?

*Chapter 15*

# *The Hewitt Ingot Company's Decision Problem**

SUMMARY

This case presents an interesting production planning problem involving storage of inventories of an intermediate product (residues) in the production process for metal products.

The aim of the case is to provide the reader with practice in developing a problem structure and evaluation model for an imperfectly specified, somewhat complex decision problem.

While attending a course on decision-making, Mr Alec Barton, head of the Casting Section at the Hewitt Ingot Company Ltd., realized that a recurring set of decisions he had to make at the end of each month could perhaps be improved by applying decision analysis. Residues from manufacturing the company's various metal products were reclaimed by ingotting. The ingotted and analyzed residues were known as 'recovered melts,' and these were stored in the Casting Section either for future use by the Company or for sale. They did not conform to any particular specification, but had a composition determined by a chance mixing of different types of alloy. Recovered melts were sold whenever the total stock of *all* materials, not just the recovered melts, exceeded £80,000.

Mr Barton felt that the decision to sell when stocks exceeded £80,000 was arbitrary and had led the company to sell recovered melts that it subsequently needed. Recovered melts are always sold at a loss, but if they can be used in making up new ingot melts to a given specification, they realize their full value. While this factor favors retaining each recovered melt until it is used, another factor works against this: the investment loss of 18 percent per annum that accrues on stored melts. Thus, if it looks as if a recovered melt will be used fairly soon, it should be kept, but if the melt will be in storage for a very long time, it should be sold at a modest loss rather than incur the heavy investment

*This case was originally developed by J. A. Morris of Glacier Metal in the United Kingdom. It is reproduced here by permission of the author.

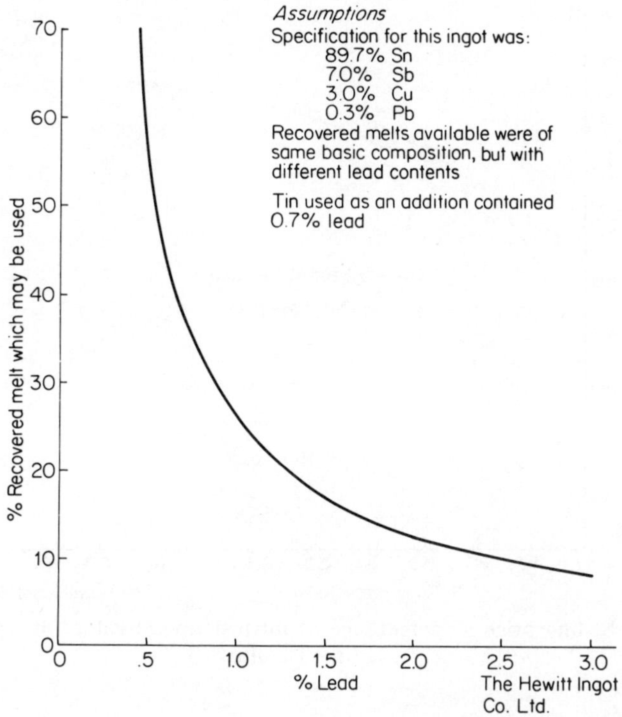


Figure 15.1 Illustration of the way in which the amount of recovered melt permitted in a tin-base alloy varies with the lead content of the recovered melt

loss later. Somehow, Mr Barton reasoned, these two factors could be made explicit and balanced off against each other in a decision and risk analysis.

In a letter to Mr Charles Durrell, a decision analysis consultant, he outlined the background of the project and asked Mr Durrell if a decision analysis would at least clarify the basis for keeping or selling the recovered melts. Here are relevant portions of the letter:

(1) Most of our metal residues are reclaimed by ingotting them. The ingotted and analyzed residues are known as 'recovered melts.' They find an outlet in the make-up of new charges made to an exact specification by adding in the appropriate amounts of pure metals.
(2) Recovered melts are more likely to be used if their degree of contamination is low, and more melt can be used in making up a new charge. This is shown in Figure 15.1. The bulk of our sales are of white-metal recovered melts, and for these the degree of contamination is determined primarily by the proportion of lead in the melt.
(3) The terms under which we sell white-metal are very much affected by their composition. In Figure 15.2 I have shown how the proportion of tin in the recovered melt affects the selling price. The selling price is expressed as a

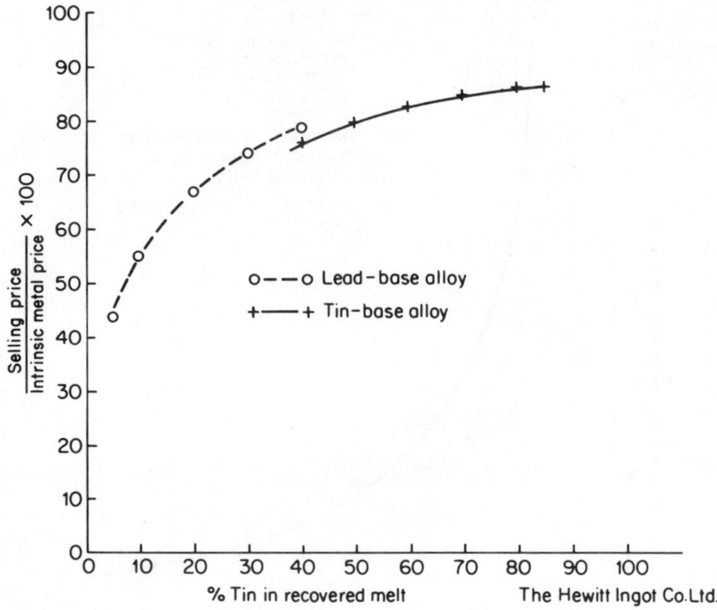


Figure 15.2 Selling price as percentage of intrinsic metal value for lead-base alloy and tin-base alloy

percentage of the intrinsic metal value (IMV), where the IMV is the total current market cost of the constituent metals.

(4) The main criterion at present used in deciding whether or not a recovered melt should be sold is that the total stock level of all materials in the Casting Section should not exceed £80,000. It is likely that, with the present methods of operating, some selling of recovered melts will always be desirable. The melts sold will be those that are so contaminated that they are never likely to be used, or, in the terms mentioned above, those where the sales loss is much less than the investment loss. However, many melts which might eventually be used profitably in new charges are, under the present policy of trimming down to £80,000, being sold off at a loss. Figure 15.3, based on the usage of white-metal recovered melts last year, gives some evidence in support of this point. The situation has worsened since that time in that melts down to about 2½ percent lead are now being sold.

(5) Figure 15.4a is a frequency distribution of the time for which metal-recovered melts are held in stock. The distribution comes from a sample of all melts received during a typical four-month period, about 200 melts in all. The melts are not generally used at one stroke, but are taken from stock gradually. In other words, the stocks gradually decay. Figure 15.4b is a distribution showing the time taken for the stock level in each case to decay to half its original value. Figure 15.4b has been prepared as a first attempt at estimating the real loss in investment value while the melt, or any

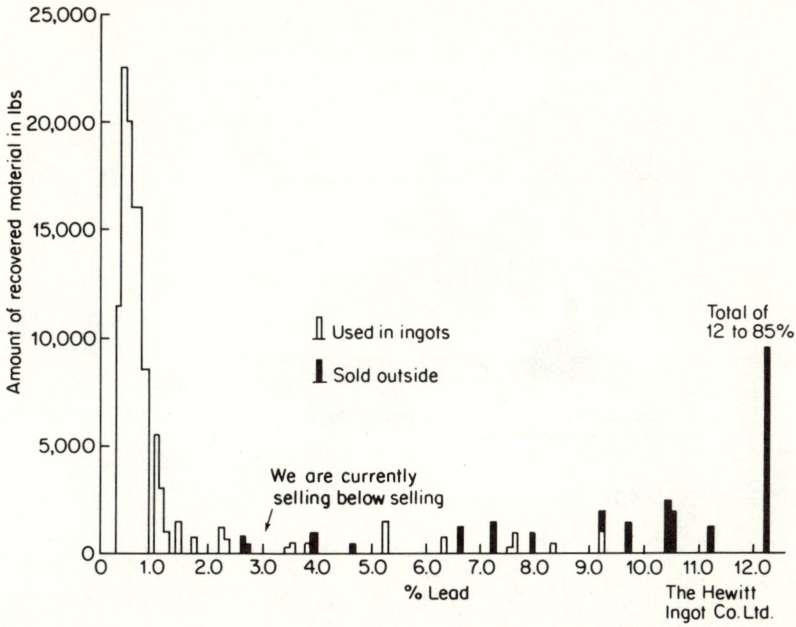


Figure 15.3 Usage of recovered melts in making ingots to specification and by selling outside at a loss

part of it, is on the books. It would be an overestimate to base the investment loss on the initial value of the melt and the time it took to dispose of it completely.

(6) The most profitable way of disposing of recovered melts is to sell them as ingots to specification outside the Company for then we get rid of them completely. If we use them in ingots which are to be used within the company, we see a large portion of them back again in the residue system. Our sales of ingots outside the company are comparatively small, possibly because we expect too high a price for them. We could perhaps increase our overall profitability by dropping our ingot prices to increase demand and so increase the opportunities for disposing of recovered melts.

(7) The remarks made here on the usage of white-metal melts relate to our present methods of processing residues. Trials are at present under way on removing lead from tin-base alloys, and on other matters.

(8) The £80,000 total stock mentioned earlier is made up of all the materials in the Costing Section: pure metals and ingots made to specification, residues awaiting processing or being processed, and recovered melts. A fairly tight stocking policy is operated for the pure metals and ingots, and it is not likely that we would sell materials which we have recently purchased or made up. Efforts are made to keep the work in progress at a minimum. It is not generally sold in an unprocessed state because it is difficult to measure its real worth; the scrap merchant's price for it tends to be lower than it would be

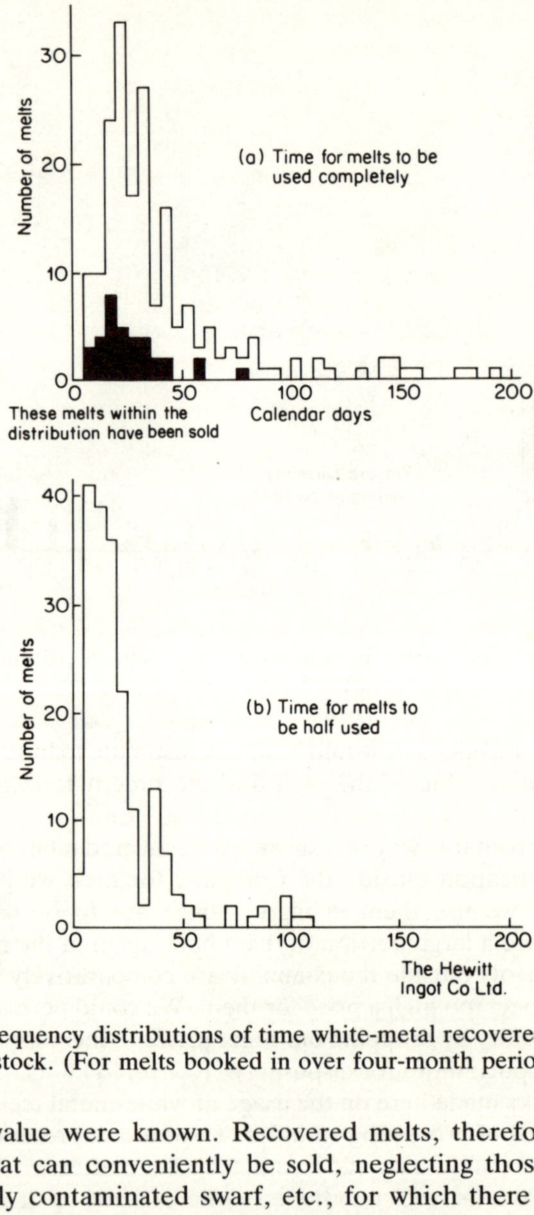


Figure 15.4 Frequency distributions of time white-metal recovered melts are held in stock. (For melts booked in over four-month period.)

if the real value were known. Recovered melts, therefore, are the only materials that can conveniently be sold, neglecting those items, such as dross, grossly contaminated swarf, etc., for which there is at present no chance of internal use. In trying to reduce total stocks to a pre-determined level, it is the recovered melts that receive the most attention.

In his reply, Mr Durrell said he thought a decision analysis might be appropriate, and a meeting was arranged to discuss the problem.

Mr Barton opened the meeting by giving some background information: 'Requests for new ingots come both from other sections of our own Company, and from outside customers. We make up a new melt to the customer's specifications, and the composition is optimal, in terms of minimizing our cost, because it is determined by linear programming.

Melts sold outside our Company rarely come back as residue. Those that do come back from our own Company are sometimes in contaminated form, and we have to make them back up into the exact specifications. We do this by adding more pure materials. Those that are left as we received them can be sold as recovered melt, but we don't get their IMV. What we do get depends on their tin content.'

'How often does a recovered melt that you have in store meet the precise specifications of a customer?' Mr Durrell was speaking.

'Very rarely,' replied Mr Barton.

'What is the size and IMV of your most valuable melts in stock?' inquired Mr Durrell.

'About £1,000 to £1,500 per ton, and the melts are often in one-ton ingots,' came the reply.

'And how many melts might be in stock at any one time?'

'About 20 to 50.'

'Do you have any limitations on storage space?'

'Not really. I wouldn't worry about that because much more space is taken by our pure metal stock than by the recovered melts. There's always space for the recovered melts.'

'Will the scrap dealer take any recovered melt you want to get rid of?'

'Yes, but he probably wouldn't bother to pick up just one or two tons. He would probably want at least four tons to make it worth the trouble. However, that's a policy I might persuade our buying office to change if you think it's worth it.'

'I'm not sure just now,' replied Mr Durrell. 'Let's get back to the recovered melts in stock. Can anything be gained by considering the ingots in combination when you decide to keep or sell them?'

'I don't see how. I have a separate record of each one showing the date when it was received, an analysis of its own composition, its weight when received and the weight remaining at the end of each month.'

'When do you review your stocks of recovered melts?'

'At the end of each month. If total metal stocks are above £80,000 at the end of the month, I weed out the least promising recovered melts, the ones I'm afraid I'll have around for a long time with no occasion to use.'

'Tell me about trends in the metal market and how they affect your decisions.'

'I take these into account when I consider the present and future IMV of each melt, but I don't think fluctuations in the market are nearly as serious in influencing my decisions as the discrepancy between selling cost and IMV, or as the investment loss, at least for the alloys I'm mainly concerned with.'

'Can you give me an example of a recovered melt that you were absolutely sure you should keep, another which appeared utterly useless, and a third that you were uncertain about? Tell me also the IMV and sale price of each.'

Mr Barton produced the three melts shown in the following table:

| Melt no: | K62 | J28 | K81 |
|---|---|---|---|
| Composition | | | |
| % Sn | 83.99 | 85.26 | 82.37 |
| % Sb | 10.28 | 7.68 | 7.82 |
| % Cu | 5.21 | 4.33 | 3.87 |
| %Pb | 0.52 | 2.73 | 5.94 |
| Original weight | 1 ton | 1 ton | 1 ton |
| Intrinsic value | £1,309 | £1,300 | £1,261 |
| Sale price | £1,130 | £1,131 | £1,092 |
| Decision | Keep | ? | Sell |

## QUESTIONS FOR DISCUSSION

1. In what way do you feel decision analysis can contribute to solving Mr Barton's decision problem?
2. Go as far as you can in solving Mr Barton's problem.
3. What decision should be made about J28?

*Chapter 16*

# *Strategic Decision-Making: Industrial and Chemical Processes Ltd.**

This case offers the reader with an opportunity to develop a problem formulation for a manufacturing investment decision situation. This investment decision was part of a series of diversification moves which had recently been considered by Industrial and Chemical Processes Limited.

The Executive Committee had not come through its first engagement unscathed. In presenting their conclusions to the Board it had soon emerged that only one person – Peter Gridley – really knew what he was talking about. He alone understood the underlying statistical techniques which had resulted in their recommendation that it was impossible to break into the domestic central-heating market with their current product range. None of the others had been capable of sustaining the arguments on which this conclusion was based.

John Sedgeley had felt this particularly keenly, as he had previously been used to pontificating on any Board Report of a quantitative nature. Now he found himself speechless. It was rumored that he had been studying M. J. Moroney's statistics text 'Facts from Figures' and he was clearly not going to be caught out again. It was noticeable that his contribution to the discussion on subsequent studies had been much more informed.

David Jones and Geoff Chisholm were discussing the next problem confronting the Executive Committee when they were joined by Sedgeley. As no alternative diversification projects had emerged since the last Board meeting, and as their market studies for the sale of scrap and by-products were satisfactory, their next task was to put forward a proposal to implement the move into car-crushing on the lines of David's report of 27 October.

'You may think that throwing out domestic boilers simplified matters', said Geoff, 'but when you look at the car-crushing situation, you quickly realize that this overall choice really covers a number of different things we could do. For a

*This case was originally developed by T. V. Ryder-Runton from an actual decision situation. It has been modified and disguised by J. C. G. Campbell and Howard Thomas.

start we have to decide on either the crushed cube or shredder type of equipment. In both cases I think we also have to consider the effects of eventually manufacturing the crushing plants ourselves at Bilkston. Have you developed any figures on this yet, John?'

'Yes,' replied Sedgeley, 'in fact I have been working on this problem for some days. Ted Summers had various operating and capital cost data from the manufacturers in the United States. I have converted this to UK terms, allowing for differences in labor wage rates and so on. Peter Gridley, who seems to be our marketing expert, has looked at scrap prices, and he and I have worked out some estimated revenue figures. Perhaps you would like to glance at these – I have them here.' (Sedgeley's statement is reproduced in Table 16.1).

Table 16.1 Statement of Estimated Capital Costs and Revenues: Car-crushing Plants

| | | | Hoskins auto baler (£000) | Miller process (£000) |
|---|---|---|---|---|
| 1. | *Capital cost* | | | |
| | (a) | Initial car-crushing system | 1,250 | 2,000 |
| | (b) | Equipment to manufacture car-crushing systems[a] | 850 | 1,750 |
| | | Total | 2,100 | 3,750 |
| 2. | *Annual average net revenue after tax* | | | |
| | (a) | Sale of scrap | 107.5 | 199.0 |
| | (b) | Sale of systems | 200.0 | 385.0 |
| | | Total | 307.5 | 584.0 |
| 3. | *Return on investment* | | % | % |
| | (a) | Scrap sales | 8.6 | 9.9 |
| | (b) | System sales | 21.0 | 22.0 |
| | | Total | 14.6 | 15.5 |
| 4. | *Life of plant* | | *Years* | *Years* |
| | (a) | Car-crushing system | 15 | 15 |
| | (b) | Manufacturing equipment | 8 | 10 |

[a]Including alteration to buildings at Bilkston plant.

Dave and Geoff were silent while they studied the figures. Finally Dave spoke: 'Surely we dare not assume just one set of circumstances, pitched at some average level. Single-point estimates are always dangerous; we ought to consider what might happen if the market was better or worse than current demands. Also I think that if we owned and operated manufacturing equipment, in fact our annual profits on the car crusher itself would be higher by about £50,000 for the Hoskins machine and around £90,000 for the Miller Process. This is because the main constituents of operating costs are certain expensive replacement parts. Obviously if we were making them ourselves the overall cost to the company would be lower than if we bought then on the open market.'

Sedgeley's reply was testy: 'Look, Geoffrey, at this stage of the game any estimates of costs or revenues are bound to be inaccurate to some extent. What is the use of unnecessarily complicating the issue by all sorts of other estimates as well? In fact Gridley looked at this point.'

Sedgeley rummaged in his brief case and produced some working papers, 'Yes, here we are: he estimated £150,000 to £65,000 as the possible high/low range of profits for the sale of Hoskins scrap: £300,000 to £100,000 for the manufacture of the equipment. Similarly for the Millerized Scrap he arrived at £300,000 to £98,000, with £600,000 to £170,000 for the equipment. None of these figures take into account your supposed cost saving on spares: I imagine that would not apply in any case to a low-demand market. In my statement I merely took mid-point averages of profits in each case. Quite sufficient I feel.'

Edward Summers had joined them by this time, and had overheard the exchange. 'Weak data never justified weak methods, John. If your estimates are subject to variation, then we must test them as far as we can. In our market survey of the scrap business we unearthed some probability estimates prepared by the National Metals Research Organization – we should apply these to Gridley's estimates. As far as I recall they said that there was a 70 percent chance of a high scrap market and only a 30 percent chance of a low one. Based on this we also worked out that the corresponding probabilities for the sale of equipment were 60 percent and 40 percent.'

'I think this opens up a whole range of alternatives. For example, if we didn't manufacture the equipment we could make £20,000 per year out of license fees for subcontracting the work without any capital expenditure on our part. We would of course lose the cost benefit of cheap spares. At any time we could pull out and cut our losses by selling the plants. I should think that a reasonable break-up value for the Hoskins process would be about £350,000 for the equipment, manufacturing plant and property; probably £650,000 for the operating crusher itself. For the Miller process the figures would be about £600,000 and £980,000.'

By the way, John, how long does each plant take to construct: when does your eight, ten or fifteen years start?'

Sedgeley had been frantically scribbling down the estimates made by Summers, and was relieved to find a subject on which he could be precise. 'In each case construction or erection time is said to be one year. The times quoted date from the end of the construction period and are based on engineering estimates from the United States.'

Ted Summers continued: 'Well, we seem to have a great deal of information to work on and lots of paths we could take. We can decide to license the Hoskins or the Miller equipment; in each case we can build and run it, or subcontract the building; at any stage we can sell off either the plant or the equipment. These decisions being dictated by the market conditions at each stage, and each one having its associated probabilities and costs, we should be flexible enough to adapt to market conditions at the end of, say, the first year. Gentlemen, we must devise a strategy that will maximize our profits whatever happens – how do we do it?'

## QUESTIONS FOR DISCUSSION

1. What approaches would you use to help the executive committee in its decision-making process?
2. What decision should be made with regard to the Hoskins and Miller processes?
3. How would you improve the formulation and evaluation process?

*Chapter 17*

# *The Rheumatogen Situation:* Pharmaceutical Research and Development*


## SUMMARY

The process of strategic management of research and development (R & D) is examined in this case in relation to a research project, Rheumatogen, in an ethical pharmaceutical company. This should be compared with the Aztech Electronics case in Chapter 2 of the complementary *Risk Analysis and its Applications* volume.

Readers should contrast the two different applications of risk analysis. The shorter term time horizon for R & D in electronics should be compared with the much longer time horizons involved in R & D in the ethical pharmaceutical industry. In both situations, there is a perceived need for the development of flexible decision and performance criteria for evaluating research and development.


## 17.1 INTRODUCTION

Amco and Sappho are two pharmaceutical companies, both with interests in the field of rheumatic drugs. Amco, an American company, has been deeply involved in the development of a compound for the treatment of rheumatism, and has taken this drug through all the stages of synthesis, pharmacology and pharmacological development, and toxicology. In addition, it has completed some preliminary clinical trials. The company is now keen to launch this drug onto the Japanese market and is looking for a partner in its venture. It has offered Sappho the opportunity to purchase the license for the compound.

Sappho have to assess whether or not the purchase of this drug would be a profitable proposition. Sappho is aware that entry into the Japanese pharmaceutical market is neither a simple nor a speedy process. Even if a compound has been accepted for registration by the health authorities of other countries, this gives no assurance that it will therefore be accepted by the appropriate Japanese authorities. The Japanese health authorities are well

*This case was originally developed by Howard Thomas in association with Dr. Max Taeschler of Sandoz Ltd. The data and chronology of the project have been disguised.

known for demanding evidence of a highly detailed standard of clinical testing and trials before any compound will even be considered for possible registration. In relation to the Amco compound under offer, these stringent requirements imply that Sappho would have to undertake a further three years of toxicological and clinical trials, which would have to be carried out at their own expense.

It must also be taken into account that as far as the Japanese patent authorities are concerned, it is the manufacturing process itself that has to be registered. This influences the current decision problem because two manufacturing processes have been involved in the development of the compound under consideration. Unfortunately though, only one of these processes has been granted a patent by the Japanese authorities. This occurred because the patent authority was not informed of the existence of the second process when the patent was granted to Amco. As a result, a new application would have to be made for a patent on the second process. Amco have told Sappho that they intend to try and negotiate the second patent; however, the problem facing Sappho is that as it is the manufacturing process which has to undergo registration, the risk exists that if the second process is not patented by Amco, then it may be used by another company in developing similar compounds.

Commercial intelligence has shown that a Japanese company called Nipo has been working in the same field. However, as far as Sappho and Amco are aware, Nipo has not developed specific manufacturing processes, nor conceived of similar applications for the developed compound.

Given that Sappho must decide whether or not to buy the license, an assessment of its worth must be undertaken before a final decision is made. If a positive decision is reached, then they must also decide how much they are prepared to pay for it.

## 17.2 THE DECISION PROBLEM

Amco are offering Sappho the license on the following basis. Firstly, rather than stipulating a lump sum payment, the terms of agreement would demand that Sappho introduce the developed drug onto the Japanese market by 1978. If this condition were fulfilled, Sappho must further guarantee royalty payments to Amco for an ensuing 20-year period. More specifically, the royalty to be paid would be gauged in terms of a percentage of sales volume during prescribed periods; namely, during 1978–90 the royalty would be 10 percent of sales volume, to be followed by a 5 percent sales volume share during 1990–97.

It must also be noted that the costs to Sappho would be higher than royalty payments alone. For example, it must be remembered that to anticipate acceptability by the Japanese health authorities would require further extensive and time-consuming clinical tests and trials; such tests would obviously necessitate additional expenditure. The possible costs in terms of current values ranged from a low value of 1,000,000 Sw. Fr. to a high value of 1,900,00 Sw. Fr., with the most likely value lying around 1,500,000 Sw. Fr. provided that these further trials were successfully completed. Given this level of expenditure, current estimates suggested that there existed an 80 percent chance of this further development being successful. If successful, then Sappho would be in a position to apply for registration for uses determined within the clinical trials. In terms of the probability of the success of the subsequent application for registration, this was forecast as being approximately 90 percent. However, if failure occurred by the end of the three years of further clinical trials, then it was estimated that the range of costs for development before success was achieved with probability 100 percent might rise to a range from a low value of 2,000,000 Sw. Fr. to a high of 3,000,000 Sw. Fr., with a most likely value lying around 2,500,000 Sw. Fr. (this would apply for a further two-year period).

Given the information presented so far, a group of research engineers within the company raised the possibility of another course of action. It was suggested that perhaps Sappho could apply for registration for the single use outlined in the Amco clinical trials, and simultaneously undertake additional clinical and toxicological trials and apply for registration at a later date. This suggestion was raised because research work already undertaken hinted that there existed a strong possibility that compounds of the Amco type might have alternative therapeutic uses. Moreover, it was suggested that amongst such uses were some that had a strong relationship to other drugs already marketed by Sappho in Japan. If this was the case, then the economic value of the license would be further increased. Given that these additional tests would also take a further three years (for the reasons already outlined), then the additional development costs for developing evidence on other therapeutic uses were estimated to be between 1,500,00 Sw. Fr. and 2,000,000 Sw. Fr., with a most likely value of 1,800,000 Sw. Fr.

A number of planners within the company suggested an alternative policy. They proposed that Sappho should, in association with Amco, attempt to negotiate with the Japanese patent authorities for the lapsed patent on the second manufacturing process. It was estimated that such negotiations stood a 50 percent chance of success. Assuming such success, then the chance of Nipo entering the field before Sappho was considered to be extremely small. The Planning Department estimated that if Sappho did not obtain the patent, then the chance of entry by Nipo was approximately 15 percent. But, if Sappho held the patent, then the probability of entry was reduced to 1 percent. If the position was reversed and Nipo gained the patent rights the situation would alter. Nipo would have a three-year monopoly on the compound and on its promotion within Japan. Consequently, Sappho would not want to wait three years before launching its product.

As yet another suggestion, some members of the Planning Department proposed that heavy emphasis be placed on the further development of the Amco compound to evaluate its potential additional therapeutic use within the rheumatic field. The cost for such development had already been estimated at around 2,000,000 Sw. Fr., but given the wealth of relevant experience possessed by Sappho, then it was calculated that the chance of development being successful could be rated as 95 percent. Taking into account the potentially increased market area for the compound, then it was considered appropriate to study the effect of any new market outlets on future sales.

As a first step in this analysis, it was considered crucial to assess the market structure in terms of a twenty-year time horizon. With an estimated launch date of 1978, the estimated range of sales volume for the year set a low value of $400,000 to a high of $650,000 with a most likely value of $500,000. It was estimated that within the three years, Sappho could possibly gain a 50 percent market share of the appropriate drug market and that with a less optimistic prediction, could in any case fairly easily obtain a 25 percent market share. The most likely market share obtained would be about 40 percent. Table 17.1 illustrates the most likely, low and high values of the sales figures for the twenty-year time horizon.

Table 17.1 Sales Volume Figures
($)

| | *Low* | *Most likely* | *High* |
|---|---|---|---|
| 1978 | 400,000 | 500,000 | 650,000 |
| 1979 | 1,250,000 | 1,500,000 | 1,750,000 |
| 1980 | 2,500,000 | 3,000,000 | 3,500,000 |
| 1981 | 3,500,000 | 4,500,000 | 5,500,000 |
| 1982 | 5,500,000 | 7,000,000 | 8,500,000 |
| 1983 | 10,000,000 | 12,000,000 | 14,000,000 |
| 1984 | 12,500,000 | 15,000,000 | 17,500,000 |
| 1985 | 14,000,000 | 17,000,000 | 19,000,000 |
| 1986 | 16,000,000 | 19,000,000 | 23,000,000 |
| 1987 | 17,500,000 | 20,000,000 | 24,000,000 |
| 1988 | 19,000,000 | 22,000,000 | 25,000,000 |
| 1989 | 20,000,000 | 23,500,000 | 27,000,000 |
| 1990 | 23,000,000 | 26,000,000 | 27,000,000 |
| 1991 | 23,000,000 | 27,000,000 | 28,000,000 |
| 1992 | 23,000,000 | 24,000,000 | 25,000,000 |
| 1993 | 16,000,000 | 20,000,000 | 21,000,000 |
| 1994 | 12,000,000 | 17,000,000 | 18,000,000 |
| 1995 | 8,000,000 | 14,000,000 | 15,000,000 |
| 1996 | 5,000,000 | 11,000,000 | 12,000,000 |
| 1997 | 4,000,000 | 8,000,000 | 9,000,000 |

The occurrence of either, or both, of two events could cause fluctuations in these exhibited values. First, assuming that Sappho had an initial three-year monopoly but was then presented with a competitor, Nipo, at the end of this time, it was estimated that likely sales would be reduced at that time by between 5 and 15 percent, with the most likely value of 10 percent. The second event which might cause a change in the values of Table 17.1 was if Sappho successfully developed and registered the anticipated additional usages of the compound by 1981. It was estimated that in the field of rheumatic drugs, Sappho could potentially increase its market share from 30 to 50 percent, with a congruent increase in sales volume in that specific area of approximately $8,000,000 per annum from 1981 onwards until 1997. It was also estimated that there existed a 50 percent chance of Nipo developing further rheumatic drugs by 1984 (allowing for retrospective registration), with a subsequent loss to Sappho's sales volume of approximately $3,000,000 annually from 1984 through 1997.

After lengthy discussion it was decided that cash flows should be discounted at a cost of capital in the region of 15 to 20 per cent per annum for the period over which this license proposal was being assessed. Company accountants suggested that Sappho's profit margin per unit of the drug would be between 10 and 15 percent with a most likely value of 20 percent.

## 17.3 SUGGESTED ANALYSIS FOR THE DECISION PROBLEM

A decision analyst had been taking part in the general discussions and he suggested that considering the amount of information available to the planning team, it would be useful to attack the problem in the following way. First, by drawing the appropriate decision tree; second, by evaluating the worth of the alternative strategies available to the company; and third, by explicitly considering the criterion by which a choice should be made between the alternative strategies.

## QUESTIONS FOR DISCUSSION

1. Evaluate this problem using whatever techniques you consider relevant.
2. Propose a solution and discuss the realism of your analysis.
3. Do you need extra information regarding the financial structure of Sappho to help you choose the criterion by which you would discriminate between alternative strategies?

*Chapter 18*

# *The Great Expectations Company Ltd:* The Evaluation of Risk in Mining Ventures*


## SUMMARY

This case examines a risk analysis model applied to the evaluation of a mining venture. The value for the reader lies in attempting to critique the model's assumptions and in assessing the sensitivity of the project's value to changes in the values of the underlying project variables.


## 18.1 INTRODUCTION

Strategic and operational-level decisions in mining ventures involve considerable uncertainty arising from various possible causes and sources. For example, in contemplating the development of a new lease for oil drilling and exploration, a major uncertainty concerns the unknown potential of the lease. Answers are sought to questions such as: How productive is the basin? What is the likely range of oil and natural gas reserves? What is the likely productive time horizon of the lease? How difficult and costly is it to retrieve the oil?

## 18.2 THE GREAT EXPECTATIONS COMPANY

In the Great Expectations case we confront the decision problem of a company which is considering whether or not to acquire a copper and nickel mining company. The price is not known and therefore the company has to make a valuation of the worth of the Company's assets, given estimates of reserves, production capacity and the quality of the copper and nickel which would be obtained.

*This case was written by Howard Thomas using as a basis an article by G. A. Brown (1970). 'The Evaluation of Risk in Mining Ventures', *CIM Transactions*, **73**, pp. 278–304.

The flow diagram showing the logic of the approach is shown below:

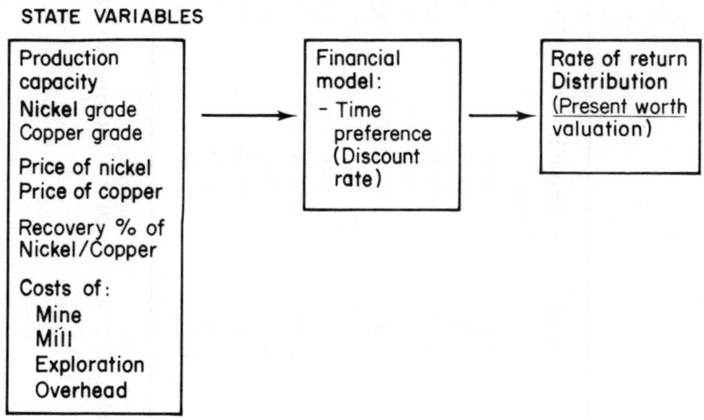


Table 18.1 shows the assessments made for the variables in relation to the mine evaluation. It was assumed also that the useful life of the mine would be five years and this was the time horizon used for discounting purposes. This was further reinforced by a plan to increase the annual production by some 50,000 tons per year with the intention of depleting the present ore reserves in five years.

Before programming the simulation program in order to obtain the present worth distribution, certain assumptions were made about the cash flow patterns:

(1) Nickel and copper grades in the final year were assumed to be such that they would completely deplete the nickel and copper remaining in the ore reserve. This may have the effect of making the grade in the final year higher than in previous years.
(2) If the production sequence were such that less than 50,000 tons would remain in the final year of operation, it would be taken in the penultimate year.
(3) Tax calculations were made allowing for depreciation, capital cost allowances and tax losses. The aim, within the constraints of tax policy, was to minimize the tax paid by the company on a per period basis.
(4) The variables in the model were assumed to exhibit some growth or decay over time as explained in the next section.

## 18.3 GROWTH OR DECAY OF VARIABLE VALUES OVER TIME IN THE PLANNING MODEL

The values of variables, such as nickel price, are known to change with time, and this must be allowed for in a model of this type. In the model, the future values are assumed to change in the following manner:

Table 18.1 Estimates of Variable Values

| Variable | | Min. | ML | Max. | Confid.[a] | Growth[b] | Disc.[b] |
|---|---|---|---|---|---|---|---|
| Annual production '000 | | 240 | 300 | 320 | 0.95 | 0.0 | 1.0 |
| Annual grade | Ni % | 1.45 | 1.60 | 1.70 | 0.90 | – 0.05 | 1.0 |
| | Cu % | 0.90 | 1.05 | 1.10 | 0.90 | −0.06 | 1.0 |
| Price | Ni $ | 1.15 | 1.28 | 1.35 | 0.95 | 0.02 | 0.95 |
| | Cu $ | 0.48 | 0.55 | 0.59 | 0.95 | 0.04 | 0.99 |
| Rec'y | Ni % | 89 | 92 | 92 | 1.0 | 0.0 | 1.0 |
| | Cu % | 89 | 92 | 92 | 1.0 | 0.0 | 1.0 |
| Mine cost | $ | 12.00 | 14.50 | 15.25 | 0.95 | 0.06 | 0.99 |
| Mill cost | $ | 9.80 | 10.20 | 11.00 | 0.95 | 0.05 | 1.0 |
| Explor. cost | $ | 2.25 | 2.40 | 2.90 | 0.95 | −0.30 | 0.99 |
| Mine overhead | $'000 | 4.175 | 4.300 | 4.500 | 0.90 | 0.08 | 1.0 |
| Out overhead | $'000 | 400 | 450 | 550 | 0.95 | 0.05 | 1.0 |

[a]The confidence figure is the probability that the range minimum to maximum contains the uncertain variable value.
[b]The combination of growth and discount factors will determine the growth or decay of a particular variable over time. The nature of the process is explained later in the case.

The growth factor in year $N = F_N$.

$$F_N = 1 + GD^{N-1}(N-1)$$

where $G$ = Growth;
$D$ = Discount.

Thus, the value of a variable in year $N$ would be

$$V_N = V_1(1 + GD^{(N-1)}(N-1))$$

If $D$ = greater than one: then the growth increases rapidly;
$D$ = one: growth is linear;
$D$ = less than one: growth reaches a plateau value;
$G$ may be positive or negative or zero.

The effects of various combinations of $D$ and $G$ are shown in Figures 18.1 and Table 18.2. Thus, by using various growth and discount values, the analyst may approximate any growth pattern. For instance, the analyst estimates that the mining cost, although at \$14.50/ton now, will probably be \$17.80 in five years, and that a discount rate of 0.99 produces the type of curve likely to express the growth pattern.

$$\text{Then, growth rate} = \frac{V_5 - V_1}{V_1} \cdot \frac{1}{D^4.4}$$

$$= \frac{17.80 - 14.50}{14.50} \cdot \frac{1}{(0.99)^4.4}$$

$$= 0.0592 \text{ or a compound growth effect of}$$

$\underline{5.92\%}$

The analyst would therefore specify:

| | Initial value | Growth | Discount |
|---|---|---|---|
| Mine Cost | 14.50 | 0.06 | 0.99 |

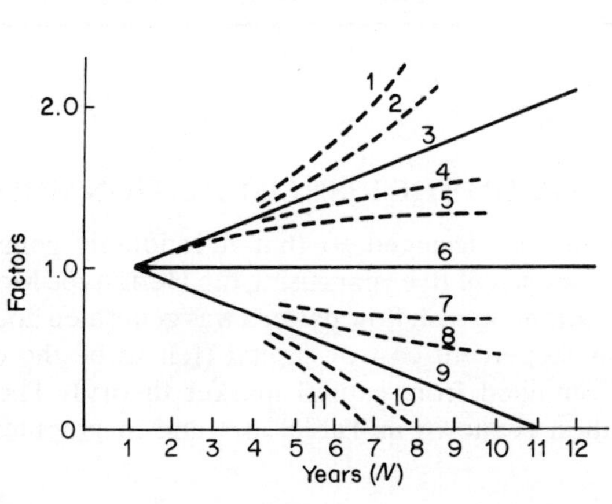


Figure 18.1

Table 18.2 Growth Factors
(Factor = $1.0 + GD^{N-1}\ (N-1)$)

| | $G$ | $D$ |
|---|---|---|
| 1 | +.10 | 1.10 |
| 2 | +.10 | 1.05 |
| 3 | +.10 | 1.00 |
| 4 | +.10 | 0.95 |
| 5 | +.10 | 0.90 |
| 6 | 0.0 | 1.00 |
| 7 | −.10 | 0.90 |
| 8 | −.10 | 0.95 |
| 9 | −.10 | 1.00 |
| 10 | −.10 | 1.05 |
| 11 | −.10 | 1.10 |

Table 18.3 Present Value ($'000)

| From | Up to | Frequency | Cumulative freq. | Percent |
|---|---|---|---|---|
| − 500 | 0 | 2 | 2 | 1.0 |
| 0 | 500 | 3 | 5 | 2.5 |
| 500 | 1000 | 5 | 10 | 5.0 |
| 1000 | 1500 | 16 | 26 | 13.0 |
| 1500 | 2000 | 51 | 77 | 38.5 |
| 2000 | 2500 | 36 | 113 | 66.5 |
| 2500 | 3000 | 47 | 160 | 80.0 |
| 3000 | 3500 | 32 | 192 | 96.0 |
| 3500 | 4000 | 7 | 199 | 99.5 |
| 4000 | 4500 | 1 | 200 | 100.0 |

## 18.4. RESULTS FROM THE RISK SIMULATION MODEL

The simulation program was designed so that it randomly generated 200 values of each variable for each of five years using the Hertz-type Monte-Carlo technique. On each iteration the cash flow pattern was generated and a present value obtained using a 10 percent cost of capital (felt to be the company's opportunity cost and obtained from capital market theory). The resulting present value distribution is shown in Table 18.3 and in graphical form in Figure 18.2.

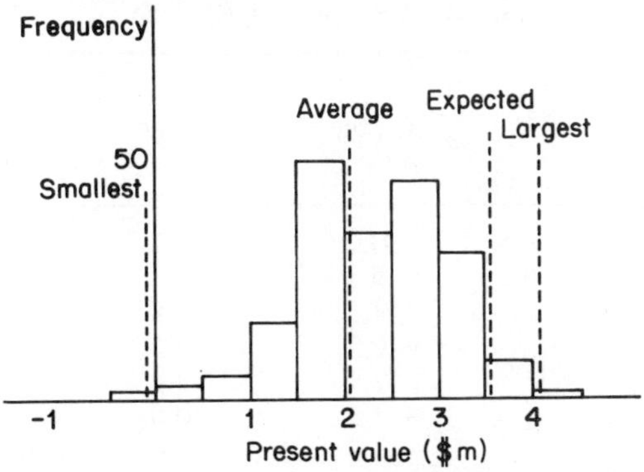


Figure 18.2 Frequency diagram of returns

Summary Statistics of Present Value Distribution

| | |
|---|---|
| Arithmetic mean | $2,012 |
| Standard dev. | 803 |
| Smallest | $−127 |
| Largest | 4,050 |
| Range | 4,178 |
| Most likely | 3,517 |

Probability of $2,000,000 (present value) or less is 38.5 percent
Probability of $3,500 000 or less is 96 percent

The summary statistics obtained from this distribution show a range of $ – 127,000 to $4,050,000. The difference between the mean of $2,042,000 and the mode of $3,517,000 demonstrates the skewness of the distribution.

For the decision-maker, the key issue is the determination of the offer price for the copper and nickel mining company. In order to help, the analyst provided him with some sensitivity analysis results. These were obtained by holding all variables, except one, at their modal value, changing the single variable from its minimum to its maximum and noting the effect on the present value.

The results shown in Table 18.4 demonstrate the sensitivity of the valuation to production rates, future copper and nickel prices and mine costs. Such sensitivities suggest that assessment efforts should be rechecked in relation to the above-mentioned variables.

## 18.5 CONCLUSION

The valuation appraisal in risk analysis terms has looked at one possible scenario for the exploration of the mine prospect. The process could equally well be applied to scenarios involving different assumptions about productive capacity, tax policies and minimum cut-off trades for mining of copper and

Table 18.4 Sensitivity Test

| | | Variable min. | Changed max. | Present Value (% change) Min. | Max. |
|---|---|---|---|---|---|
| Annual production | | −20.0 | 6.7 | −65.9 | 16.1 |
| Annual grade | Ni | − 9.4 | 6.3 | −17.8 | 0.4 |
| | Cu | −14.3 | 4.8 | − 6.5 | 0.5 |
| Price | Ni | −10.2 | 5.5 | −102.8 | 47.0 |
| | Cu | −12.7 | 7.3 | − 34.4 | 18.6 |
| Recovery | Ni | − 3.3 | 0.0 | − 29.9 | 0.0 |
| | Cu | − 3.3 | 0.0 | − 8.57 | 0.0 |
| Mine cost | | −17.2 | 5.2 | 67.2 | −21.6 |
| Mill cost | | − 3.9 | 7.8 | 10.8 | −22.7 |
| Explore cost | | − 6.3 | 20.8 | 1.6 | − 3.7 |
| Mine overhead | | − 2.9 | 4.7 | 9.0 | −14.9 |
| Outside overhead | | −11.1 | 18.2 | 3.4 | − 7.0 |

nickel. In this manner, different risk simulations can allow the manager to test and contemplate suggested changes in exploration and operation of the mine before making a decision about implementation. In essence, he gets a refined understanding of the impact of uncertainty and environmental factors on the operations and potential of the mine.

If a detailed case about acquisition has to be made then the planners must evaluate the worth of adding the prospect to the existing portfolio of activities. Thus, the addition of the prospect should be looked at in terms of its effects on such things as capital structure and the project's cash flow pattern.

## QUESTIONS FOR DISCUSSION

1. Do you think that the model has examined all the appropriate variables (i.e. maintenance and operating costs, cost of recapping etc.…)?
2. Do you find cash flow assumptions (1) and (2) on page 225 realistic? Give reasons.
3. Would you say that the approach adopted with respect to taxes is a sensible one? (*see* assumption (3) page 225). Would it be better to minimize the present value of taxes?
4. What is the role of the discount rate in the formula for $F_N$? Can it really be called a discount rate? How do you feel about the range of values used in Table 18.2 and Figure 18.1?
5. The capital asset pricing model (*CAPM*) was used in this analysis. In view of the nature of the project would you expect the discount rate so obtained to be adequate? What particular aspect(s) of mining ventures in your opinion might make the CAPM inadequate?
6. Should interactions between the various variables be included formally in the model's structure?
7. Comment on the conclusion. In particular do you consider the analysis as presented to be sufficient?

*Chapter 19*

# *Sand or Gravel:* A Case History of a Decision Problem Involving Uncertainty*


SUMMARY

This case compares two mining opportunities in the sand and gravel business. Separate risk analyses of each opportunity are undertaken followed by a comparison between them on an incremental cash flow basis.

The case shows much of the analytic detail including cash flow and profit and loss projections. By this means the reader is encouraged to question those analytic approaches and assumptions.


Digger & Sons are in the sand and gravel business. They are an old-established firm with sand and gravel pits in various parts of the West Country. They are always looking for opportunities to expand and tend to find that their financial and managerial resources are sufficient for any expansion they commonly contemplate, and that it is the dearth of new sites in their part of the country which is the limiting factor. Their established customers are in the West and they do not want to shift their business out of that part of England.

The Development Director, whose responsibility it is to find new deposits to renew the reserves of the business, comes to the Board with a problem. He has found both a gravel and a sand site near to an important market center, close together on the outskirts of the town. The Town Council, which owns the land, is willing to grant a mineral lease for either site, but not for both, because it intends to build council houses in that area and needs the land covering one site or the other. It is indifferent as to which site is developed, so long as it can have the land back within eleven years, or at the end of the mineral development, whichever is earlier, for further building. Both sites are very substantial and the Council is asking a very high price for the right to work the land.

One site, called Penrose Hill, will produce gravel, and this gravel will be bought by the local road contractor. The county is currently stepping up its

*This case was developed by T. V. Ryder-Runton in association with Howard Thomas.

road construction program and will offer a three-year contract for a large quantity. On renewal the contract is likely to be for a rather smaller annual amount at a lower price.

The other site, Tremoe Field, will yield sand, which Digger & Sons expect to sell to local builders. The sand needs to be cleaned before delivery, which necessitates some stockpiling. Digger has not had a site near this town before, and up till now a local company has had a monopoly. Digger expect to have to fight for sales initially, but potential profits are considerable if they can win a significant share of the market within a few years. The town is expanding very quickly because of a London 'overspill' scheme.

Two other members of the Board have a special interest in the Development Director's problem. These are the Marketing and Finance Directors. The Marketing Director is responsible for confirming the preliminary market estimates for these new ventures. The Finance Director is required to assess their relative profitability and present this analysis to his colleagues. For this assessment to have any validity he needs to know, not only the Marketing Director's view on the most likely sales achievement, but also the range of possible outcomes and the likelihood of any part of those ranges being achieved.

The three directors form a subcommittee of the Board to report on the two prospects. The Board would like to see a number of indices of profitability, as they believe each tends to give a different insight about the viability of the prospect.

The subcommittee reports in the form of a general description of the two opportunities open to the company and a recommendation as to which of the two the company should undertake. Its recommendations are backed up by three fairly detailed appendices (A, B and C) setting out and analyzing the data relevant to an assessment of profitability and risk. These appendices follow.

# Appendix A: Penrose Hill

## 1 THE MARKET

Our basic expectation here is that the promised contract for road gravel will be at the rate of 75,000 tons a year for three years at the current price of just over 85p a ton ex-quarry. This contract can be signed before starting construction, so we see no reason for seriously examining any alternative forecast.

At contract renewal time our most likely estimate is that the contract tonnage will fall to 55,000 tons per annum at an ex-quarry price of 80p a ton (disregarding price increases resulting from inflation). However, the range of possibilities we foresee is as follows:

| | |
|---|---|
| Range of possible tonnage | 40,000–75,000 t.p.a. |
| Range of possible prices | 75p–90p |
| Range of lengths of renewed contract | 3 years–5 years |

## 2 COSTS

The capital cost will be as follows:

| | |
|---|---|
| Fixed assets | £40,000 |
| Lease | £60,000 |
| Working capital | £15,000 (at peak in most likely case) |
| Less grant | (£4,000) |
| Total capital | £111,000 |

The exact build-up and decline of working capital is shown in the cash flow statement (Table 19.1).

Eventually a further £10,500 will be incurred in making good the surface of the land before returning the site to the Council. Operating costs will be 32p a ton direct, at the initial contract level. The increase in administrative overhead, etc. attributable to this project will be about £2,000 a year in most years.

We believe our cost estimating is sufficiently good to make a study of the effects of an overrun or higher operating costs unnecessary.

## 3 FINANCE

No permanent loan capital can be raised for this project due to its short life. However, we have been promised a £15,000 increase in our 7½ percent overdraft facilities on the condition that we repay this increase after four years. All other finance will be from the company's equity cash resources.

Table 19.1 *Penrose*: Forecast Cash Flow Statement

| Cash flows (£) | Years −1 | 1 | 2 | 3 | 4 | 5 | 6 | 7 | 8 |
|---|---|---|---|---|---|---|---|---|---|
| Lease | (60,000) | — | — | — | — | — | — | — | — |
| Fixed assets | (40,000) | — | — | — | — | — | — | — | — |
| Working capital | ( 5,000) | (10,000) | — | 5,000 | — | — | 10,000 | — | — |
| Grant received | — | 4,000 | — | — | — | — | — | — | — |
| Cost of making land good | — | — | — | — | — | — | — | (10,500) | — |
| Bank loan | 15,000 | — | — | — | (15,000) | — | — | — | — |
| Net profit before tax | — | 20,375 | 20,375 | 20,375 | 7,575 | 8,700 | 8,700 | — | — |
| Tax in year paid | — | — | (7,450) | (7,706) | (8,026) | (4,946) | (5,516) | (5,196) | — |
| Tax saved on company's other income | — | 3,200 | — | — | — | — | — | — | 4,200 |
| Depreciation | — | 16,500 | 16,500 | 16,500 | 16,500 | 16,500 | 16,500 | — | — |
| Net equity cash flow | (90,000) | 34,075 | 29,425 | 34,170 | 1,049 | 20,254 | 29,684 | (15,696) | 4,200 |

Tax is paid over to the government in cash during the year following the year in which the profits on which it is assessed are earned. Capital allowances include a mineral depletion allowance on the gravel pit calculated in the form of a notional royalty.

## 4 PROFITABILITY

Table 19.2 details the profit and loss statement for the most likely case. The results of the profitability analysis follow immediately.

### Analysis of the Most Likely Case

| | | |
|---|---|---|
| (i) | DCF yield | 16.5% |
| (ii) | Net Present Value at 10% | £14,226 |
| (iii) | Discounted payback period at 10% | 5.66 years |
| (iv) | Book rate of return, net of tax, on both initial and average capital employed | 8.75% (initial)<br>15.0% (average) |
| (v) | Traditional payback period | 3.78 years |

Note: Our cost of equity capital, net of inflation, is 10 percent. The cash flow is in real terms.

### Effect of Market Uncertainty on Profitability

The significance of the range of each variable factor, such as tonnage or price, is measured by its effect on the Net Present Value of the project as a whole. We chose NPV (Net Present Value) rather than yield, to reduce the length of the calculation. The effect of each factor is shown on the following graphs.

Figure 19.1 shows the effect on NPV of variations in tonnage on renewal of the contract, assuming a price of 80p per ton and a three-year renewal. Figure 19.2 shows the effect on NPV of variations in price on renewal of the contract, assuming 55,000 tons per annum and a three-year renewal. Figure 19.3 shows the effect of variations in contract life on renewal, assuming 80p per ton and 55,000 tons p.a.

### Full Range of Possible Outcomes

*If*, on renewal of the contract, the annual tonnage is 40,000, the price 75p and the life three years, *then*,

the NPV @ 10% is £1,003

*If*, on renewal of the contract, the annual tonnage is 75,000, the price 90p and the life five years, *then*,

the NPV @ 10% is £55,326.

Table 19.2 *Penrose: Forecast profit and loss statement in the most likely case*

| | *Years* | | | | | |
|---|---|---|---|---|---|---|
| Profit and loss | 1 | 2 | 3 | 4 | 5 | 6 |
| Sales | 64,000 | 64,000 | 64,000 | 44,000 | 44,000 | 44,000 |
| Cost of sales | 24,000 | 24,000 | 24,000 | 16,800 | 16,800 | 16,800 |
| Equals gross margin | 40,000 | 40,000 | 40,000 | 27,200 | 27,200 | 27,200 |
| Less other expenses | 2,000 | 2,000 | 2,000 | 2,000 | 2,000 | 2,000 |
| Interest on overdraft | 1,125 | 1,125 | 1,125 | 1,125 | — | — |
| Depreciation and amort. | 16,500 | 16,500 | 16,500 | 16,500 | 16,500 | 16,500 |
| Equals net profit before tax | 20,375 | 20,375 | 20,375 | 7,575 | 8,700 | 8,700 |
| Less corporation tax provision | 7,450 | 7,706 | 8,026 | 4,946 | 5,516 | 5,196 |
| Equals net profit after tax | 12,925 | 12,669 | 12,349 | 2,629 | 3,184 | 3,504 |
| *Notes on Tax* | | | | | | |
| Net profit before tax | 20,375 | 20,375 | 20,375 | 7,575 | 8,700 | 8,700 |
| Plus depreciation, etc. | 16,500 | 16,500 | 16,500 | 16,500 | 16,500 | 16,500 |
| Equals | 36,875 | 36,875 | 36,875 | 24,075 | 25,200 | 25,200 |
| Less capital allowances[a] | 18,250 | 17,610 | 16,810 | 11,710 | 11,410 | 12,210 |
| Equals taxable profit | 18,625 | 19,265 | 20,065 | 12,365 | 13,790 | 12,990 |
| Corporation tax provision @ 40% | 7,450 | 7,706 | 8,026 | 4,946 | 5,516 | 5,196 |

[a]Additional capital allowances are as follows:

(i) £8,000 of capital allowances in the year of construction, which can be offset against profits elsewhere in the company which would otherwise give rise to tax payments of £3,200 in the first year of sales. Thus, there are tax savings of £3,200 in Year 1.

(ii) £10,500 of capital allowances in year after the end of sales resulting from making good the land surface can be set off against income from elsewhere in the company in year 7. This means a tax saving of £4,200 in year 8.

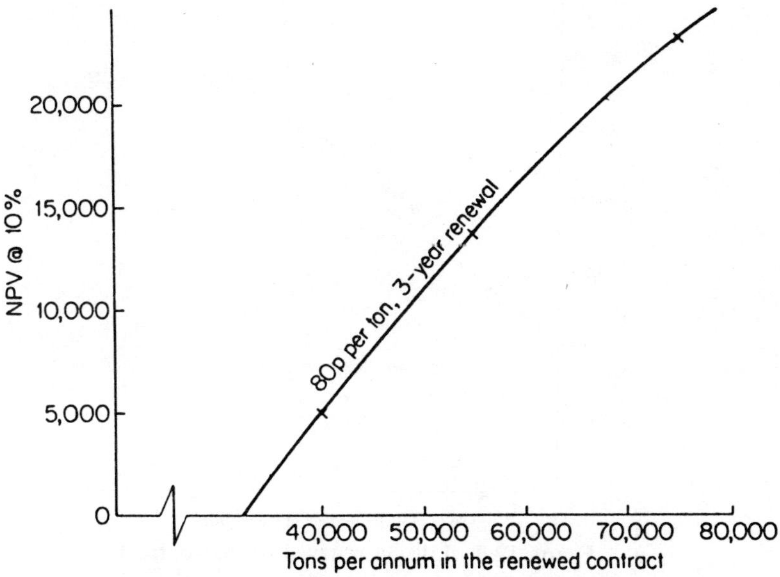


Figure 19.1 Tonnage on renewal of the contract

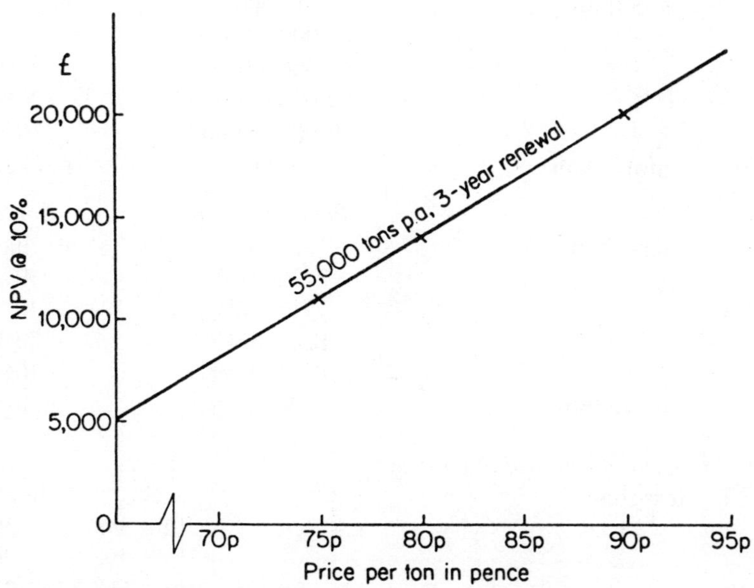


Figure 19.2 Price on renewal of the contract

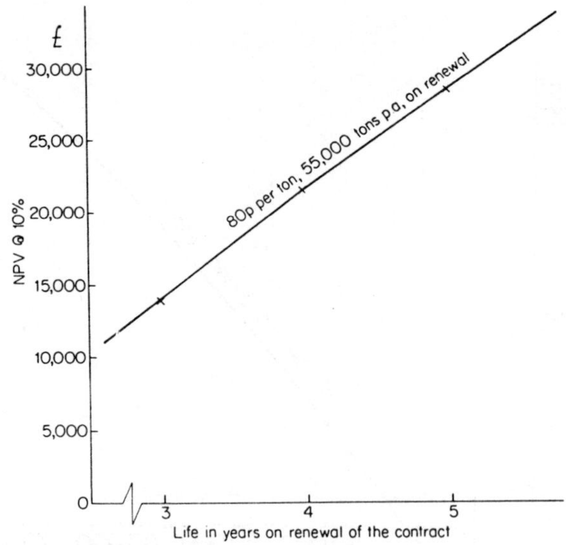


Figure 19.3 Life on renewal of the contract

**Probability of a Successful Outcome**

The following estimates are made of the likelihood of achieving a particular tonnage, price or length of renewal of the contract.

| | | | |
|---|---|---|---|
| (i) | *Tonnage* | *t.p.a.* | *Chance* |
| | less than | 40,000 | negligible |
| | | 40,000–50,000 | 20% |
| | | 50,000–60,000 | 50% |
| | | 60,000–70,000 | 20% |
| | | 70,000–80,000 | 10% |
| | more than | 80,000 | negligible |
| (ii) | *Price* | *Pence per ton* | *Chance* |
| | less than | 72½ | negligible |
| | | 72½–77½ | 30% |
| | | 77½–82½ | 40% |
| | | 82½–87½ | 20% |
| | | 87½–92½ | 10% |
| | more than | 92½ | negligible |
| (iii) | *Length of renewal of contract* | *Years* | *Chance* |
| | less than | 2½ | negligible |
| | | 2½ – 3½ | 50% |
| | | 3½ – 4½ | 30% |
| | | 4½ – 5½ | 20% |
| | more than | 5½ | negligible |

Given these probabilities, graphs can be drawn to show the probability distribution of possible profitability. (These are shown in Figures 19.6 and 19.7.)

# Appendix B: Tremoe Field

## 1 THE MARKET

Our basic expectation here is that we shall successfully break into the local sand market and take a 40 percent share in four years. We should maintain this share for as long as we can retain the sand deposit, which is ten years from today. This means we should be selling 86,000 t.p.a. in the fourth year of operations (see section (ii) below).

The current price of £1.20 a ton delivered is expected to fall as a result of competition, probably by 20 percent, so we are assuming a price of only £1.00 a ton. Clearly we face a great uncertainty here, not knowing what the reaction of our competitor may be. The range of possible prices and tons sold is our best estimate of the risks we face.

(i) *Range of Prices*
We expect the price competition to take effect during the first year, the fall being to between

90p and £1.15 a ton.

(ii) *Range of Tonnage*
Official forecast sand-consumption statistics, published as part of the local authority planning for the London overspill scheme, are as follows:

Years (adjusted to the years for this project)

| | 1 | 2 | 3 | 4 |
|---|---|---|---|---|
| Tons per annum | 170,000 | 204,000 | 204,000 | 215,000 |
| We expect our share of the market to grow as follows: | 10% | 25% | 33% | 40% |
| Thus sales should total: Tons per annum | 17,000 | 51,000 | 68,000 | 86,000 |

We face two major uncertainties. Will our share of the market rise at the pace forecast? Will we ever achieve a total of 40 percent? The range of possible shares of the market in the light of these two uncertainties we forecast as follows:

| | 1 | 2 | 3 | 4 |
|---|---|---|---|---|
| At worst | 7% | 17½% | 23% | 28% |
| At best | 12½% | 31¼% | 41¼% | 50% |

Hence the worst and best sales tonnage expectations are as follows:

| | 1 | 2 | 3 | 4 |
|---|---|---|---|---|
| At worst | 11,900 | 35,700 | 46,900 | 60,200 |
| At best | 21,250 | 63,750 | 84,150 | 107,500 |

Sales revenue is assumed to continue at a constant level from year four onwards.

## 2 COSTS

The capital cost will be as follows:

| | |
|---|---|
| Fixed assets | £45,000 |
| Lease | £80,000 |
| Working capital | £19,500 (at peak in most likely case) |
| Less grant | (£4,500) |
| Total capital | £140,000 |

The exact build-up and decline of working capital is shown in the cash flow statement (Table 19.3). Because of bad debts and unsold stocks, we expect to be able to recover only 70 percent of working capital in the final year of sales. Both the fixed asset and lease expenditure is spread over a two-year construction period.

Eventually a further £6,000 will have to be spent in making good the surface of the land before returning the site to the Council.

Operating costs will be 36½p a ton direct at the expected peak production level in the most likely case; but will be as high as 50p a ton at the lowest level of production due to the fixed element in direct costs. The increase in administrative overhead, etc. attributable to this project will be about £2,500 in the first year of sales and £1,500 a year in the remaining years.

We believe our cost estimating is sufficiently good to make a study of the effects of an overrun or higher operating costs unnecessary.

## 3 FINANCE

No permanent loan capital can be raised for this project due to its short life. However, we have been promised a £20,000 increase in our 7½ percent overdraft facilities on the condition that we repay this increase after three years. All our other finance will be from the company's equity cash resources.

Tax is paid over to the government in cash during the year following the year in which the profits on which it is assessed are earned. Capital allowances include a mineral depletion allowance on the sand pit, calculated on the basis of a notional royalty. (This explains the unusual pattern of the tax allowances.)

Table 19.3 Tremoe: Forecast Cash Flow Statement (£)

| | Years | | | | | | | | | | | |
|---|---|---|---|---|---|---|---|---|---|---|---|---|
| | −2 | −1 | 1 | 2 | 3 | 4 | 5 | 6 | 7 | 8 | 9 | 10 |
| Lease | (70,000) | (10,000) | — | — | — | — | — | — | — | — | — | — |
| Fixed assets | (22,500) | (22,500) | — | — | — | — | — | — | — | — | — | — |
| Working capital | — | (4,500) | — | (5,000) | (5,000) | (5,000) | — | — | — | 13,650 | — | — |
| Grant received | — | — | 4,500 | — | — | — | — | — | — | — | — | — |
| Cost of making land good | — | — | — | — | — | — | — | — | — | — | (6,000) | |
| Bank loan | — | 20,000 | — | — | (20,000) | — | — | — | — | — | — | — |
| Net profit before tax | — | — | (11,500) | 11,000 | 23,000 | 37,000 | 37,000 | 37,000 | 37,000 | 37,000 | — | — |
| Tax in year paid | — | — | — | — | (6,176) | (11,536) | (14,656) | (14,776) | (14,896) | (15,016) | (15,056) | — |
| Tax saved on company's other income | — | 3,600 | — | 912 | — | — | — | — | — | — | — | 2,400 |
| Depreciation | — | — | 16,000 | 16,000 | 16,000 | 16,000 | 16,000 | 16,000 | 16,000 | 16,000 | — | — |
| Net equity cash flow | (92,500) | (13,400) | 9,000 | 22,912 | 7,824 | 36,464 | 38,344 | 38,224 | 38,104 | 51,634 | (21,056) | 2,400 |

Table 19.4 Tremoe: Forecast profit and loss statement in the most likely case

| | Years | | | | | | | |
|---|---|---|---|---|---|---|---|---|
| Profit and loss | 1 | 2 | 3 | 4 | 5 | 6 | 7 | 8 |
| Sales | 17,000 | 51,000 | 68,000 | 86,000 | 86,000 | 86,000 | 86,000 | 86,000 |
| Less cost of sales | 8,500 | 21,000 | 26,000 | 31,500 | 31,500 | 31,500 | 31,500 | 31,500 |
| Gross margin | 8,500 | 30,000 | 42,000 | 54,500 | 54,500 | 54,500 | 54,500 | 54,500 |
| Less other expenses | 2,500 | 1,500 | 1,500 | 1,500 | 1,500 | 1,500 | 1,500 | 1,500 |
| Interest on overdraft | 1,500 | 1,500 | 1,500 | — | — | — | — | — |
| Depreciation and amort. | 16,000 | 16,000 | 16,000 | 16,000 | 16,000 | 16,000 | 16,000 | 16,000 |
| Net profit before tax | (11,500) | 11,000 | 23,000 | 37,000 | 37,000 | 37,000 | 37,000 | 37,000 |
| Less corporate tax provision | — | 6,176 | 11,536 | 14,656 | 14,776 | 14,896 | 15,016 | 15,056 |
| Net profit after tax | (11,500) | 4,824 | 11,464 | 22,344 | 22,224 | 22,104 | 21,984 | 21,944 |
| *Notes on Tax* | | | | | | | | |
| Net profit before tax | (11,500) | 11,000 | 23,000 | 37,000 | 37,000 | 37,000 | 37,000 | 37,000 |
| Plus depreciation, etc. | 16,000 | 16,000 | 16,000 | 16,000 | 16,000 | 16,000 | 16,000 | 16,000 |
| | 4,500 | 27,000 | 39,000 | 53,000 | 53,000 | 53,000 | 53,000 | 53,000 |
| Less capital allowances[a] | 6,780 | 11,560 | 14,160 | 16,360 | 16,060 | 15,760 | 15,460 | 15,360 |
| Equals taxable profit[b] | (2,280) | 15,440 | 28,840 | 36,640 | 36,940 | 37,240 | 37,540 | 37,640 |
| Corporate tax provision @ 40% | — | 6,176 | 11,536 | 14,656 | 14,776 | 14,896 | 15,016 | 15,056 |

[a]Additional capital allowances as follows:

(i) £9,000 of capital allowances in the first year of construction which can be offset against profits elswhere in the company which would otherwise give rise to tax payments of £3,600 in the second year of construction. Thus, there are tax savings of £3,600 in Year −1.

(ii) £6,000 of capital allowances in the year after the end of sales resulting from making good the land surface can be set off against income from elsewhere in the company in year 9. This will result in a tax saving of £2,400 in year 10.

[b]This loss can also be offset against profits elsewhere in the company, which would otherwise result in a tax payment of £912 in the second year of sales. Thus, in year 2, there is a tax saving of £912.

Tax is paid over to the government in cash during the year following the year in which the profits on which it is assessed are earned. Capital allowances include a mineral depletion allowance on the sand pit, calculated on the basis of a notional royalty. (This explains the unusual pattern of the tax allowances.)

## 4. PROFITABILITY

Table 19.4 details the profit and loss statement for the most likely case. The results of the profitability analysis follow immediately.

### Analysis of Most Likely Case

| | | |
|---|---|---|
| (i) | DCF yield | 13.7% |
| (ii) | Net Present Value @ 10% today | £20,608 |
| (iii) | Discounted payback period @ 10% | 8.6 years |
| (iv) | Book rate of return, net of tax, on both initial and average capital employed | 13.2% (initial) 20.2% (average) |
| (v) | Traditional payback period | 6.8 years |

Note: Our cost of equity capital, net of inflation, is 10 percent. The cash flow is in real terms.

### Effect of Market Uncertainty on Profitability

The significance of the range of each variable factor, such as tonnage or price, is measured by its effect on the Net Present Value of the project as a whole. Again, we choose NPV rather than yield, to reduce the length of the calculation. The effect of each factor is shown in the following graphs.

Figure 19.4 shows the effect on NPV of variations in tonnage in the fourth and subsequent years of sales. The price is assumed to be £1.00 per ton. (In each case, the build-up of tonnage follows the same pattern as in the most likely case.) Figure 19.5 shows the effect on NPV of variations in price, assuming the most likely build-up of tonnage.

### Full Range of Possible Outcomes

*If*, the annual tonnage built up from 11,980 in year one to 60,200 in year five and subsequent years, and if the price achieved averages 90p a ton,
*then*,

the NPV @ 10% is £(31,746)

*If*, the annual tonnage builds up from 21,250 in year one to 107,500 in year five and subsequent years, and if the price achieved averages £1.15 a ton,
*then*,

the NPV @ 10% is £88.075

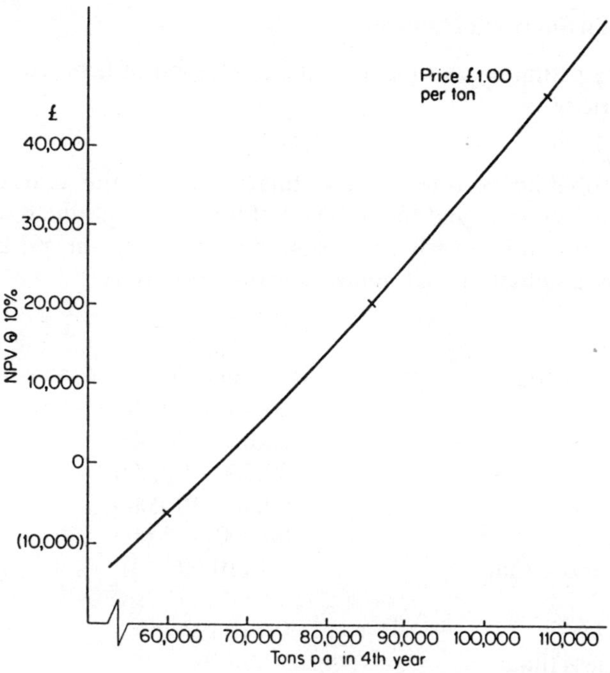


Figure 19.4 Tonnage varies

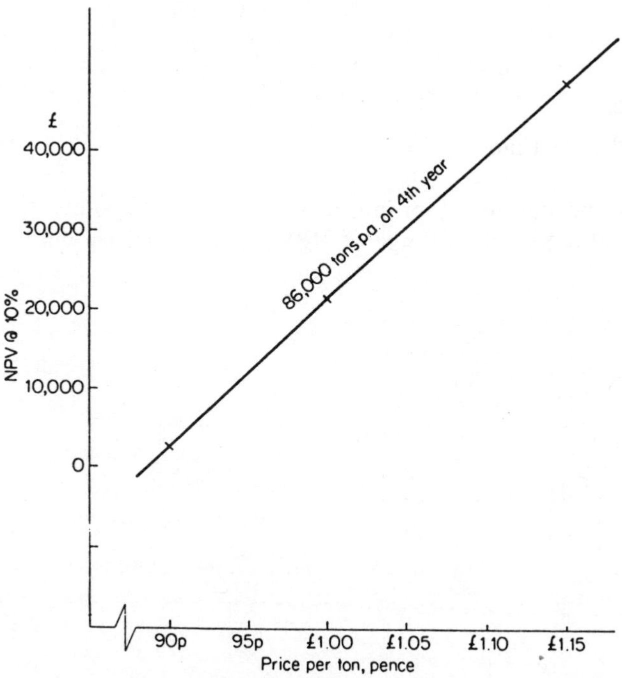


Figure 19.5 Price varies

**Probability of a Successful Outcome**

The following estimates are made of the likelihood of achieving a particular tonnage or price.

(i) *Tonnage*

The probabilities refer to the final share of the market achieved, expressed in tons, and the build up of tonnage is assumed to be an even progression in line with that assigned to the worst, most likely and best cases as assumed in the tonnage sensitivity analysis.

| | *t.p.a.* | *Chance* |
|---|---|---|
| less than | 60,000 | negligible |
| | 60,000– 70,000 | 20% |
| | 70,000– 80,000 | 20% |
| | 80,000– 90,000 | 30% |
| | 90,000–100,000 | 20% |
| | 100,000–110,000 | 10% |
| more than | 110,000 | negligible |

| (ii) *Price* | *Pence per ton* | *Chance* |
|---|---|---|
| less than | 87½ | negligible |
| | 87½– 92½ | 5% |
| | 92½– 97½ | 15% |
| | 97½–102½ | 40% |
| | 102½–107½ | 25% |
| | 107½–112½ | 10% |
| | 112½–117½ | 5% |
| more than | 117½ | negligible |

Given these probabilities, graphs can be drawn to show the probability distribution of achieving a range of NPVs. (These are shown in Figures 19.6 and 19.7.)

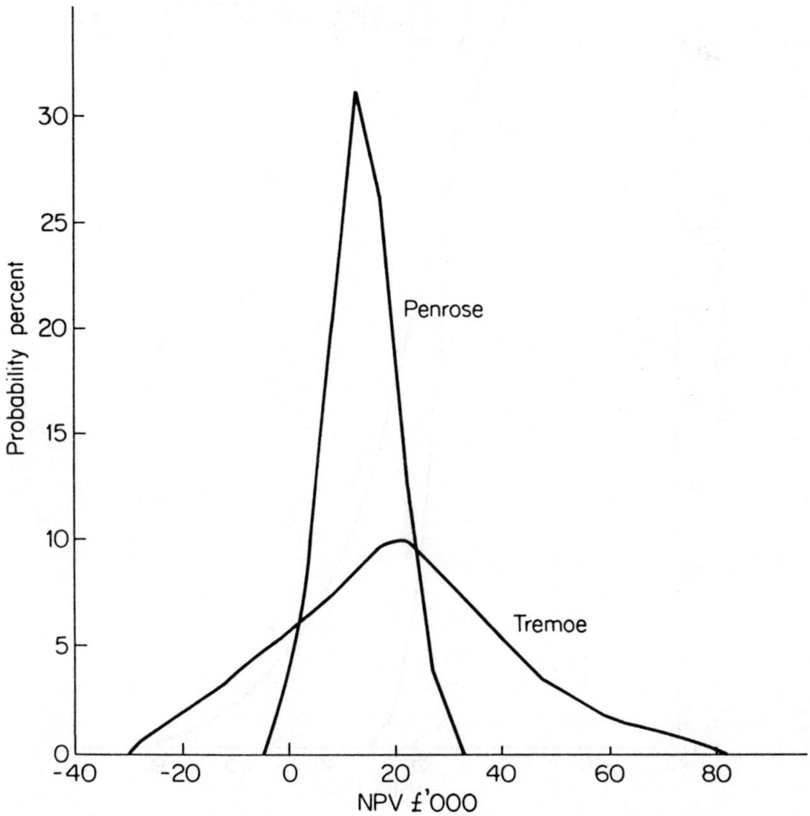


Figure 19.6 Estimated NPV probability distributions of Penrose and Tremoe

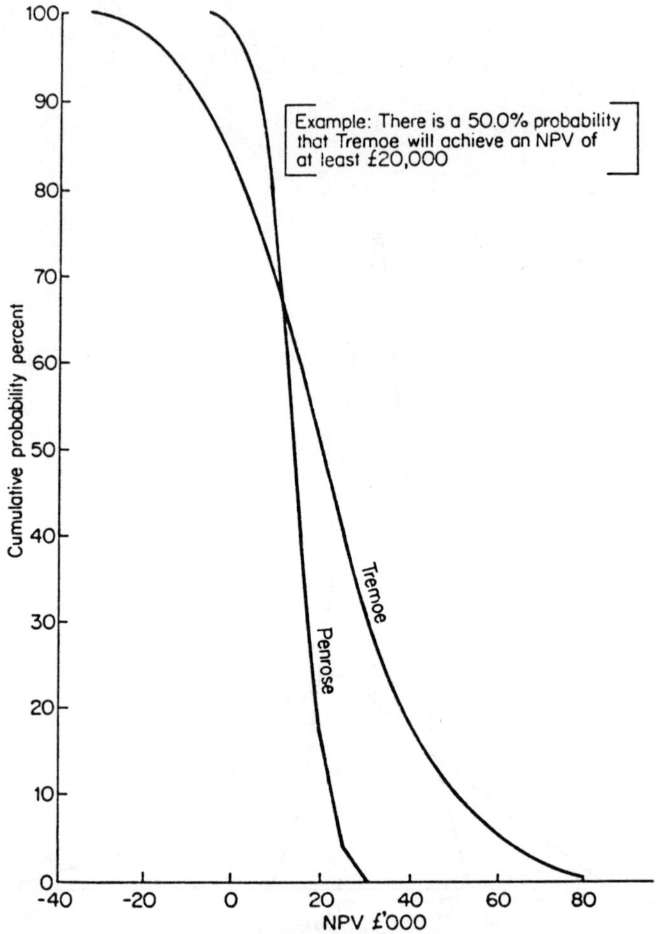


Figure 19.7 Cumulative probability of achieving at least a given NPV
[Example: there is a 50.0% probability that Tremoe will achieve an NPV of at least £20,000.]

# Appendix C: Comparison of Tremoe and Penrose

The following table compares Tremoe with Penrose on an incremental yield basis

**INCREMENTAL YIELD**

| *Tremoe* | *less* | *Penrose* | = | *Incremental cash flow* | *Adjusted* | *At 12%* | *At 11%* |
|---|---|---|---|---|---|---|---|
| £(92,500) | | £(90,000) | | £( 2,500) | £( 2,500) | £( 2,500) | £( 2,500) |
| (13,400) | | 34,075 | | (47,475) | (47,475) | (42,390) | (42,770) |
| 9,000 | | 29,425 | | (20,425) | (20,425) | (16,283) | (16,577) |
| 22,912 | | 34,170 | | (11,258) | (11,258) | (8,013) | (8,232) |
| 7,824 | | 1,049 | | 6,775 | 6,775 | 4,306 | 4,463 |
| 36,464 | | 20,254 | | 16,210 | 16,210 | 9,198 | 9,621 |
| 38,344 | | 29,684 | | 8,660 | 8,660 | 4,387 | 4,630 |
| 38,224 | | (15,696) | | 53,920 | 53,920 | 24,388 | 25,973 |
| 38,104 | | 4,200 | | 33,904 | 33,904 | 13,694 | 14,771 |
| 51,634 | | — | | 51,634 | 32,492 | 11,717 | 12,701 |
| (21,056) | | — | | (21,056) | — | — | — |
| 2,400 | | — | | 2,400 | 2,400 | 690 | 761 |
| | | | | | | (806) | £2,781 |

$$\therefore \text{Yield} = 11 + \frac{2781}{2781 + 806} = 11 + 0.78$$

i.e. 11.8%

Incremental Net Present Value at 10 percent at present time (i.e. beginning of year −1 for Penrose and beginning of year 12 for Tremoe)

| *Tremoe* | *less* | *Penrose* | = | *Incremental* |
|---|---|---|---|---|
| £20,608 | | £14,226 | | £6,382 |

Discounted payback period for incremental investment is 7.8 years.

## QUESTIONS FOR DISCUSSION

1. What recommendations would you have made in the light of the completed analysis, including the sensitivity and probability analysis?
2. Critically evaluate the analysis presented in the case.
3. How would you amend it?

*Chapter 20*

# *Sandy Creek: A Coal-mining Case Study**


## SUMMARY

This case presents the analysis of a coal mining opportunity in considerable detail. A 'first-pass' preliminary risk analysis is presented together with sensitivity analyses of the project to changes in many of the underlying project assumptions.

The case shows the role of sensitivity analysis in alerting managers to the effects of crucial sources of uncertainty upon project appraisal. Thus, the process of sensitivity analysis provides an important input to dialogue about project viability.


## 20.1 INTRODUCTION

In 1977,* an oil exploration company known as XYZ accidentally discovered a large coal seam (called Sandy Creek) in one of its exploration permits 250 km east of Rockhampton, Queensland. Following the disclosure of the discovery, XYZ announced that it had no plans to develop the mine at present or in the future.

ABC is a large mining company which has traditionally been involved with the mining of metals. Following the rocketing of oil prices, and the subsequent repercussions on other energy sources, ABC management has been looking at ways of broadening its base in the mining business in which it has achieved a high level of competence and a strong external reputation.

After consideration of the exploration data released by XYZ Tom Jones, the manager of the New Resources Department of ABC suspects that the Sandy Creek seam could provide the company with the stepping stone it needs to develop a coherent, broadly based, long-term mining strategy.

Jones's initial problem is to assess more formally whether or not the Sandy Creek seam is potentially as profitable as his subjective assessment leads him to

*This case was developed by Jean Dubourdieu and Howard Thomas at the Australian Graduate School of Management in Sydney. Though disguised (in terms of both chronology and data) it is based very closely upon the analysis of a recent large-scale mining opportunity in Queensland, Australia.

believe. Jones consequently asked Joe Smith, a mining engineer and recent MBA graduate, to investigate the potential of the Sandy Creek discovery.

## 20.2 INITIAL MEETING

In their first meeting, Jones told Smith that he wished to obtain a preliminary fix on the potential profitability and riskiness of the project. Jones indicated that if the results of this preliminary analysis were encouraging, a thorough financial analysis would then be undertaken.

To help Smith get started, Jones suggested that, as a rough rule of thumb, unless the project had the potential to return 25 percent or so before tax, it would probably not be worthy of further consideration. He also indicated that he was especially interested in the sensitivity of the project to the price-level assumption. Finally he told Smith that some preliminary contacts had been made with a few prospective buyers of coal from the seam. As a result of these discussions, some Japanese companies were interested in buying coal from Sandy Creek mainly because of its high quality. Smith thought it was therefore extremely likely that, at the going price, all the coal could be produced up to about 3,000,000 t.p.a. (tons per annum) would be immediately contracted for on a long-term basis.

## 20.3 MINE SITUATION AND ENVIRONMENT

If development went ahead, the mine would be particularly well situated. Several mines already existed in the region, operated by some of the largest Australian companies. A substantial mining town located just 11.5 km away would be able to provide the required accommodation. Furthermore, a rail link currently used to service other mines passes just 4.8 km away from the site.

The rail line links the region to the port of Gladstone which is already equipped to handle coal. The Queensland Government has made it known that the present infrastructure could meet the requirements of the present mine for a production not in excess of about 3,000,000 tons per annum. Any further output from the area would result in the complete saturation of both the rail and the electrical systems, thus necessitating the upgrading of the service facilities at the cost of significant further capital investments. This particular situation meant that a firm considering any other new venture in this area would be at a significant competitive disadvantage because it would have to invest and undertake a joint venture with the Government to upgrade infrastructure facilities.

## 20.4 COST DATA

After careful consideration the engineering department came up with the cost split shown in Table 20.1. These investments are required to enable the mining of up to 3,000,000 t.p.a., a figure which is dictated by the geology of the prospect as well as by engineering constraints.

Table 20.1 Capital costs
(Australian $)

| | | First Three Years[a] | | | |
|---|---|---|---|---|---|
| 000 19X8 A$ | | 1978 | 1979 | 1980 | Total |
| Mine | | 6,100 | 19,500 | 24,200[b] | 49,800 |
| Washery | | 400 | 17,000 | 4,400 | 21,800 |
| Utilities | | 200 | 4,200 | 2,800 | 7,200 |
| Others | | 1,300 | 12,500 | 4,400 | 18,200 |
| Engineering and general expenses | | 12,800 | 20,300 | 11,400 | 44,500 |
| | *Total* | 20,800 | 73,500 | 47,200 | 141,500 |
| Buffer provision of 8%[c] | | 1,600 | 5,900 | 3,800 | 11,300 |
| | *Total* | 22,400 | 79,400 | 51,000 | 152,800 |

[a]The capital costs for the remaining years are as shown in Appendix I.
[b]The high 'mine' capital expenditure for 1980 is due to the acquisition of the first of the three drag lines needed. N.B. in Appendix I, most of the capital costs for years 4 and 5 are due to the acquisition of drag line numbers 2 (1981) and 3 (1982).
[c]This provision is based on experience with mining ventures.

In order to achieve the production of clean coal as shown in the full investment appraisal in Appendix I three drag lines would be required, bringing the total capital expenditure on the mine itself to almost $72m. Note that the capital expenditures shown for years 6 onward (Appendix I) are incurred mainly in replacing the rolling stock. The operating costs for the whole life of the project are also given in Appendix I. Finally, the state railways indicated that the ABC company could have its coal transported to Gladstone at the flat rate of $11 per ton. A further charge of $3 per ton would be made at the port for stockpiling and loading. In other words, if a ton of coal were to sell for $50 fob, then the price at the mine gates would effectively be $36/ton.

## 20.5 PRELIMINARY ANALYSIS

With the information available from the engineering department, Smith now had enough data to start his analysis. He believed it relevant to investigate the following variables for their effect on the profitability of the project.

### Discount rate

Smith decided to use a rate of return before tax of 25 percent as a base value. However, he would subsequently investigate the impact of various alternative assumptions about the rate of return. Clearly, if the initial analysis happened to be favorable, then the rate of return for the detailed financial analysis would have to reflect the firm's weighted average cost of capital.

## Capital Expenditure

Smith examined the capital expenditure estimates shown in Appendix I and decided that in view of the prevailing conditions, he could concentrate upon the first 5 years of the project's life. He also thought that most of the capital expenditure in years 4 and 5 was due to the acquisition of the drag lines which are tendered for when required. Thus, almost all of the expenditure of years 1981, and 1982 was defined as fixed as was the greater proportion of that of 1980.

The general consensus was that for the first three years of the project, inflation would be unlikely to exceed 10 percent p.a. Furthermore, there was also a buffer provision on capital expenditure. In view of these facts, Smith decided that for now the analysis could be simplified by ignoring capital expenditure increases as the resulting error would be at most about \$10m or roughly 5 percent of the total capital investment.

## Production

Smith believed that the strong probability of winning long-term coal contracts meant that the quantity of coal produced would be sold fairly easily. Consequently he could safely assume the sales figures to be reliable estimates and for inventory holding costs to be relatively low. Furthermore, in a project such as this one, completion of the various mine construction phases was unlikely to be significantly behind schedule.

## Operating Costs

As can be seen from Appendix I operating costs are significant throughout the life of the project. These costs include haulage and port loading costs, which account for about one-third of the overall figures given. The remaining two-thirds are mostly made up of labor costs and utilities.

Haulage and port rates, as in the case of utilities, are determined by government bodies. These could therefore be expected to follow the Consumer Price Index, the CPI. In the absence of any further information, Smith decided it would be reasonable to assume that wages would also follow the CPI.

Over the next 10 years or so the 'most likely' estimate for inflation was put at about 10 percent p.a. People agreed that they also expected the present government to return in office in the election of 1980.

## Price

In 1977, the price of clean coal fob was \$45 per ton. Smith decided to use \$50 per ton as the base price for 1978 as this was given by the experts as the most

Table 20.2 Standard values

| *Variable* | *Standard value* |
|---|---|
| Price | $50/ton fob |
| Price growth | 10% |
| Operating cost inflation | 10% |
| Discount rate b/t | 25% |

likely value for 1978. Smith also thought that short of any catastrophe (e.g. Middle East war), the price of coal would also reflect increases in costs due to inflationary pressures.

**Summary of Standard Values**

Smith thus reduced the number of variables to be examined through sensitivity analysis to four. These are shown as standard values in Table 20.2.

## 20.6 SENSITIVITY ANALYSIS

Smith carried out a sensitivity analysis of project profitability. He estimated project sensitivity to each variable by varying one variable at a time whilst keeping all other variables constant at their standard value. The sensitivity analysis results are summarized in Table 20.3 and the four graphs in Appendix II.

Table 20.3 A sensitivity analysis

| Variable | Base value | Variation | Resulting NPV change | % of capital Investment |
|---|---|---|---|---|
| ROR | 25% | 1% | $ 8m | about 5% (ROR and Price) |
| Price | $50 | $1 | $ 8m | |
| Price inflation | 10% | 1% | $18m | about 10% (Price inflation and Operating cost inflation) |
| Operating Cost inflation | 10% | 1% | $18m | |

Table 20.3 was in fact derived using the graphs of Appendix II. Furthermore, the NPV for the project for the base case was found to be about $60m and the project appeared to be marginally profitable if inflation was kept at reasonable levels.

## 20.7 RISK ANALYSIS

At this stage Smith was encouraged by the results. However, he was somewhat disturbed by the potential volatility of the projects to assumptions about the base coal price. When questioning people about the other variables, he found fairly widespread agreement with his own predictions. For example, in the case of inflation, people did not believe it would fall below 5 percent nor did they expect it to go above 15 percent or so under most reasonable expectations. When he enquired about price projections most people had a high degree of uncertainty about future priçes. Certainly, most people expected the base price for 1978 to be about $50, but no-one was prepared to bet that it would not be as low as $40/ton or as high as $60/ton. The price of coal was thought to be closely related to that of oil and, as one manager pointed out, with the Middle East situation, just about anything was possible. Effectively there could be another Israeli/Egyptian war, the Saudi monarchy could collapse, or there could be further unrest in Iran; any one of these events would more than likely result in a price rise for oil. Alternatively, there could be a concerted reduction in the price of oil by the producing states to stimulate consumption and this might also significantly reduce the coal price.

Through further discussions Smith was able to assess the probability of a price change in any one year as follows:

| | | |
|---|---|---|
| *P*(reduction in price) | = | 0.05 |
| *P*(no change) | = | 0.80 |
| *P*(increase in price) | = | 0.15 |

The next step was to try to estimate by how much the price would change if something happened in the Middle East. In view of the prevailing equilibrium already existing between supply and demand, it was estimated that if the price fell it would probably fall by about 5 percent in that year with 15 percent being a very unlikely occurrence. Smith represented this information with the following distribution.

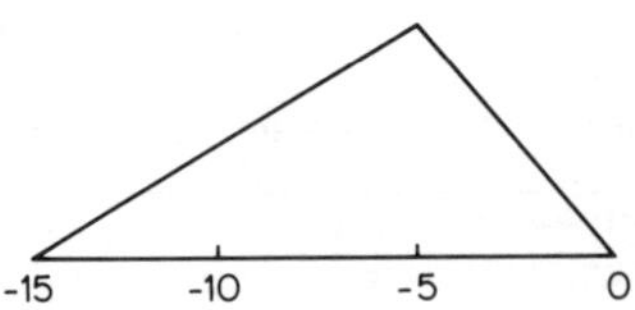


Similarly Smith believed that if the price increased, it would probably go up by about 5 percent in that year, with 20 percent being again a very unlikely occurrence. This information is shown below.

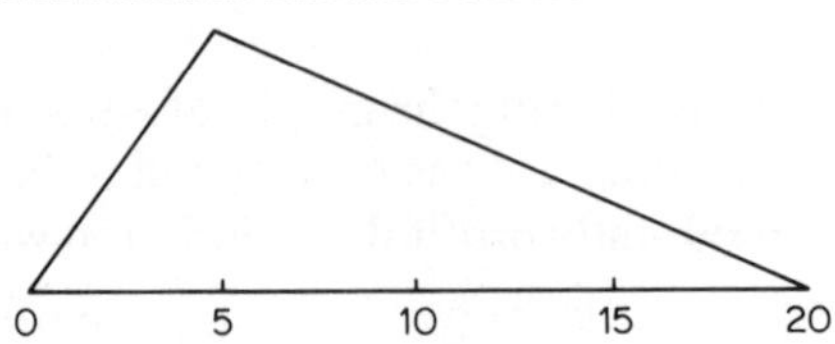

In view of the roughness of the information, Smith felt that he was justified in using triangular probability distributions. Because of the lack of information, he decided to assume independence between events from year to year; in reality, however, the dependence is evident. For example, the longer nothing happens, the more one would expect the probability of, say, a new Arab-Israeli war to be modified. Smith incorporated this information in the project simulation.

The output of the analysis is shown in Appendix III. It is of interest because it shows that the international situation is favorable to the project. The expected NPV becomes \$90m. In other words, the project profitability would be favorably affected by a deterioration in the international situation provided of course that it remained of a manageable kind. At this stage Smith presented Jones with the results.

After taking note of the results, Jones indicated that further analysis was appropriate. In particular, he wished Smith to look at the company's cost of capital, required rates of return and treatment of depreciation and other investment allowances.

## 20.8 FURTHER PROJECT APPRAISAL CONSIDERATIONS

### Cost of Capital

To estimate the cost of capital, Smith first had to determine the cost of equity capital for the company. While at university, he had collected a series of articles by Professors Ray Ball and Philip Brown*, one of which gave a list of alphas and betas (coefficients required from the capital asset pricing model (CAPM)) for most Australian companies. This information was obviously extremely important since Smith wanted to use the (CAPM) for this analysis. The following values were listed for the ABC Company.

$$\text{Alpha}_{\text{ABC}} = -0.6$$
$$\text{Beta}_{\text{ABC}} = 1.3$$

The cost of equity $K_E$ could therefore be determined from the CAPM formula:

$$K_E = \text{Alpha}_{\text{ABC}} + \text{Beta}_{\text{ABC}} \times R_{mt}$$

where $R_{mt}$ is the market return. In the present case $R_{mt}$ should be specific to the mining industry. Fortunately, Smith had another paper on the mining industry, by the same authors, which contained the relevant information. $R_{mt}$ for the life of the project had been estimated at 12 percent. Obviously this value was an expected value and the variance for this estimate was given as 15 percent. Initially, however, the variance of $R_{mt}$ was to be ignored. In 1977 shareholders' equity represented 45 percent of total funds and liabilities (TF & L). Using the above formula, Smith calculated the cost of equity as follows:

*See articles by R. Ball and P. Brown in the Australian Accountant and the Australian Journal of Management.

$K_E = -0.6 + 1.3 \times 12$
giving $K_E = 15\%$

Debt represented 55 percent of total funds and liabilities and Smith evaluated their cost as follows. The bank overdraft rate of 11.5 percent was applied to the total of current liabilities plus income tax equalization provision and accruals (these items represent 40 percent of total funds and liabilities).

Debentures accounted for another 3 percent (of TF & L) at a cost of 8.75 percent. Finally, loans accounted for the final 12 percent (of TF & L) at a rate of 10.75 percent.

The prevailing tax rate was 42.5 percent and consequently the weighted average cost of capital $K_C$ was easily calculated using the familiar formula.

$$K_C = \frac{E}{E + D} K_E + \frac{D}{E + D} K_D(1 - T)$$

where $E$ is equity, $D$ is debt, $K_E$ is the cost of equity $K_D$ is the cost of debt and $T$ the tax rate. Using the above information $K_C$ was found as follows:

$$\begin{aligned} K_C &= 0.45 \times 15 + [(0.4 \times 11.5) + (0.03 \times 8.75) + (0.12 \times 10.75)] \times (1 - 0.425) \\ &= 10.1\% \end{aligned}$$

thus $K_{C_{A/T}}$ is 10.1%, where $K_{C_{A/T}}$ refers to the after-tax ($A/T$) cost of capital.

The risk-free rate as determined by the 20-year bond rate was taken to be 8.9 percent. Smith carried on with the analysis on the explicit assumption that ABC was using the optimum gearing in view of its activities and financial requirements. He furthermore assumed that this project would not subject the portolio of investments to any significant change (e.g. risk) thus warranting the use of the *ex-post* weighted average cost of capital for the analysis. One consequence of the above assumption is obviously that the cost of equity for ABC would not be expected to change in any significant way should this project be undertaken. Finally, Smith assumed this project to be independent of any other project undertaken or about to be undertaken by ABC and that no capital-rationing restriction existed at that time.

For simplicity, he assumed that taxes were to be paid at the end of the year in which they were incurred and, finally, tax benefits ensuing from depreciation allowances were discounted at the risk-free rate.

## Depreciation

Under the tax act legislation, mining companies were allowed to choose between several depreciation procedures as shown by the Table 20.4.

The choice gives rise to four allowable depreciation methods combinations, all of which Smith tested in an attempt to find the approach that would maximize the tax benefit to ABC. The table of Appendix IV shows the split between tangible and intangible capital expenditures.

Table 20.4 Allowable depreciation methods

| Tangible investment expenditures | Intangible investment expenditures |
|---|---|
| SL10 | SL05 |
| RB15 | SL17* |

Where:
RB = Reducing balance
SL = Straight line
* Life of the mine
(Numbers refer to a number of years)

Table 20.5 Summary of sensitivity to depreciation method

| Tangible expenses | Intangible expenses | *E* (NPV)* \$ m | σ(NPV)** \$ m |
|---|---|---|---|
| SL10 | SL05 | 252.0 | 79.2 |
| SL10 | SL17 | 243.3[a] | 81.8 |
| RB15 | SL05 | 258.3[b] | 78.1 |
| RB15 | SL17 | 250.1 | 81.0 |

[a]Worst
[b]Best
*E(NPV) is the mean NPV
**σ(NPV) is the standard deviation of NPV.

The output of the best and worst combinations of depreciation methods is shown in Appendix V.

Table 20.5 summarizes the output from the simulation runs. The summary showed Smith that depreciation combination of RB15 and SL05 is optimal for this project. It also showed that the variation between the two extreme cases is relatively small and is equivalent to a difference, in terms of 1978 dollars, of about \$1m per year over the life of the mine. Finally, Smith was pleased to see that the preferred depreciation combination is not only best in terms of expected values, but that it also reduces the variability (i.e. risk) of the project as shown in the last column of the table.

**Investment Allowance**

In 1977, mining companies were entitled to an investment allowance of 20 percent on tangible capital expenditures. However, no-one could guarantee that this allowance would remain in force throughout the early years of the project when all the tangible expenditures would be incurred.

Smith consequently re-evaluated the profitability of the project, using the optimum depreciation method without the investment allowance. The output for this run is presented in Appendix VI.

By comparing the output of Appendix VI with that of Appendix V (p. 268), it can be readily observed that the expected NPV has decreased only slightly (i.e. \$3m), thus not affecting the profitability of the project in any significant way.

**Cash Flow Management.**

One very important aspect of planning is that of cash flow management. In an ideal situation where a decision-maker would know with certainty his future cash flows, it would be possible for this very fortunate manager to optimize (among other things) the use of funds from the firm. Smith was aware of this and ensured that it was not overlooked in the present context.

The output shown in Appendix VII presents the distributions of the after-tax cash flows generated in each year of this project. By combining the cash flow distributions from all projects in a particular year, it is possible to determine the overall financial requirements for the firm in that year and thus plan for it. With these aggregate distributions it becomes possible to minimize the cost to the firm of borrowing funds and also to determine the borrowing requirements for the risk the firm is prepared to bear (for example, the risk of cash flow falling below a pre-specified level).

**Sensitivity to $R_m$**

The cost of equity was calculated using the CAPM on the assumption that $R_m$ was known with certainty (12 percent). Over a period of time as lengthy as the life of the mine however, this assumption is obviously an oversimplification. Smith consequently removed this constraint in order to evaluate its impact on the expected profitability of the project.

The variance of $R_m$ over the life of the mine was assessed at 15 percent and $R_m$ was subsequently introduced in the calculation in the form of a distribution. The output of this run, using the optimum depreciation methods, is presented in Appendix VIII.

Smith found the distribution shown in Appendix VIII interesting as it indicated that the expected NPV had not changed but that the spread of the return had increased as shown by the greater standard deviation (now \$90m versus \$78m previously).

Although this last result did not significantly change the attractiveness of this project, it does highlight the fact that in the case of a marginal project, such a change could mean all the difference between an acceptable and an unacceptable risk.

## QUESTIONS FOR DISCUSSION

1. Comment upon the sensitivity analysis aspects of the study.
2. Do the analyses with respect to depreciation methods and cash flow modelling help in the evaluation process?
3. Should a more extensive risk analysis model be built?

# Appendix I: Initial Investment Appraisal

Sandy Creek Mine Project: Evaluation of Profitability on B/T Basis

| Project year | 1 | 2 | 3 | 4 | 5 | 6 | 7 | 8 | 9 | 10 | 11 | 12 | 13 | 14 | 15 | 16 |
|---|---|---|---|---|---|---|---|---|---|---|---|---|---|---|---|---|
| Capital costs × $10^6$\$ (1) | (22.4) | (79.4) | (51) | (18.7) | (14.5) | (1.5) | (0.8) | (2.2) | (1.8) | (3.5) | (4.7) | (1.0) | (4.2) | (1.8) | (0.2) | (0.1) |
| Contribution To NPV at 25% (2) | (17.9) | (50.8) | (26.1) | (7.7) | (4.8) | (0.4) | (0.2) | (0.4) | (0.2) | (0.4) | (0.4) | (0.1) | (0.2) | (0.1) | — | — |
| Clean coal sold × $10^6$Tons (3) | — | — | — | 2.7 | 2.6 | 2.4 | 2.2 | 1.9 | 2.0 | 1.8 | 1.9 | 1.7 | 2.5 | 2.0 | 2.1 | 2.1 |
| Revenue × $10^6$\$ at \$50/Ton (4) | — | — | — | 135 | 130 | 120 | 110 | 95 | 100 | 90 | 95 | 85 | 125 | 100 | 105 | 105 |
| Operating[a] costs × $10^6$\$ (5) | — | — | (7.9) | (67.9) | (71.2) | (70.4) | (66.5) | (62.9) | (63.9) | (69.,6) | (63.1) | (59.3) | (69.4) | (61.3) | (62.6) | (62.6) |
| Trading profit × $10^6$\$ (6) | — | — | (7.9) | 67.1 | 58.8 | 49.6 | 43.5 | 32.1 | 36.1 | 29.4 | 31.9 | 25.7 | 55.6 | 38.7 | 42.4 | 42.4 |
| Contribution to NPV at 25% (7) | — | — | (4.0) | 27.5 | 19.3 | 13.0 | 9.1 | 5.4 | 4.8 | 3.2 | 2.7 | 1.8 | 3.1 | 1.7 | 1.5 | 1.2 |

$NPV^{25\%} = \Sigma$ Row (2) + $\Sigma$ Row (7) = −18.3

[a]Inclusive of haulage and port charges.

# Appendix II

(See Page 255). Graphs of Net Present Value (NPV) sensitivity in relation to price, price inflation, discount rate and cost inflation

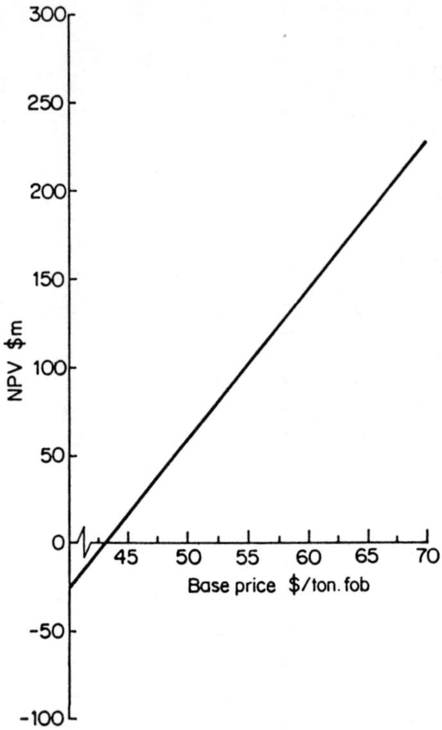


Appendix II.1 *Sensitivity of NPV to base price*
NPV (in $m) vs Base price (in $/ton fob)
All other variables standard

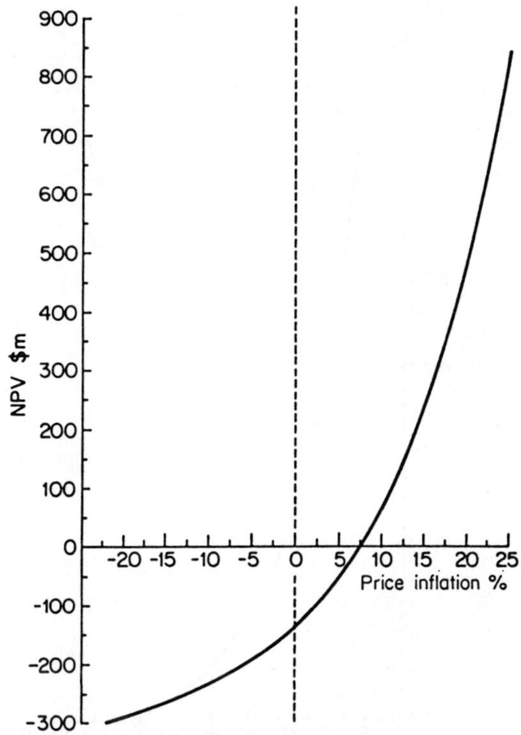


Appendix II.2 *Sensitivity of NPV to price inflation*
NPV (in \$m) vs Price inflation (%)
All other variables standard

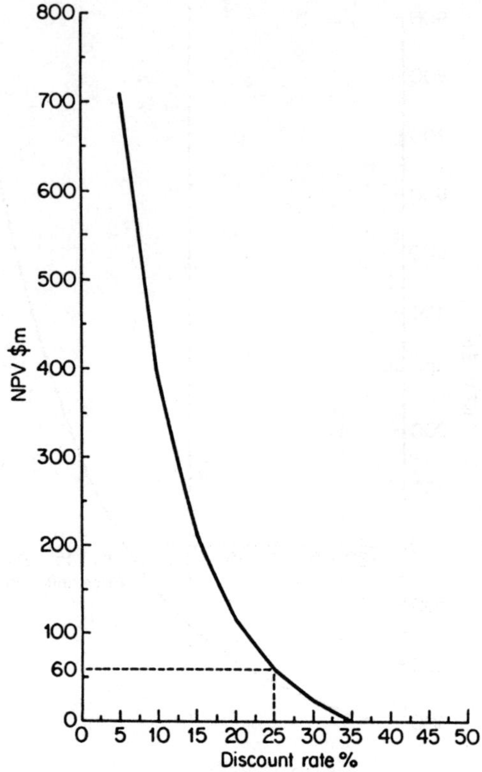


Appendix II.3 *Sensitivity of NPV to discount rate*
NPV (in $m) vs Discount rate (%)
All other variables standard

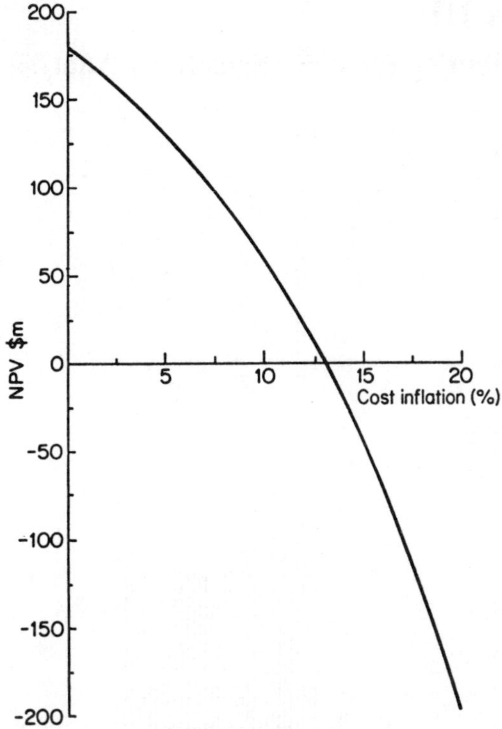


Appendix II.4 *Sensitivity of NPV to cost inflation*
NPV (in $m) vs Cost inflation (%)
All other variables standard

# Appendix III:
## NPV Distribution for Price Sensitivity Analysis

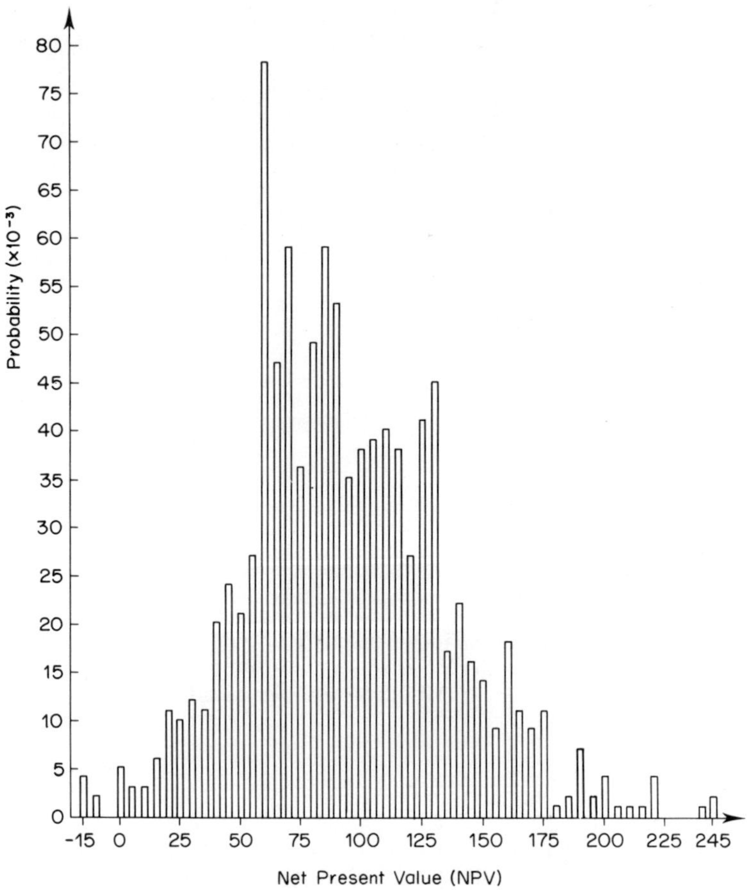


Appendix III *Price Sensitivity Analysis*

[Note: Mean NPV = 91.38
Standard Deviation of NPV = 42.95]

# Appendix IV: Split of Capital Expenditures: (Tangible v Intangible)

Split of Capital Expenditures

| Year | 1978 | 1979 | 1980 | 1981 | 1982 | 1983 | 1984 | 1985 | 1986 | 1987 | 1988 | 1989 | 1990 | 1991 | 1992 | 1993 | 1994 |
|---|---|---|---|---|---|---|---|---|---|---|---|---|---|---|---|---|---|
| Tangible costs × $10^6$$ | 6.5 | 36.5 | 28.6 | 12.0 | 12.0 | — | — | — | — | — | — | — | — | — | — | — | — |
| Other costs × $10^6$$ | 15.9 | 42.9 | 22.4 | 6.7 | 2.5 | 1.5 | 0.8 | 2.2 | 1.8 | 3.5 | 4.7 | 1.0 | 4.2 | 1.8 | 0.2 | 0.1 | — |
| Total capital expenditures × $10^6$$ | 22.4 | 79.4 | 51.0 | 18.7 | 14.5 | 1.5 | 0.8 | 2.2 | 1.8 | 3.5 | 4.7 | 1.0 | 4.2 | 1.8 | 0.2 | 0.1 | — |

# Appendix V: NPV Distributions for Different Depreciation Assumptions

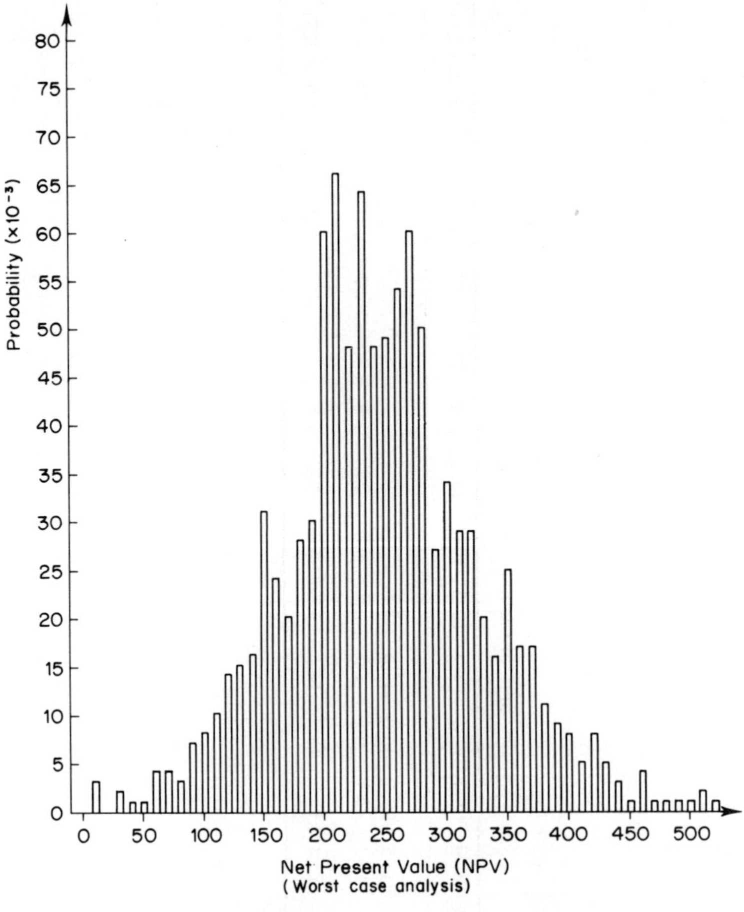


Appendix V *Worst Case Analysis for Depreciation*

[Note: Mean NPV = 243.291
Standard deviation of NPV = 81.760]

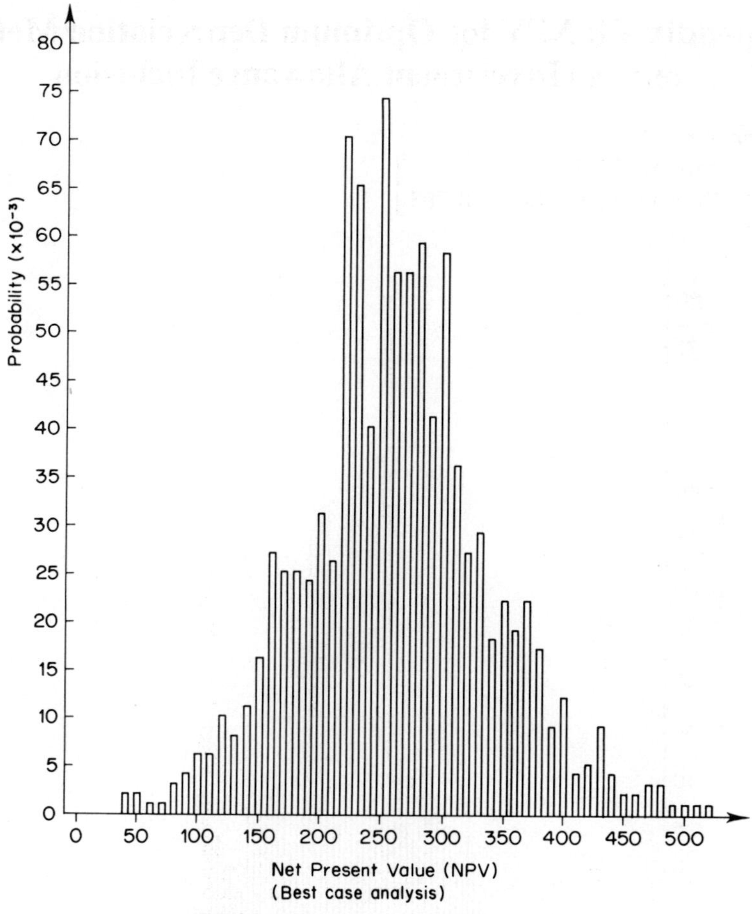


Appendix V *Best Case Analysis for Depreciation*

[Note: Mean NPV = 258.296
Standard deviation of NPV = 78.124]

# Appendix VI: NPV for Optimum Depreciation Method and No Investment Allowance Inclusion

*Summary result*

[NPV Mean: 255.339
NPV Standard deviation: 78.763]

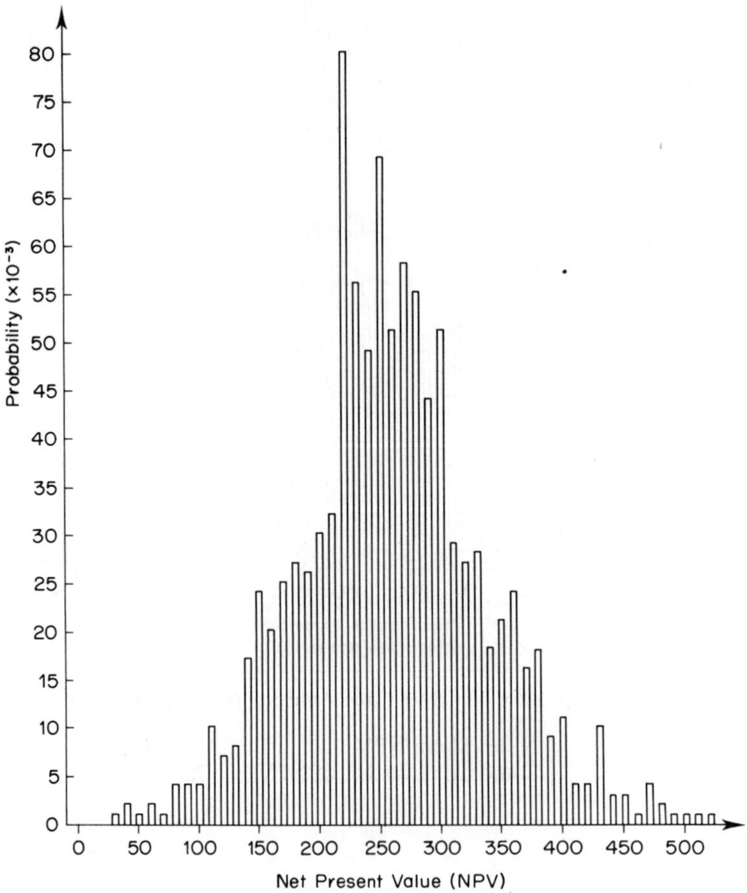

# Appendix VII: Project Cash Flow Profile

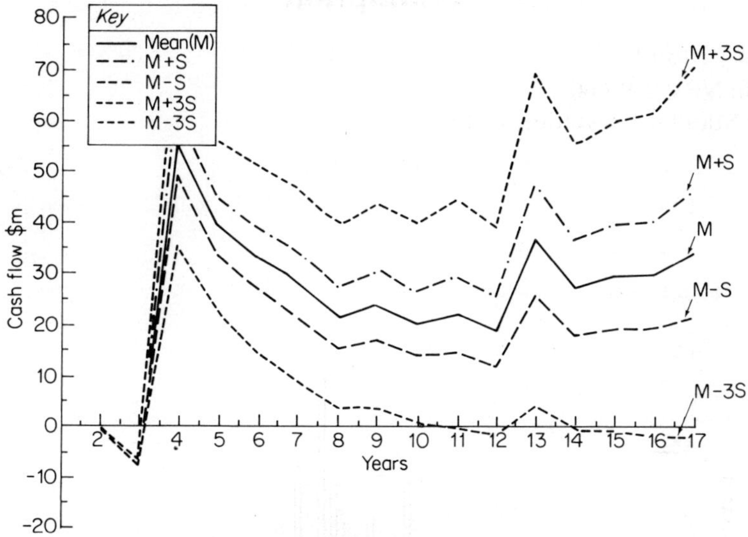


[ Note M: denotes Mean Cash Flow
S: denotes Standard Deviation of Cash Flow ]

# Appendix VIII: Sensitivity of NPV to Mining $R_m$ Assumption

*Summary Results*:

$$\begin{bmatrix} \text{Mean NPV } 259.060 \\ \text{NPV Standard deviation } 90.135 \end{bmatrix}$$

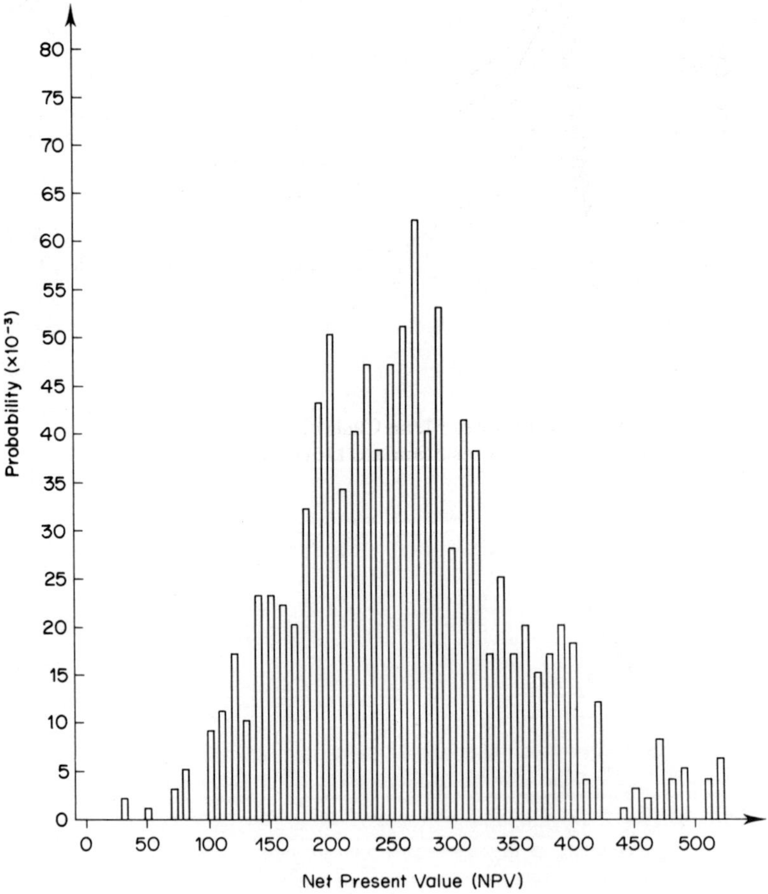

*Chapter 21*

# *National Feeds Ltd:* A Bargaining Decision*


## SUMMARY

This case examines possible structural changes in the operations of National Feeds resulting from the decline of the market for animal feeds. The emergence of much larger localized agricultural units exploiting scale economies had shifted the supply advantage for feeds to the smaller local producers known as 'local compounders'. National Feeds was, therefore, considering investment in a series of smaller localized feed-mills as replacements for the larger port-mills which they currently owned. As a result, National Feeds had to analyse their strategy options in the light of many cost, market and personnel uncertainties.


## 21.1 INTRODUCTION

National Feeds is a company whose main interest is in the animal feeds industry. It has recently been amalgamated with another company in the same industry and, as a result, has created a new management structure in which line responsibility has been given to each area of the business, for example, cattle, pig, poultry, etc.

The amalgamation was brought about because of the simultaneous occurrence of a declining market situation combined with structural changes in the animal feeds industry. More specifically, the profits of National Feeds in constant terms had fallen from £6,000,000 in 1966 to a figure of £3,000,000 in 1970. At the same time, the yield had dropped from 6 percent per annum to 4 percent per annum. In addition, there were ever-increasing indications to suggest that the animal feeds industry was becoming more localized in nature. In contrast to this, the majority of the National Feeds mills were large sites

*This case was originally written by Howard Thomas in conjunction with two National Feeds executives, John Hollier and Alan Coates

which were based close to ports. Indeed, in a general sense and as the name suggests, the company could be described as a 'national' feeds company. In the jargon of the trade, National Feeds was a national compounder, and because of the extent of its operations was burdened with the inevitable administrative costs incurred by any large-scale business.

In summary, the environment in which National Feeds had to operate could be described as an industrial market in which margins were generally low and even declining, and in which the principal competition – the local compounders – had a distinct cost advantage.

The Corporate Planning Department of the company had been given the brief of analyzing the structure of the feedstuffs industry, with a view to making recommendations about how the company should adapt to the changing requirements of the industry. After careful examination of the task to be undertaken it was realized that a number of problems would emerge during the investigation. First, it was recognized that because of the changing nature of agriculture within the United Kingdom it could be expected that in future years farmers would regard animal feed as a raw material. Over the years, the growth in the size of the agricultural units had encouraged improved efficiency and, at the same time, had allowed the units to take advantage of the benefits to be reaped from the economies of large-scale production. The implication is that these units will in the future tend to bargain for the best possible deal in terms of price, rather than buy according to brand loyalty. The second problem to emerge related to the structural changes which had occurred over time. The Corporate Planning Department came to the unassailable conclusion that National Feeds had been somewhat slow to react to changes in its environment. There was abundant evidence to suggest that the medium-sized mill, based near to its sources of raw materials and its markets, provided an excellent site from which a local compounder could launch his attack on the market. As a national rather than a local compounder, National Feeds had larger overall costs – both in terms of administrative overheads and salaries. As a result, its competitiveness had suffered from shortfall both in its market share and in its profits.

## 21.2 THE DECISION PROBLEM

Given the above factors, the Corporate Planning Department decided to review the alternative strategies available to the company. After much discussion with the Management, the following options were considered. The first was to embark upon a policy of aggressive expansion involving the use of the greater R & D, marketing and financial resources which National Feeds, as a large company, possessed. A second choice was to adopt a strategy in which the company would critically assess various aspects of its organization, and subsequently attempt to simplify the structure on a selective basis. The third option was to do nothing, and merely sharpen up areas of financial control and management organization. An example of such action would be the adoption of a policy of the decentralization of management, and the thinning of management resources to a bare minimum.

Whilst there was general consensus that these were a feasible set of alternatives, it was recognized that the choice of the most appropriate approach would depend to some extent upon a number of uncertain factors. The first such uncertainty related to the nature of the market. Although the market had remained relatively static (or declined in absolute terms) over the preceding five years, amalgamations had occurred within the feedstuffs industry. It could be argued, therefore, that the changing structure of competition in the animal feeds industry might itself convey the possibility of an increasing market. In addition, sales forecasts for feedstuffs for the coming five years might themselves have considerable in-built inaccuracies. Members of the Planning Department expressed strong beliefs about the need to view the market in its entirety, and it was stated that if at all possible, it would be useful to quantify their views about the market uncertainties in terms of subjective probability assessments.

Quite apart from the market uncertainties outlined above, there existed other uncertainties which had also to be considered. First, what levels of cost saving should be achieved by policies of either simplification or expansion? Second, if structural changes were made to the company, what would be the manufacturing costs per ton of feedstuffs at each mill, and would the new structure be capable of handling any tonnage which had to be diverted as a result of mill closure elsewhere? Thirdly, if selected mills were closed, what might be their asset values, and what degree of labor unrest would exist at such sites?

The Review Team studied the possible alternatives and put forward the following points. It was argued that it was unnecessary to quantify uncertainty about such things as market growth until the various options under discussion had been accepted as potential solutions. For example, the majority of the Review Team saw the 'do nothing' strategy as economic nonsense in that it took no account of the known factors relating to the environment and structure of the industry. It was therefore generally agreed that this particular strategy should be eliminated. Greater interest was generated by the suggestion of an expansionist strategy, and attention was centered on the appropriate criterion for choosing between expansion and rationalization. It was strongly argued that the company wanted to improve its yield to 15 percent per annum, and that it wanted to meet certain cash flow targets. Upon agreement of this financial objective for the five-year planning period, it was felt that the policy of aggressive expansion was inappropriate. Such a policy would necessitate the up-grading of production facilities, obviously incurring massive investment costs, and such expenditure would make the attainment of any financial objectives very difficult. Furthermore aggressive expansion would be a risky option without a clear analysis of the cost economics of the new local structure of the feeds industry. Also, price level rather than brand loyalty had appeared as the dominant reason for purchasing a specific firm's product.

Table 21.1 Production cost figures for a sample of National Feeds' factories

| | £ per ton |
|---|---|
| Cheltenham | 4.00 |
| Doncaster | 3.40 |
| Oldham | 4.25 |
| London | 4.17 |
| Glasgow | 5.17 |
| Ipswich | 2.80 |
| Kings Lynn | 2.95 |
| Gainsborough | 4.65 |
| Liverpool | 4.00 |

Initially, therefore, it was decided to concentrate on the strategy of selectively simplifying the company's structure in order to move towards the principal financial objectives of:

(i) maximizing the turnover of capital;
(ii) increasing pre-tax yield of 15 percent of gross capital employed, and therefore maintaining a yield of at least 15 percent;
(iii) achieving a profit growth of 5 percent per annum in real terms;
(iv) maintaining a positive cash flow through the period.

It was concluded that these objectives could best be attained by maintaining market leadership, by increasing turnover in areas where increased sales were profitable, by maintaining product advantage through R & D, by disposing of all assets that could not be put to profitable use, and, finally, by maintaining tight control over working capital.

Continuing to dominate the market and using research and development to maintain product advantage are in essence, market objectives rather like those of continuing to service only the profitable sales outlets. In effect they are operational objectives once the feedstuffs have emerged from the factory. It was suggested that it would be useful to assess the efficiency of production in existing company mills, and Table 21.1 outlines the production cost figures for various factories within the group. Table 21.2 itemizes the areas which each of these mills service. These Tables form a basis for assessing which sites might be short-listed for possible closure. These are shown in Table 21.3.

Given that a decision had been made that it might be necessary to consider the closure of certain sites, it was felt appropriate to consult the company's personnel manager. He had some immediate comments to make. First, he argued, the Review Team should make realistic assessments of the cost savings for each site. Such assessments should include the uncertainties of unknown site value, savings on the direct and indirect costs, and uncertainties about the possible losses in market share which might result from closure. He stated that he could not make these assessments, but he felt that appropriate experts should meet to quantify the uncertainty in terms of subjective probability

Table 21.2: Areas Serviced by Various National Feeds Factories

| *Factories* | *Area serviced* |
| --- | --- |
| *Northern area* | |
| Doncaster | |
| Oldham | North of England |
| Glasgow | and |
| Gainsborough | Scotland |
| Liverpool | |
| *Southern area* | |
| Cheltenham | Wales, |
| London | the Midlands |
| Ipswich | and |
| Kings Lynn | Southern England |

NB: In general, all southern area mills (including those omitted from the above list) have moved more towards the country-mill type of organization. In contrast, the northern area mills tend to have a national compounding orientation.

Table 21.3 Short list of Potential Closure Sites

| | |
| --- | --- |
| | *Northern area* |
| OLDHAM | High cost, but serves a wide area efficiently. |
| GLASGOW | High cost, difficult distribution and administrative problems. |
| GAINSBOROUGH | High cost, poor and inefficient distribution. |
| | *Southern area* |
| LONDON | High cost, likely that more efficient production and distribution could be obtained by using country mills. |

assessments. He emphasized quite strongly that some of the sites itemized in Table 21.3 were well known for their history of poor industrial relations. He stressed that uncertainty must exist regarding the union reaction at mills where closure notices were issued. Furthermore, an element of uncertainty must also exist as to the extent to which the unions might use the political process to try and force the company to reconsider its decision. He speculated that the level of redundancy payments and pay-out costs for factory closure, added to the possibility of prolonged strike action, might in fact cost the company far more than any savings which might be achieved from closure. He suggested that it would be useful to convene a joint meeting of personnel and production specialists from each of the sites under consideration, together with a decision analyst from the Central Planning Department. This group of experts could then attempt realistic assessments of the nature of potential union reaction.

Mr Sadler, a company corporate planner, put forward another point of view. He believed that the company wanted to move towards becoming a conglomerate local compounder, and in effect, away from serving as a national compounder. He argued that if some sites were closed, then it would be necessary to establish new local factories to take up some of the diverted tonnage previously handled by those mills. He emphasized that it might take time first of all to find these sites, and then to obtain planning permission to build. His suggested strategy was that the company should work some of the national mills less intensively for a few years, at least until they could commission the new local plants. Mr Sadler was asked to review the situation and present his evidence at the next meeting of the Review Team.

## 21.3 ANALYSIS OF THE DECISION PROBLEM

The meeting reconvened two weeks later when there was detailed discussion regarding the 'short list' of potential sites for closure shown in Table 21.3. The decision analyst then explained that, given this short list of four possible sites for closure, it was possible for the company to choose between sixteen alternative strategies. That is, the company could choose to keep all four mills operational and close none; it could close one mill only; or two of the mills, or three, or even close all four. Put another way, this implied that the company was faced with the option of either closing all four (one strategy), closing three of the four (for which there were four strategies), closing two of the four (six strategies available), closing one mill (four strategies possible), and finally, of keeping all mills in operation (one strategy) – hence the sixteen strategies as illustrated in the decision tree shown in Figure 21.1.

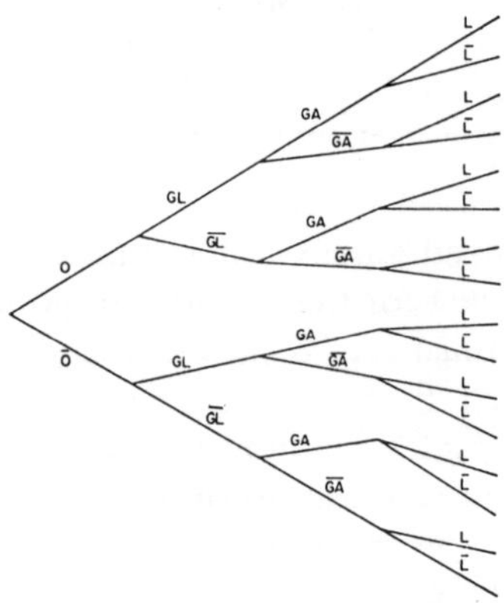

*Notation*

| | |
|---|---|
| $\underline{O}$ – keep Oldham open | $\underline{GL}$ – keep Glasgow open |
| $\overline{O}$ – close Oldham | $\overline{GL}$ – close Glasgow |
| $\underline{GA}$ – keep Gainsborough open | $\underline{L}$ – keep London open |
| $\overline{GA}$ – close Gainsborough | $\overline{L}$ – close London |

For example, O, GL, GA, L is the strategy of keeping all four sites open. There is only *one* way of doing this.

Figure 21.1 Tree of options for National Feeds

Table 21.4 Further Information About the Short-listed Sites

| |
|---|
| Mr Sadler reported that:<br>(i) On the basis of 100,000 tons capacity size and assuming that modular minimum cost design techniques were used in the construction of the country mills, then it was a reasonable assumption to anticipate that these mills might be operational within 20 months.<br>(ii) The London capacity, and a significant proportion of that of Cheltenham, could be serviced by 8 strategically placed mills capable of serving a 30-mile radius.<br>(iii) As far as the competitors of National Feeds were concerned, Glasgow was becoming redundant as a centre for operations and was increasingly being serviced from other points.<br>(iv) As a general statement, the northern mills, in contrast to their southern counterparts, tended to be large port-based sites. |

This analysis of problem structure generated much interest, and the conclusion that was drawn by the Review Team was that in short-run terms the company could feasibly close only one mill, primarily because of the time lag involved in constructing new localized facilities. It was felt that in the future it would be possible to consider alternative strategies, but it was decided that the urgency of the present situation necessitated immediate action regarding the short-term decision already made to close one of the four mills.

At this point in the meeting Mr Sadler interjected and offered further information regarding the short-listed sites, and also the nature of country mills. This evidence is presented in Table 21.4 and after studying this report the team saw the need to give serious consideration to possible short-run losses in tonnage if the mills were closed. As Table 21.4 illustrates, Oldham in particular would suffer large losses, as would Glasgow, though to a lesser extent.

This discussion prompted the planners to think more carefully about the nature of the uncertainties confronting them. Each of the short-listed mills was relatively large in terms of tonnage output; the move to smaller, more localized mills seemed to be a prerequisite for improved efficiency and competitiveness, given the reasons outlined earlier. It was felt reasonable to assume that the value of the site and any equipment could be traded off against the costs of replacing the larger sites with a series of smaller, more strategically placed, country mills. This assumption was made on the expectation that the gains from the disposal of the redundant sites would be more or less balanced by the investment costs incurred in the building of the new facilities. As there was general consensus of opinion about the issues discussed up to that point, the conference became more specific and focussed on what appeared to be the two major uncertainties involved in the analysis. First, it was argued that for each of the sites an assessment should be made of the uncertainty about the cost savings that would be obtained by putting the production facilities to more efficient use. It was then argued that this cost saving should be traded off against the uncertainty about the possible losses in market share, if the diverted tonnage could not be effectively handled by other outlets within the group. This information is shown in Table 21.5.

Table 21.5 Cost Savings and Market Share Changes for Each Potential Closure Site

| Sites | Cost savings (£) | | Losses in market share (£) (money terms) | |
|---|---|---|---|---|
| | Mean | Standard deviation | Mean | Standard deviation |
| OLDHAM | 375,000 | 35,000 | 225,000 | 19,500 |
| GLASGOW | 500,000 | 45,500 | 150,000 | 20,500 |
| GAINSBOROUGH | 400,000 | 25,500 | 50,000 | 15,500 |
| LONDON | 250,000 | 13,500 | 125,000 | 12,500 |

Table 21.6 Estimated disinvestment savings. (Normal distribution Assumed)

| Close | Mean (£) | Standard deviation (rounded) (£) |
|---|---|---|
| OLDHAM | 150,000 | 40,000 |
| GLASGOW | 350,000 | 50,000 |
| GAINSBOROUGH | 350,000 | 30,000 |
| LONDON | 125,000 | 18,000 |

Table 21.6 shows the decision analyst's summary of these distributions given in terms of the distribution of the gain from the closure of each site. In simple terms and taking Oldham as an example, the Table showed that there was approximately a 95 percent chance of the gain lying between £150,000 *less* twice times £40,000 giving £70,000, and £150,000 *plus* twice times £40,000 giving £230,000.

When the Review Team was convinced that the distribution did in fact offer reasonable assessments of the attainable gains from short-term closure, discussion then centered on the second major uncertainty facing National Feeds. That is, the industrial relations aspect of the situation, and more specifically, the formulation of tactics to be adopted for negotiation with the appropriate unions. It was assumed that the proportion of possible redundancies as a result of site closure was small in relation to the total employed population in that area; it would probably affect between 300–500 people. It was agreed, given this information, that there existed little likelihood of extra political pressure from the union to keep the plants operational. The assumption was made that any industrial action contemplated by the unions would instead be mainly directed towards obtaining generous redundancy terms for their members. Such industrial action might take the form of work-ins, sympathy strikes, etc. For the purpose of deciding bargaining terms it was agreed that the values shown in Table 21.6 would set the ceiling as to estimated gain from closure, thus at the same time setting the upper limit on total possible redundancy expenditure. Taking Oldham as an example again, £230,000 would be the estimated maximum gain that could be achieved on the basis of assessments made in Tables 21.5 and 21.6. Similar calculations made for the other three sites would indicate that the maximum pay-off for Glasgow would be as high as £450,000, for Gainsborough £410,000 and finally, for London it would be £161,000.

Returning again to the problem of the uncertainty of the extent and nature of possible industrial action, Mr Sadler told the meeting that experience suggested that of the four sites involved, Glasgow was potentially the most likely source of any intensive militant action. Bearing this in mind, the Review Team decided that as an initial step, the company would offer the union some multiple of the national norm for redundancy settlements, as set down in the Redundancy Payments Act. The Act itself proposes the following terms: employees of age 41 years and over – 1½ weeks pay for each year of service; for employees in the age bracket 22–41 years suggested settlement is 1 week's pay per year of service, and finally, for employees between the ages of 18–22 years, settlement is suggested as half a week's pay for each year employed by that company. The unions would either accept or reject this, with some potentially measureable probability of acceptance or rejection. If the offer was rejected, then it was likely that the union would bring various pressures to bear on the company through industrial action, with the obvious intention of obtaining higher settlements. In simple terms it could be assumed that the company would then increase its offer by an integer unit of the national norm, that is, it would offer twice, three, or even four times the national terms. In behavioral terms it is reasonable to assume that the probability of the union accepting the offer at the first round of bargaining is very small; but at each subsequent stage the probability of acceptance by the union must increase. In other words, the bigger the offer the more probable the settlement; however, it is also reasonable to assume that the probability of settlement does not necessarily increase at the same rate as changes in the offer. That is, militancy and other factors might be influential in the formulation of any decision to accept or reject offers, and it might be the case that the union is not solely concerned with the monetary aspects of an offer. Thus it is not valid to assume that doubling an offer necessarily doubles the chance of settlement.

At this stage, the decision analyst asked the Review Team to reaffirm that they considered the best tactical bargaining approach would be to offer a redundancy package which would, for each of the sites, not exceed the maximum attainable gain from closure. In reply, the Chairman said that general consensus was that the above method of 'maximum gain' would provide a highly satisfactory first approximation for planning the conduct of future bargaining negotiations. However, should circumstances of a strategic nature occur, such as a board decision to disinvest whatever the cost, it might then be necessary to alter the criterion for estimating the size of settlements.

Finally, and in view of the information given in Tables 21.5 and 21.6 and taking into account the assumptions that had been made regarding the nature of the bargaining process, the decision analyst was asked to formulate appropriate recommendations regarding the decision-making problem facing National Feeds.

It was decided to hold another meeting later, when the longer term aspects of the decision problem would be studied.

## 21.4 ANALYSIS OF THE LONGER TERM PLANNING PROBLEM

The Review Team met again one week later to discuss the structure of the longer term planning problem. In the long term, it was clear that all 16 strategies outlined in the probability diagram (Figure 21.1) were feasible. It was evident from the report given by Mr Sadler (Table 21.4) that the country mills took approximately 20 months to be made operational, assuming that it was easy to resolve any problems connected with the new sites, obtain planning permission, and so on. Should difficulties arise the time horizon could be lengthened.

Mr Sadler's earlier evidence suggested that the London capacity could be serviced by 8 strategically placed country mills, and these same mills could also serve a significant proportion of Cheltenham. The basic problem was one of evaluating the time horizon involved in reaching the operational stage for each new mill, and of deciding whether or not total closure of the London plant was in the firm's best interests. It seemed a feasible solution to phase out the London capacity at the same time as the new country mills were being established. A similar solution seemed applicable to Oldham and Glasgow. However, it was quite clear that in the case of Gainsborough the diverted tonnage could readily be handled by Doncaster and Ipswich.

Given the extent of available information, the decision analyst suggested that the Review Team should attempt to construct a crude decision tree for the longer term problem under consideration.

## QUESTIONS FOR DISCUSSION

1. In relation to the information given in National Feeds Limited particularly Sections 21.1 to 21.3, use the tools of decision analysis to analyze the problem of which site to close in the shortrun. Make appropriate recommendations to the Review Team, and include any reservations that you think should be considered. Comment on the realism of the analysis and factors under consideration by the Review Team.
2. In relation to the information given in National Feeds Limited particularly Section 21.4, construct a crude decision tree for the longer term problem. Make whatever assumptions you regard as realistic about the uncertainties facing the company in the longer term period. In other words, see yourself as a member of the Review Team and assess not only the potential uncertainties, but also consider the criterion by which the appropriate strategies should be determined in the long run.

*Chapter 22*

# *Developing a Computer Model to Simulate the Civil Litigation Process**

## SUMMARY

This case describes an extremely interesting and novel application of the risk simulation approach to the legal system. In particular, the approach aims to identify blockages in the operations, and hence efficiency of the current Federal civil litigation system. This is undertaken as a prelude to the more detailed examination (in later 'passes' of the approach) of a number of alternative structures for the more efficient and timely operation of that system.

## 22.1 INTRODUCTION

In July 1979 McKinsey & Company, Inc., with the cooperation of the Federal Judicial Center, embarked on a project to develop a computer model of the civil litigation process. The model aims to show the relationships and interdependencies among resource requirements and uses in the Federal civil litigation system and the system's administration, organization, processes and procedures. The computer model permits the simulation of many 'cases' from a procedural point of view in a matter of minutes. If the model is sufficiently realistic, we can compile statistics from a large number of cases (e.g. 100 or more) and test how proposed changes in rules, processes and procedures might affect resource requirements, case-elapsed time and other performance measures. This understanding could ultimately be applied to studying potential modification of the Federal civil litigation system so that it operates more efficiently while continuing to provide – as its first priority, of course – fair resolution of civil disputes.

The Phase I version of the model contains all the programs necessary to carry the progress of cases from beginning to end. For purposes of demonstration,

*This case was written and directed by David Hertz at McKinsey and Co. Ltd. It reflects David's more recent interest in legal matters and in applications of analytic approaches to the resolution of legal problems.

the activities in a case have been carried only as far as the pre-trial stage.

This memorandum summarizes in non-technical language the work on Phase I. The following sections are included:

(i) Defining the civil litigation process for modeling purposes (Section 22.1);
(ii) Applying the model to cases (Section 22.2);
(iii) Next steps (Section 22.3).

Two appendices provide a more technical description of the programs and procedure for operating the model and the procedures for modifying data files.

## 22.2 DEFINING THE CIVIL LITIGATION PROCESS

Each element in the civil litigation process is described in the model as an 'activity', e.g. activity #1 is '*plantiff files complaint.*' An activity can be regarded either as the initiation or completion of an event, e.g. activity #1; or as a step, which consumes resources and time, in a process, e.g., '*plaintiff lawyer prepares a motion for summary judgement.*'

Each activity is described in three ways: its activity name, its consumption of resources and time, and its consequences. Historical case and summary statistic files are kept separately.

It cannot be overemphasized that it is upon the accurate description of activities and the data they require that the utility of the model rests. The computer programs are largely 'bookkeeping' routines to facilitate carrying out, recording, and printing the effects of the instructions contained in activity data files. Thus the art of 'exercising' the model to obtain useful insight into the civil litigation process lies in understanding and describing the activities which control the results produced by the model.

This section of the case discusses the three data files that constitute the description of an activity:

(i) File A1 – Activity Resource Data;
(ii) File A2 – Activity Decision Data;
(iii) File A3 – Activity Name Data.

### File A1 – Activity Resource Data

File A1 contains information on an activity's requirements of resources and time.

The Phase I model allows any activity to utilize up to six different resource types: 1 = plaintiff lawyers, 2 = defense lawyers, 3 = judges, 4 = court personnel, 5 = expert witnesses, 6 = fact witnesses. If an activity requires exclusive access to a resource type for the activity to occur, the activity is said to have a 'restricted resource.' Table 22.1, which shows File A1 for Activity #7, 'Defendant decides on strategy in response to complaint,' indicates that this activity has no restricted resource.

Table 22.1 File A1, Activity #7

| | | | | *Information Field* |
|---|---|---|---|---|
| Activity has no restricted resource. | | | | [1] |
| Number of resource types = 6 | | | | [2] |
| Resource type number | Restricted (1=Y;0=N) | Average number of days | Distribution type | [3–26] |
| 1 | 0 | 0.0 | 0 | |
| 2 | 0 | 1.0 | 5 | |
| 3 | 0 | 0.0 | 0 | |
| 4 | 0 | 0.0 | 0 | |
| 5 | 0 | 0.0 | 0 | |
| 6 | 0 | 0.0 | 0 | |
| Minimum elapsed days for this activity = 1 | | | | [27] |
| Basic calculation sub-routine number = 0 | | | | [28] |

The second information field in this file merely defines the number of resource types that the Phase I model allows an activity to employ. In the Phase I model this number is always six.

Information fields 3–26 show, for each resource type in this activity:

(i) Whether the resource is restricted. The entry is either 1 = yes or 0 = no.
(ii) The average number of days the resource type requires to accomplish the activity.
(iii) The designation of a table (distribution type) from which the model can determine the actual days required based on the average days.

The next information field, [27], specifies the minimum elapsed days that this activity requires for completion, regardless of resource requirements.

Last in File A1 is a reference number for a calculation subroutine. It permits the determination of resource requirements in cases for which the previous steps do not apply. For example, a large number of discovery actions would affect both parties' resource requirements, which the subroutine would calculate. If the subroutine is not used, the entry in this field will be 0.

**File A2 – Next Activity Decision Data**

File A2 outlines the decision process that occurs in determining what activity or activities follow the one being described. Table 22.2 shows File A2 for Activity #7.

The first information field shows whether the activity ends the case. In the Phase I version of the model, only one activity (#99) signals case termination.

Next are shown the number of possible outcomes (or subsequent activities) and the number of decision conditions that determine the possible outcomes. Activity #7 has four possible outcomes and three decision conditions.

Table 22.2 File A2 Activity # 7

This is not a termination activity
Possible outcomes = 4 Decision conditions = 3

| Condition type | Prior/ prob. | Prior (Y/N) |
|---|---|---|
| 2 | 0.50 | −1 |
| 2 | 0.20 | −1 |
| 1 | 8.00 | 1 |

| Outcome number | Field 7 Decision Conditions | Field 8 Steps | Field 9 Next Activities |
|---|---|---|---|
| 1 | — | 1 | 12 |
| 2 | 1 0 0 | 1 | 18 |
| 3 | 0 1 0 | 1 | 13 |
| 4 | −1 −1 1 | 1 | 106 |

Next activity descriptions

| | |
|---|---|
| 8 | PL/△ meet |
| 12 | △ Files answer with court |
| 13 | △ Interviews witness |
| 106 | △ Moves for dismissal and files |

Y/N denotes Yes/No
PL denotes Plaintiff
△ denotes Defendant

For each decision condition the file contains three kinds of information to instruct the computer.

(i) *The decision condition type code*. If the code number is 1, the condition relates to a prior activity, e.g. 'Has defendant already met with plaintiff?' If the code is 2, meeting the condition depends on probablity; e.g. 'Should the defendant meet with the plaintiff?'

(ii) *The prior event or probability*. For type 1 conditions, the number in this column is that of the prior activity which must have happened. For type 2 conditions, the number is the probability of their occurrence.

(iii) *Yes/No Response*. For type 1 conditions, a (1) in this column means that the computer should generate a 'yes' response to the condition if the prior event is discovered, and (0) means a 'no' response to the condition. For type 2 conditions, since a 'yes' response is always assumed, this field has no relevance.

Based on these instructions, the computer determines a yes or no (i.e. 1 or 0) answer for each of the decision conditions. These answers are then compared with what is required for an outcome to be selected for this case-activity.

The next group of information fields deals with the choice of the outcome and the initiation of the next activity or activities.

(i) Field 7 shows the combination of decision condition answers that is required for each outcome to be chosen. (1 = yes, 0 = no, −1 = either yes or no).
(ii) Field 8 tells how many subsequent activities are to be initiated if the corresponding outcome is chosen.
(iii) Field 9 gives the identifying number(s) of the activity or activities initiated if that outcome is chosen.

Outcome #1 is always the 'default' outcome, which is selected only if *no* combination of decision condition answers generated for this case/activity matches one of the combinations specified in Field 7.

The last item in the activity description provides the names of the next activity choices as an aid to the user.

**File A3 – Activity Name**

File A3 contains only the name of the activity and is referred to when printing results.

In summary, an activity is described in three files: File A1, which calculates the resource and time requirements; File A2, which outlines the process of deciding upon the next activity; and File A3, which contains the name of the activity.

## 22.3 APPLYING THE MODEL TO CASES

The model can now be used to compute resource requirements for cases in progress, to generate case histories and to compile summary statistics for all cases generated. In addition, several auxiliary programs allow the user to modify file data upon which the model operates. Below is a very brief outline of what the model does; the computer programs and method of operations. Procedures for modification are discussed in more detail in the Appendices.

When the simulation begins, the computer programs start the first day of a specified simulation period, e.g. 40 days. Each day proceeds as follows:

(1) All cases to be started that day through the filing of complaint are generated. For each such case, a case history record describing the type of case (e.g. tort), numbers of fact and expert witnesses, and on which day during the simulation period the case began is created.
(2) Resource requirements are computed for all case activities starting today.

(3) Individual case activities are scheduled, testing, if required, for resource availability. For example, if a case's activity today requires one day of a judge's time on a 'restricted resource' basis, the program refers to a resource inventory to determine whether a judge is available today. If the judge is not available today, the activity is rescheduled for the following day and one 'delay day' for this resource type is added to the case history. If the activity is completed, the program so indicates.
(4) Subsequent activities for all activities completed today are initiated and recorded as starting 'tomorrow'. If a case has terminated today, records are adjusted accordingly.
(5) Advances to next simulation day and repeats actions described above.

At the end of the simulation period, case histories (Table 22.3) and summary statistics (Table 22.4) are printed for all cases generated.

Table 22.3 Case history

*Example Case*

Case number 1
Complaint filed on day 1
Case type code = 1
Number of fact witnesses = 3
Number of expert witnesses = 2

| Resource type | PL | ΔL | J | C | EW | FW |
|---|---|---|---|---|---|---|
| Delay days | 0.0 | 0.0 | 0.0 | 0.0 | 0.0 | 0.0 |
| Workload requirements | 5.0 | 1.0 | 0.0 | 4.0 | 1.0 | 1.0 |

| *Activity Name* | *Activity number* | *Initiation day* | *Completion day* |
|---|---|---|---|
| Plaintiff files complaint | 1 | 1 | 1 |
| Court records complaint | 2 | 2 | 2 |
| PL Decides litigation strategy | 10 | 2 | 3 |
| Court attempts to serve Δ | 3 | 3 | 4 |
| Δ Receives complaint | 5 | 5 | 5 |
| ΔL Interviews witnesses | 11 | 4 | 5 |

Δ denotes Defendant; PL denotes Plantiff; ΔL denotes Defense Lawyers; J denotes Judges; C denotes Court Personnel; EW denotes Expert Witnesses; FE denotes Factual Witnesses

By modifying the data which the model uses, one can test assumptions about the effect of changes in rules, processes or procedures. New activities can be created, current ones deleted, or any of the descriptive files about an activity changed, e.g. add another decision condition, restrict a resource type, or change the next steps that an outcome initiates.

Table 22.4 Summary statistics

Seed for basic random number generation = 1234
Number of days in simulation period = 5
Average number of cases per day = 1
Average number of fact witnesses = 3
Average number of expert witnesses = 2
Number of ficlds for each activity in F3 = 9
Number of restricted resource types = 1
Allowable concurrent activities per case per day = 15
Number of judges = 1
Number of lawyers for plaintiff = 100
Number of discovery actions per witness = 2
Fraction of discovery actions rejected by counsel = 0.2
Fraction of rejected discovery actions on which action is compelled = 0.5
Number of lawyers for defendant = 50
Number of court personnel = 100
Number of expert witnesses = 100
Number of fact witnesses = 100

| By resource type | Plaintiff lawyers | Defendant lawyers | Judges | Court personnel | Expert witnesses | Fact witnesses |
|---|---|---|---|---|---|---|
| Sum of days delay | 0.0 | 0.0 | 0.0 | 0.0 | 0.0 | 0.0 |
| Sum of resources required | 17.0 | 1.0 | 0.0 | 23.0 | 2.0 | 2.0 |

## 22.4 NEXT STEPS

In developing this Phase I version of the simulation model, we deliberately, for the sake of simplicity, left out certain capabilities which we knew could be added later (e.g. different resource time distributions based on case or judge type). In addition to these conscious omissions we recognized during the development work that the following other desirable capabilities should be added to the structure of the model.

(1) As another outcome option, allow for the cancellation of specific activities in progress.
(2) Add a third type of decision condition, namely, type of case.
(3) Provide a 'maximum allowable time' for activity completion as well as minimum required time.
(4) Modify the case history output to show which activity triggered each of the activities that make up the case. This addition would help in identifying illogical decision rules in the definition of activity.

Without question, many other capabilities will be identified as the Center gains experience in utilizing the model, and in our opinion, this evolutionary development is desirable and easily achievable in terms of the model design and architecture.

## QUESTIONS FOR DISCUSSION

1. Discuss and critically evaluate the approach with regard both to the assumptions and the analytic framework.

# Appendix A: Description of Programs

Appendix A describes the functions performed by each of the five operating subprograms, and how to run the model.

## OPERATING PROGRAMS

The programs are:

(i) GO – starts the simulation exercise;
(ii) MAIN – controls the simulation exercise;
(iii) Subroutine A – calculates and schedules case activity resource requirements;
(iv) Subroutine B – initiates next activities for the case from completed case activities;
(v) OUT-1 – prints out case histories and/or summary statistics for all cases generated.

Figure 22.A.1 should be referred to in reviewing this material.

## GO – INITIATE SIMULATION

This subprogram starts the simulation run and requests the user to indicate if he wants to modify any of the factors controlling the simulation – these factors are contained in the file designed as F1. If the user chooses to modify, the computer prompts him to enter the changed factors. Once this is completed the program automatically initiates the MAIN subprogram.

## MAIN – CONTROLS SIMULATION – GENERATES NEW COMPLAINTS

This subprogram sets-up and maintains control over the number of days to be simulated and the number of cases generated to date. In addition, it generates the 'complaint activity' (File F3) for new cases started today, and creates a case history record (File F2) describing the case type (e.g. tort), numbers of fact and expert witnesses and the day on which the case was started.

Once all of the cases started today have been generated this subprogram sets up a control to examine all cases to date and proceeds to subroutine A to compute and schedule activity resource requirements. If the total cases to date have been processed through subroutine A this subprogram proceeds to subroutine B to initiate the next activities for each case that are generated by case activities completed today. If all cases to date have been processed through subroutine B, this subprogram advances to the next simulation day and reinitiates itself. If all simulation days have been processed this subprogram advances to OUT-1 to print the output results of the entire simulation.

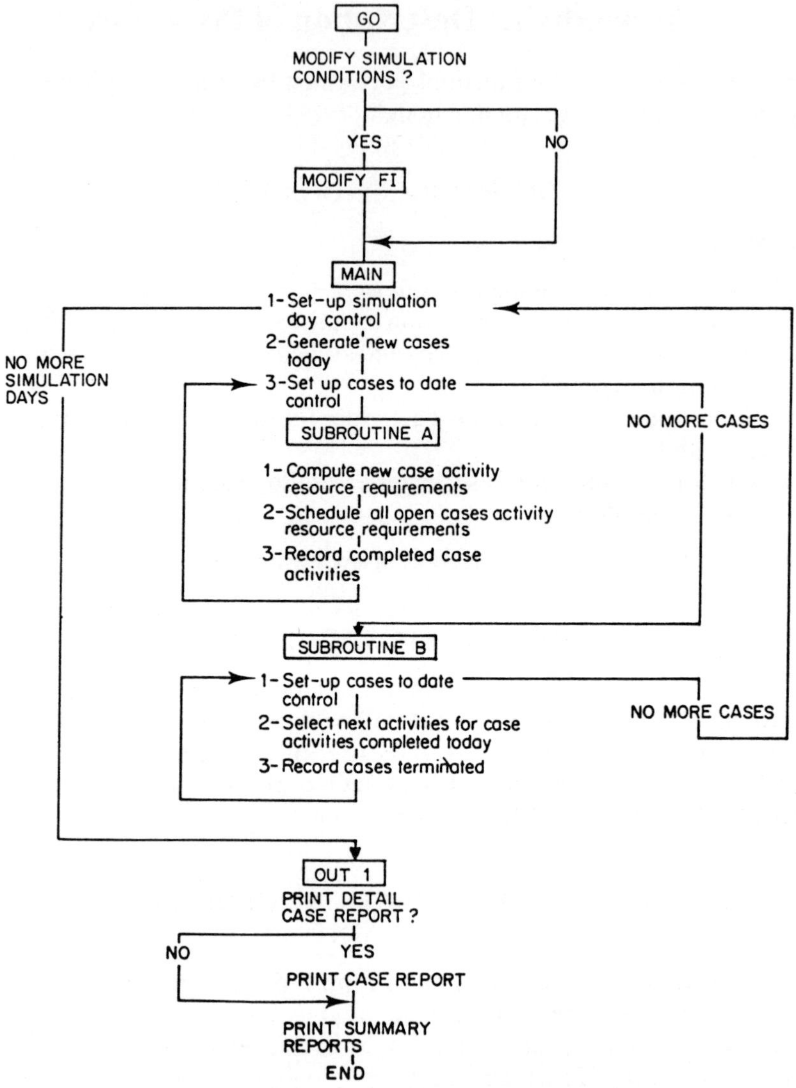


Figure 22A.1 Overview of litigation simulation model

## SUBROUTINE A – CALCULATES NEW ACTIVITY RESOURCE REQUIREMENTS AND SCHEDULES ALL ACTIVITIES ACTIVE TODAY

This subprogram examines all cases generated to date and if the case is still in process (i.e. has not reached a termination activity), it examines each of its 'in-process' activities in file F3 for today to determine if it was just initiated; if it was, then its resource requirements have not been computed and this subprogram computes the needed resource requirements (i.e. from file A1 and associated frequency distributions or from a special calculation subroutine for this activity type). These resource requirements are then accumulated by resource type for this case in the case history file F2, and stored for this activity in the case/activity in process file F3 for today.

Once all new activities' resource requirements have been calculated this subprogram reviews all activities in the 'today' column of in-process file F3 for this case and:

(1) On the basis of the activity data from A1 determines whether this activities' resource requirements for today must be tested against the number of this resource type that is available today. For example, if the activities require one day of a judge's time today, and on this activity type a judge's time is considered to be restricted, then the program refers to the resource inventory file F4 to determine if there is a judge as yet unassigned today. If the judge is available the resource file F4 is reduced by today's judge requirement for today (i.e. this is never greater than one in any one day). If the judge is not available today the entire activity record is moved to the tomorrow column of the in-process file F3 and erased from the today column. In addition, a delay day for this resource type is added to the case history file F2. For activities that are not restricted today by resource requirements or for those that are restricted but have available resources, the program advances to step 2.

(2) Reduces each resource requirement for this activity by one day or by the remaining resource requirements if it is less than one day and computes the remaining resource requirements to be used. These new acitivity resource requirements are placed in the tomorrow column of the in-process file F3. If no resource types for this activity have any remaining resource requirements (i.e. the required resources have been utilized) and if the current simulation day number is equal to or less than the activities' initiation day number plus the 'minimum elapsed acitivity days' from A1, then this activity record is transferred to the case history file F2. Note, however, that the activity record remains in the today column of the in-process file F3 to serve as a 'trigger' for generating the next activities in subroutine B.

The above routine is processed for each of the currently scheduled activities for the case that is in process. The routine returns to the main routine to initiate this process for the next open case. As we noted in the main routine, once all cases to date have been processed through subroutine A the simulation for this day proceeds to subroutine B.

## SUBROUTINE B – GENERATES NEXT ACTIVITIES FROM ACTIVITIES COMPLETED TODAY AND HANDLES CASE TERMINATIONS AND THE SIMULATION END CONDITION

This subprogram again sets up a control over all cases processed to date and examines the activity data for each case that is in the today column of the in-process file F3. For each case with in-process activities it:

(1) Determines if there is a termination activity. If there is, the program subtracts all of the remaining resource requirements for all activities for this case from the resource type requirement fields in the case history file F2. It then transfers all of today's activities for this case in F3 to the case history file F2 as completed. Then both the today and tomorrow columns of F3 for this case are erased.
(2) If this case does not have a termination activity, the program reviews the A2 file for each completed activity and generates the next activity numbers that are to be started as a result of this activity's completion. These activity numbers are recorded in the tomorrow column of the in-process file F3 for this case. Any activity which has not been completed is ignored in this process. Phase II of the model should provide a subroutine exit for unusual logic routines for selecting next activity numbers in subroutine B. This will require a change in file A2.

Once all activites for a case are processed the next case is initiated for processing in this subprogram. When all cases to date have been processed this subprogram returns to the main routine; where as we noted before the simulation day is advanced by one. Simultaneously the program transfers all case activities still present in the tomorrow column of the in-process file F3 to the today column of F3 and then the tomorrow column is set to zeroes.

When the main routine calculates that the simulation is finished it proceeds to subroutine B and considers all in-process cases as being terminated. Once this is done the main routine advances to OUT-1.

## OUT-1 – PRINT CASE HISTORIES AND SIMULATION SUMMARIES

This final subprogram is initiated only at the end of the simulation run. It requests the user to indicate if he wants either:

(1) Detailed case histories and simulation summaries;
(2) Only the simulation summary.

It should be noted that if the user requests the 'only' simulation summary option and then after it has been printed he decides he wants case histories, these can be obtained by recalling program OUT-1.

## RUNNING THE MODEL

The description given here assumes that the user has decided on the structure of the process to be modelled as defined by the activity descriptions and data in Files A1, A2, and A3. Further, it is assumed that he is satisfied with the values shown in the frequency distribution tables in the DISTRIB file and called upon by the main routine and A1 files. Given these conditions he proceeds as follows:

(1) initiates the GO program;
(2) Decides whether or not to modify the simulation run values in file F1, enters modified field numbers and values in response to the computer queries;
(3) responds to computer query as to whether detailed case histories are required;
(4) if he requests only summary data he may, after reviewing the results, recall the print program OUT-1 and obtain detailed case histories.

Any given simulation run will presumably be aimed at either:

(1) testing the reasonableness of the litigation system definition as expressed in activity files A1, A2, and A3, in which case detailed case histories are required; or
(2) developing summary statistics under some changed A1, A2, A3, F1 or DISTRIB file data to compare with an earlier or later run under different file conditions to determine the relative effect of these changed conditions on the simulation results. Where this is the use only summary statistics will usually be needed.

It is difficult to specify further actions that might be taken in either specific type of use of the model. However, it is certain that the user will at some time want to add to, change, or delete the activity and distribution files and their data entries.

# Appendix B: Procedures For Modifying Data Files

Basically, there are three types of file data used by the model which the user may want to modify:

(i) Activity data contained in files A1, A2, and A3.
(ii) Simulation run data contained in file F1.
(iii) Frequency distribution data contained in file DISTRIB.

We do not discuss here the detailed procedures that must be used to add new records to these files; to change, add data to or delete it from existing records in these files; and to delete records from these files. However, copies of the programs and instructions are available from the authors.

*Chapter 23*

# *Investment in Indonesia:* An International Business Problem*


## SUMMARY

This case examines the value to a multi-national corporation (MNC) ABC plc of investment in local, host-country manufacturing facilities. The current arrangements involved the MNC in the export of the product, transistor radios, to the local, host-country.

A decision tree analysis is presented which fomulates a negotiating strategy for MNC management and models the actions of the MNC in its future dealings with the host-country government. A feature of the analysis is the assessment of the political risks associated with the investment opportunity.


## 23.1 INTRODUCTION

Indonesia at the time (mid-1970s) was a fairly stable nation, developing under a ruler who had been in power for some years. However, there were economic problems in the nation, ambitious officers in the armed forces and a small revolutionary party. The President wished to provide employment both for its own sake and to help in damping down discontent. It had been suggested that ABC should set up a transistor-radio manufacturing operation in Indonesia and that favorable terms for this might be arranged. The company knew that transistor-radio manufacture was possible in Indonesia only at a cost higher than that achievable elsewhere. The higher costs were due to the unskilled labor, lack of supporting facilities and the small scale of manufacture. The operation would be feasible only if a monopoly was given to the local manufacturer for about ten years, a tariff placed on imported radios and a quota placed on imports. ABC had wondered whether to negotiate with the President to see if these terms could be agreed, or to leave matters alone and continue with its reasonably satisfactory profit from importing.

*This case was originally developed by Bill Byrnes and Keith Chesterton of Unilever as the 'Transistors in Alterland' case. It has been used in training programs at London Business School and the Australian Graduate School of Management for a number of years. The current version, modified for use in Australia by Howard Thomas, is reproduced here by permission of the original authors.

ABC's management thought that if they did not negotiate, someone else would. As the government was already thinking on these lines it was thought there was a good chance of success. The company did not think it stood to lose any secrets by negotiating and decided to do so.

## 23.2 FINANCIAL PICTURE

The total market was 200,000 radios a year and it was expected to remain at about that level. There were no local manufacturers and ABC was the leading importer with 25 percent of the market or 50,000 radios. The selling price of radios was $6.00 compared with the direct cost to the company of $5.00 per radio. As there were no significant overheads to meet on this relatively small addition to the total output, the $1.00 difference was virtually all profit. The company was making a profit of $25,000 a year on its sales to Indonesia, after tax at 50 percent. There was no tariff in operation on radios.

The company had worked out that if it were to agree to manufacture in Indonesia, it would need sole manufacturing rights, a quota reserving two-thirds of the market for local production and a tariff of $2.00 per radio. These would be 'satisfactory' terms. As a result of the tariff, the price of radios could rise to $7.00. Importers would have to sell at $7.50 per radio. The total market was then expected to fall to 150,000 a year. The home manufacturer would have two-thirds of this reduced market and would thus sell 100,000 radios a year, or double ABC's previous sales. At this level of production, the costs would allow a profit per radio of $1.50, and a total profit of $75,000 p.a. after tax to be made. This would give a 15 percent yield after tax on capital employed. These figures are shown in Table 23.1. This figure also shows the cash flow (profits after tax, plus depreciation).,

The company felt that the difficult point in the negotiations would be the quota and that it was quite likely that a quota arrangement would not be agreed to. If the company manufactured in Indonesia without a quota, it could only expect to keep half of the market or 75,000 radios a year. With these sales, the company would make only $1.20 per radio before tax. The total profits after tax would be $45,000 a year. This was only $20,000 more than the profit on exporting, despite the $400,000 investment that had to be made in a new factory. These would, therefore, be regarded as 'unsatisfactory' terms.

But whatever the terms, if ABC did not take up the manufacturing offer and another company did, it still expected to keep 25 percent of the market open to importers. If the competitors' terms were the terms which have been called 'satisfactory' the company would have a very considerable reduction in profits.

Overall, the company would have preferred to carry on exporting, but if it seemed likely that protected local manufacturing would start, it wished to be the manufacturer and to do so on 'satisfactory' terms. This was a preliminary conclusion. It was reached without any consideration of the risks and uncertainties. However, management felt able to assess the probability of

Table 23.1 Profitability of radio market

| | Export as now | Factory 'satisfactory terms' | Factory 'unsatisfactory terms' | Export after 'satisfactory terms' for someone else |
|---|---|---|---|---|
| Price/unit | \$6 | \$7 | \$7 | \$7.5 (tariff \$2) |
| Total market size | 200,000 | 150,000 | 150,000 | 150,000 |
| Market share | 25% | 66⅔% | 50% | 8⅓% |
| Our market size | 50,000 | 100,000 | 75,000 | 12,500 |
| Factory cost | — | \$500,000 | \$400,000 | — |
| Fixed costs p.a. | — | \$100,000 | \$80,000 | — |
| Variable costs/unit | \$5.00 | \$4.00 | \$4.20 | \$5.00 |
| Depreciation | — | \$50,000 | \$40,000 | — |
| Total cost | \$250,000 | \$550,000 | \$435,000 | \$62,500 |
| Total receipts | \$300,000 | \$700,000 | \$525,000 | \$68,750 |
| Gross profit | \$50,000 | \$150,000 | \$90,000 | \$6,250 |
| Profit after tax | \$25,000 | \$75,000 | \$45,000 | \$3,125 |
| Cash flow p.a. | +\$25,000 | +\$125,000 | +\$85,000 | +\$3,125 |

other manufacturers accepting the terms offered, if our company did not. These were, 0.7 that another company would manufacture locally under 'satisfactory' terms and 0.3 that it would manufacture locally under 'unsatisfactory' terms.

## 23.3 RISKS

The risks were chiefly political ones. The most serious risk was that a new government might expropriate a local factory either for revolutionary reasons or in an excess of nationalistic fervor. The profitability of the investment would also be affected if profit remittances were severely controlled (with limited alternative opportunities this would severely worsen the cash flow), if a 50 percent local shareholding were forced on the company (another popular nationalistic move), or if an orthodox conservative government removed both tariffs and quotas to reduce prices for the customer. The probabilities of these actions occurring depended very much on the political complexion of the government. If it were the present one it would probably stand by the agreement it made as far as it was able. If a new government were created by a military coup or by a revolutionary takeover, the risks would be correspondingly greater.

The company's political advisers assessed the probabilities of these changes of government at 0.6 for no change in government and 0.4 for a change in government. They said that if a governmental change did take place, there was a 75 percent chance that this would be by a military coup and 25 percent that it would be by a revolutionary takeover. The advisers and ABC management then jointly estimated the probabilities of the different types of government taking different forms of action affecting profitability. These are shown in the 'probability tree' in Figure 23.1. Five government actions were considered, including leaving any agreement unaltered.

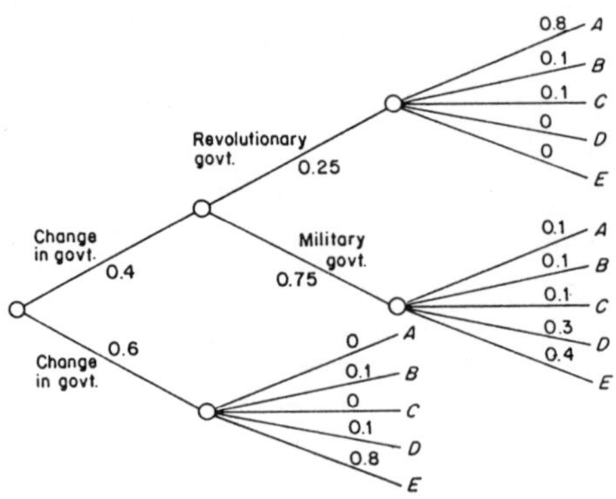


| | A | B | C | D | E |
|---|---|---|---|---|---|
| Total probabilities, wholly owned factory | 0.11 | 0.1 | 0.04 | 0.15 | 0.6 |
| Total probabilities, 50% owned factory | 0.11 | 0.1 | 0.04 | 0 | 0.75 |

Where: *A* represents Expropriate (no compensation)
*B* - - - Control profit remittances
*C* - - - Remove tariffs and quota
*D* - - - Force 50% local shareholding
*E* - - - Agreement continuing unaltered

Figure 23.1 Political events

An example of a government action is the possibility of expropriation with no compensation. It was estimated that, if a revolutionary government took over, there was a 0.8 chance of such expropriation. If a military coup took place the probability was put at 0.1. It was put at zero if the present ruler continued in power. This gave a total probability of expropriation of $0.8 \times 0.25 \times 0.4$ (the probability that a revolutionary government would expropriate, times the probability that a revolutionary government would take over if there was a change in government, times the probability of there being a change in government) + $0.1 \times 0.75 \times 0.4$ (similarly for a military coup) + $0 \times 0.6$ (similarly for no change in government). This gives a probability of 0.11 for expropriation without compensation. One point to note in the diagram is that the probabilities are different if the factory is started as a 50 percent locally owned factory. If it started this way, the company would not need to be forced into 50 percent local shareholding.

## 23.4 CASH FLOW CALCULATIONS

Cash flow calculations were then made for each eventuality. The outcome of these calculations is summarized in Table 23.2.

Table 23.2 Net Present Value Figures

| | Political Events | | | | |
|---|---|---|---|---|---|
| | A | B | C | D | E |
| Continue exporting with no local competitive manufacturer under satisfactory terms | 187 | 187 | 187 | 187 | 187 |
| Continue exporting with local competitive manufacturer under satisfactory terms | 65 | 65 | 153 | 65 | 65 |
| Continue exporting with no competitive local manufacturer under unsatisfactory terms | 187 | 187 | 187 | 187 | 187 |
| Continue exporting with local competitive manufacturer under unsatisfactory terms | 74 | 74 | 151 | 74 | 74 |
| Build own factory under satisfactory terms | −232 | 18 | −29 | 87 | 269 |
| Build own factory under unsatisfactory terms | −200 | −30 | −18 | 25 | 141 |
| Build 50%-owned factory under satisfactory terms | −76 | 71 | 76 | n.a. | 217 |
| Build 50%-owned factory under unsatisfactory terms | −63 | 39 | 78 | n.a. | 141 |

The decision analysis and planning team were asked to recommend a negotiating strategy for management given a managerial policy decision seriously to consider negotiations with Indonesia's ruler.

## 23.5 THE FINANCIAL INFORMATION

An example of the cash flow calculations is shown in Table 23.3. These calculations are summarized in Table 23.2. This example shows the cash flow which would occur if the company built a factory on 'satisfactory' terms but were forced to accept a 50 percent local shareholding in year 4. It also indicates the likely profits from exporting in the first two years while the factory is being built; the cash flow from the factory (halved from year 4 onwards) and the expected sum received for the 50 percent share. The total cash flows were calculated for the life of the project and discounted at 10 percent. The discounted cash flows for each year are summed to yield the Net Present Value of the profit ($87,000) under these conditions. In the calculations a 'management fee' of 3 percent of sales revenue was assumed to be paid to a 50-percent-owned venture to the company.

## 23.6 THE DECISION TREE

The decision tree is drawn in Figure 23.2. It displays the returns for the various options open to the company, namely for the events 'satisfactory' or 'unsatisfactory' terms of negotiation; for the company manufacturing alone or with a 50 percent shareholding or for the option to continue exporting. Each consequence of these events is the Net Present Values for the five different political events. For example, the first table shows them for the situation where 'satisfactory' terms are granted to another company and ABC continues to export while the other company is building the factory. The NPV is 65 in all cases except case C where the tariffs and quotas are removed in year 4. This would be a fortunate case for ABC. It would regain its lost export market. The figure of 153 reflects this beneficial effect. However, this was only expected to occur with a probability of 0.04 (from Figure 23.1), so its influence on the expected NPV for this course of action is small. The expected value of 69 shown on the right is, of course, obtained by multiplying each value in the table by the probability of its occurrence.

Another point to be observed from the tree is the effect of the presence of political risks. The value of building a factory on 'satisfactory' terms is reduced from 269 to 150 by the presence of political uncertainty. For example, if the factory were expropriated (Case A) a net present *loss* of 200 would be incurred. If it was possible to ensure that no competitors built a factory, the 'best' strategy, that is to say, the strategy which maximizes the expected NPV,

Table 23.3 Cash Flow for Building a Factory and Forced 50 percent Local Shareholding After 4 Years

| | Figures in 000's Years | | | | | | | | | | | |
|---|---|---|---|---|---|---|---|---|---|---|---|---|
| | 0 | 1 | 2 | 3 | 4 | 5 | 6 | 7 | 8 | 9 | 10 | 11 |
| Profits from export | +25 | +25 | | | | | | | | | | |
| Cost of factory | −250 | −250 | | | | | | | | | | |
| Cash flow from factory | | | +125 | +125 | +62.5 | +62.5 | +62.5 | +62.5 | +62.5 | +62.5 | +62 | |
| Cash from 50 shareholders | | | | | +100 | | | | | | | |
| Total | −225 | −225 | +125 | +125 | +162.5 | +62.5 | +62.5 | +62.5 | +62.5 | +62.5 | +62.5 | +62 |
| 10% discount factor | 1 | .91 | .83 | .75 | .68 | .62 | .56 | .51 | .47 | .42 | .39 | .35 |
| (Present value, discounted at 10%) | −225 | −205 | +103 | +94 | +111 | +39 | +35 | +32 | +29 | +27 | +24 | +22 |

Total Net Present Value is +67

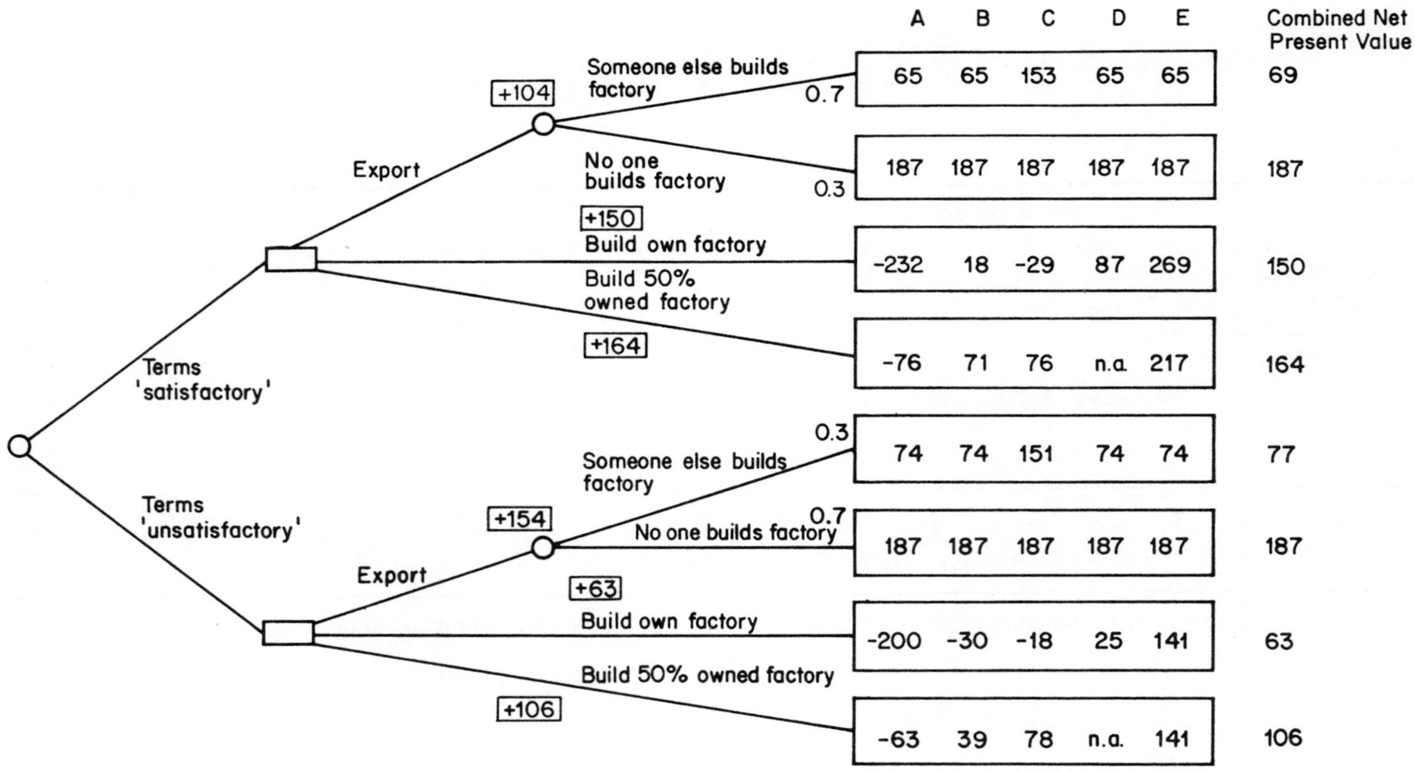


Figure 23.2 Transistor radio decision tree

would be to continue to export. Although possible in a very close-knit group of manufacturers in collusion, this was not the case in this instance and hence the optimum strategies were:

(1) to build a factory with 50 percent local shareholding if the terms were 'satisfactory' with a 164 payoff;
(2) to export if the terms were 'unsatisfactory' with a payoff of 154; or
(3) to build a 100-percent-owned factory, on 'satisfactory' terms with a payoff of 150.

The other strategies were clearly inferior, especially if 'unsatisfactory' terms were negotiated. The return from building a 100-percent-owned factory was less than that obtained by exporting, if a competitor built a factory.

Comparing the top three strategies, strategy 3 was inferior to strategy 1 both because of its lower NPV and because of the higher risk involved. Strategy 3 offers an 11 percent chance of a loss of 232 whereas strategy 1 has a maximum loss of 76. Clearly then, if satisfactory terms were offered, ABC should build a factory with 50 percent local shareholding. If only unsatisfactory terms were offered, it should carry on exporting. This conclusion confirmed most of management's feelings, but there was the crucial difference that a 50-percent-owned venture was better than a 100-percent-owned factory. This was an important change.

## 23.7 NEGOTIATING STRATEGY

The company was thus left with two strategies with little real difference in net NPV. Building a 50-percent-owned factory on 'satisfactory' terms had an NPV of 164, made up of a 70 percent chance of 187, 29.4 percent of 74 and 0.6 percent of 151. Overall, it incurred rather less risk than the first strategy. The two strategies were about equally desirable. This left the company in a comfortable position for negotiation. Whether it gained 'satisfactory' or 'unsatisfactory' terms, it had an equally good option available. It did, however, have to make clear to the Indonesian government that it would only build a factory if 'satisfactory' terms were offered. ABC could offer to make the factory a 50 percent locally-owned one, if the political leader accepted 'satisfactory' terms. But the company did not have to try to force any particular conclusion. It could afford to be relaxed in the negotiations. This was a considerable asset to the negotiator.

## QUESTIONS FOR DISCUSSION

1. In terms of the negotiating strategy, do you feel that the approach suggested is useful for the company?
2. What are your comments about the political risk analysis shown within the case, i.e. the assessments of the occurrence of the events A, B, C, D and E?

*Chapter 24*

# *Postscript: Some Guidelines for Getting Started on Risk Analysis*

For those readers who feel they would like to implement risk analysis in their own organizations, the following guidelines about getting started are suggested:

(1) Make sure that your colleagues are enthusiastic about, and interested in, risk analysis. Ensure that your superiors and other colleagues are able to recognize the value of, and payoff to be derived from, risk analysis. Some prior education and training is useful in alerting the organizational decision-making team to the rationale of risk analysis.

(2) Once this has been achieved, make sure that the decision problem has been correctly defined and structured. In other words, it is important that the correct problem is being analyzed. The greater proportion of analytic effort should be directed towards the structuring phase. Problem identification and formulation are the creative phases of the risk analysis and require that decision-makers have sufficient time to think clearly about the problem.

(3) Try several alternative decompositions and formulations for the problem before going through the assessment process. It is sometimes useful to hire the services of a consultant for the first attempt at risk analysis. The experienced analyst will be able to offer guidance and discuss problem structure as a non-involved third party.

(4) It is important that thorough training in the concepts and meaning of probability has been undertaken before any attempts are made to obtain probability assessments from decision-makers. Often such training is given from within companies by staff members who are competent at probability assessment.

(5) When probabilities have to be assigned for some uncertain quantities, e.g. price, it is important that decision-makers have access to all the objective, quantitative information about price levels which is available in the firm.

Such information might come from varied sources, e.g. accounting records, past sales data, etc. but will serve as a useful decision aid in the judgment process.

In summary, reasons for successful implementation of risk analysis can be characterized as *organizational, personal* and *technical*.

From the organizational perspective, there must be commitment and enthusiasm from senior managers for the analysis to be carried out and implemented. Many management techniques have failed to gain implementation because they have been pursued by rather isolated specialist groups; the typical operational research group is an example. It is essential for the success of decision and risk analysis that there should be none of this 'arms-length' consultancy. In so far as the approach is mainly one of elucidating managerial expertise, it requires a close working relationship between analyst and manager. Therefore, there must be sufficient time (and freedom from undue pressure) in which to carry out the analysis and this factor alone suggests an important role for decision and risk analysis. It will tend to be most effective in the resolution of those more complex and strategic decision problems in which the problem structure is 'fuzzy', the organizational mechanism for decision-making unclear and both the level of risk and the scale of the decision significant. In other words, risk analysis should encourage dialogue about the most appropriate policy options. Analysis, in this vein, is an aid to problem formulation and resolution and *not* an end in itself.

At the personal level, managers must understand the approach and communicate effectively with analysts. One expert has likened the analyst's role in such communication as being closely akin to the skills of the psychoanalyst.

At the technical level, the major need in application is to provide aids for the manager fully to understand and formulate the problem. Current research on such decision aids as dialectic and devil's advocate processes and creativity approaches, e.g. synectics, should provide an improved future climate for effective organizational problem formulation.

## PROS AND CONS OF RISK ANALYSIS

At this stage it is useful to question whether decision-analysis techniques should be used in practical analyses of decision problems. The main arguments for and against these techniques are presented in the following table.

| Pro | | Con | |
|---|---|---|---|
| 1. | Provides a systematic and logical approach to decision-making | 1. | Sometimes provides few guidelines to aid problem formulation |
| 2. | Permits a thorough analysis of alternative options particularly in complex decision problems | 2. | Sometimes time-consuming. More useful for complex decision problems |
| 3. | Enables the decision-maker to confront risk and uncertainty in a realistic manner | 3. | Lack of acceptance by some organizations |
| 4. | Helps communication within the organization – experts in other areas are consulted in decision-making | 4. | Difficulties sometimes exist in obtaining probability assessments |
| 5. | Allows decision-makers to judge how much information to gather in a decision problem | 5. | Managers sometimes find difficulty in interpreting the output of the risk analysis process |
| 6. | Allows judgment and intuition in decision-making to be presented in a meaningful way | | |

# *Short Bibliography*

The literature on decision and risk analysis is extremely large and is found in a wide range of journals in business, economics, operations research, planning, psychology, statistics and systems analysis.

The first source of further reading should be the references from our text volume *Risk Analysis and its Applications*. Some additional references can also be obtained through searches of abstracting services such as 'International Abstracts in Operations Research', 'Business Periodicals Index' and 'Social Sciences Abstracts'.

We also suggest that readers refer to the volume *Modern Decision Analysis* by G. M. Kaufman and H. Thomas (Penguin, 1977). This provides a series of up-to-date readings and an annotated bibliography listing useful books and articles, sources of articles and finally addresses of the major research groups and consulting organizations in the field.

# Short Bibliography

[illegible]

# *Author Index*

# *Subject Index*